Furcraea longaeva at Tresco Abbey, in 1944, from the first edition of *Shrubs for the Milder Counties*. See page 330.

SHRUBS
FOR THE MILDER COUNTIES

by
W. Arnold-Forster

A New Edition

Introduction
by
Val Arnold-Forster

Addendum of Plant Name Changes
by
Peter Clough

Colour Photographs
by
Susanna Heron and John Packer,
Roger Phillips and James Hodge

ALISON HODGE

Dedicated to
CANON ARTHUR BOSCAWEN, of Ludgvan,
JOHN CHARLES WILLIAMS, of Caerhays,
P. D. WILLIAMS, of Lanarth
and other Cornish gardeners
who have helped to enlarge our
inheritance of plants from
many lands.

First published in 1948 by Country Life.
This edition published in 2000 by Alison Hodge
Bosulval, Newmill, Penzance, Cornwall TR20 8XA
in collaboration with Neil Armstrong.
© First edition Octopus Publishing Group.
© This edition Alison Hodge, 2000.
© Introduction Val Arnold-Forster, 2000.
© Addendum Peter Clough, 2000.
Photographs copyright © Susanna Heron, numbers 1–12;
James Hodge, number 24; John Packer, numbers 13–17, 20–23 and 25–29;
Roger Phillips, numbers 18 and 19.
Eagles Nest, 1958 © Estate of Patrick Heron 2000.
All Rights Reserved, DACS.

All rights reserved. No part of this publication may be
reproduced, stored in a retrieval system, or transmitted in any form
or by any means without the prior permission in writing
of the publishers.

ISBN 0 906720 28 1

British Library Cataloguing-in-Publication Data
A catalogue record for this book is available from
the British Library.

Printed and bound in the UK by Short Run Press Ltd., Exeter.

The publishers gratefully acknowledge the help and support of
South-West Horticulture in the production of this book.

Contents

	List of Illustrations	iv
	Introduction to the 2000 Edition, by Val Arnold-Forster	vii
	A Note about the Photographs	x
	Foreword by The Rt. Hon. Lord Aberconway	xi
	Preface	xiii
I	Opportunities and Problems	1
II	Wind and Shelter	6
III	Planting for Roadsides and Towns	39
IV	A General Planting List	79
V	Acacias	188
VI	Camellias	194
VII	Ceanothus	206
VIII	Eucalyptus	217
IX	Magnolias, by G. H. Johnstone	228
X	Metrosideros	249
XI	Nothofagus—Southern Beeches	257
XII	Olearias	261
XIII	Prunus, Pyrus and Sorbus	269
XIV	Rhododendrons and Azaleas	282
XV	Some Uncommon, Untried, or Tender Shrubs	314
XVI	Addendum—Plant Name Changes, by Peter Clough	350
	Index	365

List of Illustrations

Furcraea longaeva at Tresco Abbey, in 1944 — Frontispiece

The 'Giant's Snuff Box': the garden at Eagles Nest, *c.* 1940s — vi

Pencil drawing, *Eagles Nest, 1958*, by Patrick Heron — vii

Starting the garden: Eagles Nest, *c.* 1920s — ix

The garden takes shape: Eagles Nest, *c.* 1920s — ix

between pages 112 and 113

1. *Olearia* x *haastii*, *Olearia* x *scilloniensis* (*Olearia stellulata*), *Olearia cheesmanii*, *Olearia* x *mollis* 'Zennorensis'
2. *Olearia albida* hort. (*Olearia* 'Talbot de Malahide')
3. *Senecio elaeagnifolius* (*Brachyglottis elaeagnifolia*) and *Senecio rotundifolius* (*Brachyglottis rotundifolia*) growing in full exposure
4. *Rhododendron* 'Princess Alice'
5. *Rhododendron maddenii* subsp. *maddenii*, Polyandrum group
6. *Kerume azaleas* under rhododendron
7. *Rhododendron sanguineum* with *Corokia*
8. *Eucryphia cordifolia*
9. *Rhododendron Cubittii* (*Rhododendron veitchianum* Cubittii Group), *Pieris Forrestii* in the background

10 *Rhododendron 'Loder's White'* and
   Drimys winteri (*Drimys winteri* var. *chilensis*)
11 *Rhododendron 'Blue Tit'*
12 *Camellia oleifera*

                    between pages 208 and 209

13 *Abutilon vitifolium*
14 *Embothrium coccineum* at Fox Rosehill Gardens, Falmouth
15 *Gaultheria forrestii*
16 *Grevillea rosmarinifolia*
17 *Clianthus puniceus*
18 *Leptospermum flavescens* var. *obovatum* (*Leptospermum obovatum*)
19 *Lapageria rosea 'Nash Court'* in an unheated vinery at Sellindge, Kent
20 *Sophora tetraptera* at Penlee Gardens, Penzance
21 *Camellia japonica 'Adolphe Audusson'*
22 *Viburnum tomentosum 'Lanarth'* (*Viburnum plicatum 'Lanarth'*) at Fox Rosehill Gardens, Falmouth
23 *Metrosideros tomentosa* (*Metrosideros excelsus*)
24 *Camellia 'J. C. Williams'* (*Camellia J. C. Williams* var. *Williamsii*)
25 *Rhododendron johnstoneanum*
26 *Rhododendron 'Loderi Pink Diamond'*
27 *Magnolia mollicomata* (*Magnolia campbellii* subsp. *mollicomata*) alongside *Butia capitata*
28 *Rhododendron davidsonianum*
29 *Brugmansia sanguinea*

The 'Giant's Snuff Box': the garden at Eagles Nest, c. 1940s, photographed by W. Arnold-Forster.

Introduction to the 2000 Edition

by Val Arnold-Forster

'It may be on rough moorland,' said my husband, Mark Arnold-Forster, as he persuaded Patrick Heron, the distinguished artist, to take over Eagles Nest, 'but it's a painter's garden'.

Mark's father, Will, had studied at the Slade under Tonks; the Great War took him into the Navy. Like most of his generation, he had lost too many friends and family, and his reaction was to depart to distant west Cornwall, where he installed his wife and their new baby in a windswept, bleak house high above the cliff, with few trees, neighbours or modern conveniences. There he worked for the League of Nations and other international good causes, wrote articles, built his own studio—and, of course, his garden. He was a skilful portraitist, though later concentrating on

Pencil drawing, Eagles Nest, 1958, *by Patrick Heron.*
© Estate of Patrick Heron 2000. All Rights Reserved, DACS.

finely-coloured, remote landscapes, mostly in pastel. But his foremost work of art was surely his garden. Certainly it was where his heart was.

He was a keen correspondent, especially to his mother who presided over a large, but more conventional, garden in Wiltshire. His letters might well start with plans, for exhibitions, visits to London or Geneva, but his true enthusiasm was for his—and other people's—plants. His advice was sought by other gardeners, from those with small plots to those in charge of public gardens. And the advice was copiously given, often accompanied by sketches and detailed plans.

For Will Arnold-Forster was not just a plantsman. The design of his comparatively small garden was both intricate and ambitious, and constantly revised. However much his garden had to cope with the practicalities of his awesome site, it still had to please the eye. His last gardener, Percy Edwards, remembered him as a frail man who could yet find the energy to uproot big shrubs. To get a subtler colour contrast or a different profile, he would think nothing of moving a full grown camellia a few feet. If he didn't like it there, he moved it back.

Happily, a few years after Will's death, the Herons did move to Eagles Nest. With Delia, Patrick and their daughters Katharine and Susanna Heron, the garden has thrived: the same devoted care, the same rigorous intelligence applied to replanting. Even better, both Patrick and Susanna Heron have put into words their own artistic involvement with the garden, and its importance to both of them. That rough patch of moorland has been fortunate in its owners.

VAL ARNOLD-FORSTER

LONDON
SEPTEMBER 2000

Starting the garden: Eagles Nest, c. 1920s, photographed by W. Arnold-Forster.

The garden takes shape: Eagles Nest, c. 1920s, photographed by W. Arnold-Forster.

A Note about the Photographs

Shrubs for the Milder Counties was first published in 1948, illustrated with black and white photographs. The 2000 edition is illustrated with archival photographs of Eagles Nest, and colour photographs of many of the same species as in the first edition. Many of Susanna Heron's photographs, taken at Eagles Nest between 1992 and 2000, are of the very shrubs planted by W. Arnold-Forster. These were mostly cut to the ground by the frost of January 1987, but have revived.

Note: Chapters I–XV are reprinted from the original. References to photographs (Plates) have not been removed.

Foreword

by The Rt. Hon. Lord Aberconway

I felt greatly honoured to be asked to write the Foreword to Mr. Arnold-Forster's book, but I felt even more honoured when I had read the manuscript and had realised its great value. The book should be a classic, if only because it is founded on real knowledge—the result of personal observation and research strengthened by advice and information from the author's Cornish friends.

The book is one which not merely records—though it does this fully—but which also teaches. Much of its teaching is of very special interest at this particular time, which may well be the beginning of an era of widespread public planting.

W. Arnold-Forster deals with this most important section of his subject in detail, and with great ability and artistic sense; and those who propose planting our roads in the country or our roads and parks in towns would do well carefully to study his words of wisdom on the matter.

Readers will be especially glad that he draws so definite a distinction between town and country planting.

In all such planting two things are essential. Firstly, that the planting should really succeed, without which qualification the whole thing is an eyesore; and secondly, that when it does succeed, it should be felt to be the right planting.

In the country the planting should look as if it grew there by itself; but in towns and the smaller parks it might well look as if it had been placed there by man, though here too planting must not look fussy.

The book points the moral that in public planting in the mild counties the choice of plants should not be too closely limited to the plants commonly used for such purposes in colder counties.

The writer of the book also devotes very special attention to the important question of shelter. Chapter II and its illustrations most usefully suggest some extensions in the repertory of wind-resisting plants—extensions based on severe tests. In very mild gardens near the sea, plants escape the frost but feel the wind; but, given a little thought and suitable planting, they can escape much of the ravages even of a salt-laden wind. One wishes that as much could be done in inland gardens to protect plants from frost.

Mr. Arnold-Forster's account of the plants which can be grown successfully in mild climates will make those who garden inland feel very envious. A certain number, however, of the plants that are supposed to grow only in climates of Cornish quality will grow elsewhere if only they are boldly tried, especially if the shelter of a wall is possible.

As an instance of this, one may remark that certain of the fragrant rhododendrons of the *Edgworthii* series and their hybrids, dealt with so fully in the book, will stand without undue damage a zero frost against a north or north-west wall, and will carry their flower buds unharmed through an ordinary winter. *Embothrium coccineum* too, especially in its narrow-leaved forms, will stand in the open unharmed by a zero frost.

Of course, a really hard winter will bring much tribulation to those who try to grow others of these border-line plants; but to grow them even for some years is a pleasure and an achievement, and it may be that not for a generation may we have again the severe winters that have visited us in the last six years.

Several species of plants in the garden that I know best, which had grown to great size and beauty, some of them forty years old, have been wiped out by the frosts of recent winters; but they have given great pleasure in the past, and they will be replanted in the hope that they will give pleasure in the future.

One much hopes that the publication of this book will increase the interest in such plants, even though we may recognise what losses an especially hard winter may entail.

Finally, one must needs welcome a book designed under the auspices of the very active Cornwall branch of the Council for the Preservation of Rural England. Cornwall has always set a noteworthy example in the skill of its great gardeners and in the beauty and number of its great gardens, and it is perhaps the best compliment that I can pay to this book to say that it is most fully worthy of the gardeners and of the gardens of Cornwall.

Preface

This book is meant chiefly for those who live in the milder parts of the British Isles—in climates such as those of Cornwall and Devon, the coastal districts of southern England, Morayshire, West Scotland, and Wales, and much of Eire and Northern Ireland.

The book has three aims.

Firstly, I hope it will be of assistance to local authorities in planning new plantings, and in preserving good existing planting. With the end of the war, with the launching of new housing-schemes, and with the extension of public control of land and building, there has come an exceptional opportunity for such planning and planting. But the range of plants that will grow in the milder parts of these islands is so large that the task may be found confusing unless there is available a review of this kind—not simply a summary catalogue of plants suitable for the average British climate, but an annotated selection specially adapted to conditions in counties comparatively frost-free, but subject in many cases to sea-winds.

Secondly, the book is offered to private gardeners who, free now to think again of planting, want to choose plants for their gardens with a comprehensive view of the immense repertory available for the milder parts of these islands. I do not claim that the book meets this need adequately; I have not the expert knowledge for so large a task. But a good many streams of experience have contributed to these pages, both through the generous help I have received from many quarters during the writing, and through my good fortune in having known, well or slightly, some of the great gardeners of a past generation, of whom three are mentioned in the Dedication. In attempting to cover so wide a field, partly new, and in offering so many estimates of the probable behaviour of plants under diverse conditions, I cannot hope to have avoided errors; but I trust that fellow-gardeners, in comparing the book's generalisations with their own experience, may at least find some interest in it as another gardener's annotated catalogue.

Thirdly, the book attempts to contribute something fresh on the subject of planting in exceptionally windy places. Having experimented for twenty-eight years in what must surely be the windiest garden in Britain, I venture to claim that I do not underrate the difficulties due to sea-winds. The milder parts of Britain are the maritime parts; and Cornwall in particular, lying between sea and sea, is swept by winds much stronger and more salt-laden than those which trouble up-country gardeners. There is still much need for the kindly protection and colour of trees and shrubs in many of the mild but wind-swept parts of Britain, especially in Cornwall.

It was with these aims in view that the Cornwall Branch of the Council for the Preservation of Rural England asked me to write the book. I have throughout been helped and encouraged by my colleagues of the C.P.R.E., especially by the Committee's Chairman, the Bishop of Truro, an ardent and learned gardener.

Whilst the book is meant for planters anywhere in the milder parts of the British Isles, I make no apology for referring repeatedly to Cornish conditions. For much of whatever gardening experience I possess has been gained in Cornwall; and Cornwall provides in exceptional degree both mildness of climate and severity of wind. Perhaps those who live in other counties will excuse this local emphasis, for the sake of the additional precision which it allows.

At the request of the Cornish C.P.R.E. Lord Aberconway—who, besides being President of the R.H.S. and owner of one of the finest gardens in the world, has long been a close friend of Cornish gardening—kindly agreed to write a Foreword. I owe to him, not only the honour of having this Foreword in the book, but also many notes on the manuscript, drawn from his great experience.

I am especially indebted to two men who carry on the succession of pioneers of gardening in the milder parts of Britain. One is Major Arthur Dorrien Smith, D.S.O., V.M.H., who is owner and in large part the maker of a garden, Tresco Abbey, in the Scilly Isles, which is at once a lovely scene and a unique treasury of plants. The other is Mr. G. H. Johnstone, of Trewithen, Grampound Road, Cornwall, who has contributed, from his unri-

PREFACE

valled knowledge of the subject, the chapter on magnolias—forerunner of a book about them which he is preparing.

I offer very warm thanks also to Mr. Campbell, Curator of Kew, and to Mr. C. P. Raffill, V.M.H., who has helped me with many comments, drawn from his wide experience of half-hardy shrubs in the Temperate House, Kew. I gratefully acknowledge, too, generous help from Dr. Van Rensselaer, Director of the Santa Barbara Botanic Garden, California; he contributed material for the eucalyptus chapter, and the chapter on ceanothuses owes very much to his authoritative book on the genus. For help with some of the plant names and identifications I have to thank the Royal Botanic Gardens, Edinburgh; also Mr. Chittenden, of the R.H.S. Garden, Wisley, and Mr. B. Mulligan, now Director of the University Arboretum at Seattle.

Others to whom I am much indebted include Captain Collingwood Ingram, for his most expert counsel on the pages about cherries[1] and crabs; the late Mr. E. L. Hillier, V.M.H., of Winchester, who spent some of his last strength before his death in annotating the chapter on shelter-planting; to Mr. H. Hillier, his son, for notes on this and other chapters; Mr. W. J. Marchant, of Keepers Hill Nursery, Wimborne, for much valuable comment on the general planting list; Mr. L. Slinger, of the Slieve Donard Nursery Co., Newcastle, County Down, for comment on the pages about escallonias; Treseder's Nursery, Truro, for notes based on much experience of planting in windy sites; Mr. Charles Eley, V.M.H., for comments on the chapter on town and roadside planting , Dr. F. Crossman for valuable notes of his experience with clematises; Mr. J. Comber, V.M.H., for notes on the behaviour of Chilean barberries and other plants at Nymans, Sussex; Mr. H. F. Comber for notes on plants he introduced from Tasmania; Mr. Roland Bryce for much information on the behaviour of tender shrubs in his very mild island garden in Bantry Bay; Mr. E. H. Walpole, of Mount Usher, Wicklow, for notes on the hardiness of the numerous species of eucalyptus which he grows; Mr. H. Armytage Moore, of Rowallane, near Belfast, for counsel about embothriums, etc.; Major C. E. Radclyfle for notes of his long

---

[1] Captain Collingwood Ingram's recent book on cherries will no doubt be a standard work on the subject.

experience of planting conifers in very exposed coastal sites in Caithness; the British Fuchsia Society for help with the pages on fuchsias; Mr. M. Haworth-Booth for help on the garden forms of hydrangea; Messrs. Waterer and Crisp, Bagshot, for advice on which rhododendron hybrids will best stand sunlight; Mr. D. Martin, of the Australian Scientific Research Liaison Office, for expert advice about hardiness of eucalyptus; and Mr. Michael Williams, of Lanarth, Cornwall, for the privilege of studying the garden book kept by his father, the late P. D. Williams, V.M.H., during his long experience of Cornish and other gardens.

The book has been written at a time when the world is shadowed by recent griefs of war and by new anxieties of the peace, and when, more than ever, our first call on the earth's fertility must be for "our daily bread." Yet I do not think such a book is too inopportune now. We need not just bread alone, but the rose as well. The corn and the grass, the potatoes and the apples, will all be duly tended; but even in a world so hungry, the gardeners will see to it that our varied flower-garden is tended too, and they will still replenish it with flowers chosen from the whole world's treasury of plants—a camellia, maybe, or a clematis, or the miracle shut up in a packet of nasturtium seed.

I have enjoyed many flowers. My hope is that some seeds of such enjoyment may be found lodged between these pages, and will presently spring up in bright shoots of cheerfulness elsewhere.

W. ARNOLD-FORSTER

EAGLES NEST
CORNWALL, 1948

CHAPTER I

Opportunities and Problems

THOSE who can plant shrubs and trees in the milder parts of the British Isles enjoy exceptional opportunities; for they can count with some confidence on frosts being less than in other parts of Britain and much less than elsewhere in northern Europe, and so they can draw upon an extraordinarily wide range of beautiful plants. But at the same time these planters, fortunate as they are, have to allow for certain special difficulties. The milder parts of these Atlantic islands are those which are near the sea, especially the western sea; which means that they are all more or less subject to sea-winds—winds that are often abnormally violent and sometimes charged with salt. Thus, planters in our milder counties have to pay much more heed to wind-shelter and wind-hardiness than planters inland find necessary.

THE OPPORTUNITY

Few regions of the earth can draw upon so rich and varied a repertory of plants as we can in these mild counties. That is specially true of Cornwall, the coasts of Devon, West Scotland, and various parts of Ireland; but the good fortune extends in varying degree to many other favoured spots, as may be seen at Abbotsbury, on the Dorset coast, in various gardens of Hampshire and Sussex, in part of Morayshire, and at some places near the sea in Wales. Of course there is much, very much, that we cannot grow here nearly so well as it can be grown in drier, hotter or more extreme climates. Yet the mildness and dampness of the Atlantic air offers rich compensations. In particular, it allows planters in our mild maritime counties to grow rhododendrons perfectly, and the most splendid of magnolias. Indeed, coming to live in the south-west, a gardener from "up-country" finds that he has to enlarge his ideas of what flowers can be. I shall never forget seeing for the first time, in a Cornish wood in March, thousands of the huge rose-pink flowers of *Magnolia Campbellii* up against a light-blue sky. Here in May one may see the light shining through the translucent white bells of that incomparable flower, the Himalayan *Rhododendron Griffithianum*. Here in the south-west, and in southern Eire, the Chilean fire-bush, *embothrium*, grows over 30 ft. high, unbelievably vermilion. I know a Cornish wood where the grandest of camellias, *reticulata*, makes bushes 20 ft. high, splashed all over with glowing pink flowers 5 or 6 inches across. Some of the *mimosas* (*acacia*) flower in our mild gardens as lavishly as on the Riviera. The loveliest of heaths, *Erica canaliculata* from the Cape, reaches 12 ft. or more, a cloud of violet-pink in spring; in mid-summer the "Rata" trees (*metrosideros*) from New Zealand and the bottle-brushes (*callistemon*) from Australia show their splendid scarlet; in late summer the lily of the valley tree from Madeira (*Clethra arborea*) is plumed all over with its scented sprays, *eucryphias* from Chile are whitened with flowers like single roses, and tree myrtles sow themselves as lavishly as if they were at home in Andean forests. In September–October *Schima khasiana*, a bushy tree with flowers like small white camellias, flourishes in the few gardens which yet possess it. And by November–December camellias and *Rhododendron Nobleanum* are starting the pageant which will continue, ever-changing, into the New Year.

Some of these plants, such as the *clethra*, thrive only in the mildest gardens of the mild counties; but there is an enormous range of shrubs of rare beauty, such as *lapageria*, lantern tree (*Tricuspidaria lanceolata*), tree myrtle, *Clematis Armandii*, the *eucryphias*, and the hybrids of the finest red rhododendron species, which can be grown perfectly in most of the milder gardens of these fortunate islands.

Is it not astonishing that plants from such diverse countries, soils, climates and altitudes should settle down as neighbours here? Nowhere can one see the miracle of acclimatisation more strikingly displayed. Within the space of a few feet plants from Switzerland, Ecuador, South Africa, the Chinese Alps, Chile, Corsica, and Siberia are all thriving in the writer's garden on a Cornish moor; and such a triumph of adjustment by plants is so common that we take it too much for granted. A century ago Sir Joseph Hooker brought to Kew seeds of rhododendrons from Sikkim; seedlings of these were tried in various woodland gardens, and experience showed that under cultivation here the visitors grew quite as well—even better, it is claimed—as their parents do in the fiercely competitive conditions of the Indian forest. A similar claim has been made for some New Zealand shrubs. Canon Boscawen, of Ludgvan Rectory in Cornwall, after forty years of growing New Zealand shrubs sent to him by his brother in that country, compared notes with that brother on his return to England; and the Canon concluded that some of the plants under his care here made a braver show than ever they did in the New Zealand bush. But one need not go to the mild counties to find such examples of acclimatisation. Fifty years ago our gardens had no purple buddleias; today these Chinese plants are not only at home in our gardens everywhere, but have become wildlings, self-sown on ruins and railway embankments. Certainly we have much cause to be thankful for the singular fortune that plants from such different homes can flourish together in this alien land.

Besides being able to grow a very wide range of plants, we are fortunate in having many mature, long-established trees and shrubs. For our people have been playing the garden game for centuries—collecting plants, trying them in various conditions, hybridising and selecting them. It took a century or more of favourable air and uncommon skill to produce some of the monuments of English gardening—the huge old rhododendrons and camellias, for instance, the *Pieris formosa* at Pentillie Castle, the *Sophora japonica* trees at Kew. Many such grand old plants, and noble old gardens with their trees, survive. But they survive now amidst increasing difficulties and dangers. Already before the war pressure of taxation and other social causes were making it difficult for the owners of large private gardens to maintain them. In consequence, rare and beautiful plants, long loved and tended, are being smothered and killed year by year as brambles take command; only a few plumes of myrtle or the crown of a great magnolia emerge still above the rising jungle, and only birds and rabbits can make their way along the overgrown garden walks. Moving now (for good reason) into a more equalitarian age, we shall certainly see further diminution of gardening on the old lavish scale by private owners, and we shall not be able to retain nearly all the widely spread treasure of long-established plants that gardeners of the past have left to us. But the community will waste a unique inheritance if it sets no limit to the destruction of the finest gardens made by private owners. In selected cases the community should, I suggest, take action to make possible the maintenance of fine old plantings, on terms which will ensure that they can be seen by those who will enjoy them and who will respect the conditions necessary for the well-being of the plants.

The Problems

No one who has experience of planting in the maritime counties is likely to be under the illusion that it is all easy. Anyone who knows Cornwall, for instance, knows that it is far from being all "Riviera," all "palms and sunshine and the South"; he will remember, besides sleepy sheltered valleys and lush growth, miles of country almost or quite treeless—country with hardly a bush taller than gorse. Anyone who was in West Cornwall in May 1943 may recall how every native tree and hedge was blackened and stripped by a salty gale, just when the green was fresh; and anyone who has seen Cornish woodlands of native trees in August will know that, weeks before autumn really begins, they are apt, unless in sheltered spots, to look umber-brown like an old English water-colour from which the blues have faded. Almost everywhere within direct influence of the sea-wind its power is visible, either in the absence of trees, or in the bent shapes and diminished stature of the native trees and shrubs, or in the failure of seaside towns and villages to furnish themselves with the comfortable green of shrubs and trees. I think of the seaward side of the towns and villages of the north Cornish coast, so bleak and arid—needlessly so, as the next chapter will show. And, having had experience of starting plants in a small, very windy garden, I realise how limited are the opportunities for planting unless there is enough space and time for shelter-planting.

There are other drawbacks, besides wind, in such a climate. For one thing, in so mild a climate, planters are tempted to rely too much upon plants which are on the border-line of hardiness. Abnormal frosts, like those of December 1938, and January–February 1947, do far more damage in a county planted largely with exotics than in a county such as Yorkshire; and if injury is repeated by heavy frosts in successive winters, as happened after 1938, the chances of recovery are destroyed. The moral is, not that no tender plants should be tried, but that too much reliance should not be placed on them, especially for shelter-planting. For instance, the use of *Pittosporum crassifolium* as a hedge plant has proved a great success in the daffodil fields of the Scillies; but after the frost of 1938, which killed this plant and *P. Kirkii* on the English mainland, we shall have to learn to put no such trust in it here.

Another drawback of a temperate, damp climate is that plants which require a thorough ripening of their wood in summer and a long rest from growth in winter do not get it, and so do not flower

Opportunities and Problems

or fruit as freely as they do in a more extreme climate. Many berrying shrubs fruit far better in the severe cold and heat of the Eastern United States than they do in this country; *Lonicera tatarica*, for instance, which is little valued here, makes a magnificent show of orange-scarlet berries over there (especially the variety "*bella*"). And here such plants as lilacs, *philadelphus, deutzias,* and many roses flower much better up-country, generally speaking, than they do in such a climate as Cornwall's.

As for the trees and shrubs which commonly flare into scarlet and orange and pink up-country when autumn touches them, most of them—such plants as *cercidiphyllum, liquidambar, parrotia, Vacciniums pennsylvanicum* and *corymbosum,* and *Aronia arbutifolia*[1]— can be seen in much fuller glory at such places as Westonbirt, in Gloucestershire, and Sheffield Park, in Sussex, than anywhere in Cornwall.

So it comes to this. The planter of trees and shrubs in these mild counties is blessed with extraordinary opportunities *provided* that the problem of wind-shelter has been mastered and *provided* that the normal mildness of the climate does not tempt him to rely overmuch on plants that may be knocked out by an abnormal frost. Let us begin therefore by considering, in the next chapter, the problems of wind-shelter and wind-hardiness. Then in later chapters, we will review the plants available in these mild climates for various purposes, including the planting of towns and roadsides.

[1] A notable exception is the Japanese maple, *Acer* "*Osakazuki,*" which colours magnificently even in the mild Cornish air.

CHAPTER II

Wind and Shelter

ALL the milder parts of the British Isles are near the sea and are therefore more subject than the rest of the country to persistent and often violent winds. Moreover, the wind off the sea is often charged with salt. Thus, planters in our milder counties (for whom this book is primarily intended) are specially concerned with wind-shelter; and, if they live close to the sea, with the capacity of plants to endure wind-borne salt. So it is appropriate that the book should deal first with problems due to wind.

In considering the planting of windy places, one has to decide:
(1) Whether any planting is *desirable* on the site in question;
(2) Whether successful planting is likely to be *practicable* on that site, given such attention as will probably be available;
(3) *What plants* would grow there and would look appropriate.

IS PLANTING DESIRABLE?

In very many places, especially near the sea, more planting would be desirable. But in recognising this we should also recognise that there are some places, treeless now, whose "amenity value" would not be enhanced but injured by planting, however well done. In our small, much-domesticated islands some of the treeless wild places have a special value for at least a part of the community—a value largely dependent on their remaining treeless and wild. Further afforestation in parts of the Lake District is now widely recognised as injurious to amenities which are a precious national asset, especially if the trees planted are conifers; and the afforestation of certain coastal lands should likewise be recognised as injurious. If you have visited those Cornish headlands where you can look westwards "from the shore that hath no shore beyond it set in all the sea," you will have done so, probably, in cheerful expectation that the winds you will face will be fresh off the Atlantic, winds untempered as yet by trees or hills; and when there you will not regret but enjoy the characteristic absence of growths taller than thrift and wind-nibbled gorse. The austere quality that makes these exceptional places precious should not lightly be destroyed or changed by planting. If their afforestation were proposed, it should not be permitted unless an impartial weighing of economic needs against the other values involved had shown compelling reasons why such sacrifice must be tolerated.

So much for the exceptional places where planting would be definitely *injurious* to amenities. Now, are there many places along our seaboard where more planting would be definitely *advantageous*? Surely the number of such places is great. In particular, many of our seaside towns and villages would be enormously improved in appearance, in comfort, and in economic value, if they were more amply furnished with trees and shrubs. I think, for example, of a Cornish seaside village. The old part of that village, huddled down by the cove, is pleasant and full of character; but the new part consists of white boxes spattered all over the place without coherent plan; and the whole place is far less attractive than it might be if it were better planned and better planted. Not a tree or shrub to give the white boxes screen or shelter. Good planting is specially called for in such a place; for this village, with its brilliant sands and almost frost-free climate, is likely to attract more visitors and more permanent residents in future.

That is but one example out of very many that might be given. A headland may have a beauty that is close-cropped; but few towns can afford to look positively bald, and little of our seaside architecture can well afford to dispense altogether with the softening shape and colour of trees or shrubs. Towns which live largely by attracting visitors should be at special pains, for economic reasons if for no others, to ensure that their seaward side does not become an unrelieved grey mass of cement and stone.

Is Planting Practicable?

So we come to the second of our three questions. Assuming that in many seaside places more planting would be desirable, would it be practicable?

Well, of course there will be difficulties to surmount, some normal, some special. There will commonly be the problem of protection against rabbits; there may be a risk of damage by hooligans; and there is the difficulty of obtaining plants during a period immediately after a long war, especially those plants which were always comparatively uncommon. And besides these difficulties which many planters anywhere may have to face, there are the difficulties peculiar to planting in sea-wind.

Those special difficulties are serious. It is true that in the bleakest seaside exposures none of our native hardwood trees will thrive—not even ash or sycamore. It is easy to understand why some Cornishmen, accustomed to living on a coast now almost treeless, are content to say "We don't belong to have trees here."

But—and here comes the point of this chapter—I am convinced that even in these bleak places good planting is practicable; practicable, that is, without excessive trouble. It is much more practicable now than it was in the past, and much more practicable in mild maritime districts than it would be in colder climates, thanks to certain plants from New Zealand and elsewhere which have by now been thoroughly tested in this climate. I suggest that Plates I, II, III, and IV, illustrating plants growing in an exceptionally severe exposure—that of my own garden, high on a Cornish moor—are evidence in support of this claim.

Look, for instance, at the shrubs illustrated in Plate III. These bushes of *Senecio rotundifolius* are growing at an altitude of 600 ft., facing north, and exposed to every wind except from the south. Northwards, the sea is half a mile away; north-eastwards, there is nothing between the bushes and Newquay, and north-westwards nothing between them and New York. Some twelve years ago they were planted when small in shallow peaty soil on top of a big rock, without even sticks to steady them (though this help would generally be advisable); now they are 8 ft. high and growing fast. The outstanding fact about this and other plantings of this shrub in similar exposures is that the plants are wholly undistorted by wind or draught: in a spot where blackthorn and hawthorn would be sheared to a height of 2 ft. or 3 ft., this New Zealand shrub stands up, a perfect round. Look also at Plate II, illustrating a tree of *Olearia Traversii*, another New Zealander. The site is so exposed that, when I began making a garden here twenty-five years ago, a most expert Cornish gardener warned me not to expect to be able to get an *ilex* to reach 6 ft. in twenty years. Behind the tree lies open moorland, without a bush taller than dwarf autumn gorse; yet here is this tree, 20 ft. high, a fast-growing evergreen. No native tree—not even ash or sycamore—could have achieved so much. And in sandy soil close to the sea this plant will reach 10-15 ft. in four or five years.

Certainly, planting in such exposures involves more initial trouble and more after-care than planting in shelter. But it is a manageable

Wind and Shelter

enterprise, given such simple care as is suggested in the Notes at the end of this chapter, and given such plants as are recommended in List A below.

What Plants?

So we come to the third question: What plants have been found to be best fitted to provide shelter in severe maritime exposures in our milder counties? What plants are likely to thrive behind the first line of defence but within close range of spray-drenched air? And what plants would be most suitable for the windiest parts of fairly sheltered gardens farther inland?

The list that follows is meant to be a help in answering these questions. A large proportion of the plants here included figure, of course, in previously published lists of plants recommended for maritime sites. But this list, being meant only for the milder counties, can include without reserve some plants which would be too tender for such inclusion in a list meant for general use. And a few of the recommendations here made, based on experiments by myself and other Cornish planters, are likely to be new to most readers.

It will be seen that the repertory of wind-hardy plants is a fairly large one. I believe that it could be enlarged considerably if only there were provision for long-term experiment on an ample scale by some public body such as the Royal Botanic Garden, Kew, or the Royal Horticultural Society.

Throughout the book a standardised system of symbols has been used to indicate the idiosyncrasies of certain trees and shrubs. These symbols are as follows:

* * Specially recommended.
* ¶ Recommended for planting on sand-dunes, or sandy foreshore.
* § Wind-hardy.
* † Needs shelter.
* ‡ Frost-tender.

LIST A

WIND-HARDY PLANTS

ABIES. SILVER FIR.

Some of the firs can well be used in windy places as a plantation for giving shelter or for timber. Like other conifers they stand a much better chance in windy sites if protected at the outset by a wind-break 3–4 ft. high. Some look well as isolated trees when young, even in exposed places, but I doubt if any can be relied upon to remain shapely trees when old unless fairly well sheltered. Those worth considering include:

A. cephalonica, Greek Fir, from the Greek mountains.

A. Forrestii, or the almost identical *A. Georgei*. This is probably the finest of the Silver firs. I find that, surprisingly, it does very well as a young tree in severe exposure here on the moorland near Land's End; but this is no guarantee of its ultimate behaviour.

A. grandis, Giant fir, a native of the Pacific coast from Vancouver to California. It wants deep damp soil.

A. nobilis, another from N.W. America, does well as a plantation on the windy coast of Caithness, and can be recommended for trial elsewhere in windy maritime sites where the soil is deep and the climate damp.

A. pectinata, Common Silver fir, from mountains of Central and S. Europe, is likely to succeed, given a damp climate and some shelter. It does so even in Caithness.

A. Pinsapo, Spanish fir, from limestone mountains in S.E. Spain, is very wind-hardy, and handsome in its rigid distinctive style. It transplants pretty well, and can thrive without free lime. Worth trial as a more isolated tree, as well as in plantations.

For *Douglas Fir* see *Pseudotsuga*.

ALNUS. ALDER.

A. glutinosa. Common alder. The native alder grows well in full exposure in several exposed places on the Cornish coast. It may be helped by the fact that it comes into leaf late in spring.

A. oregana, which ranges from Alaska to California, is a handsome tree, both in flower and in foliage, and might well be tried here near the sea, as in California.

ARBUTUS

A. Unedo stands a good deal of wind, though not very severe exposure. See page 82.

ASH. See FRAXINUS.

ATRIPLEX

¶ *A. Halimus*, purslane, with silver-grey semi-evergreen foliage, is extremely wind-hardy, and useful for a hedge in full sun on dry soil, even pure sand. Easily propagated from cuttings.

Baccharis

B. patagonica, another good hedge-plant near the sea, has neat, deep-green, evergreen foliage, and reaches 8 ft. or more; a dull plant but useful.

Beech. See Fagus.

Berberis

B. Darwinii is extremely wind-hardy, though it does not flower where exposed to the full blast. See page 84.

Brachyglottis

B. repanda. A large evergreen bush, about 12 ft. high and across, with big leathery leaves, white beneath, and very large terminal heads of small whitish flowers. Used for wide hedges in the Scillies; hardy in such climates as Cornwall's except in an abnormal frost; handsome in foliage when slightly sheltered, and very wind-hardy; but likely to get tattered and shabby in full exposure. There is also a form with purplish leaves.

Buddleia

B. globosa, the one with honey-scented flowers like orange balls in May and June, is very wind-hardy. *B. Davidii (variabilis)*, especially var. *nanhoensis*, is suitable also; and there are hybrids between *globosa* and *Davidii*.

Bupleurum

¶ *B. fruticosum.* An evergreen bush with blue-green leaves and umbels of small, dull-yellow flowers; useful as a wind-stopper near the sea, even in sandy soil, or for temporary interplanting (with, say, *Rhododendron Roylei*). It needs staking to begin with, unless planted quite small.

Cassinia

¶ *C. fulvida.* A New Zealand bush up to 6 ft., with small crowded leaves, dark green, yellow beneath, the whole bush yellowish in effect. Flowers small, white. Not very pretty, but useful as a hedge close to the sea. *Olearia Solandri* is very like this. *C. retorta* is similar, but has grey foliage.

Cistus

¶ *C. pulverulentus* (formerly *C. crispus*), with grey leaves and lilac-pink flowers, proves able to stand exposure right down on a sandy foreshore; and others, such as *laurifolius*, *corbariensis*, and *populifolius*, are worth trying. See page 96.

Clematis

C. Flammula, though not of course able to afford shelter, thrives without shelter itself, even in severe exposure. See page 99.

Coprosma

‡ *C. Baueri.* A New Zealand shrub with round leaves, rather fleshy bright green, glazed and glittering. Very wind-hardy and suitable for gardens on sand-dunes, but may be knocked out by frost, even in the mildest counties.

Cordyline

C. australis (*Dracæna*) is among the very wind-hardy plants for mild maritime sites, and it has a remarkable capacity for carrying its trunk bolt upright even in full exposure. But it is not a plant which always looks appropriate in the English garden picture. See page 104.

Cornus

C. capitata (syn. *Benthamia fragifera*), with cream-white flower-bracts and red fruits, is one of the plants which proves much more wind-hardy than one would expect; so that, like *Tricuspidaria lanceolata*, *Myrtus Luma*, the *hoherias*, and the garden *hydrangeas*, it can be used in mild windy gardens behind the first line of shelter. See page 104.

C. stolonifera, the red osier dogwood, which makes a thicket of red stems conspicuous in winter, can be used as a wind-break in a rough place; also *C. s. flaviramea*, its yellow-barked variety.

Corokia

**C. virgata*, with small leaves, small stars of yellow flowers, orange berries, and stiff growth, is first-rate for a hedge in a windy garden.

‡ *C. macrocarpa*, with olive-like leaves, white underneath, and yellow flowers, is a handsome upright bush, suitable for a wind-

screen, and beautiful in colour with such plants as *Olearia Traversii* and *O. semidentata*. See also *C. buddleoides*, page 106.

COTONEASTER

These include some of the most wind-hardy and valuable shrubs for exposed gardens.

*C. lactea is outstanding in this respect, making a wide mound of grey-green, loaded with small red berries; try it as a wide hedge. Also *C. serotina*.

*C. pannosa, with tall plumes of small grey-green leaf, can stand wind and draught as few shrubs can; and *bullata*, with fine scarlet berries as early as September, is remarkably tough. See also *C. salicifolia*, *Wardii*, *conspicua*, etc., pages 108–109.

C. integerrima, the only species of cotoneaster which is a native of Britain, might seem a poor plant in sheltered gardens, but is a pleasant sight when hugging a large wind-swept rock.

CRATÆGUS. THORN.

C. Oxyacantha and *C. monogyna*, our two hawthorns, are amongst the most wind-hardy of native shrubs; but even these get shorn and deformed into flame-like shapes when fully exposed to sea-wind.   For their varieties, and for other thorns worth trying, e.g. *prunifolia* and *cordata*, see page 69.

CUPRESSUS

C. Lawsoniana stands wind fairly well; the grey and golden-leaved forms, such as the blue-green *C. L. Allumii*, resist wind and spray better than the green ones (Thuyas, on the contrary, are useless in sea wind).

*C. macrocarpa. Monterey cypress. This plant, so familiar in mild climates here, is extremely fast-growing, and in favourable conditions makes a stately forest tree or isolated specimen. Planted as a tall screen and allowed to grow freely, it makes an excellent wind-break, though it will be blasted on the seaward side if close to the sea. But in exposed positions it is apt to blow over when about 20 ft. high, having grown too fast for its root-system. *C. macrocarpa* is often used as a hedge because it grows so fast, and because of the bright green of its juvenile leaf (which is very different from the much darker leaf on mature growths). But such hedges are often unsatisfactory, dying off brown in patches. This is probably due either to draught, or to attack by

grey aphis, or to hard pruning which this tree resents. Hedges of *macrocarpa* should be clipped twice annually, say at the beginning of July and about the second week of August, only a few inches of growth being removed at each clipping. This will leave time for further small growths to be made before winter. It is a mistake to allow the hedge to grow to the full height desired before the first clipping is made.[1]

C. macrocarpa lutea, a variety with a good deal of yellow in its young growth, is considered to be less liable to browning than the typical form, but even this is unreliable as a hedge, being ruined where a persistent draught strikes it.

ELÆAGNUS. OLEASTER.

*E. glabra. A rampant evergreen bush, reaching 10–15 ft. or more if among trees; leaves green with rust-brown undersides and shoots; small, tubular flowers in late autumn, inconspicuous but fragrant.

*E. pungens is more spreading, usually spiny, with dull white and brown scales on the underside of the leaf. Like *E. glabra*, it is very useful as a wind-stopper. Its variegated form is much better than most variegated shrubs.

E. macrophylla, with beautiful foliage and small scented flowers in late autumn, can also be used in windy sites, and will stand shade. Its large leaves are grey-green above, silvered beneath, and the young growths look as if washed with aluminium.

ELM. See ULMUS.

ESCALLONIA

These, as every seaside gardener knows, provide some of the most valuable of all shrubs for sheltering windy gardens in a mild climate.

---

[1] In California, where this plant is native, it has been commonly used for hedges, but it is being wiped out by a fungus disease (*Coryneum cardinale*), and, according to a study by Dr. Carl Wolf, of the Rancho Santa Ana Botanic Gardens, California, it "is apparently doomed in cultivation and no further plantings should be made." Experiments have been made to find a disease-resistant substitute from amongst the other cypresses native to California; and it was reported in 1938 (*Proceedings of the 5th Western Shade Tree Conference, Sacramento*) that "Sargent's, Dutton's" (a form of *C. Sargentii*), "and the Tecate cypress" (*C. Forbesii*) "seem to be the most promising for wind-breaks and hedges, but little is known as yet as to how well they will stand trimming."

E. macrantha. This and *E. rubra* (so-called) are two of our most familiar and useful hedge-plants. *Macrantha*, with its gummy leaf, is proof against all storms except the saltiest, when it may get scorched. Its foliage is handsome, and gives off an aromatic gummy smell when new. It is often so red with flowers in June as to be conspicuous from a distance; and bees love it. It grows fast when once it gets started, reaching 14 ft. even in severe exposure. Some fifty years ago it was planted as a hedge on a site 600 ft. up on Zennor Moor, where there was not a tree, not a bush bigger than gorse, and where even sycamore cannot thrive. The hedge remains today an almost perfect evergreen windbreak, 14 ft. high.

But the plant has serious defects. Its roots are wide-spreading and greedy; it needs fairly frequent attention, for it spreads horizontally as well as upwards, quickly overgrowing its allotted space, blocking pathways and smothering other plants. Fortunately, it stands cutting back very well. Branches spent with flowering should be cut out. It transplants badly, often taking a year to settle down after a shift, but when it does start it grows fast. Few plants more detest having their roots exposed to drying winds. Plant it small, and if you want a specially good specimen for a special place, choose a seedling rather than a plant raised from a cutting.

E. Ingramii is a hybrid of this (*E. macrantha* × *punctata*), with an erect vigorous habit. Still more erect, with small scarlet-red flowers, is *E.* "Red Hedger," a form selected by Messrs. Treseder, of Truro, probably a similar hybrid: it makes a tall hedge, very upright, and narrower than the usual *macrantha* hedge, but may prove not stiff enough for its height.

"C. F. Ball" is a vigorous, wind-hardy hybrid of the *macrantha* type, reaching 9 ft. or more, with large lasting flowers, very bright red; good for clothing a tall espalier.

E. rubra. The plant commonly known in Cornwall under this name is not *rubra*, but a form of *E. punctata*. It is a very valuable hedge-plant, e.g. for the top of an earth-filled hedge. The leaf is much smaller than that of *macrantha*, the flowers pinker, and the habit more suitable for a medium-sized hedge. It stands clipping perfectly, and cuttings strike as easily as willow. (Prunings stuck straight into the ground in some shade will generally grow.) It has two defects: it gets badly browned in a salty gale, and it grows outwards too much, so that it needs fairly frequent cutting.

E. erecta is another small-leaved hedge-plant, offered by the Donard Nursery Co., with well-furnished shoots bolt upright; excellent in habit, but unfortunately wind-tender.

E. "Crimson Spire" is another erect grower, now offered by Treseder's Nursery, Truro: a tall vigorous plant with red flowers, very promising.

Other *escallonias* which are notably wind-hardy include: *exoniensis* (*E. pterocladon* × *punctata*), an erect grower with dark leaves and small, white, pink-flushed flowers. This is good for a tall screen. Growths that have flowered heavily should be cut out immediately after flowering.

E. Iveyana, a natural hybrid found by Mr. Ivey, gardener at Caerhays, has exceptionally handsome, dark, polished foliage and conspicuous trusses of white flowers in July–August; fairly wind-hardy, but not suitable for the first line of defence.

E. newryenis is an erect tall grower, with small leaves and small pinky-white flowers; fast growing, little scorched by wind and very useful for a high screen.

E. pterocladon, with small white flowers, stands a lot of wind.

E. revoluta, like *macrantha*, but with greyer duller leaves and poorer flowers, is another very wind-hardy one.

E. organensis makes a large rounded bush well furnished down to the ground, with a showy cluster of pink flowers at the end of every shoot. This is surprisingly wind-hardy, and is recommended for trial as a hedge in severe maritime exposures. Not very hardy.

Lastly, the garden hybrids, red, pink, and white, from the splendid new *"Glory of Donard" to the old *langleyensis*, are exceptionally good for windy gardens. *"Donard Seedling," pink and white, flowers with wonderful freedom even in so exposed a site as the south side of St. Michael's Mount, and *"Apple Blossom," stiffer and bushier in habit than most, is first-rate.

Eucalyptus

E. coccifera will stand much exposure and does not grow too tall. Try planting this thickly as a wind-screen.

Also *E. Gunnii* var. *montana*. But both are greedy soil robbers. For these and others, see Chapter IX.

Euonymus

E. japonicus. This familiar evergreen is invaluable for extremely windy gardens, keeping remarkably trim even near salt spray, and thriving in sand on the foreshore as well as in loam or peat. It makes a tall dense bush, and can be moved when fairly large; but it is a bad neighbour, since it robs much ground, and is a host to the sugar-beet fly. It may lose its leaves in frost, but usually recovers.

Fagus. Beech.

F. sylvatica. This is much less successful than ash in severe exposure to sea-winds; its soft young leaves are generally spoilt so early in summer that the tree makes little growth, affords almost no shelter, and cannot show its characteristic beauty. In positions with some shelter it does quite well; and in full shelter, on soil that is not too acid, beech grows magnificently, even in Cornwall.

Fraxinus. Ash.

F. excelsior. Ash and sycamore are much the best of our native or naturalised hardwood trees for exposed positions. In West Cornwall, for instance, ash or sycamore is generally the only tree around the more wind-swept farms. Ash will just grow in these severe exposures if closely planted and given some wind-shelter at the outset, such as a low wall. Trees grown under these conditions will remain stunted to 15 or 20 ft. They may have a good deal of dead wood at the top, and their new leaves may get blasted by a briny gale in May; but even so they are much better than nothing. In places where there is some land-shelter, such as the small valleys running down to the Cornish sea, ash and sycamore can make very sightly trees, though of course not nearly so big as those up-country.

Fuchsia

F. Riccartonii, the familiar red fuchsia, which is one of the outstanding flowers in climates such as Cornwall's or West Scotland's, stands a surprising amount of wind, though it may get seared by a briny gale in mid-summer; and though deciduous, it is valuable as a wind-sifting hedge. In cold places it may be cut to the ground by frost, but it comes up again perfectly. In some places it is now naturalised here, e.g. beside sheltered streams.

F. gracilis, the more slender common *fuchsia*, looks soft, but is in fact as wind-hardy as blackthorn. This, too, has run wild in some places.

GARRYA

*G. Thuretii is a very fast-growing evergreen with large greyish-green foliage; no beauty of flower; useful as a quick stop-gap or nurse for other plants, though in severe exposure the windward side will get seared.

*G. elliptica, with long green catkins on the male plant in winter, and with leaves like Ilex, is a much more decorative plant than *Thuretii*, but slower-growing. Get the male form: in mild gardens its catkins may be a foot long. Plant it from pots, for it resents root disturbance. It will do in light dry soil.

GENISTA

¶G. hispanica. Spanish gorse. Even in pure sand close to the sea this invaluable plant will make wide prickly cushions of deep green, yellow all over in summer. Extremely wind-hardy and easily satisfied. Unlike many members of its family, it grows equally well on alkaline or acid soils.

GRISELINIA

*G. littoralis. This is well known as one of the most reliable plants for wind-shelter. Its evergreen leaves are round, thick, yellowish green: the male form has dwarfer, smaller leaves, and is a more erect grower. No beauty of flower. This can make a handsome tree, 20 ft. or even 40 ft. high. One advantage of *griselinia* is that it can be moved without injury when fairly large: having a heavy mass of roots it is less likely to blow over when so moved; so it is one of the few which may be worth getting in oldish plants, where quick shelter is required in a new garden.

*G. lucida has larger foliage, and is a handsome upright-growing plant; rather more frost-tender than *littoralis*, but equally wind-hardy.

HIPPOPHAE

¶H. rhamnoides, Sea buckthorn, is deciduous, but very useful for sifting wind, and very decorative with its narrow grey leaves and orange berries. It will grow from 8 ft. to 20 ft. or even more.

To get berries, grow one male to every five or six female plants. *Clematis Flammula*, with milk-white flowers, looks well climbing through this, and stands wind equally well.

HOLLY. See ILEX.

HYDRANGEA

The garden varieties (*H. macrophylla*) rank with *Fuchsia Riccartonii* as the most decorative of all the shrubs that will stand much exposure. They serve remarkably well as a hedge, even close to the sea, and, though not evergreen, sift wind to a considerable extent, even in winter.

HYMENANTHERA

¶*H. crassifolia*. A dense, stiff-growing bush, wider than its height, eventually 6 ft. or 8 ft. high, but likely to remain much lower in full exposure; small sub-evergreen foliage, and quantities of small white berries along the branches in autumn. It is very wind-hardy and will thrive close to the sea, even in almost pure sand.

ILEX. HOLLY.

I. Aquifolium, the common holly, stands wind well, though not the severest exposure. Many of its hybrids and varieties are valuable for windy sites, such as *I. Shepherdii, Hodginsonii*, the small-leaved *ovata*, and (surprisingly) the very handsome large-leaved *camelliæfolia*. Planting in late spring is often advised, but may involve trouble if dry weather follows.

I. crenata major, a Japanese evergreen holly, and *I. cornuta*, the Chinese horned holly, might well be tried.

I. glabra, the American ink-berry, was recommended by E. H. Wilson (the great collector) for planting close to the sea; but it is a very slow-growing evergreen, and in our mild climate can well be replaced by *phillyrea*.

"ILEX." See QUERCUS ILEX.

JUNIPERUS

J. Pfitzeriana. A number of junipers are exceptionally wind-hardy, and some, such as *horizontalis* and *litoralis* (*conferta*) thrive

by the edge of the sea. Pfitzer's juniper is a vigorous, wide-spreading, bushy plant, dark green, very tough.
For other junipers, most of them very wind-hardy, see page 145.

LARIX. LARCH.

L. leptolepis, Japanese larch, does well as a plantation even in the very windy climate of Caithness, where it has reached 40–50 ft. in twenty-five years.

LAUREL. See PRUNUS LAUROCERASUS, page 28.

LAURUS

L. nobilis. Bay. One of the most beautiful of evergreens (besides being useful for flavouring marinated pilchards, etc.). It stands a good deal of wind, though not full exposure. Excellent for a tall screen on the lee side of the first line of shelter.
L. nobilis angustifolia, the willow-leaved bay, has narrow wavy leaves and an erect flame-like growth: a distinguished-looking plant for flanking a terrace or gateway.
‡*L. maderensis* is a very handsome species, with larger rounder leaves than *L. nobilis*, and quite showy flowers, especially in the male form. It makes an extremely vigorous and fast-growing bushy tree in woodland, but apparently (so far as I have tried it) can also stand very considerable exposure. Recommended for trial in mild gardens near the sea.

LAVATERA. TREE MALLOW.

¶*L. arborea*, the native tree mallow, makes a very fast-growing hedge by the edge of the sea; a coarse plant, but useful as a nurse.
¶*L. assurgentiflora*, the Californian tree mallow, is wind-hardy, rather weedy in habit, but very effective with its veined carmine mallow flowers. It is used as a hedge on the Californian coast, as *arborea* is here. It will reach 5 ft. in the first season from seed or cuttings.

LIGUSTRUM. PRIVET.

L. ovalifolium, common privet, is too familiar in towns, oppressively scented when flowering, and a soil-robber; but it deserves very high marks as a wind-resister, making good hedges grow on exposed headlands. Cheap and most easily propagated.
L. ionandrum, a stiff bushy grower with very small leaves, is a good hedge plant.

Lonicera

L. yunnanensis is another good hedge-plant for exposed sites—stiffer and better furnished down to the ground than the very similar and more familiar *L. nitida*. Both are useful.

Lycium

L. chinense. The Chinese box thorn is so completely naturalised on parts of our coast that one might suppose it to be a native. It is a shrub of loose rambling habit, somewhat spiny, with small greyish foliage, small purplish flowers, and showy, pendent, orange-scarlet berries. A very wind-hardy plant for the seaside, most easily grown, and useful as an informal hedge.

Medicago

¶ *M. arborea*. This bush, like a shrubby, yellow-flowered, evergreen lucerne, looks soft, but is in fact one of the most wind-hardy. In a very draughty position between buildings close to the sea near Godrevy Head, on the north coast of Cornwall, where *Senecio laxifolius* and *Olearia macrodonta* were cut to pieces, this survives as a good bush, though it has to grow there in pure sea-sand. The spikes of small yellow flowers are fairly freely borne for a very long period, including mid-winter.

Metrosideros

*‡ *M. lucida*, described in Chapter XI, is extremely wind-hardy and very beautiful, but slow to flower. When established in a mild garden it makes an excellent wind-shelter. See also *M. robusta*.

Muehlenbeckia

¶ *M. complexa*. A most rampant climber, making dense masses of wiry interlaced stems with minute leaves. If allowed to run up trees or supported on a strong fence, it will form an impenetrable screen 20 ft. high or more, even close to the sea. It thrives in sand.

Myrsine

‡ *M. africana*, which ranges from the Cape to Abyssinia, is a bright glittering evergreen like a small-leaved box, neat, useful for

stopping wind, and easily moved. Normally it makes a dense 3-ft. bush, but it can grow a good deal taller. Frost-tender, but likely to spring anew if posted in the milder counties.

NOTELAEA

‡*N. excelsa* looks like *Phillyrea decora* in leaf, but instead of remaining a large bush it makes a tree (over 40 ft. high at Tresco, in the Scillies). It is a handsome evergreen, very wind-hardy, and sufficiently frost-hardy· to have survived for many years in a cold garden at Truro. Though much injured in West Cornwall by the frosts of 1947, it is worth trial in mild gardens.

OAK. See QUERCUS.

OLEARIA. Olearias rank with escallonias as the most valuable shrubs for wind-shelter in mild counties.
O. albida (*O. oleifolia* in some catalogues). Very few shrubs can stand so much exposure. Even high up on Land's End moor it thrives in the full blast of every gale, as may be judged from Plate I. It makes a dense bush 8–10 ft. high—sometimes 20 ft. in its New Zealand home. The leaf is green above, buff-silver below; and the flowers, white in large corymbs in August, are mildly fragrant, especially after rain. The white is not brilliant and turns to brown, but this and the fluffy seed tone with the browning colours of moorland in August and September.

The plant sows itself freely, is easily propagated by cuttings, and needs only one attention: when it gets a bit leggy cut it hard back, or, better still, give it a hair-cut annually after flowering. *O. avicenniæfolia* is equally wind-hardy, but less satisfactory.
O. Forsteri, with tough leaves waved at the edge, and inconspicuous but fragrant flowers in November, makes excellent wind-shelter. There is a vigorous large-leaved form of this which is one of the best shrubs for a tall wind-breaking hedge. Not very hardy.
O. macrodonta. Another of the few first-class shrubs for shelter in severe wind. Big holly-like leaves, dark grey-green with silvered undersides; large flower-heads in June, so profuse that the bush becomes a mound of white. The flowers spread a refreshing scent, and the whole bush smells faintly of musk. The

fluffy seeds are quite decorative too, making an effect like pale-brown velvet. There are three forms of this, one with larger leaves and flowers than the type, and one quite dwarf: the large one is much the best; the dwarf flowers seldom, if ever. In many gardens *macrodonta* becomes leggy, but it can be kept bushy by pruning after flowering, or can be allowed to grow into a small tree, in which case the trunks look better for having the loose bark stripped off. The plant is easily propagated from seed or cuttings.

O. ilicifolia is similar in flower, but has long narrow leaves; it is equally wind-hardy.

¶O. *Solandri*, with erect twiggy growth and minute leaves, all yellow in effect, makes a good wind-screen hedge even on a sandy foreshore. Better than *O. virgata*, which is very similar but greener.

*¶O. *Traversii*, makes a tree 20–30 ft. high (see Plate III), with leaves green above, white beneath, so that in a wind it flashes against the sky like silver poplar. It has no beauty of flower.

This is one of the most valuable plants for wind-shelter, and is very fast-growing. How tough it is may be judged from the illustration, which shows a tree some 20 ft. high on Zennor Moor, at an altitude where the sea-wind keeps common blackthorn down to 2½ ft. high. It grows in any soil, including sand. Planted in pure sand close to the sea near Godrevy Head, Cornwall, it has made fine bushy plants 15 ft. high in four seasons; plants from cuttings will form a hedge 6 ft. high in two years. It is easily propagated by cuttings, but flags quickly on moving, and should be planted small. Pot-bound plants are useless for an exposed site. Being so quick a grower above-ground, it is apt to blow over unless severely topped several times until well developed underground; cut its head off ruthlessly when it reaches, say, 5 ft., and again later.

This is the best tall plant we have for providing shelter and greenery in sites where the soil is blown sand; and it might well be used here, as in New Zealand, for reclaiming sand-dunes. *Senecio rotundifolius* (q.v.) may well be interplanted with the *olearia*, since it never shakes at the root, and serves, with its stocky growth, to steady the taller grower.

In West Cornwall it was severely damaged by the great frosts of January–February 1947.

PHILLYREA
P. latifolia and var. *media*. These make large bushes of small dark leaves, eventually becoming small trees, beautiful in silhouette, like a fine-cut evergreen oak. They stand wind well.

P. decora has much larger evergreen leaves, dark green, with small white flowers in spring, not showy but very profuse and fragrant, followed by purple berries.

P. angustifolia has smaller leaves, and is slower growing than *P. latifolia*. A good bush for formal planting beside buildings. The variety *rosmarinifolia* has still smaller leaves.

PHORMIUM TENAX
New Zealand flax. This may be included here, though it is not a shrub, since it is commonly used for rough wind shelter. Its huge metallic swords of leaf stand all the winds, and it will grow in pure sand and increases fast. But it is a coarse plant, and the leaves make such a clatter when thrown together by wind that it is likely to be a nuisance if planted close to the house. Keep it for a wild place at the garden's edge.

P. Cookianum is a hardier and dwarfer plant, generally not exceeding 3–4 ft.; so it is better suited to a small garden.

PICEA. SPRUCE.
Some spruces are useful for shelter-plantations in windy exposures.

P. alba, White spruce, is extensively used for plantations on wind-swept dunes and heaths in Jutland.

P. excelsa (syn. *Abies Picea*), common or Norway spruce, comes from mountains in Europe, and is often used in Sweden for wind-breaks; but it is liable to blow over, and is not recommended for coastal planting.

P. nigra, Black spruce, which extends to severe climates in Alaska and Labrador, is one of those which succeeds as a plantation on the windy coast of Caithness.

P. sitchensis, Sitka spruce, from coastal ravines of Alaska to California, has grown very well as a shelter plantation on the coast near Thurso, and deserves trial in maritime exposures elsewhere, in moist soils. A tall narrow "Noah's Ark" tree.

PINUS. PINE.
Some of the pines, especially *P. radiata* and *P. Laricio*, are of outstanding value for shelter-plantations in mild exposed sites.

P. contorta, var. *latifolia* (syn. *Murrayana*), an extremely wind-hardy pine from altitudes of 5,000-11,000 ft. in the Rockies, is a quicker grower than *P. montana*, and can be recommended for shelter-belts, even in dry sites.

P. halepensis, Aleppo pine, common on Europe's southern coasts, e.g. in Dalmatia and Greece, proves remarkably wind-hardy near the sea in Cornwall. It can stand sandy soil.

*P. *Laricio*, Corsican pine, is first-rate for a shelter-plantation, one of the best conifers for windy sites. It grows fast and does well in sandy soil: in very poor soil the variety *calabrica* may be better. Plant small, when not more than 1 ft. high, in spring.

*P. *Laricio nigricans*, Austrian pine, may not be a very attractive-looking tree, but it is of exceptional value for wind-shelter. For a lime-saturated soil it is the best wind-hardy conifer; and it will thrive even on poor rocky soil in bleak exposures. Its value as timber is much less than the Corsican pine's. Plant in spring when the top bud is beginning to open; 1 ft. high is big enough. In ten years the plants will be about 12 ft. high in an exposed position, and still bushy; but when they get older they will shed their lower branches and draughts will come in at ground level. So if a shelter-belt of these pines is planned, provision should also be made for an outer screen of such evergreens as *Griselinia* or *Olearia*, which will remain bushy. See also *P. radiata*.

*P. *montana*, Mountain pine, should, I believe, be extensively used for shelter-planting in exposed dry sites. It is not one of the more beautiful trees of its kind, but it stands exposure and drought to an extraordinary degree, thriving on the driest heights in South-east Switzerland, above the levels at which even the tough *P. Cembra* gives up the struggle for existence. Mr. E. L. Hillier (in his *Suggested Combinations for Forestry Planting*) wrote thus about *P. montana*, var. *uncinata*, the tall-growing form which reaches 60-80 ft. in mountainous country in Spain and France: "At about 5 ft. apart [it] makes the best possible wind-break, even at very high altitudes and against the fullest possible sea exposure. This taller variety of mountain pine, with the dwarfer form, are much used in Denmark, with success, on the most exposed coasts of Jutland and elsewhere. In similar localities *Pinus contorta* var. *latifolia* (*Murrayana*) may be planted with the above-named pines, especially where the plantations are of considerable width."

This estimate of the toughness of *P. montana* is borne out by experience in several places in this country. Thus, near Dundee it has been used with notable success as a large shelter-belt. In North-west Wales it makes a perfect shelter even on a bleak hill-top, 1,100 ft. up, with very little soil. It thrives too in the Scillies, in conditions of extreme drought and exposure.

It is a variable plant, some forms making upright trees 80 ft. high, others (var. *mugho*) remaining dwarf enough to furnish ground cover for chamois.

*¶*P. muricata*. Bishop's pine. This, the most decorative of these pines, comes from the stretch of coast in California which is also the home of *Pinus radiata* and *Cupressus macrocarpa*, and like them it stands wind and even spray. In Guernsey it is said to endure salty winds even better than *P. radiata*[1]; and on the North Cornish coast it makes dense bushy plants on sand close to the sea.

P. Pinaster (*maritima*). Maritime pine. This is the tree which, planted in 1826 in quantity on the northern slopes of Helford Estuary in Cornwall, provided much of the shelter which has made possible the luxuriant growth of such gardens as Glendurgan and Trebah. It constitutes the resin forest of the Landes country south of Bordeaux and the pine-woods of Bournemouth. Mature trees bear all their foliage high up, on top of a tall bare trunk, so that a narrow belt of it does not provide shelter at ground-level.

**P. radiata* (syn. *insignis*). Monterey pine. It is this splendid pine which makes the dark mass on the landward side of St. Michael's Mount, the plantation within a few miles of Land's End, and much of the wood which grows out in the Atlantic on Tresco Island. That shows how wind-hardy it is. It has been extensively planted on waste ground of disused Cornish tin mines, and is doing excellently so far in these conditions. In sheltered places it makes one of the grandest of large isolated trees. In very severe exposures *P. radiata* may get blasted and deformed on the windward side, so in such places it is better in a plantation of some size than in isolation. But it is very intolerant of crowding: if too close to other trees, even of its own kind, it grows poorly. In light or shallow soil it is apt to get blown down by a gale when full-grown.

[1] *Trees and Shrubs Hardy in the British Isles*, W. J. Bean, Vol. II, p. 186, citing a Guernsey correspondent.

As a garden plant *P. radiata* needs careful placing, for its needles can be a curse, blowing about the garden, and near the tree they make a dense mat through which hardly anything will grow. Moreover, when the trees in a plantation get fairly big, in fifteen years or so, the lower branches are apt to die, making an ugly blackness and letting through draughts which may be damaging in the garden. So if a shelter-belt of this pine is planted, give it an outer shelter-belt of such plants as *Olearia Traversii, O. albida*, and *O. macrodonta*, and another belt, if space allows, on the inner, sheltered side, consisting of such shrubs as gorse, *griselinia*, and *olearia*.

It grows extremely fast—faster than any other pine. It cannot bear root disturbance. Plant it in March, when it is not more than 2 ft. high. If obtained from a nursery, the plant should come with roots tied up in a ball of hessian, having been lifted from open ground, not pot-grown. It is easily raised from seed sown in a bed in the open.

*P. sylvestris. Scots Pine. Very wind-hardy. Prefers light acid soils. Succeeds sown on coastal sands if thickly planted. Healthy mature trees are always decorative in silhouette, even when distorted by wind.

¶*P. Thunbergii.* Black pine. This is the Japanese pine whose stiff horizontal growth is familiar through Japanese prints and pictures. A good wind-break, and content with sandy soils.

PITTOSPORUM

The pittosporums include some of the most useful of evergreens for wind-shelter in mild gardens. Unfortunately the finest species are too tender to be reliable except in favoured gardens.
P. bicolor, with small leaves and small yellowish flowers, is a hardy, very wind-resistant species; not one of the most decorative, but excellent for a tall hedge.
*P. Buchanani and *P. Colensoi*, between which and *P. tenuifolium* there are many intermediate forms, stand wind extremely well, and are amongst the hardiest. *P. tenuifolium*, and its variety *nigricans*, stand a lot, but not the full blast.
*P. Ralphii is outstanding as a wind-resister, and is hardier than the two similar species, *P. crassifolium* and *P. Fairchildii*. With its silvery shoots and grey-green colour it is a very decorative plant; and it stands extreme exposure even on sand near the sea. It

should be planted when quite small, from pots or seed-bed; plants with a twisted tap-root are almost certain to get blown over when they grow tall in an exposed site.

*P. Tobira, with large polished leaves and cream-white flowers scented like orange-blossom, is another first-rate shrub for a windy place, fairly hardy and amenable to moving. In Mediterranean climates its flowering is conspicuous.

P. Dallii, a large round bush with very dark leaves, is wind-hardy, and certainly very frost-hardy. It is very slow to produce its scented white flowers, and remains very shy-flowering.

‡P. Kirkii is never seared by the severest gale, and it quickly makes a most decorative deep-green upright bush; but it was killed in most places by the great frost of December 1938, and cannot be recommended as a reliable wind-screen even for the mildest mainland gardens, since it may be destroyed by abnormal frost. For other *pittosporums* see page 341.

POPULUS. POPLAR.

The poplars include some wind-hardy and fast-growing trees; but, as noted in Chapter III, they have some serious drawbacks, notably the habit in some species of sending up a forest of suckers.

P. trichocarpa, best of balsam poplars, with its gummy leaf, thrives in windy seaside sites, here and in France (e.g. in the Cherbourg peninsula). See also pages 59–60.

P. alba. White poplar. On the North Cornish coast, in sites almost at sea-level, where whatever soil there is has long been overlaid by 3 or 4 ft. of blown sea-sand, white poplars reach 40 ft.

PRUNUS

P. Laurocerasus. Common laurel or cherry laurel. This plant, so often misused and despised, can be of great value as a windscreen in woodland, though it may not stand full exposure. I have seen a wall of it 50 ft. high in a Cornish wood; what other plant could surpass that as a screen for such trees as magnolia and *schima*? Left unpruned, it makes a most decorative tree in the milder counties: even in a Cornish garden rich in rarities some ancient laurels with twisted trunks leaning out from a bank hold their place amongst the outstanding plants. But laurels are notorious soil-robbers, and to make a tall wind-screen of them involves a considerable annual labour of pruning.

P. lusitanica, Portugal laurel, can likewise serve as a tall wind-screen in woodland.

PSEUDOTSUGA

P. taxifolia (Britten), (syn. *P. Douglasii*, Carrière). Douglas fir. This great tree does well as a plantation, for timber and shelter, in damp climates with fairly good soil. In southern England it grows very fast, and in the climate of Perthshire it is one of the grandest conifers.

QUERCUS. OAK.

*Q. *Ilex*. Ilex. Evergreen oak. This is one of the mainstays of our shelter-planting and one of the most wind-hardy and beautiful of evergreen trees. It succeeds even up on the high wind-swept moor, though of course it cannot there grow into great tree-masses as in sheltered places. Close to the sea, too, it thrives where few other trees can survive, though the plants on the sea-ward side, fully exposed to salt-spray, will get stunted and browned. Ilex was the nurse of the remarkable gardens at Abbotsbury, close to the sea, in Dorset; and it should be planted more freely near the sea elsewhere. But it needs time and space. It must be planted when small—not more than 1 or 2 ft. high; it grows quite fast when once it is well established. And it needs room, not only because it grows big, but because other plants apparently dislike growing close to it.

Several other evergreen oaks, such as *Q. phillyræoides*, a large bush or small tree, deserve trial for wind-shelter. As for the deciduous oaks, *Q. sessiliflora*, one of the two native species, affords a good wind-break when growing in a low dense mass, as it does in parts of Cornwall (e.g. on the northern shore of the Helford Estuary).

For other oaks, see pages 61-63.

RHODODENDRON

R. ponticum. It is remarkable that a family in which the large-leaved plants are notoriously shy of wind should include one species which is amongst the most wind-hardy. The common

purplish-pink *ponticum*, and its seedlings in purer shades of pink, thrive on bleak Cornish moorland just as the dwarf alpine rhododendrons do in the Chinese mountain-meadows. It sows itself as the foxgloves do, and under a June sky contributes as appropriate a colour to the scene as the foxgloves. In the shadow and glitter of a wood it is equally at home, and quickly makes a draught-proof screen for other plants. Like others of its tribe, it moves well even when quite large; but it needs watching if used as a screen, since it quickly spreads and multiplies, and is most difficult to eradicate when once it has taken firm hold. Don't over-plant it, valuable though it is. And don't get its purplish-pinks mixed with purer pinks or scarlets.
See also page 283.

Rosa. Rose.

¶*R. rugosa* and its hybrids, including I believe some fine American sorts little known as yet in this country, do well close to the sea, even on almost pure sand.

¶*R. virginiana* (syn. *R. lucida*), an American species with glossy foliage and bright-pink flowers, is another good plant for the shore. Make a thicket of it, such as blackthorn might make near the sea.

Rosmarinus. Rosemary.

Common rosemary does well even quite near the sea, and can be used for a low hedge.

R. corsicus, a hardy dwarf sort with bright-blue flowers, is excellent, e.g. for planting in the face of a dry wall; and so is the better-known *R. prostratus*. But *prostratus* is much less hardy than the common one.

Salix. Willow.

Some of the willows are excellent seaside plants. In particular, the common pussy willow, *S. Caprea*, stands severe exposure, and can be used as a deciduous wind-break in a rough place, preferably damp. *S. daphnoides* and *S. acutifolia* have very effective silver pussies, as bright as flowers against a Spring sky.

Senecio

*S. rotundifolius. Here is a plant, too little known as yet, which can contribute a great deal to the planting of exposed places in

mild climates. Its large round leaves are tough as leather, polished green above and pale gilt underneath when young. It has no beauty of flower; but the firmly drawn leaves are beautiful in pattern, and the golden shine of their undersides can make a sunlit sea look deeper blue by contrast. It will reach 20 ft. or more in a sheltered site, but will keep lower and much more in character in an exposed position.

The extraordinary wind-hardiness of this shrub is indicated by Plate III. Even in the severest exposure it keeps a trim rounded shape, undistorted by prevailing winds; and it can look after itself without further attention if planted small, with perhaps a stake to steady it until established. Its close rounded shape, when it is grown in the open, has the further advantage of making it suitable for formal planting beside buildings in seaside exposures. It might well be used in some of the new housing schemes in maritime towns in the south-west, and might be introduced, if space still allows, on built-up sea-fronts that need more planting. But it should be realised that the bush will get quite big some day. It is sufficiently hardy to have come through the great frosts of January–February 1947 without injury in fully exposed positions in the writer's garden, when common gorse browned, but I have known old plants killed in an inland Cornish garden.

The plant is easily propagated by cuttings, so that a stock of small plants can be raised quickly. And small ones, not pot-bound, are much the best for very exposed sites.

A variety of *S. rotundifolius*, var. *ambiguus*, has leaves not so round but broadly oblong or obovate (i.e. egg-shaped, with the broadest part towards the apex). The plants illustrated are probably this variety.

S. elæagnifolius. This is very similar to *S. rotundifolius*; but for some positions it is even better suited, since it grows into a wide pudding of a bush, broader than its height, half as tall as the other species. The leaves are more distinctly veined on the upper side. It is as wind-hardy, but I think rather less frost-hardy.

One form of *elæagnifolius* which is in cultivation here is very distinct and handsome; the leaves are longer and more pointed than in the type, brighter and more glittering green on the upper surface, and much whiter underneath.

S. elæagnifolius var. *Buchanani* is dwarfer again, normally reaching only 3–4 ft., with leaves only 1–2 inches long.

S. Bidwillii has the character of a mountain plant; it makes a stocky bush not more than 5 ft. high, with very thick leaves generally less than 2 inches long, of a bluer green than *elæagnifolius*, veined, greyish-buff underneath.

S. Greyii, S. laxifolius, S. compactus, and *S. Monroi* are low-growing and useful for breaking wind at ground-level.

S. Greyii is the familiar silver-leaved shrub with masses of showy, but rather coarse, yellow daisy-flowers in June; *laxifolius* is similar; *compactus* is dwarfer, and a very useful edging plant in front of grey-leaved shrubs such as olearias; *Monroi*, which is even tougher than the others, has green leaves, waved at the edge. Mr. Foster Melliar, in his book *My Garden By the Sea* (in Cornwall), records that a friend of his tried to make a garden near the sea's edge, but could get nothing to grow till he recommended *S. Monroi*. "It was trying it very high, but it stood the test, broke and sifted the wind so effectively that now she has a charming garden in which all manner of unseaworthy plants find a happy home."

SKIMMIA

These, with their dense evergreen foliage, can make handsome bushes even in seaside exposures. See page 174.

STRANVÆSIA

*S. salicifolia. A handsome evergreen, more erect than *S. Davidiana*, with narrow grey-green foliage, flowers like hawthorn, and red berries. Many of the leaves colour in winter. This makes an excellent wind-screen, 8–12 ft. high. *S. Davidiana*, a wide bush, is fine where there is room for a large wind-break in woodland.

TAMARIX. TAMARISK.

These are extremely wind-hardy, standing full exposure on the sea's edge, and thriving in sand; and they are most beautiful in flower when well-grown, making a smoke of muted pink. But they must be pruned if they are to flower well and not get ragged.[1] And the pink is not easy to mix, being easily killed;

---

[1] A correspondent on the North Cornish coast writes: "Most of my land is now bounded by a fine tamarisk hedge planted by me twenty years since, but the labour involved in keeping it trim is enormous, and I do not recommend this shrub as a boundary shrub to a private garden."

it can look just right against an old pinkish-red brick wall, or against sea and sand.

T. parviflora (syn. *T. tetrandra* var. *purpurea*). A tall shrub with arching purple stems; flower racemes lateral on last year's branches. This flowers in May, and should be thinned and relieved of old wood after flowering. The others here listed flower chiefly in terminal panicles, and should be cut back almost to the old wood in winter.

In late summer and autumn come *T. anglica* and the similar but taller *T. gallica*, much used for seaside hedges. *T. hispida* (syn. *kashgarica*) is the most free-flowering, bright pink in terminal plumes in August–September. *T. pentandra*, syn. *hispida æstivalis*, resembles this but is less compact, much taller, and a month earlier.

THUYA.

T. plicata and the like, unlike Lawson's cypress, cannot stand sea-winds.

ULEX. GORSE.

U. europæus, and the dwarf autumn gorse, *U. nanus*, are the most wind-hardy of all native shrubs, and need no recommendation for their effect in the wild. Neither is a good garden plant, but *europæus* can be very useful as nurse for other plants outside the garden proper.

U. europæus flore-pleno, the double form of the spring-flowering gorse, is a first-class garden plant, since it is even more showy, though for a shorter season, and does not sow itself.

ULMUS. ELM.

U. campestris, Common English elm, is useless in full exposure.

*U. montana, Wych elm, is worth growing in fairly severe exposures. On the south side of St. Michael's Mount there is a small thicket of it, ancient and stunted, but healthy and of some use as shelter.

*U. stricta, Cornish elm, and the more narrowly upright **U. Wheatleyi*, are much more suited for windy sites than English elm, and succeed well around Penzance. In full shelter, *stricta* can make a noble tree. But it is often short-lived, being apt to rot at the core after thirty or forty years. The trees which frame the view of Salisbury Cathedral in Constable's famous picture are the true Cornish elm.

VERONICA

V. "Autumn Glory." An excellent dwarf hybrid, 2 ft., with small heads of violet-blue from mid-summer till winter. It is hardy, and stands wind but not full exposure.

V. Andersonii. A vigorous large-leafed hybrid (*V. salicifolia* × *speciosa*), with violet-blue spikes fading to white. Wind-hardy, but not the toughest. A rather effective form, with white-variegated foliage, is often seen.

*V. "Blue Gem." This hybrid of *V. elliptica*, so familiar in climates such as Cornwall's, stands any amount of wind, and should not be despised simply because it is familiar. A plant which flowers in mid-winter as well as in mid-summer and can be grown so easily in full exposure is one for which many up-country gardeners would be thankful. But do not plant it where it will suffer from drought. And try enlivening its rather lightless colour by putting with it such plants as the giant cat-mint, *Nepeta macrantha*, which takes up the purple-blue, and some pink flowers, such as pinks or mallow or a pink rose.

*V. brachysiphon (formerly *V. Traversii*). This plant, widely known under the name *V. Traversii*, is one of the best, making a big rounded bush smothered with small white flower-heads in late summer. It is frost-hardy (even up-country), and wind-hardy enough for all but the severest exposures. It can be beautiful on a Cornish hedge together with *Fuchsia Riccartonii*. "White Gem" is a compact, early-flowering form of this, generally about 2½ ft. high.

Among the species which stand extreme wind, *V. Dieffenbachii*, *V. elliptica*, and *V. salicifolia* are outstanding.

*V. Dieffenbachii makes a large bush, wide and rounded, from 5 to 8 ft. high, with thick lanceolate leaves, rather greyish-green, and 4-inch spikes of flowers in July. The typical wild plant generally has purplish flowers, but the one grown here, on hedges at Marazion and Zennor, is pure white with brown and purple anthers. The illustration shows a plant on a very exposed hedge at Zennor. It is one of the best shrubs for providing wind-shelter quickly in mild climates; for it grows very fast, making a 2-ft. bush in one season from cuttings, and it is remarkably tolerant of drought, thriving even on top of a Cornish hedge, which may dry out in summer—a position which *Veronica* "Blue Gem" might be unable to stand.

V. elliptica is another exceptionally wind-hardy species, from South America and the Falkland Islands as well as New Zealand. In the wild it varies from a bush a few feet high to a round-headed 20-ft. tree. Leaves grass-green, oval-pointed, ½–1¼ inches long, symmetrically set at right angles to the stem, with a minute edge of white down. Flowers large, white, or touched with purple, sometimes fragrant, in small heads. The true *elliptica*, in its fragrant form, should be extensively propagated here for hedging in severe exposures. Rabbits, unfortunately, have a passion for it.

V. macrocarpa is a striking bush 4–8 ft. high, apt to be gaunt in habit, with narrow, thick, dark-green leaves up to 6 inches long, and white flower-spikes 6 inches long in April–May, followed by large seed-capsules. *V. m. latisepala* is a variety of this, with shorter purple flower-spikes: perhaps not in cultivation here.

V. salicifolia is a very variable erect bush, with narrow light-green leaves up to 5 inches long; small flowers, generally white but lilac in some forms, on narrow spikes often drooping like catkins, 4–10 inches long. This is frost-hardy and extremely wind-hardy. *V. salicifolia Kirkii* is a small-leaved variety of the type, making a tough bush some 8 ft. high. Yet another of the many varieties, *longiracemosa*, has catkins of flower sometimes more than a foot long.

V. gigantea, from the Chatham Islands, closely resembles *salicifolia*, but makes a round-headed tree, 20 ft. high or more, with a stout trunk. This was introduced to cultivation here by Major Dorrien Smith, of Tresco; if, as I fear, it has been lost, it should be reintroduced, since it must be very wind-hardy.

V. speciosa, with broad glossy leaves and splendid spikes of wine-crimson flowers, is the parent of many garden hybrids. The species grows wild on cliffs close to the sea, sometimes almost touching the water.

The hybrids (dealt with in Chapter IV) are very showy and fast-growing, and are very valuable for a windy garden, though not in full exposure.

V. Traversii (now renamed *V. brachysiphon*, q.v.).

The foregoing selection is only a draft: there is need for much more trial of *veronicas* as regards resistance to both wind and frost; and I expect that some species and varieties not in cultivation here, including sub-alpine species, will prove as wind-hardy as any we have already got. The attention of hybridists is drawn to the illustration of *V. Dieffenbachii* (Plate VI). Give us plants as wind-hardy as that, but with the colours of the *V. speciosa* hybrids.

Notes on Shelter-planting

In venturing to add to this chapter some notes on methods of shelter-planting, I ask the indulgence of the readers who are practised in this job already. I can say nothing new.

Soil

Firstly, if the planting site is pure sand, give the plants a chance by bringing in some soil with humus in it. A little will commonly suffice to make a great difference. Once they get started, they will probably reach down to the soil that underlies the sand, if there is any; and then they will be all right, anchored. Since sandy soil is specially liable to dry out, it is worth giving a mulch of cut fern to plants newly put out in such soil for their first summer.

If the planting site is hard and rocky, break it up a bit. A stone-worker with a little dynamite can save a lot of labour in specially difficult cases.

Size

It is specially important in exposed sites to start with small plants. Cuttings of *Senecio rotundifolius*, for instance, when once they are well rooted, can be planted just as they are, without even a stake or with only a steadying stick. *Pittosporum Ralphii* is best planted as a seedling less than a foot high. So too with Corsican pine and *Pinus radiata*: plants 1 ft. high or at most 2 ft. are enough to start with. The same with *Quercus ilex*. There are, however, a few plants which can safely be planted in larger size even in considerable exposure. *Griselinia littoralis* is one, *Rhododendron ponticum* another.

Deciduous plants such as poplars, ash, and willow can of course be planted when considerably taller, for they do not have to carry so much sail during winter gales.

Topping

As was noted in the foregoing list, *Olearia Traversii* must not only be planted small but must be beheaded before it gets tall;

Wind and Shelter

otherwise it will probably blow over before it has a chance of getting sufficiently anchored.

If a plant does blow over, do not simply straighten it up and leave it as it was; lighten its top-hamper by drastic pruning, or the trouble is likely to recur.

Staking

In ordinary exposures, tie sufficiently staked till established, with one strong post, creosoted at the base and firmly driven down before earth is filled in over the tree's roots. But in exposed sites a cage of four posts is much better. Keep the posts rigidly in position by cross-bars at the top, and fasten the ties to the cross-bars, the tree being held in the middle of the ties. The bark must not be chafed anywhere, or constricted by the ties.

If you live near your plants all the year round, look to their ties after any severe gale: if you have to leave your garden for months untended, then you will have to take special care in staking, and may have to omit some plants.

Walls

A wall is of course an enormous help; indeed, where a garden is fully exposed to the north, a wall may be an almost indispensable preliminary to the growing of the finer and more fragile plants. Even a low wall may be of great value, breaking the force of wind at ground-level and enabling tall shelter-plants, such as *Escallonia macrantha* and *griselinia*, to get a good start.

But walls have their drawbacks too. They throw wind back in full force instead of sifting and taming it; so that new draughts have to be reckoned with, and space has to be spent on planting that will prevent the damaging sweep of wind along the wall and round its ends.

Hedges and Plant Screens

No need to stress the value of a good hedge. What would one not give, in a bleak new garden, for a wall of holly or yew clipped and fed for fifty or a hundred years. Fortunately, in mild climates, one can make a tall evergreen hedge or screen in ten years or so, with such plants as *escallonia, griselinia, Senecio rotundifolius,*

Pittosporums Colensoi and *Ralphii, Olearia Traversii*. Some of the forms of *escallonia* lately selected are likely to prove exceptionally valuable for this purpose, being more upright in habit than the old *E. macrantha* and the so-called *E. rubra* (see page 16).

A combination of wall and hedge is often very useful. Build a wide stone hedge, earth-filled; and plant the top with a double staggered row of such plants as *Escallonia rubra*, or *Fuchsia Riccartonii*, or *Veronica Dieffenbachii*, or *V. Traversii*, or *V.* Blue Gem. In this way one gains extra height, and saves the ground thus sheltered from much of the root-robbing that would otherwise be caused by the hedge plants.

Hurdles

As temporary screens, hurdles are very useful, both in new gardens and in old ones where wind and draughts are troublesome. When they are no longer needed for giving initial protection to shelter planting, they may still be useful for stopping local draughts; and if they are in a conspicuous place they can be erected in November and removed in April.

Wattle hurdles imported from up-country are less durable and more expensive than hurdles that one can easily make at home. Get some lengths of wood 3 inches × 1 inch; some bundles of builders' laths, say $3\frac{1}{2}$ ft. long (when these become obtainable again); a pound of inch nails, and some iron bars. Make the wood into long oblong frames, say 3 ft. × 8 ft. long, with a vertical bar in the middle and with end-posts long enough for driving into the ground. Nail the laths to the top and bottom rails, leaving, say, $\frac{1}{4}$ inch between them so as to let wind through. The iron bars, driven in on both sides and wired to the wood, will help to keep the hurdles steady.

Another good way of breaking the force of wind is to stretch coir-netting between strong uprights. This can be used on a boundary wall, or within the garden as a special protection for such plants as large-leaved rhododendrons or tree ferns.

CHAPTER III

Planting for Roadsides and Towns

AS part of the post-war development of town and country some new planting of trees and shrubs will certainly be needed; and Local Authorities, concerned with the planning of this development, will therefore have to consider what plants would be suitable for such purposes as roadside planting, street planting, and the open spaces in housing schemes. Here, then, is a review of this problem, especially as it affects Local Authorities in the mild maritime counties, followed by lists of plants recommended for various uses.

1. KEEP GOOD EXISTING PLANTS

The first need is to retain and look after good existing planting. Fortunately, even after the war's heavy demands have been met, and despite much road-widening, England still possesses a wealth of fine trees and a unique beauty of hedgerows. But care and replacement of this inheritance are needed, particularly in regions, such as West Cornwall, where sea-winds have helped to make trees and hedgerows scarce. And that care will only operate if the need for it is adequately recognised and if there is an effective curb on forces making for needless destruction of good planting.

Fortunately, the need for such care is becoming better recognised, and it has been emphasised in several recent publications by the Ministries of Transport and of Town and Country Planning. But there is still a lamentable insensitiveness to the loss that results from ruthless destruction of roadside trees and long-matured hedgerows.

Often, of course, it is impossible to save existing trees which stand in the way of a housing scheme or road-widening. That is one reason why new planting should be provided for.

But often it would be possible, without excessive trouble or expense, to save good trees or a pleasant old hedge, either by a slight readjustment of plans, or by a little extra care in building. The result is rewarding. I recall, for instance, a row of houses built by a Cornish Local Authority; they have no distinction of design or material, but they always look pleasant—far pleasanter than more expensive houses near by—largely because trouble was taken to spare a few tolerably good Cornish elms.

Road-widening has been responsible for the greater part of recent losses of good roadside planting, and this process will now be accelerated. Much loss is inevitable because of changing traffic needs. But every care should be taken to minimise this loss, and to make good such losses as cannot be avoided. To ensure that such care is taken, County Highway authorities and Planning authorities should, I suggest, co-ordinate their policies, so that, with all due regard for the efficiency of the roadway system, there may be agreed action to conserve so far as possible the irreplaceable charm and character that time and the farmer's unending labour have given to the English scene. No utility formula by itself, particularly no rigid standardisation of rural road-widths, can be a sound criterion for a road programme in this country.

Sometimes, when a road must be widened, an established hedgerow with trees can be saved from destruction by making the road into two one-way-traffic lanes, with a strip between. Properly managed, this kind of roadway has, of course, great advantages for traffic.

2. Appropriate Public Planting is Worth Some Public Expenditure

That is the starting-point. If you do not think that any public planting could make your town or countryside pleasanter to live in and to visit, and if you do not agree that suitable planting, well-sited, can be a sound investment of public money—why then, what follows will not interest you.

That public planting is worth while is being increasingly recognised by the public and by local authorities, and it is now being strongly encouraged by the Government.[1] Such planting would not be "appropriate" if its maintenance required more expenditure or more skill and labour than could be counted upon in the locality in question. Seaside resorts such as Torquay, Bournemouth, Eastbourne, and Scarborough have long found it a good investment to maintain elaborate public gardens; but these are special cases. I am not suggesting that what is appropriate for a Torquay should be copied in towns with quite different conditions and rateable value.

---

[1] Even since this chapter was written, there has been further official encouragement of "tree planting in roads and streets in urban and suburban areas." See Circular 24 (May 24, 1946) issued by the Ministry of Town and Country Planning to Local Planning Authorities.

Nor do I recommend the kind of planting that looks like an overspill from a private garden into public places; rock gardens, lily pools, elaborate herbaceous borders, are not likely to be appropriate for public planting, except in special cases where they can be conveniently dealt with as part of a public garden. And enthusiastic plan-makers would, I fear, be heading for trouble if they submitted plans involving heavy expenditure on plants, planting, and upkeep to Local Authorities unaccustomed to such a budget, especially if the Authority concerned had previously had disheartening experience of damage wantonly done to earlier essays in public planting. What I mean here by "appropriate planting" is planting substantial enough to make a manifest improvement in the general appearance of town or roadside, and simple enough to put no severe strain on the local budget or the local resources of gardening skill.

I must add, however, that in Britain—in this country where gardening is the most native and widespread of arts, and where most townsmen still feel themselves to be countrymen transplanted—we are still far behind our European neighbours as regards public planting in towns and villages. When we try, we can do the job magnificently, as may be seen in, say, St. James's Park. But how seldom we try. How restricted and unadventurous our public planting generally is.

Recently I passed by train through an industrial town in Switzerland. Forty feet from the edge of the railway platform rose the high blank wall of a factory. They might have walled in the platform and plastered the wall with advertisements. They might have left the space empty, with just the blank wall, or an advertisement on it, to look at. Instead they had used the space for an admirably planned and planted garden, with a backing of shrubs, three birch trees grouped on a little lawn level with the station platform, and a bright border of the long-flowering Poulsen roses. That garden was easy to keep up, and not costly to plant; I maintain that it was worth the trouble. So refreshing a sight, so civilized an achievement, in so unpromising a place.

Do consider, when next you walk through your town, whether it would not be a pleasanter place if there were just one cherry-tree in that open space, or a fuchsia-hedge, or a mound of hydrangeas. Why be content to assume that such things need remain "nobody's business"? The beauty that can be publicly shared is not less important than the beauty nursed in our back gardens.

3. Bad Planting is Worse than Useless

I say "worse than useless," since bad planting wastes money and labour, and wastes plants at a time when they are exceptionally scarce. "Bad planting" covers inadequate preparation of the plants for planting, bad preparation of the planting hole and bad setting of the plant, inadequate or inexpert after-care, and bad choice of plants. Far better not to plant at all if the requirements for good planting cannot be met.

(If I venture here to indicate what planters commonly mean by "bad planting," I ask the indulgence of every experienced planter who reads this. The elementary notes which follow are not, of course, meant for him. I only hope he will not quarrel with them, so far as they go.)

4. Trees for Important Positions must be Prepared for Some Time Beforehand

A tree suitable for roadside planting takes several years to produce. That is specially unfortunate just now, since labour has not been available during the war for the usual nursery practice of transplanting trees every other year (or in some cases every year). So for some years after the war trees worth planting will inevitably be expensive and scarce. That cannot be helped; the process of preparation cannot be dispensed with. For a roadside tree must start with a strong, compact root-system—not simply a few long trails, but plenty of fibrous roots; and this can only be achieved by transplanting, and by cutting back long roots. Moreover, if the tree is to stand in a fairly windy place, it must have a stout trunk; if it is to grow into a good shape, it should have a leading shoot, without competitors; and if it is to grow vigorously, it must have branches properly spaced, carrying plenty of leaf, which means that it must have been competently pruned if the need arose during its early growth. It is an illusion to suppose that a self-sown seedling tree growing in a wood is likely to thrive if simply howked up and planted beside a road. Preparation of the tree is indispensable and cannot be short-circuited.

5. Planting

(*a*) *Roots*. Don't let the roots of plants lie exposed to drying winds whilst planting holes are being prepared: cover them until all is ready.

(b) *Hole.* The old planter's maxim—"a pound on the hole and sixpence on the plant"—was on the right lines. Don't be content with a hole less than 6 ft. across for a roadside tree, 2½ ft. deep; and if there is a hard pan below that, it should be broken up.

(c) *Soil.* Don't fill the hole with sterile subsoil; give the plant a fair start with fertile stuff containing some humus. (I recall a trunk road in Cornwall before the war, with a wide sloping verge. An attempt was made to plant trees on this verge, but practically every one died. That was not because trees wouldn't do in that situation: anyone with experience of tree-planting could have predicted their death, since there was no proper cutting and filling of the planting holes.)

Above all, do not commit the crime of wasting that precious stuff, top-soil. It takes ages to make good fertile top-soil. If grass is cut in road-making, don't bury it, but stack it for use in the holes when rotten.

(d) *Depth.* Don't plant the tree deeper than it was before lifting. It is sometimes supposed that deep planting is a good precaution against a tree getting blown over; but it is not: it deranges the root-system, which is the tree's permanent anchor.

(e) *Staking.* Of course trees must be protected from being rocked by wind until they are perfectly established: they must be staked. But a mere pole up against the tree, with a tie or two, won't suffice to prevent rocking if the site is windy, and is likely to chafe the life-carrying bark of the tree. The only kinds of staking which prevent both rocking and chafing are the cage or tripod.

Such staking is really an economy, not a waste, of labour and money, especially in a windy climate.

(f) *Bindweed.* There is one weed which is so rampant and smothering, and so difficult to eradicate, that it is well-nigh useless to plant small trees or shrubs where it has got a hold. Beware of bindweed—the lovely and detestable big white convolvulus. If you find its growth above ground or the brittle white strings of its root in the soil, it is generally better to give up the idea of planting in that infected place.

6. After-care

The requisite after-care must also be provided for. In the case of trees and shrubs planted beside country roads, they should have been chosen with adequate regard for their capacity to look after themselves, despite rough weather, rabbits, and competition with plants already on the spot, since no great amount of labour is likely to be available for their care. But they must have some care, at least during the first four or five years. Staking and tying must be seen to fairly often, especially in exposed sites after a gale. Grass and weeds should be kept clear from the base of the tree for several years. A little pruning may be necessary, e.g. to remove a branch hanging across a footpath, or to remove one of two leading shoots; and this pruning must be competently done.

As for trees in street planting, they need more care; in particular, they must be expertly pruned, in so far as pruning is required.

Do consider this question of after-care before embarking on a planting scheme. Pruning is not a difficult job, given some expert training and some supervised practice, but an inexpert pruner can quickly waste several hundreds of pounds of public money, and permanently ruin growth that has been carefully tended for years. I recall, for instance, a housing scheme in which an admirable planting enterprise was deprived of its due effect. Each street was provided with an avenue planting. The trees were chosen with expert help; they were well grown when they arrived from the nurserymen; and for all I know they were well enough planted. A good many were ruined by children, the trees being ill-protected and the children insufficiently taught. Many were ill staked, and in war-time all suffered, inevitably, from lack of after-care. But these were not the worst injuries. All the surviving trees were deliberately cut to pieces, not by hooligans, but by a man paid for the job; every leading shoot was decapitated, each tree being sheared into a close mop-head, regardless of its character, by some unskilled hedge-trimmer. There are very good reasons for having good trees in those streets; there is something to be said for having no trees; but there is nothing to be said for having slaughtered trees.

7. Principles of Choice

There remains the crucial question—what are the chief requirements to bear in mind in choosing the kinds of plant for country roadsides and for towns?

(*a*) *Soil.* The plants must be such as can be expected to take

Planting for Roadsides and Towns

kindly to the local soil. In making the selections of plants which follow, I have had in mind the fact that in much the greater part of our maritime counties, including Cornwall, the soil is more or less acid. This means that plants of the heath family (*Ericaceæ*), such as rhododendrons and heaths, can be included, whereas certain lime-loving plants would be much more at home on chalk.

(*b*) *Climate*. The plants must be adapted to the climate, which is likely in this case to be equable and damp, perhaps windy. For exposed maritime sites they must be abnormally wind-hardy. I have indicated probable endurance of wind in the notes that follow, and Chapter II on wind and shelter has already listed plants specially wind-hardy.

(*c*) *Appropriateness to the scene*. The plants should look appropriate to their setting. Yes, of course, but how is appropriateness to be judged? Here is a difficult question.

First, let us be clear about this. The English scene, as affected by plants, has been changing for centuries; and it would be idiotic conservatism to rule out as inappropriate all the plants that we do not happen to be familiar with as constituents of the local picture. Year by year, consciously or not, we come to accept more plants as old friends, and that process will and should go on. If you question that, just try this simple experiment, if you live in a mild, maritime county. Lift your eyes now from this book and look out of the window. The chances are that your glance will fall first upon some "foreigner." That pine-tree over there is *Pinus radiata*, and the cypress is *Cupressus macrocarpa*—both from California. Your *escallonia* hedge came from South America, *euonymus* from Japan, *veronica* and *pittosporum* from New Zealand, hydrangeas from China, dahlias from Central America. Even your potatoes were foreigners once. If there is a rhododendron in sight, Asia Minor, the United States, India, or China will have bred its ancestors. The old red *Fuchsia Riccartonii*, which is at home beside so many a Cornish and Scottish cottage, is said to be a hybrid raised near Edinburgh in 1830 from a Mexican species. The purple buddleia which is now so familiar to you (and to English butterflies) first reached this country from China so lately as 1893. Imagine what the familiar scene would lose if all these "foreigners" were wiped out from our repertory.

Of course, we have much to be thankful for in our native trees and shrubs. Spring gorse, seen as a mound of pure yellow against a sunlit sea, is one of the finest shrubs in the world; and the hawthorn of English hedgerows is another. Pussy willow and catkins and blackthorn take a lot of beating; and one may travel far before seeing such a glow of colour from shrubby plants in flower as one may see each summer on a Cornish or Scottish moor, when the three common heaths are out, or such as one may see each autumn in places where the deep yellow of dwarf autumn gorse mixes with heather-crimson. In Cornwall, on Goonhilly Downs, we have the lavish pink and white of Cornwall's special heath, *Erica vagans*; and even in the bleak Land's End country, wherever the land gives some shelter, we have Cornish elm, and ash and sycamore,[1] and in some parts beech and oak.

But we need the foreigners too. In particular, the windy counties need them because they include plants far more wind-hardy than any of our native ones.

As regards planting in towns and in such places as railway stations, I urge planters in the mild counties to be a bit venturesome and imaginative, making use of the unusually varied range of plants that they can draw upon. We could make our public places so much more enjoyable for ourselves by more interesting and resourceful planting: and as for our holiday visitors, though we cannot always lay on sunlight for them, we can provide in winter as well as in summer the most attractive show of *unfamiliar* flowering plants that they can see anywhere in Britain. Certainly, the range of trees suitable for planting as standards in streets is a restricted one, whether in the mild counties or the colder ones; but planters in mild places throw away an opportunity if they confine all their planting to the almonds, laburnum, pink may, double pink cherry, etc., which are so plentiful now in the suburbs of London or Birmingham. Take Cornwall's case for an illustration. How many people, travelling past Doublebois railway station in the first months of the year, have enjoyed the white heath (*Erica lusitanica*) which some benefactor started there years ago. How many people, looking out at the platform of St. Austell station, must have been grateful for the screen of blue *ceanothus* which flourished there till lately. How many, noticing palm-like *cordylines* at St. Erth station, have seen in them a cheering sign that they were indeed coming to a mild sunny land! Why not go on with that kind of

[1] One thinks of sycamore as a native tree, but it is said to be one of the "foreigners."

planting? Not simply at railway stations, but at bus stops; not only in enclosed public gardens but in public squares and in reserves of planted ground in the new lay-out of our towns; not merely with *cordylines* (which are apt to look scraggy unless well backed with evergreens as they are in the planting beside Penzance's municipal buildings), but with trees and shrubs that will make a cheerful decoration in the town, will be unfamiliar to many visitors, and will require a minimum of after-care. A shrub could hardly require less attention than the hydrangea, and none makes a braver show; but remember that in most parts of England, hydrangeas are pot-plants, quite expensive, the sort of plant one sees at the front of concert platforms. Why shouldn't Penzance, say, lay itself out to provide, as part of the rebuilding now necessary, a really fine show of hydrangeas, blue and white, with a few good shrubs such as *hoheria*, *Eucryphia cordifolia* or *E. nymansensis*, Lantern tree (*Tricuspidaria lanceolata*), and tree myrtle (*Myrtus luma*). Why shouldn't the rebuilding of Newlyn provide a space for, say, a hedge of red fuchsia? A windy place such as Sennen could make itself more attractive if its new building plan allowed for such extremely windhardy plants as *Senecio rotundifolius* and *Olearia albida*. In some open space (such as the Moor at Falmouth) where people have to wait for buses, let us have something gay to look at, such as a bed of *agapanthus* (African lily) with white anemones. In a situation not fully exposed to the sun there might be *Rhododendron Nobleanum*, to cheer our winter visitors and ourselves; many other noble rhododendrons, such as "Loder's White" and "Britannia," can be used where light shade and annual mulching can be provided; others, such as "Mother of Pearl" and "Alice," need less shade; and some, such as "Lady C. Mitford" and "Mrs. J. Millais," stand almost full sun. (See pages 301–302.)

What I have said about extending the range of town planting can only be applied with reservations to planting in the open country, along roadsides. In particular, there are some plants which, though perfectly "in the picture" in a town or garden, look misplaced if planted in open country. Tastes differ much on this point. Everyone enjoys the sight of a copper beech near houses, and this tree can make a fine effect as an avenue in the countryside; but would you consider that a beech-wood, with its incomparable new green in spring, would be improved by some copper beeches interspersed with the green ones? For my part, I should not. I should say, keep copper beech, generally speaking, for town and garden. Again, take the case of the green- and purple-leaved forms of the cherry-plum, *Prunus cerasifera*. The green-leaved type is one of the most beautiful flower-sights of early spring and is strongly recommended in this book for hedgerow planting in soils where it will thrive. And *Prunus cerasifera* var. *Pissardii*, the commonest of its purple-leaved varieties, is a beautiful plant also, so much valued indeed as a decoration of our towns and gardens that it is perhaps over-planted there; but in a green English hedgerow this would, in my opinion, look much less appropriate than the common green-leaved one.

Nothing in all our hedgerows is more beautiful than a crab-apple tree; some of the imported species, such as *Malus hupehensis* or *Malus micromalus*, adorn a tall hedge, if suitably placed; but *Malus Lemoinei* or other crabs with bright purplish-rose flowers, lovely as they are in a garden, look too sophisticated, too gardeny, in the wild. The native wild cherry, white in April, is perhaps the best of all large flowering trees for a wild place (in soil which is not very acid); but the double Japanese cherries, especially pink ones such as the much-planted "*Kwanzan*" (miscalled "*Hisakura*"), are plants for the town and the garden, not for the wild.

(*d*) *Size of trees.* The very worst mistake in planting roads, especially streets, is to plant trees without allowing for the fact that they will grow to the stature of the tree in question. Consider what the road, and the view from the road, will look like when the trees are 30 ft. high, 50 ft. high, according to the kind and the exposure. Think especially what the tree-planted street will be like when the trees are big enough to show their character. Assume that the trees you propose to plant will have to be pruned a certain amount, but should not be so mutilated as to destroy their characteristic beauty; and then ask yourself whether those trees, reasonably pruned, will unduly obstruct the lighting of houses and gardens in summer. Will they make an excessive obstruction on the footpath when their trunks become fairly mature?[1] Will their branches droop too much in the way of passengers? If so, then *don't plant those trees*. Plant smaller growers, or none.

[1] The Ministry of Town and Country Planning, in Circular 24, says: "It is desirable that on classified roads carrying a fairly large volume of traffic and in towns where the footways are normally crowded, no planting should take place on footways of a width of less than 10 ft."

That warning may seem redundant; but though it seems elementary, experience shows that it is called for. Many a street in London and elsewhere can only keep enough light for its windows in summer by an annual mutilation of plane trees so severe as to destroy their characteristic beauty. I know of lime trees in a Cornish street which have to be kept to a mere lump of leafage on top of a fat post. What is the good of that?

I do not mean, of course, that street-planting should be avoided. Far from it. Even tall trees such as planes can look splendid in a town, if properly pruned, in such a setting as the Mall in London or the Boulevards of Paris; and planes drastically topped and grown as wide formal umbrellas can serve very well for shade on a promenade, such as the lakeside at Geneva. A planting of big trees makes half the charm of little squares and piazzas in France and Italy; many an English village green owes its beauty mainly to some great elm or oak.

Moreover, there are plenty of plants of smaller stature that can be grown in towns, especially in the climate of our milder counties. The point is—don't choose plants for street-planting that will grow intolerably big for their place. And when you have chosen plants of suitable stature, take care that they are not ruined either by gross neglect or by ill-judged pruning.

(e) *Mixture*. In street-planting, an avenue of one kind of tree nearly always looks better than an assortment. I recall a country town where the entering roadway has been planted with many standard trees of suitable moderate growth, but of too many kinds—crabs, cherries, hawthorn, laburnum, etc. The effect, which is only too common in some London suburbs, would have been far better if only one kind, such as *Prunus yedoensis*, or hawthorn, red and white, had been used for a length of roadway.

This is still more true of the planting of roadsides in open country. A lane between towering elms, a road through a beech-wood or between sycamores planted around a Cornish farm—are not these the kind of roadside tree-plantings that you have noticed with pleasure? Scots pine or Spanish chestnut, poplar or ilex—each species makes its best effect when it grows in company with its own sort. In parts of Cornwall, such as Helford Estuary, there are woods densely grown with little oaks, nothing but oaks (*Q. sessiliflora*); and though these have a negligible stature as trees, the roadways through them remain in one's memory as pleasant and distinctive places just because the plantations are not "mixed shrubberies" but simply oak woods.

(*f*) *Damage by the plants.* Be careful, in choosing plants for a particular place, not to use kinds liable to cause damage or annoyance.

All tree-planting near roads has this drawback: it does delay the drying of the road surface; a road surveyor can justifiably claim this. But quick drying is not the only factor to be taken into account, and local authorities will, I think, be justified, generally speaking, in holding that the improvement in general appearance which results from tree-planting in appropriate places amply outweighs this minor drawback.

But there are some injuries to road-surface and road verges which should be recognised as serious enough to rule out the use of certain plants. Common lime is a bad road plant because its fallen leaves are peculiarly slippery; and horse-chestnut leaves, though not sticky as those of common lime often are, are large and liable to cause skids. English elm is a bad road tree, not only because of its liability to the fatal elm disease, but because of its habit of suddenly dropping a branch, and because, with its shallow roots and wide-spreading head, it is apt to blow over. (This applies to the English elm, *Ulmus campestris*, very much more than to the Cornish elm, *U. stricta*, or its excellent variety, *Wheatleyi*, the Guernsey elm.) Silver poplar (*Populus alba*) can be a nuisance as a roadside plant, since it makes a thicket of powerful suckers, which may impede a footpath and may disrupt roads or paths. Ash has the drawback that its roots are greedy explorers, so that it is a bad neighbour for fields. Common yew should never be planted where cattle can eat it, since it is poisonous.

The native *berberis* (*B. vulgaris*), beautiful as it is, should not be planted at all, since it is the host of wheat rust. *Euonymus japonicus* is a host of the sugar-beet fly. Shrubs such as *Berberis stenophylla* and *Berberis Darwinii*, excellent in an appropriate place, are spreaders, and should not be planted where their prickly growth would be likely to invade a footpath. The rampant roses are unsuitable for hedges near a footpath because of their thorns.

Lastly, in planting trees in towns, the possibility of injury to sewers and mains should be remembered.

(*g*) *Damage to the plants.* There are some plants which are so specially attractive to children or to adults that they may get too much damaged. There is always the difficulty that if handsome plants are put in public places children may damage them, more or less for fun, and that grown-ups may steal the flowers. That is a trouble which, more perhaps than any other, has discouraged good planting for the enjoyment of the community; and there is no simple infallible way round it. *Some* damage, some theft, there probably will be, especially at first. (When one puts out new plants in a place full of rabbits, the new-comers are much more liable to get nibbled than they will be later.) Education (whether of children or grown-ups) cannot be instantaneous, and the habit of respect for public property of this kind cannot grow strong enough until there is common opportunity for its exercise. It will require the steady courage of conviction for members of Local Authorities to advocate public planting in places which have previously suffered from vandalism. But it would surely be a mistake to go on for ever being inhibited from planting beautiful things in public places because not everybody can yet be trusted to use this privilege properly. Planters should avoid offering needless temptations. They can plant the double-flowered horse-chestnut, for instance, if it is thought necessary to avoid the risk of damage by children chucking things at the tree or breaking the branches down to get at "conkers." It may be advisable to avoid planting crab-apples with showy fruits, such as "John Downie," for the same reason. But planting should go on. The British are not more incurably liable to anti-social behaviour than the people of other countries, where public planting has been persisted in, and has won adequate respect. In America private gardens are commonly open to the main street, without gate or fence. In a town such as Manchester, Vermont, for instance, the main street has its avenue of American elms; and shady lawns, planted with hydrangeas, day-lilies, and hollyhocks, border the side-walks. Those people have learnt the good manners necessary for making the best use of the opportunities of life in a modern town; and we can do so too. All that is needed is faith and persistence on the part of the authorities responsible for the planting, and sustained help in the schools. There will be some set-backs, probably, but the net improvement will, I am confident, amply justify the decision to accept this hazard.

So much for the principles which it is suggested should be borne in mind in choosing plants for roadside and town planting.

But, you may say, there is a snag in all this. Can the plants be got now?

8. Scarcity of Plants

Unhappily, there is a real, though for the most part only temporary, difficulty about getting good plants. Only well-grown plants are worth spending public money on; and the propagation and careful preparation of trees and shrubs have been almost impossible for nurserymen during the years of war, owing to shortage of labour and restriction of the area that might be used for such purposes. Transplanting is (as was emphasised above) a necessary preparation for the planting of trees in positions such as roadsides; but that preparation has not been done. It will be done, and done on an ample scale, *if* nurserymen know that, when they have raised a stock of certain plants, with all proper care, those plants will be marketed. But it will not be done if the demand is not indicated some time in advance. It will not be done if public authorities (and private planters) are not prepared to pay a fair price for the products of a laborious and sometimes chancy process. And whilst quick results are looked for by the public, and by impatient Councillors, the process cannot be hurried. Some of the handsomest and most wind-hardy plants are slow growers; and transplanting can only be done at certain seasons, and should in many cases be repeated before sale.

One way of mitigating the difficulty is by giving nurserymen sufficient encouragement, by firm *advance orders*, to grow the kind of plants that will be wanted. The nurseries have the stock-plants and the skilled staff and the equipment: they can do the job economically and quickly if—but only if—they know in good time what plants will be required.

Another way is to enlist the *co-operation of private gardeners*, who can propagate many of the shrubs required without much trouble, and can then give them to the public authorities. The C.P.R.E. in Cornwall is operating a temporary scheme of this kind.

A third way is to start a *County Nursery*. In Suffolk this was planned before the war, and the project is now being revived.

If we are to have adequate provision for conservation, planting, and after-care of trees and shrubs on our main roads, we shall need, besides more plants, more people equipped for the job—people with the requisite time, knowledge, and authority. Private individuals and societies can contribute much, but they cannot be expected to give all the time required, and they lack the authority which is needed in carrying through a national road programme. At present, few local authorities in this country have the staff sufficiently qualified for such a task, and the building up of such a staff will, I hope, be recognised as an urgent need. The Ministry of Transport is giving a progressive lead in this respect; and we may expect to see, in the development of England's new national roads, new applications of that native genius for "landscape architecture" which has given us in the past the most beautiful and resourceful roadside planting in the world.

9. The Plant Lists

After this general review of the problem, we can turn to selection of plants for roadsides and towns.

The first of the three following lists, covering LARGE TREES FOR ROADSIDES, owes much to the help of the book, *Road Planting*, published by the Roads Beautifying Association.

I have dealt with large trees separately, believing that *the common native deciduous trees are by far the most important element in the planting of country roads.*

The second, covering SHRUBS AND SMALL TREES FOR COUNTRY ROADSIDES, was specially difficult to compile: every judgment as to the suitability of a plant for such a purpose requires knowledge of many factors, and depends largely on the personal taste of the selector. I expect many readers will consider that this or that plant should be omitted or included.

In the third list, covering TREES AND SHRUBS FOR TOWNS, I cannot hope to do more than stir the imagination of planters with a few suggestions and then point to the range of plants listed later in this book and more fully described there.

All these recommendations can, of course, be no more than generalisations: all have to be made without knowledge of the precise situation for which the plants will be chosen, and planting conditions vary enormously within each county, within each town, and even between the southern and northern aspects of a single street.

LIST B

LARGE TREES FOR ROADSIDES

* Specially recommended.
§ Wind-hardy.

Acer. Maple.

A. campestre, native field maple, is bushy, usually a low tree or bush, common in hedges on chalk soils; *cappadocicum* (syn. *lætum*), yellows well in autumn; **dasycarpum* (syn. *saccharinum*) (silver maple) has silver undersides to its leaves and glowing autumn colour; *Opulus* (Italian maple) makes a rounded spreading tree, beautifully yellow with flowers in March; **platanoides* (Norway maple) is easily satisfied as regards soil, and is free from the black leaf-spot which disfigures sycamore; also *platanoides* var. *Schwedleri*, with red young leaves.

§A. Pseudo-Platanus, Sycamore, stands wind better than any other native tree except ash; but it makes a very much smaller tree in wind-swept localities such as West Cornwall than it does in such a climate as Wiltshire's; and in the windy climates its leaves turn muddy brown and shabby as early as August, giving the impression that summer is ending prematurely.

Æsculus. Horse-chestnut.

**A. Hippocastanum*, the common one, is one of the grandest trees for an avenue or single specimen; but it should be set well back if planted by a road, so that its large leaves will not make the road-surface slippery in autumn. In towns, the double-flowered form may be preferred, since it produces no chestnuts.

A. indica is a magnificent tree, too little planted, with large foliage and white pink-flushed flower panicles more than a foot long, a month later than the common horse-chestnut. It needs good soil with plenty of moisture.

A. plantierensis is a good pink hybrid between the white horse-chestnut and the red, *A. carnea*. *A. Briotii* is the best form of the red one.

AILANTHUS. TREE OF HEAVEN.
This makes a large, very handsome tree. The female form is one of the best town trees, thriving in London, but the male form's flowers smell unpleasantly. It is fast growing, is apt to produce suckers, and may seed itself too freely.

ALNUS. ALDER.
A. cordata (syn. *cordifolia*), Italian alder, grows very fast, making a handsome pyramidal tree some 80 ft. high, and can put up with poor dryish soil as well as boggy ground. It is the only alder durably successful on poor chalky soils.
A. glutinosa, the native one, though less attractive, may be worth using in boggy soil; *nitida*, with catkins in autumn, is a handsome tree where it thrives; and *incana*, grey alder, has catkins in spring. None of these is recommended for streets.

BETULA. BIRCH.
Birches, especially the silver-barked sorts, are amongst the best roadside trees, and thrive even on poor heath-covered ground (together with Scots pines). The common sorts are easy to propagate from seed and cheap to buy; and their white trunks are useful as well as decorative near roads, since they catch the light of headlamps at night.
*B. verrucosa, common silver birch, is the commonest and as good as any; its variety *dalecarlica* has graceful pendulous branches and cut leaves, but is not a tree for streets; *fastigiata* is an upright variety.
B. pubescens, white birch, is better for heavy soils.
B. papyrifera, paper birch, has a very white trunk, but makes a rather less graceful tree.
B. Ermani, japonica szechuanica, nigra, and *albo-sinensis septentrionalis* which has most beautiful grey and tawny bark, are fine kinds for special planting, but are more expensive.

CARPINUS. HORNBEAM.
*C. Betulus makes a noble round-headed tree when full-grown, and is useful also when kept down as a hedge. It stands wind pretty well. There is a very erect form, *C. Betulus pyramidalis*, much more suitable for street planting.

CASTANEA. SPANISH CHESTNUT.
C. sativa is one of the handsomest of deciduous trees that can be grown in southern England. It needs lots of room, making a large head and massive trunk; but if space can be found for an avenue of full-sized trees on, say, the approach to a town or village, no tree would be more suitable than this. It can stand dry, hot soil, and must have good drainage.

CUPRESSUS
C. macrocarpa (Monterey cypress) is fast-growing, wind-hardy, and very handsome when well-grown, but is more satisfactory as an isolated tree or a woodland tree or in an unpruned screen of separate plants than as a hedge. I do not think the English landscape would be bettered if this became a common roadside or hedgerow tree in the countryside; but in some special sites, near buildings, or where the shine of the sea shows between dark masses of the trees, it can be excellent.
C. Lawsoniana, familiar as a tall dark pyramid in gardens, is not recommended for country roadsides; but it, and especially its erect green variety, *erecta viridis*, can be very effective in some formal plantings.

DAVIDIA
D. Vilmoriniana and *D. involucrata*, described on page 115, look hardly more alien than the native lime tree, and could well be used for an important approach to a town if the soil is good and not dry. But *Davidia* is not a tree for quick effect or for exposed sites.

FAGUS. BEECH.
F. sylvatica, common beech, grown as woodland or as a belt, provides some of the most beautiful road decoration in Britain, or indeed anywhere. It grows best in soil that is limy or neutral rather than very acid; but whilst it stands a good deal of wind, it cannot show its proper beauty when exposed to salty gales off the sea. Where beech does well, superb isolated trees are not uncommon; but in general this is a tree for woodland or groups or belts rather than for single file. Beside a road, the planting of beeches fairly close together has the advantage of encouraging the formation of trunks unbranched up to a considerable height;

whereas isolated trees are likely to make wide-spreading branches too near the roadway.

F. sylvatica, var. *purpurea* (purple beech) and *F. s. cuprea* (copper beech) are splendid trees for town and garden; and the cut-leaved beech, *F. s.* var. *heterophylla*, makes a well-shaped distinctive tree, besides having a ferny grace in detail.

FRAXINUS. ASH.

*§*F. excelsior*, common ash, is one of the two best native hardwood trees for standing wind. Even when wind-swept it is generally beautiful in line, and when grown on heavy soil it makes a magnificent tree with valuable timber. But it is a bad neighbour for fields, having very greedy roots; and its leaves come late and fall early.

F. angustifolia, with narrow leaves, is elegant.

F. Ornus, manna ash, makes an effective show of whitish flowers in May; good for road- or street-planting where there is room for a round-headed tree with an eventual spread of 20–30 ft.

HORNBEAM. See CARPINUS.

ILEX. See QUERCUS ILEX.

JUGLANS. WALNUT.

J. regia, common walnut, is long-lived, has youngf oliage of a beautiful coppery colour in May, has a pleasant smell, produces valuable timber besides its nuts, and does well as a road tree in good soil with not much exposure. But it must be planted small, so that it needs attention for some time after planting.

**J. nigra*, black walnut, is better for road-planting, making a finer tree, with first-rate timber but without the nuts.

LIRIODENDRON. TULIP TREE.

L. Tulipifera is one of the handsomest trees we can grow, reaching 80 or even 100 ft. in some English gardens, and making a huge trunk (e.g. at Glendurgan near Falmouth and Killerton near Exeter). The flowers, greenish with an orange spot, are beautiful, but not conspicuous. The tree fits perfectly into the English scene, and might very well be used for an avenue or specimen planting near or in a town; but the wood is brittle, so it must have a sheltered site. *L. T. pyramidale* is an upright form.

MALUS. APPLE. See Chapter XIII.

NOTHOFAGUS. SOUTHERN BEECH. See Chapter XI.

These comprise some magnificent trees for sheltered sites, generally on lime-free soils, notably *N. Cunninghamii, Dombeyi, fusca, Menziesii, obliqua, procera*. A public authority here would do notable service by experimental planting of southern beeches as roadside trees or as a war-memorial.

PICEA. SPRUCE.

Like most conifers, spruces seldom look well or thrive as roadside trees unless in a plantation. An ill-grown spruce, such as one often sees, is a scraggy object; but *P. excelsa*, common spruce, can make a good wind-screen or hedge; and *P. Omorika*, Serbian spruce, is effective where a narrow upright evergreen is needed for a restricted space. For other spruces, suitable for plantations in windy sites, see page 24.

PINUS. PINE.

**P. sylvestris*, Scots pine, which is the only truly native cone-bearing tree in the British Isles, looks much more at home in this country than any other conifer, and is generally the best of them for roadside planting. It can do with poor soil. Some groups of this would much improve some of our new by-pass roads.

The three following species deserve consideration for roadside planting, but are generally better in plantations or belts than as isolated trees:

P. Laricio, Corsican pine, stands wind extremely well, and makes a handsome tree when mature; but its formal Noah's Ark shape when young makes it difficult to fit into the roadside scene except in a plantation. (This formality of shape make *Wellingtonia*, Lawson's cypress, and the grand Douglas fir quite unsuitable for roadside planting here.)

The maritime pine, *P. pinaster*, may serve as a roadside plantation.

P. radiata (*P. insignis*) is very wind-hardy, very quick-growing, and content with poor soil. It is better for a shelter-belt or plantation than as a road tree. For further notes on these and other pines, including *P. Laricio nigricans*, Austrian pine, see pages 24–26.

Platanus. Plane.

Both *P. acerifolia*, London plane, and the more beautiful *P. orientalis*, Oriental plane, can make superb trees with massive trunks, when grown in good soil and left unpruned. The variety *insularis*, from Cyprus, which has smaller leaves, is particularly attractive, but not hardy enough for the colder counties. *P. orientalis*, like Spanish chestnut, is one of the trees that would be excellent as a solitary tree for a large unused space set well back from a road. There is a pyramidal form of *P. acerifolia*, *P. a. pyramidalis*, useful where width is restricted.

In England the plane tree, so often used as a street tree in towns, is seldom seen along country roads. Perhaps it is felt that one sees enough of this tree in the town. A more substantial reason is that the leaves are thick, so that for fast motor traffic the risk of skidding would be increased in autumn. But in all other respects the plane is well suited for country roadsides. In particular, the trunks of fairly mature trees, free from branchlets and silver-pale when grown in clean air, light up exceptionally well at night. And no tree is more amenable to pruning. In France planes are much used along country roads as well as in towns. Formally planted at regular intervals (e.g. twelve paces apart each way), and periodically pruned and looked after by the Roads and Bridges service of each Department, they provide some of the finest of the avenues that adorn France's national roads. (Travellers by road from Paris to Grenoble may remember the magnificent plane avenues near Bourg.) I do not suggest that such formal roadside planting as is common in France and Italy would be appropriate generally in the English landscape; but I do think more use might well be made of plane trees beside our country roads, especially if they can be set well back and grouped somewhat informally.

Populus. Poplar.

Many kinds of poplar grow extremely fast, stand a good deal of wind, and are very easily propagated. But let us avoid overplanting these trees, which has happened in parts of France. As roadside trees they have serious drawbacks, besides their evident merits. There are four groups—white, black, balsam, and aspen poplars. Few of the black or balsam poplars can thrive for long on shallow chalky soils.

WHITE POPLARS. §*P. alba nivea*, the best form of the white poplar, has leaves dark green above, brilliantly white beneath, usually shaped like a maple leaf on young trees. It does not reach more than about 40 ft. It is beautiful, wind-hardy, and quick, but has the serious drawback of producing suckers very freely, so that footpaths get obstructed and a macadam road surface may even be disrupted.

P. Bolleana (*P. alba pyramidalis*) is an upright form of *alba*, like a Lombardy poplar in shape, but with flashing white-sided leaves, attractive for a road edge where space is restricted, and less productive of suckers.

P. canescens, grey poplar, is similar to *alba*, but with grey undersides to its leaves; a commoner plant, taller, handsome, but troublesome with suckers.

BLACK POPLARS. *P. nigra* var. *italica*, Lombardy poplar, the familiar columnar tree, is used now to mark cross-roads; so it should not be planted promiscuously. Fast-growing, and so vigorous underground that its roots may disturb foundations if it is planted near buildings, especially in clay soils.

P. berolinensis, Berlin poplar, is another columnar one. Among the many other black poplars and their hybrids, the native *P. nigra betulifolia* is recommended as being neater and denser than others, some of which are very rank growers. *P. Eugenei* is a very vigorous columnar tree, one of the best; *generosa* and *robusta* are also good quick-growing hybrids, with spreading heads, suitable for roadsides. For chalky soils *P. robusta* is undoubtedly the best poplar.

BALSAM POPLARS. These are aromatic in spring. Best of them is *P. trichocarpa*, an extremely fast upright grower, very fragrant; of outstanding value where quick effect is necessary. *P. candicans*, Balm of Gilead, is another, but it is very free with suckers.

ASPEN POPLARS. *P. tremula* and *P. tremuloides*, with leaves always trembling, are attractive.

PRUNUS

This great genus, comprising the cherries, plums, and almonds, etc., supplies many of the most valuable of all decorative trees for town and roadside planting. Prunuses, Pyruses, and the related Sorbuses, are dealt with in a separate chapter (Chapter XIII), which will, I hope, be referred to by any reader who may be planning public planting.

For town planting the following amongst the larger Prunus trees should be considered: *P. Avium flore pleno* (the double form of our native gean); and such Japanese cherries as *yedoensis*, *Sargentii*, *Hillieri*, and *"Tai-haku,"* any of which might well be used for memorial plantings.

For country roadsides note especially, amongst the larger Prunuses: *P. Avium* (gean) and *P. mahaleb pendula*, both of which are sufficiently wild-looking. (Some more bush-like trees, *P. cerasifera* (the type) and *P. padus Watereri*, a form of bird cherry, are referred to on pages 271 and 277.) *P. Avium* can be bought cheaply, and should be planted freely in such places as uncultivated chalk slopes and in hedgerows; but it is not suitable for very acid soils.

PYRUS. PEAR.

The true pear, *P. communis*, and some of its varieties, make handsome upright trees, very decorative at flowering time; much used along roadsides in central Switzerland. See also *Malus hupehensis* and *M. micromalus*.

QUERCUS. OAK.

No trees are better worth taking trouble over for country roadside planting and conservation than the oaks, both deciduous and evergreen. No need to recommend them, either for beauty or for durability. English oak has long been recognised as one of England's precious assets, and few evergreen trees that can be grown here are more beautiful, none is more wind-hardy, than *ilex*, the evergreen oak.

The chief difficulty about using oaks for roadside planting is that they transplant badly. They have long tap-roots; so if they cannot be started as acorns set in their permanent quarters, which is the ideal way, they must be carefully transplanted, and then planted out when still small. This means that care is needed for some time to prevent the small plants from getting smothered.

Not all kinds of oak grow slowly; but the two native species are slow-growing besides being very long-lived. This slowness should not deter public authorities from planting the slow-growers; on the contrary, at a time when private planters are becoming less likely to plant for posterity, there is special need for such planting to be undertaken by public authorities, as trustees for the public interest in having good trees.

Q. sessiliflora and *Q. pedunculata* (syn. *Q. Robur*) are the two native British oaks. Much the commoner up-country is *pedunculata*; but in Cornwall, in Wales, and in hill-country elsewhere, *sessiliflora* is much the commoner. (*Sessiliflora* has comparatively long stalks to its leaves and *no stalks* to its acorns; in *pedunculata* these characters are reversed.) Special care should be taken by public authorities and by private planters to protect these deciduous oaks, and to start new ones growing beside roads, where a tree of fairly wide spread would not be out of place.

Q. fastigiata is a handsome upright form of Q. *pedunculata*, which can well be used where the type would spread too wide.

Other very fine oaks suitable for roadsides here include:

Q. Cerris, Turkey oak, a noble tree, more upright than English oak, fast growing on good loam.

Q. *coccinea*, the true scarlet oak, whose leaves die off red and remain on the tree for a long time. (Not to be confused with Q. *rubra*, red oak, often supplied in its stead.) It is better, at least for roadside planting, to get plants of Q. *coccinea* raised from seed than grafted plants of the selected form, Q. *c.* var. *splendens*. Also Q. *conferta*, Hungarian oak; *Lucombeana*, the handsome Lucombe oak, an almost evergreen hybrid between the cork and Turkey oaks; *Mirbeckii*, one of the best, with fine dark foliage retained until the new year has begun; *palustris*, the American pin oak, and *rubra*, the red oak, the leaves of which die off a good red, turning to brown.

§Q. Ilex, evergreen oak, stands in a class by itself amongst the evergreen trees that can be grown in this country. As was pointed out in Chapter II, it is one of the best shelter trees we have, and makes in time a roadside avenue of uncommon beauty, not too sombre if well-spaced and planted in a sunny climate. Public authorities should be specially careful to protect existing *ilexes*, which take long to mature, and should be on the look-out for opportunities to plant them and to make use of them as background for such flowering trees as *Prunus yedoensis*, P. *Hillieri*, P. "*Tai-haku*," P. "*Jonioi*," *Eucryphia cordifolia*, and *hoherias*.

As a tree in the garden *ilex* has the disadvantage that it sheds its leaves in May, just when litter is least wanted: over ivy-covered ground this matters little, but on a lawn it is a nuisance. Few other plants thrive close to *ilex*.

Like the native oak it transplants badly. It should be planted from a pot when not more than 1 or 2 ft. high, in early May or early autumn. When once it starts, it grows away quite fast.

Other evergreen oaks for roadside planting include Q. *Suber*, cork oak, a handsome tree of marked character which does well in fairly sheltered places in Cornwall (e.g. beside the road going into Fowey). Q. *densiflora*, tan-bark oak, a rare species, is likely to be very good for this purpose when easier to get. Q. *agrifolia*, Californian live oak, might well be tried here beside a road; it makes a picturesque tree and stands wind.

ROBINIA. "FALSE ACACIA."

*R. *Pseud Acacia*. This, with its feathery leaf and its profuse show of fragrant white flowers, excellent for bees, in June, is not only one of the most valued flowering trees for town and garden, but also a delightful hedgerow tree for country roads. On the Continent, millions of it are thus used. But it is a fast grower, with brittle wood; so it should not be used where there is much wind. The best way to grow it, where labour can be spared for such a purpose, is to train it to a simple straight trunk up to a considerable height, so as to minimise the tendency of branches to split off. It is a variable plant; the variety *Bessoniana*, more compact than the type and less apt to break, is the best for road- and street-planting. *Decaisneana*, with pink flowers, is good too.

SALIX. WILLOW.

*S. *cærulea*, cricket-bat willow, is a first-rate upright tree for roadside planting, not long-lived but very fast-growing, and not in need of damp soil.

S. *alba*, white willow, and its rather less robust but very silvery variety, *S. *alba argentea*, are among the loveliest of native trees, excellent for a damp place.

S. *daphnoides*, a robust arching tree with early yellow catkins and whitened stems, can be used for street planting.

*S. *Matsudana*, a Chinese species, is recommended also: it does not mind dry soil, and makes a pyramidal tree of excellent shape.

S. *babylonica*, weeping willow, has a lovely streaming habit and early green, and is most effective hanging over water. But the tree is very subject to willow disease; and a high proportion of the willows which pass under the name *babylonica* are, I am told, not true to name.

S. Salamonii, a hybrid between *babylonica* and *alba*, is another excellent weeping sort. There is also *S. vitellina pendula*, a weeping willow with pendulous branches hanging straight down, bright golden-yellow. This is most effective in winter. But these too are liable to willow disease.

Lastly, there is **S. vitellina britzensis*, with glowing orange-scarlet branches, one of the best of trees for winter effect. Plant this beside water or where damp ground adjoins a road.

SORBUS. MOUNTAIN ASH AND WHITEBEAM. See page 73.

TILIA. LIME.

T. vulgaris, common lime, cannot be recommended as a tree for roadside or town. Well grown, it makes a very fine tall tree, and its flowers are delightfully scented; but its leaves are often made sticky and blackened by aphis, they often fall early, and when falling on road or pavement they make it slippery. Other limes should be used instead.

**T. euchlora*, with darker glossy leaves, is much better for this purpose, being free from attack by aphis. **T. petiolaris* (pendent silver lime) is an upright tree with graceful pendulous branches and very fragrant flowers, which unfortunately have the effect of stupefying bees. As a street tree it may get in the way unless pruned.

Limes can be used as mop-head trees, drastically pruned (or "pleached"); but it is a pity to plant them in the pavement of a narrow street, for then they cannot be allowed to show their character, and obstruct the footway.

ULMUS. ELM.

U. campestris, English elm, is not recommended now for roadside planting because of its dangerous habit of dropping a branch suddenly, because of liability to Dutch elm disease (at least in infected areas), and because it may blow over, having a wide head and shallow roots. A much better roadside tree is **U. stricta*, Cornish Elm, and U.S. *Wheatleyi*, the Jersey or Guernsey elm. Both Cornish and Jersey elms are narrower, more upright, than the English, Jersey elm being particularly columnar in habit. Both are comparatively firm at the root, and free from the branch-dropping habit. Being much less spreading, they make less dampness on roads than English elm. So, though they do sometimes provide suckers, they can be recommended for roadside planting. But in Cornwall the Cornish elm seems to be short-lived.

*§*U. montana*, wych elm, is a grand wide-headed tree when full-grown, wind-hardy, and fortunately free from suckering. Its upright form, *U. montana fastigiata*, Exeter elm, is useful where the spreading tree would occupy too much space or catch too much wind.

LIST C

SHRUBS AND SMALL TREES FOR COUNTRY ROADSIDES

It is most difficult to select decorative shrubs and small trees for addition to the usual repertory of roadside plants; for here the question of appropriateness to the rural scene arises most acutely.

On the one hand, our bush hedges are lovely as they are, with blackthorn, hawthorn, honeysuckle, and other fine plants, native and foreign. Generally, it will be found that there is very little room for more. And our stone "hedges," decorated with foxgloves, stonecrop, blue *jasione*, thyme, and much else, do not admit of any more growth of shrubs, generally speaking, than the wild gorse so well provides. Moreover, the maritime counties of the West are not those in which we may expect great "park ways," with a planted strip between two traffic lines, such as one sees around New York and begins to see near London; so that some of the problems of using garden plants in open country do not arise there.

On the other hand, as was stressed in earlier pages, the English road scene is not static: its flora has been changing for centuries and is changing now. I see no good reason against, and excellent reasons for, adding the beauty of some plants such as arbutus, snowy mespilus, mahaleb, cherry plum, *Cotoneasters bullata* and *Wardii*, pyracantha, and (in woodland on acid soils) yellow *azalea*, to the stock of plants used beside our roads; and native plants such as broom and Cornish heath might very well be more widely distributed. There are bleak coastal roads which can be much improved by planting, but only with plants such as *Senecio rotundifolius* and *Olearia albida*. Let us treat these plants as if they were natives: they behave as such, and fit perfectly into a scene such as that of the West Cornish coast. And there are sandy roadsides which would be much improved by starting sea-buckthorn and tree lupin. Why not?

The descriptions in the following list are purposely very summary, most of the plants being more adequately described elsewhere in the book.

AMELANCHIER. SNOWY MESPILUS.
A. vulgaris, European snowy mespilus, which is a common hedge plant in Dauphiné and elsewhere, would be a delightful addition to hedge plantings in our own countryside.
A. lævis, *A. oblongifolia*, and others could well be used; they have the appropriate look of wild plants. See page 82.

AMYGDALUS. ALMOND.
A. communis. Common almond. No flowering tree is more valued for suburban roadsides than this. It can take a puff of spring into the middle of London. But it is not a plant for every soil.
For this and the magnificent hybrid, *A. Pollardii*, see page 270.

ARBUTUS
A. Unedo, with its splendid rounded masses of dark evergreen lighted by ivory flowers and scarlet fruits, is sometimes used as a hedge plant in the Killarney country, where it is native. Why not use it so in wide hedgerows in other mild counties? I hope very much this will be done, even though some damage to berried branches may have to be allowed for.

AZALEA, yellow. See RHODODENDRON FLAVUM.

BERBERIS
B. Darwinii makes a most decorative hedge beside the approach to a town. It is evergreen, brilliant in flower, wind-hardy, cheap

to buy. It is prickly (which has advantages for the plant's protection), and is rather a spreader, so it should not be put where it might overgrow a path. It is not very easy to establish.

B. *stenophylla*, with its great arching shoots, all golden-yellow in May, is another grand plant, well able to take care of itself and very suitable for a large embankment on the outskirts of a town. It can make a tall hedge if kept severely pruned, but that robs it of much of its beauty.

Several other *berberis* are suitable for certain roadside positions, e.g. B. *Thunbergii, Jamesiana, xanthoxylon* (syn. *Knightii*). But avoid B. *vulgaris*, beautiful though it is, owing to the wheat rust.

BUDDLEIA

§B. *variabilis*. This plant is already so much at home that it sows itself as a lovely weed; seedlings managed to reach flowering stage before the end of the war on the bare rubble of bombed sites in many towns, including London. B. *variabilis* var. *nanhœnsis* is particularly suitable for naturalising on embankments and road cuttings, being more compact than the others and looking more like a wild plant.

B. *alternifolia*, with long willowy shoots strung with violet flower-clusters, is a good plant for a large embankment, but it needs all the sun it can get, and lots of room.

CHERRY. See PRUNUS, pages 60–61, 71–72, and Chapter XIII.

CISTUS

C. *salvifolius, corbariensis*, and *laurifolius* would be good for naturalising in sunny stony places, e.g. beside excavated by-pass roads. C. *laurifolius* may sow itself in exposed gravelly subsoil.

COTONEASTER

Cotoneasters include some of the best shrubs and small trees for roadsides—plants that are easily propagated, can take care of themselves, and look sufficiently at home amongst native shrubs. The species can be raised in quantity from seed, and are therefore even more valuable for roadside planting than the garden hybrids which have to be propagated by cuttings.

Tall Cotoneasters

C. frigida, a small tree, effective and lasting in berry; *salicifolia*, a large bush of graceful habit, profusely berried, excellent for a tall hedge or screen; *pannosa*, with tall graceful growths, small grey-green leaves, white flowers, and red berries, extremely wind-hardy.

The hybrids include some magnificent plants for this purpose: *"St. Monica," a small tree of spreading growth, with a load of vivid berries generally spared by birds; "Cornubia," a similar plant; *Watereri*, and *Aldenhamensis*.

Cotoneasters of Medium Height

C. bullata, with sprays of large scarlet berries in September, is a first-rate bush for hedgerows and banks, sufficiently wild-looking, and self-sowing.

C. Francheti resembles *pannosa*, but is lower and stiffer.

C. glaucophylla makes a rounded bush up to 9 ft. high, late-flowering, with orange-scarlet berries carried well into the new year.

C. Henryana is very decorative in a place where it can show its spreading growth, with crimson berries in autumn and bronzed leaves in winter.

§C. lactea is one of the most useful evergreens, whether for acid or alkaline soils. It makes a large rounded bush with arching growths, 10 ft. or even 15 ft. high in time. It can also be trained into a small tree. The small red fruits are borne in great quantity. Easily raised from seed. Allow plenty of width for the bush.

C. multiflora, a graceful bush, is almost as white as hawthorn when in flower, and bears red berries early.

§*C. serotina* is another valuable evergreen, resembling lactea, excellent in habit, with orange-red berries, very wind-hardy.

C. Simonsii, brilliant in berry and autumn leaf.

C. Wardii is perhaps the best of the medium-growers for effect of berry. The leaves are grey-green, white beneath, and often colour well in autumn, together with the large orange-scarlet berries. This plant sows itself freely, perhaps too freely for its retention in the garden.

Dwarf Cotoneasters

C. conspicua, *C. horizontalis*, *C. Dammeri*, *C. præcox* are excellent dwarf sorts for roadside banks. *C. horizontalis* will sow itself when established. The familiar *C. microphylla* makes a convenient covering for a bank, but is rather blackish in effect.

For further notes on these and other Cotoneasters, see pages 107–110.

CRATÆGUS

*§*C. monogyna* and *C. Oxyacantha*, our two native hawthorns, are in a class by themselves—easily the best of small trees or hedge plants for this countryside. But these we have already. The coloured varieties, including the single scarlet, are familiar and excellent decorations of our gardens, but look too tame, I think, for hedgerows in open country. There are, however, some other white-flowered species which rank high for country roadside planting; notably **C. prunifolia*, splendidly crimsoned in autumn; *cordata*, the handsome Washington thorn; *Crus-galli*, the cockspur thorn; *mollis*, beautiful in flower, and *Carrierei*, with large orange-red berries carried till late in winter.

CYDONIA

C. cathayensis hybrids. The new hybrids of this species of flowering quince make vigorous wind-hardy bushes, with red, pink or white flowers, and are likely to prove suitable, very decorative, and sturdy.

CYTISUS

*§*C. scoparius*. No broom is so suitable as the wild yellow one, and no native shrub is better worth naturalising beside roads here. Road authorities would do a public service by sowing seed of it or starting it with small pot-grown seedlings, e.g. on the banks of new by-pass roads.

C. albus, tall white Portugal broom (T), is another lovely plant which can take care of itself. Try it with *Cotoneaster pannosa* up a steep bank.

CORNUS

C. mas, which makes a cloud of yellow flower in early spring, would make a delightful hedge-planting. *C. alba atrosanguinea*, the best form of Siberian dog-wood (from Westonbirt), has crimson stems, very showy in winter; best suited for a damp place where it can spread.

Erica. Heath.

Out of all the heaths, two only are here recommended for country roadsides. One is *E. vagans*, the Cornish heath, which is vigorous enough to take care of itself, and will sow itself when established: *E. vagans rubra grandiflora* is a good form for this purpose. The other, *E. codonodes*, is the species which has naturalised itself along the railway bank at Doublebois; it will do the same on a road-cutting if given a chance. Small kinds, such as *E. carnea*, are unsuitable, since they need to be kept clear of weeds.

E. mediterranea superba, with *E. darleyensis* in front of it, makes a splendid long-lasting show of heather-pink in spring; but these are perhaps better suited for some public garden or suburban road, where a mass effect is called for. They require little labour when well started in suitable soil free from weeds.

Euonymus

E. europæus, common spindle tree, with the beautiful fruits, rose-scarlet and orange, is one of the most welcome hedge-plants; but it is apt to get spoilt by caterpillars. *E. latifolius* is a bigger plant with larger fruits, effective and less subject to caterpillars. *E. japonicus* is invaluable as an evergreen garden hedge-plant in extreme exposures, and can thrive in almost pure sand; but it is a soil-robber, and a host of the sugar-beet fly.

Escallonia

E. macrantha is another useful plant, either in a town or where an exposed road needs hedge-shelter; and *E. Iveyana* is a handsome evergreen for a tall hedge in a not very exposed site.

Genista

§G. hispanica, Spanish gorse, makes wide low mounds, all yellow in summer: useful for a roadside bank on poor soil, even on chalk. *G. cinerea* and *G. virgata*, tall yellow brooms flowering in late summer, would make a superb show beside a road, and might be put with *Erica codonodes*.

Hippophae. Sea Buckthorn.

§H. rhamnoides, with its grey leaves and its showy orange berries when the two sexes are planted, is excellent even in very poor or sandy soil. But it is an invasive plant, and should not be used where it can block a footpath. It is naturalised in some places.

Hoheria

H. glabrata, sexstylosa, and *angustifolia.* I have never seen these used for roadside planting, but I hope that an experiment will be tried with them here, e.g. in Cornwall. They are most beautiful with their profuse white flowers; they grow extremely fast, and are easily propagated from seed or from cuttings, and they stand wind well. Try them in a tall hedge, mixed with other plants such as hawthorn, or at the edge of a wood adjoining a road.

Ilex. Holly.

§I. Aquifolium, common holly, is the best of hedgerow evergreens, and should be more planted. Put both sexes, if berries are wanted; but berried branches are liable to get mauled in the weeks before Christmas. Plant small at the end of September or in May.

Lonicera. Honeysuckle.

Best of native hedgerow climbers, honeysuckles should of course be encouraged. *L. Periclymenum belgica* and *L. p. serotina* are worth planting as additions to the wild sort.

Lupinus. Lupin.

§*L. arboreus,* tree lupin, is first-rate for naturalising in sandy soil, e.g. beside a road crossing dunes. (See also *Olearia Traversii* and *Hippophae rhamnoides* for this purpose.)

Olearia

*§*O. albida, O. avicenniæfolia,* and *O. macrodonta* are among the few shrubs that will stand extreme exposure on a cliff road, and they fit very well into such a scene, together with *Senecio rotundifolius* (q.v.). Strongly recommended for roadside planting in seaside places in the mild maritime counties. *O. Traversii* is suitable also, but requires some pruning if it is to get established in very windy sites.

Prunus

(a) Cherries. In list B, several of the taller-growing cherries have already been specially recommended for town and roadside planting. The smaller growers are not less important, e.g. *Conradinae*, *incisa*, and the spring cherries, *P. subhirtella* (which should in time become biggish trees). Don't fail to consider these for town or village planting. These are plants of more grace and style than the double-flowered pink sorts, familiar in gardens, such as "Kwanzan." See Chapter XIII.

(b) PLUMS. *P. cerasifera* (myrobalan) is the green-leaved type, of which *P. c. Pissari* is the purple-leaved form, common in gardens. *Pissari* looks out of place, I think, in the open country, but *cerasifera* itself is one of the earliest and most welcome of flowering bushes, white, and then quickly green in February or early March. It makes a bushy tree 20–30 ft. high, and is strongly recommended for hedgerow planting.

(c) BIRD CHERRY. *P. padus Watereri* is the best form of one of the most beautiful native flowering trees. *Albertii* is another good one. These are hedge trees which look—and are—at home.

§PYRACANTHA

These are the most effective of berrying plants for roadsides; *P. Lalandii*, *atalantoides*, or *Rogersiana* should certainly be considered in planning the planting of a trunk road, especially where there is a bank with a fair amount of space. Don't plant where the thorny growths may be a nuisance to passengers.

PYRUS

MALUS, CRABS. **M. baccata*, Siberian crab, makes a splendid hedgerow tree, much more suitable for the countryside than *M. floribunda*, or than the purplish-pink garden forms.

**M. micromalus* (syn. *kaido*) is a tree up to 30 ft., pink and white in April, like a glorified wild crab: excellent for a tall hedgerow.

**M. hupehensis* (syn. *theifera*), with white flowers, and its pink form, *M. h. rosea*, is later flowering than the others, fragrant, and vigorous; one of the first flowering trees to choose.

RHODODENDRON

§R. ponticum, now a naturalised plant, makes a splendid show beside many a Cornish road, in woodland or in the open, and is one of the most wind-hardy evergreens. It is an invasive plant, impossible to get rid of without much labour when established.

R. flavum (syn. *Azalea pontica*), the common yellow azalea, is

Planting for Roadsides and Towns

a splendid plant for bordering a road through a not too shady wood. It is very fragrant, flowers without fail, and is vigorous enough to look after itself when started, reaching 8 or 10 ft. Easily propagated from seed.

Rosa
The following species are good for a bank, given plenty of room. Plant each sort in some quantity by itself, 5 ft. apart. *R. Helenae, moschata* (these two will ramp up an evergreen bush), *Moyesii*, and *highdownensis* (which make brilliant hips), *filipes*, *Willmottiae*. Be careful not to plant these where they may get in the way with thorny growths.

Sorbus
No trees of moderate stature—30 to 40 feet—are more appropriate for planting beside our country roads than the native *Sorbus Aucuparia*, Mountain Ash, and the native *Sorbus Aria*, Whitebeam. Do use these. And set them in loose natural groups rather than in conventional files as an avenue. For others, more expensive, see pages 380–381.

Spartium
*§*S. junceum*. Spanish broom. First-rate for dry banks, with yellow broom-flowers long and late. Raise from seed.

Tamarix
T. gallica is useful for seaside hedges, even on very sandy soil, but it gets ragged unless cut back.

Ulex
U. europæus, gorse, needs no recommendation. The double form is even more effective, but more fastidious, and much more expensive to start.

Veronica
V. Dieffenbachii is first-rate for the top of wide earth-filled hedges in the mildest counties. *V.* "Blue Gem" can be used so, but is impatient of drought. *V. Traversii, salicifolia*, and *elliptica* are also very good ones for a windy climate. See pages 34–35.

Viburnum
**V. betulifolium*, perhaps the finest berrying shrub we can grow, would make a magnificent addition to tall hedge-plants, and is

easily propagated. Recommended for roadside trial. The native *V. Lantana*, wayfaring tree, is worth adding to hedge-plants; and **V. Opulus*, wild guelder rose, besides purplish leaf-colour in autumn, has effective flat white flower-heads and makes a splendid show of translucent scarlet or yellow berries. In damp ground this is an outstanding shrub.

LIST D

SOME TREES AND SHRUBS FOR TOWN-PLANTING

Abutilon vitifolium	For public and private gardens.
Amelanchier lævis	For public and private gardens.
Arbutus Unedo var. Croomei	For public and private gardens.
Berberis Darwinii	For public and private gardens.
B. stenophylla, corallina, and others	For public and private gardens.
Buddleias, e.g. "Ile de France" *nanhoensis*	For public and private gardens.
Camellias, e.g. "J. C. Williams," "Apollo," Kelvingtonii, "Preston Rose," "Adolph Audusson," "Jupiter"	Some shade preferred. See Chapter VI.
Caryopteris clandonensis	For mass effect in full sun.
‡*Cassia corymbosa*	For sunny walls in the mildest places.
Catalpa bignonioides	Tree for public square, or on grass in public gardens.
Ceanothus, e.g. *dentatus, floribundus, thyrsiflorus,* "Delight"	For public and private gardens, railway-station fences, etc.
Cercis siliquastrum. Judas tree	For public and private gardens in full sun.
Cordyline australis. Dracæna.	But see page 104.
Cotoneaster, "St. Monica" or *Cornubia, Watereri*	As a tall hedge or bush.
C. Simonsii	As a 3–4-ft. hedge: and others.

Cratægus, hawthorn	e.g. the single red.
‡*Cytisus racemosus* and "Porlock"	For public and private gardens, with some shelter, in mild places.
Davidia	Tree for public gardens.
Drimys Winteri, or its variety *latifolia*	Upright bushy tree, for public and private gardens in mild places; might be used with hydrangea in a public square or in a large planting recess provided for in a new street-plan.
Escallonias, e.g. *Iveyana, organensis*, "Apple-Blossom," "Donard Seedling," " Glory of Donard"	
Eucalyptus coccifera and *Gunnii montana*	
*Eucryphia cordifolia, *nymansensis, and *intermedia*	These, with their upright habit, might well be tried in a public square or street recess. They flower in August–September when visitors come. Also for private gardens.
*E. glutinosa	For public and private gardens.
Eupatorium micranthum	For public and private gardens. A late-flowering bush, good for butterflies.
Exochorda macrantha	For public and private gardens.
Forsythia intermedia spectabilis, ovata, etc.	For public and private gardens.
Fraxinus ornus. Manna ash	Street tree where space allows, and public gardens.
*Fuchsia Riccartonii	Should be amply used in town planting schemes, e.g. as a hedge.
Ginkgo biloba	Tree for public gardens.
§*Griselinia littoralis*	Public or private gardens, as wind-shelter. Pruned to a single trunk, clear of growth to a height of, say, 9 ft., this makes a handsome evergreen street tree, very wind-hardy.
*Hoheria glabrata, sexstylosa, populnea, angustifolia	E.g. with hydrangeas.

*Hydrangea, Gen. Vicomte de Vibraye (blue), "Lanarth White," and other varieties of good colour	Recommended for mass planting, two kinds only, in beds provided for in new planning of streets, and by central bus stops in towns. Some taller shrubs might be planted with them, such as Hoheria, Griselinia littoralis, Pittosporum Colensoi, Tricuspidaria lanceolata, Eucryphia cordifolia, E. nymansensis, Drimys Winteri.
Hypericum, "Rowallane Hybrid" and patulum Forrestii	
‡Leptospermums, e.g. Nichollsii grandiflorum, Chapmannii and ericoides	Public and private gardens, especially near the sea.
Liquidambar styraciflua	Small tree, for public or private gardens, including damp sites.
Liriodendron tulipifera	Large tree for public gardens, sheltered.
Magnolias, e.g. grandiflora, var. "Goliath"	For house walls, and in the open, in public and private gardens; also denudata, alba superba, kobus, etc.
‡Metrosideros lucida and M. robusta	Evergreen trees, with scarlet flowers in summer, wind-hardy but tender. Both might be tried in the mildest seaside towns. See Chapter XI.
*Myrtus luma. Tree myrtle	One of the best opportunities we have for decorative public planting in mild places is afforded by tree myrtle; and private gardeners in towns such as Penzance do a service by planting it near their hedges or walls adjoining the street.
M. communis and tarentina	Are excellent also. Tarentina stands wind.
Nothofagus	Trees for public or private gardens, fairly sheltered. See Chapter XI.
Olearia albida, macrodonta Haastii	For windy sites.
Paulownia	Tree for public garden, with wind-shelter.
Philadelphus	For public or private gardens.

Platanus, Plane.

Prunus — Many sorts, including the following, as standard street trees: **P. yedoensis*, *Sargentii, "Kwanzan," *"Tai-haku," *Hillieri.
For public and private gardens: **P. amygdalus* and *Pollardii; *P. Avium flore pleno* (where it will thrive; makes a large tree); *Conradinae*, *"Jonioi," "Shimidzu," *subhirtella, *mahaleb pendula.

Pyrus — For public and private gardens: **P. floribunda, magdeburgensis*, "John Downie," *hupehensis*.

Pyracanthas, e.g. *Lalandei, atalantoides,* and *Rogersiana*

Quercus ilex — Large tree for public gardens and street recess.

Rhododendron — The following hybrids stand practically full sunlight, are unhurt by spring frosts, and need the minimum of attention: *"Lady C. Mitford," blush pink; *"Mrs. John Millais," white, yellow flare; "Essex Scarlet," late red; "Doncaster," dwarf red; "Lord Roberts," crimson; "Midsummer," carmine; "Purple Splendour," dark violet.
The following prefer light shade and an annual mulching of leaves over the roots: *"Loder's White"; *"Mother of Pearl"; "Britannia," red, slow-growing; "Corona," bright pink, low-growing; "Betty Wormald," pale pink, dark blotch; *"Mrs. A. T. de la Mare," white with green spot; "Mrs. L. de Rothschild," white, red spot; "Gomer Waterer," blush white, late; "Mrs. C. B. van Nes," deep pink, early.
See also *R. præcox* and *emasculum*, page 288; *R. ciliatum*, page 289; *R. Nobleanum*, page 302.

*Robinia pseudacacia and Bessoniana	Fine for street or garden, unsuited for windy places.
Salix daphnoides	For streets.
Senecio rotundifolius	Large bush, for very windy sites, in conjunction with buildings, or as shelter. Also, S. elæagnifolius for lower growth.
Sophora japonica	Wide-headed tree for public gardens, or memorial planting,.
*Sorbus aucuparia. Mountain Ash	For streets.
*S. commixta	Upright Mountain Ash, recommended for streets.
*§S. Aria Whitebeam	For streets, even in windy places; leaves silvered underneath. See page 281.
*S. A. Decaisneana	
*S. A. lutescens	
Tilia (lime), e.g. T. euchlora	Tree for street or park.
*Tricuspidaria lanceolata, lantern tree	One of the best flowering shrubs for public as well as private planting in the mild counties. Bushy upright growth; stands wind; red flowers in May.
*Viburnum Tinus	Laurustinus—e.g. French White, and, in shelter, lucidum.
*Wistaria sinensis	For house walls and along railing on top of walls.
Yucca, gloriosa, filamentosa, and others	
Zelkova crenata	Tree for public gardens.

CHAPTER IV

A General Planting List

ASSUMING that the site you have to plant has some shelter from wind, or is fully sheltered, what plants will you choose for it?

The following annotated list is an attempt to help in answering that question, so far as gardens in the milder counties are concerned. Of course, the list is only a selection; and every practised gardener will have additions to make and perhaps subtractions; but certainly it contains many of the best shrubs that can be grown in such climates.

The list omits all but a few trees. (Some have been briefly dealt with in Chapters II and III.) In particular, this book does not attempt to review the vast tribe of conifers, although conifers are amongst the outstanding features of some of the most notable gardens in the country.

The list also omits some of the main genera, such as *camellia* and *rhododendron*, since these are covered by separate chapters.

It omits various plants likely to prove tender or difficult to get, since there is a special list for the use of the more venturesome gardeners in a later chapter.

The notes on plants common to mild gardens and those up-country are very summary, since such plants are amply dealt with in other books. Here the emphasis is on the plants which, generally speaking, are more at home in the mild maritime counties than in the frostier ones.

Up-country, when a planter chooses shrubs, he has to consider first whether the shrub in question, besides being happy in his soil, is likely to prove sufficiently frost-hardy. But in many of the mild counties, particularly Cornwall, the question of wind-hardiness is often the primary one. So special consideration has here been given to this factor in the planter's choice. Plants marked § are recommended for gardens where some shelter is available, but where a good deal of strong wind must be allowed for. Plants marked † are thought to be unlikely to show their character well enough except in full shelter, whether in some woodland garden in a valley or in some specially protected corner in a more exposed site.

I offer these generalisations for what they are worth, as a rough guide; they cannot be expected to meet each situation exactly. Any such classification of plants according to their capacity to stand strong and salty winds is a difficult essay, since experiment on the subject is still very inadequate and little has been written about it.

As for frost-hardiness, I have ventured to put ‡ to some plants as a warning that they are likely to prove more susceptible to frost than others in this list. But every practised gardener knows that the value of such a classification is limited. For a plant's capacity to stand frost varies, not only from garden to garden within one parish, but from one spot to another within a single garden: a plant may come through unscathed on a hump of ground, whilst its fellow is killed a few yards away in a frost-pocket.

So the prefix ‡ should be regarded as a pointer rather than as a stuck-on label. Its omission is no guarantee.

LIST E

A GENERAL LIST

Abelia

A. floribunda is a lax evergreen shrub with very effective hanging clusters of tubular flowers, bright magenta. It is usually treated as a wall plant, but is hardy enough for the open in mild gardens. I have seen it very good as a sprawling bush amongst silver-grey granite boulders, with silver-pink *mesembryanthemums*.

*A. grandiflora (*A. chinensis* × *uniflora*) is a vigorous evergreen bush reaching 6–8 ft., sometimes more, with glittering evergreen foliage and pinky-white flowers, flowering for many months and until late in autumn. This excellent hybrid is commonly seen under the name "*chinensis*" or "*rupestris*" or "*uniflora*."

A. Schumannii, with pale lilac-pink flowers, is pretty but washy in colour.

A. triflora is not at all showy, but the small white flowers are fragrant.

Abutilon

*§A. vitifolium is one of the best of shrubs for mild gardens, whether windy or sheltered. The bush grows quickly to 8 ft.

or more, and may reach 20 ft. on a wall; but it is apt to get leggy at the base. Leaves large, grey-green, shaped like a maple leaf; flowers like single hollyhocks, lilac or white, borne for a long season in early summer. It is remarkably wind-hardy, thriving even in open ground on the south side of St. Michael's Mount and in draughty gardens near the sea at Penzance; but in exposed positions it should, of course, be well staked. Frost-hardy enough for any of the mild counties, though needing a wall in colder gardens. Not long-lived, but easily raised from seed. Plant small. Single bushes of this earn their place very well in a small garden; and in larger gardens it would make a fine effect freely planted on either side of a walk, with a few bushes of *Rosa Moyesii* or *R. Hillieri*.

A. megapotamicum, with hanging flowers, yellow and maroon-red, is hardy in the open in mild gardens and hardy on a sunny wall elsewhere; it will thrive in poor stony soil, and is most persistent in flowering. Unfortunately, the form most often grown has an unhealthy-looking yellow variegation of the leaves.

‡*A. Milleri* has well-shaped flowers, orange-buff, with red stamens.

‡*A. speciosum* hybrids, which used to be common in greenhouses, are hardy enough for walls in mild gardens, though not proof against an abnormal frost. The large, veined, bell-shaped flowers are borne for a very long season. "Insigne" is a fine blood-red, "Boule de Neige" a white.

ACER. MAPLE.

Amongst the many very decorative maples, four only must suffice for this selection. Other trees are mentioned in List A.

**A. palmatum septemlobum* "Osakazuki" makes a bush up to 10 or 15 ft. high, with green leaves turning to the most vivid scarlet in autumn; an outstanding plant, which colours well even in the damp air of Cornwall.

A. palmatum atropurpureum is a good crimson-leaved form, coloured in spring and summer.

A. griseum is a small tree with peeling cinnamon-brown bark and vivid autumn leaf-colour. In Cornwall it often needs coaxing to make an adequate leading shoot, but in good soil, in such a climate as Dorset's, there is generally, I understand, little or no such trouble with it.

A. nikoense is one of the best maple trees for autumn colour, flaring up in October.

ÆGLE

A. sepiaria, syn. *Citrus trifoliata*. A very spiny bush, up to 8 ft. or more high and through, with white flowers like orange blossom, fragrant, sometimes very profuse. More curious than beautiful when out of flower, having little foliage, but very effective when flowering freely in a hot place, in sandy acid soil.

ÆSCULUS

A. parviflora is the shrubby chestnut, a wide vigorous bush with handsome spikes of white flowers in July–August. *A. indica* is a noble flowering tree.

AMELANCHIER. SNOWY MESPILUS.
*A. lævis (*A. canadensis* of Gray) is a lovely small tree which should be more planted; besides its profuse but short-lived white flowers in dropping racemes in April, it has brown-pink young leaves and good autumn colour (though perhaps not in mild damp climates). **A. oblongifolia* is similar and equally good.
A. asiatica is another good one, flowering in May and often again in September. Also *A. grandiflora* (*A. canadensis* × *lævis*), with pink-tinted flowers, and its beautiful form **A. grandiflora rubescens*.

AMYGDALUS. ALMOND. See page 270.

ARBUTUS
§A. Unedo var. *Croomei*. Any mild garden which has room for a large evergreen should have a place for an *arbutus*, for no evergreen that is hardy here is more beautiful in leaf and in mass, and where it fruits well the orange and scarlet balls among the dark leaves are an incomparable decoration at Christmas. It is wind-hardy, though not suitable for severe exposure. In Kerry it is a native woodland plant. The best form for most gardens is *Croomei*, which makes a smaller bush than the type, with red-flushed flowers and a more certain show of fruit.
A. andrachnoides, a hybrid between *A. Unedo* and *A. Andrachne*, is perhaps even handsomer, with conspicuous cinnamon trunks.
*A. Menziesii (Madroña), as it grows in California and British

A General Planting List

Columbia, its native country, or in New Zealand, is one of the noblest trees in the world. There it sometimes reaches a height of 60 or 70 ft., occasionally even more, and a tree in California has a girth of 28 ft. The branches are shining cinnamon-red, paler where the bark has flaked off in strips; the ivory-white flower-clusters are followed by bunches of orange fruit deepening to vermilion. Any gardener who has seen this tree doing well, e.g. on Mount Tamalpais, overlooking San Francisco Bay, will want to grow it here; and though I have yet to see a good one in Cornwall, I question whether this is not due to some avoidable error in culture rather than to the climate. It has reached 60 ft. at Rostrevor, in Ireland, and near Southampton. As a wild plant it stands Pacific gales even at considerable altitudes; but it should be noted that wind-velocities on the Californian sea-board are in general much less than they are in Cornwall; I would not recommend trying Madroña in full exposure here. But try it where the wind is tempered. Plant it, when small, in, say, a group of four where the silhouette will show against the sky, and give it coarse well-drained soil. It is sensitive to root disturbance.

ARCTOSTAPHYLOS

A. manzanita is, like *Arbutus Menziesii*, a Californian. It is a distinguished-looking shrub, ultimately reaching 8 ft., but generally less, with thick ovate leaves, dark green, but covered with a conspicuous glaucous surface; flowers white or pink-flushed; bark red and peeling like that of the *arbutus*. It comes from open stony places exposed to sea-winds; so it is not a plant for coddling in a sheltered wood in the deep peaty soil provided for rhododendrons. It does very well at Kew, but is hard to establish, being sensitive to root disturbance. There are a number of other species worth considering.

ARONIA. See page 281.

AZALEA. See Chapter XIV.

AZARA

All these are Chileans, and do well in climates which suit such plants as *tricuspidaria*. They like leaf-mould.

A. dentata is a tall bush or low tree with oval evergreen foliage, saw-edged, bright green with downy underside; flowers a fluff of yellow stamens in May, slightly scented and showy. Hardy in the open in mild counties, fast-growing, and tolerant of drought.

A. Gilliesii has dark shiny leaves 3 inches long, toothed, rather like holly, and catkins of yellow mimosa-like flowers in the leaf-axils. A plant for mild gardens only.

A. integrifolia flowers in January–March, producing racemes of golden-yellow fragrant flower-balls like mimosa, followed by lilac-white berries, each with a blackish spine. The shrub is evergreen, and generally does not grow taller than 15 ft., but may reach 30 ft. or more. There is a variegated form.

A. Brownea has oval leaves, dark above and pale green beneath: the yellow flower-clusters in the leaf-axils show well above the foliage.

A. lanceolata, first found by Charles Darwin, has decorative fronds of bright-green evergreen foliage, and profuse, bright-yellow, fluffy flowers, slightly scented, in May, followed by lilac-white berries. This sows itself in mild gardens. It is the most effective of the *azaras* in flower, the flowers being well displayed on the upper side of the arching growths; but the yellow is rather harsh and not easy to mix.

A. microphylla—the commonest, and still, I think, the best—makes a small evergreen tree up to 30 ft., with frond-like branches of small dark leaves, very elegant in effect. The minute flowers, borne under the leaves, are vanilla-scented in February. A variety of this is strikingly variegated with pale yellow—one of the best variegated shrubs.

Up-country, *A. microphylla* is usually grown on a wall, but in mild climates it thrives as a tree in the open, with some shelter.

BERBERIDOPSIS. CORAL PLANT.

*B. corallina, a handsome Chilean climber, has toothed leaves that become dark-green and leathery, and flower-sprays like small jets of coral-red drops. In the humid Cornish climate it flourishes in sun as well as shade, but up-country it needs shade. It should be started in lime-free soil, but when established will grow out into limy soil. It can be used on a wall or for scrambling through a bush. In colour it goes well with *Tacsonia mollissima*.

BERBERIS

Here is only a brief selection: there are many others of great value for the garden and for wilder planting.

§B. Darwinii is not only the best barberry for general cultivation,

but one of the best of hardy flowering shrubs. Of all the garden plants that William Lobb, the Cornish collector, introduced from Chile a century ago, this is the most generally valuable. It is beautiful always, whether in polished evergreen leaf, or orange with flowers, or loaded with grape-purple berries. It varies considerably: the best form I know is "Flame,"[1] which has fiery red buds and an excellent habit of growth. *B. Darwinii* is a woodland plant, but proves to be extremely wind-hardy; it stands even the first shock of sea-wind pretty well, but is then, of course, much stunted. Behind the first line of wind-defence it does perfectly, reaching 8 ft., or in woodland conditions 12 or 15 ft. It is apt to run at the root, and sows itself with a freedom sometimes tiresome; but it is not very easy to establish, and should be planted small, preferably in spring. The hot orange colour of its flowers is all right with milk-white, pale yellow, or blue, but swears violently with the pinks and reds of heaths, rhododendrons, and camellias.

*B. linearifolia. This very beautiful Chilean plant, introduced in 1925-7 by Mr. H. F. Comber, is akin to *B. Darwinii*, but has larger flowers of a burning orange-flame colour. The leaf is pointed and entire (never toothed as the leaf of its hybrids commonly is). The wild plant reaches 4-8 ft. in moist shady woods, growing at higher altitudes than *Darwinii* (3,400 ft.) and standing more frost. In this country it is frost-hardy at Kew. Its habit is something like that of a brier-bush, the older branches drooping and gradually becoming spent with flowering, whilst younger ones, usually erect, take their place. It does best in open spaces in woodland, requiring light but not the fullest exposure to the sun. In some places it does not do well, but in others (e.g. in the heath country of Dorset) it is considered less exacting and a faster grower than *B. lologensis*, its hybrid, or even than *B. Darwinii*. So far as my experience goes, it cannot stand exposure to sea-winds as *Darwinii* can. The plant is easily propagated from cuttings: if it is grafted on *B. vulgaris*, suckers of the stock give endless trouble. Seed is unreliable, as the plant crosses very readily. The hybridist should find it excellent to work on.

*B. lologensis is another outstanding shrub, found in Chile as a natural hybrid between *B. Darwinii* and *B. linearifolia*. It is very variable from seed, some forms being almost pure *Darwinii*, others

[1] From W. J. Marchant, Keepers Hill, Stapehill, Wimborne, Dorset.

double the size of *Darwinii* in leaf and flower, some equalling *linearifolia* in size and colour of flower. "Nymans variety" (a form selected at Nymans from the seedlings raised from the seed collected by Mr. H. F. Comber) is a fine, easily grown plant, stiffer in habit than *Darwinii*, with flowers rivalling *linearifolia's*. Given a cool root-run, *lologensis* can stand full sun; as with *linearifolia*, an open space in woodland should suit it.

*B. *chillanensis*. This is another Andean plant introduced by Mr. Comber; but unlike the last three it is deciduous. It is very variable, some forms being dwarfed and alpine in character, others free-growing, reaching 15 ft. The flowers are yellow and pale orange, ½ inch across, very profuse. A fine form, with hairy shoots and larger flowers, has been distinguished as var. *hirtipes*. The plant is quite hardy. Some growers have found it difficult to grow; but seedlings raised at Nymans have, I am informed, thrived there, despite "a rough time."

*B. *montana* is another deciduous Andean barberry, introduced by Comber in 1925–7, akin to *chilensis*. The flowers, yellow and pale orange, are exceptionally large—sometimes ⅞ inch across. In the wild it reaches 15 ft. in height. It is expected to prove one of the best barberries. At Nymans and at Winchester it has grown well, presenting no difficulties of culture; but if left unpruned, plants may become ungainly in habit, and some growers have, I gather, found it difficult to satisfy.

*B. *stenophylla*. This famous hybrid (*B. Darwinii* × *B. empetrifolia*), with its long arching wands hung with golden-yellow in April–May, needs no commendation. It is one of the heartiest of evergreens and one of the showiest of flowering shrubs. Prune after flowering. It is rampant and hard to eradicate, so do not put it where it could overrun treasured plants or obstruct a path. It goes well with white *Clematis montana* and *Osmanthus Aquifolium*.

*§B. *stenophylla coccinea* is a very fine *stenophylla* variety, slow at first, but making in time a dense bush 4–6 ft. high, with small blue-green leaves, brilliant vermilion buds, and honey-scented flowers. Very wind-hardy, becoming in time an excellent wind-break.

*B. *s. corallina* is another dense bush, up to 7 ft., with whippy arching growths set thickly in spring with yellow coral-flushed flowers. Both these are excellent for bees.

*Mahonia japonica (true), often confused with *M. Bealei*, is a rounded bush of good habit, with large, decorative, pinnate leaves, and long sprays of lemon-yellow flowers, pendulous, not erect, from November till March. The flowers smell like lily-of-the valley, and rank with winter sweet (*chimonanthus*) and *Daphne odora* amongst the most fragrant flowers of winter. Plant small in May, and avoid root disturbance.

M. Bealei is similar, but is generally gaunt in habit: its leaflets are broader, often whitened underneath, and the flower spikes are stiff and upright.

* *Mahonia lomariifolia*, not long introduced from West China, makes a well-furnished bush 6–7 ft. high, with magnificent pinnate foliage. I know of no shrub more decorative in leaf-design. The flowers too are very handsome from October onwards, making a dozen or more yellow spires a foot long in the centre of each leaf-crown. A first-class introduction, hardy in the mild counties, but liable to be cut or killed or to have its flowers frosted elsewhere.

*Mahonia pinnata, syn. *M. Aquifolium* var. *fascicularis*, is like an enlarged and improved *M. Aquifolium* (the berberis commonly used as ground cover). It grows to 4–6 ft., with large clusters of honey-scented flowers all over the bush—not only at the ends of the growths. This is easily grown in some shade and shelter, but cannot stand windy exposures.

**Mahonia napaulensis* resembles *Bealei*, but is taller, sometimes reaching 20 ft. or more. Its bright-yellow flowers, unscented, are borne in upright spikes in October–November.

Amongst the many berberises grown chiefly for their berries, none is more beautiful than the common *B. vulgaris*, but this should not be planted, as it is the host of wheat rust. Other fine ones include: "Comet," "Fireflame," *orthobotrys, *Prattii, *rubrostilla var. *Crawleyensis*, *suberecta (formerly known as *B. rubrostilla* var. *erecta*), which makes a fine hedge, and *Vernæ*. At their best these are splendid in autumn. In the Cornish climate they grow lavishly, but I have not seen them nearly as decorative with berries as in climates such as that of Gloucestershire.

Those grown chiefly for autumn leaf colour include: *B. dictyophylla*, *Forrestii* (formerly misnamed *B. pallens*, a species which is probably not in cultivation), *Sieboldii, the true plant of which is dwarf, about $2\frac{1}{2}$ ft. high, with marbled foliage and autumn colour of an astonishing scarlet, even in Cornwall, and *Thunbergii*, another dwarf, which has a crimson-leaved form now overplanted.

Billardiera

‡*B. longifolia.* A slender twiner for growing through a shrub: it needs a wall except in mild maritime gardens. Decorative in August, with glazed, oblong, purple-blue fruits. There is a white-berried form and a pink one.

Bowkeria

B. Gerrardiana. A tall evergreen with inflated white flowers like calceolarias: these are generally spotted about the bush, making little show, but it is sometimes an effective plant. It has an unpleasant smell.

§Brachyglottis repanda. See page 11.

Buddleia

**B. alternifolia* makes a large bush or small tree, with willow-like shoots carrying clusters of lavender flowers all along their length. Give it a hot place and plenty of room, and cut out flowered wood immediately after flowering. It prefers a hotter summer and a drier climate than Cornwall's, and is unsuited to damp, sheltered, woodland gardens; but it is a grand plant for a ledge high up in a disused quarry, or for a sunny bank beside water. There is a form, *argentea*, with foliage silvered on both sides.

‡*B. auriculata*, with off-white flowers, is not showy, but it is well worth growing for its honey smell and late flowering. Hardy in mild counties in the open, but usually grown on walls up-country.

B. Colvilei makes a large coarse-leaved bush with large drooping flowers, pink or deep red, like pentstemons. Hooker rated it as "the handsomest of all Himalayan shrubs"; but here, though it grows very freely (e.g. at Trebah, near Falmouth), I have not seen it flowering freely enough in proportion to the room it takes. It flowers on unpruned growth. Weak wood should be cut out.

B. C. kewensis is a good red form.

B. Davidii (syn. *B. variabilis*). Varieties and subspecies of this type are now familiar to every gardener here, though the plant was only introduced in 1893 (its good form, *Veitchiana*, in 1903); and self-sown seedlings have been quick to flower in the rubble of bombed buildings. *"Ile de France," with deep purple spikes, is perhaps the best form: it makes a compact free-flowering bush if hard pruned. *Magnifica* and *amplissima* are first-rate also. *nanhoensis*, with paler purple flower spikes, has a good compact habit and flowers late. All these are favourite plants for Red Admirals and other butterflies. They make a good backing for *Anemone* "Queen Charlôtte" or *Lavatera olbia*, and for purple gladiolus, such as "Pelegrina" or "Baron Hulot," with dark clematis, such as "Gipsy Queen" or *Jackmanii superba*. But these buddleias do not thrive in an acid peaty soil as they do on chalk or good loam. Prune in February.

B. *globosa* is familiar to very many seaside gardeners, being very wind-hardy. It makes a large bush, rather coarse in growth, with orange balls of flower in early summer, strongly honey-scented, and excellent for bees. Some growers advocate pruning this as little as possible, but perhaps the best effect is produced by cutting the bush (or alternate bushes, if several are grown) down to the ground every other year.

There is a washy yellowish form to be avoided. And the hybrids between *globosa* and *Davidii* are too undecided in colour; the best of them is "Golden Glow," buff coloured.

B. *madagascariensis*. See page 320.

BURSARIA

B. *spinosa* makes a very elegant small tree, with a cloud of small, white, fragrant flowers in September–October, and reddish seed-capsules like those of the weed shepherd's purse. It is a scarce plant, not suited for cold gardens.

CÆSALPINIA

‡C. *Gilliesii*. A big shrub or small tree with deciduous pinnate leaves like an acacia and foot-long racemes of yellow flowers with long scarlet stamens. This striking plant prefers a hot wall.

‡C. *japonica* (syn. C. *sepiaria*). A straggly, very thorny shrub, deciduous, with pinnate leaves and racemes of 20–30 canary-yellow flowers with red stamens. A grand plant, too seldom seen; hardy in the mild counties. It likes lime. Beware of its thorns. In a hot climate such as that of La Mortola it makes a fine effect scrambling through high trees.

CALCEOLARIA

*‡C. *violacea*, a Chilean evergreen, makes a 3-ft. bush, covered at the beginning of May with small lilac bells, spotted inside with

yellow and purple. It has a smell something like a dead-nettle. In lime-free soil, in shade or sun, in the mild maritime counties, this is a rampant grower, able to find its way through a thick dry wall. It looks much better as a bush in the open than flattened on a wall; but needs a wall except in the mild maritime counties. The colour looks well as a backing to dark-purple tulips.

‡*C. integrifolia* is the familiar and very showy sub-shrubby one, with brightest yellow flowers for months in late summer. It will reach 4 ft.

Callistemon. Bottle-Brush.

*‡*C. citrinus splendens* (syn. *lævis*) is much the finest kind of bottle-brush, and is worth trying outside in very mild gardens, though it may be knocked out by an abnormal frost. It makes a bush 10 ft. high or more, with stiff leaves, broad and pointed, smelling of *eucalyptus* when bruised; the young shoots are pink and silky. The large bottle-brush flowers around the ends of the shoots are shining vermilion, each stamen tipped with pollen. In mild sheltered gardens, and even in the writer's bleak one near a wall, this flowers with great freedom, making a magnificent show, as it does in the Temperate House at Kew. It is easily grown in a cold greenhouse, but makes rather a mess with fallen stamens.

‡*C. citrinus* (syn. *C. lanceolatus*), the typical form of the species, is a fine plant too. It is the coastal bottle-brush from moist places in Victoria, N.S. Wales, and Queensland, and makes a rather straggling bush with strong drooping branches ringed with the clusters of wooden seed-capsules of past seasons.

‡*C. linearis* is a loose bush with stiff leaves narrow as grass, channelled on the upper side, and pinkish-red brushes smaller than those of *citrinus* and less effective.

‡*C. rigidus* is another small-leaved one with vigorous upright growths and bright-red flowers: a showy plant and fairly hardy.

‡*C. salignus* makes a tall bush or small tree, up to 30 ft., with papery bark, narrow grey-green leaves, red young shoots, and pale-sulphur flower-brushes 2–3 inches long. Young plants of this were killed in Cornwall in the abnormal frost of 1938, but at least some old ones survived, and it is certainly worth replanting in mild gardens if lost.

*‡*C. speciosus* is the plant often sold as a pot-plant under the

wrong name of *Metrosideros floribunda*.[1] The leaves are smaller than those of *C. citrinus splendens*, and the flowers are of the same vivid rose-scarlet but smaller. It stands exposure in mild seaside gardens, making a brilliant flower show for many weeks in summer and always decorative in leaf. An excellent choice if you want to try something out of the ordinary in a small seaside garden, in shelter, in a southward aspect; in such conditions the bush keeps compact, generally 3 ft. or 4 ft. high, but it can reach 10 ft. It is a superb decoration as a pot-plant.

CALLUNA. See under ERICA, page 125.

CAMELLIA. See Chapter VI.

CAMPSIS

*C. *grandiflora* (Thunberg) Loisel (syn. *Bignonia chinensis*, Lam.). On a warm sheltered wall here this grand climber produces its clusters of orange and red trumpets in quantity; but it needs all the sun and ripening it can get, and I have not seen it flower in Cornwall with the lavishness that it shows at, say, Lymington in Hants, or in France. This, doing well, is one of the best climbers we have.

C. *radicans* (*Bignonia radicans*, L., *Tecoma radicans*, Juss.) is a rampant climber, self-clinging by aerial rootlets, with orange and red flowers. It is hardier than *grandiflora*, but generally shy-flowering in this climate, needing more heat. Its varieties include *atropurpurea*, with larger scarlet flowers; *flava*, orange-yellow; "Mme Gallen," salmon-red; *præcox*, scarlet, June-flowering, and *speciosa* (Voss), orange-red, more a bush than a climber.

C. *Tagliabuana* (*Bignonia radicans grandiflora*) is a hybrid between *grandiflora* and *radicans*, hardier but probably less free-flowering than *grandiflora*.

All these should be pruned in spring like a vine, the growths being spurred back to a couple of buds from the old wood.

CARMICHAELIA

C. *australis*, with small lilac pea-flowers, from New Zealand, is almost leafless, but a decorative bush when well grown. Don't

[1] *Metrosideros* have flowers in umbels, generally at the end of the shoots; *Callistemons* have their flowers *round* the terminal shoots, making a cylinder of stamens, not an umbel.

let it get shaken at the root by wind. There are other species, including the very dwarf *C. Enysii*.

CARPENTERIA

*C. californica. This is a superb plant, especially for maritime climates. I do not know why one so seldom sees it in Cornwall. It makes a tall shrub with clusters of white flowers something like *Anemone japonica* in June–July. Too often the leaves get browned by sunburn, especially in time of drought. It likes well-drained soil, but don't let it dry out. There is a finer form, unfortunately very scarce, known as "Ladham's Variety."

CARYOPTERIS

*§C. × clandonensis, which is a hybrid between *C. Mastacanthus* and *C. mongholica*, makes a bush some 3 ft. high, with greyish-green leaves and fuzzy spikes of blue flowers in late summer. First-rate for a sunny spot, even in exposed seaside gardens; but I have never seen it so good in the Cornish climate as in hotter counties, and it wants loam, not heath soil. Prune it almost down to the ground every spring. It roots readily from sappy cuttings, and is easily raised from seed, but seedlings show much variation. It goes well with such plants as the claret-leaved vine, *Ceanothus* "Autumnal Blue," or *C.* "Gloire de Versailles," or with *Perovskia atriplicifolia*, and pale-yellow *gladiolus*.

CASSIA

*‡C. corymbosa. One of the showiest and most long-flowering of wall plants in very mild climates; most profuse with buttercup-yellow flowers from late summer till far into autumn. In the mildest counties it is easily grown on a wall, except in bleak places, and can be used as a sprawling bush in the open in sheltered spots.

CATALPA

*C. bignonioides, Indian bean tree, makes a round-headed wide tree, with soft light-green leaves sometimes as large as 10 inches long and 8 inches across. The flowers, borne in spikes like a chestnut's, are large, white, spotted with yellow and purple. The leaf is produced in May, so that grass grows well under the tree. This is the tree which does well in Palace Yard, Westminster.

It is not of course an Indian tree, or of the Orient at all, but a native of the eastern regions of the United States. There are several forms, but it is doubtful if any are better than this type. Recommended for town planting, where space allows, even in windy places. Note, however, that it does not flower freely every year, takes a good many years to reach flowering age, and is not very long-lived as trees go. It is hardy, but wants all the summer heat it can get. In the mid-European climate it flowers with astonishing freedom: in the streets of Basel, for instance, it can be seen from a distance, at the end of June, as a huge splash of white, whiter in effect than a horse-chestnut.

In America, *C. speciosa*, a taller more erect tree, is preferred. Here it was thought to be less-flowering; but this is by no means certain, now that trees in this country, e.g. at Kew, have reached maturity. It flowers two or three weeks before *bignonioides*, and has larger more tapered leaves and larger flowers. It grows wild in the alluvial soil of river-bottoms, and might well be tried here in such conditions.

C. Duclouxii, from Szechuen and Hupeh, in East China, has large corymbs of lilac-pink flowers, spotted with rust-red: a beautiful tree 20–30 ft. high.

CEANOTHUS.   See Chapter VII.

CELASTRUS

C. orbiculatus, miscalled *C. articulatus*, is a vigorous twining climber, reaching 30–40 ft. up a tree, with long trails of seed-clusters which split open in November: the inside of the seed-capsule is bright yellow and the seeds coated with scarlet. This show remains for weeks on the plant undamaged by birds, and can provide a curious and vivid decoration for the house. Other species include *C. Loeseneri*, which is similar, perhaps preferable, and *C. Rosthornianus*, of more trailing habit.

CERASUS.   See PRUNUS, Chapter XIII.

CERATOSTIGMA

C. Willmottianum is first-rate for a hot place, making a round 3-ft. bush with gentian-blue flowers for a long season in late summer and autumn. Most easily grown.

C. Griffithii can show a pretty reddening of leaf against blue flowers, when somewhat starved, but the flowers are too sparse for the plant to be worth the space it takes.

CERCIDIPHYLLUM
C. japonicum. In the climate of Gloucestershire or of West Scotland this is one of the most brilliantly beautiful of autumn-colouring trees, the leaves turning red, yellow, or pink; but in many gardens it is a disappointment. There is a Chinese form, *C. sinense*.

CERCIS
**C. Siliquastrum.* Judas tree, redbud. We should see more of this lovely and distinctive small tree in the mild counties, especially in hot places. It is deciduous, bushy at first, eventually making a low round-headed tree with a short trunk; leaves heart-shaped, borne just after the flowers; flowers vivid magenta-pink in a cloud all over the tree and even on the trunk. A gay, delightful colour in sunlight but not one that easily mixes with other plant colours, except white and grey-green. Judas trees might well be planted in some quantity in public gardens. They must be planted small, and raised from seed, but the flowering is worth waiting for. They want all the sun they can get. Perhaps we overfeed them; they grow wild on stony slopes.

C. chinensis, the Chinese redbud, is a rather bigger tree with pink flowers, more tender than *Siliquastrum* and less satisfactory.

C. racemosa, another Chinese species, with longer flower clusters, is very slow to flower, but may prove a fine plant.

CESTRUM
‡*C. elegans*, an evergreen climber from Mexico, is hardy enough for warm walls. The tubular flowers are purplish-pink in terminal clusters in late autumn.

C. Newellii is crimson.

C. Parqui has greenish flowers, not pretty but strongly scented at night. This too is hardy enough on a wall in mild gardens.

CHERRY. See Chapter XIII under PRUNUS.

CHIMONANTHUS. WINTER SWEET.
**C. fragrans.* No great show of flower colour here, but a scent sweeter than any other flower's in mid-winter, except perhaps

Daphne odora's—a smell as unforgettable as that of *boronia*. The small downward-looking flowers on bare twigs are translucent horn-colour with purplish centre. If the plant is grown on a wall, prune back the flowered shoots close to the main stem immediately after flowering, so as to encourage the new summer's growth on which next winter's flowers will be borne. But it grows well in the open, and then needs no pruning. I have seen it as much as 14 ft. high as a bush in Cornwall.

The variety *grandiflora* has larger yellower flowers; the scent is less strong, but quite good enough.

A fine variety, *luteus*, has quite conspicuous flowers, clear sulphur-yellow.

CHIONANTHUS. FRINGE TREE.

*C. retusa. The Chinese fringe tree makes a large deciduous bush or small tree, with erect panicles of small white flowers in June–July. I have not seen this magnificent shrub in Cornwall; probably this is because it does better in more extreme climates, such as that of Eastern U.S.A., where it becomes white all over. It should be more often planted. Forrest introduced a fine form.

*C. virginica, the species native to the Eastern U.S.A., is similar, but is easier to grow, and has pendent flower-panicles in dense masses. If on its own roots, not grafted, it will quickly attain 10 ft. or 15 ft., and will be white with flowers when only 4 ft. high. Its yellow autumn colour is another glory of the plant.

CHOISYA. MEXICAN ORANGE BLOSSOM.

C. ternata. This quickly makes a large spherical bush, handsomely evergreen; and if the growths get well-ripened, its dead-white slightly fragrant flowers are very profuse in spring. Often it flowers again in autumn. A common shrub now, but not to be neglected. Its tidy habit and rounded shape make it suitable for such positions as court-yards and recesses beside doorways; and it is one of the white flowers that can be used to relieve the terrific magenta of a mass of *Azalea amœna*.

CISTUS

These are so free-flowering in mid-summer, and so fast-growing, that they are exceptionally useful for making a show quickly in new gardens; they are good, too, for nursing more permanent plants, since they do not make large roots. Some, such as *C. ladaniferus* and *Loretii*, are very aromatic.

Tall whites are **C. ladaniferus*, the big "gum *Cistus*," with splendid flowers splashed with crimson at the centre; *C. ladaniferus maculatus*, without the crimson; **C. cyprius*, with flowers not quite so fine, but with more of them; *C. laurifolius*, very hardy, and quick to sow itself; *C. populifolius*.

Medium growers include *purpureus, with large flowers of bright purplish-rose with a dark blotch; *florentinus* and *corbariensis*, free-flowering white hybrids; and the lovely *"Silver Pink," with flowers of clear rose-pink free from purple.

Skanbergii, with small pink flowers, is pretty but not very effective. *C. pulverulentus* (syn. *crispus*), with grey-green leaves waved at the edge and heather-pink flowers, succeeds even in pure sea-sand in severe exposure.

**C. Loretii* (syn. *lusitanicus* var. *decumbens*, Maund) is a compact low bush, aromatic, with flowers like a reduced version of *C. ladaniferus*.

**C. salvifolius* has a dwarf form, hardier than the type, which is valuable as a low mat; and another excellent dwarf is a hybrid between *Cistus salvifolius* and *Halimium umbellatum*. This plant, *Halimiocistus Sahucii*, is robust and hardy, wide-spreading, but only 1 ft. high, very free with its small white flowers.

Halimiocistus Wintonensis is a beautiful cross between *cistus* and *helianthemum*, white with a dark crimson zone; but it is tender and a weak grower, best in good soil that is not too dry.

The shrubby *halimiums*, like yellow *cistuses*, are amongst the best dwarf shrubs for hot exposures; e.g. **H. lasianthum* (syn. *formosum*, Dun), yellow with a brown spot, and grey leaf; *H. ocymoides* (syn. *algarvense*, Dun), yellow with grey leaf; and *H. halimifolium*.

CLEMATIS

**C. Armandii*. The form of this clematis which was first introduced into English gardens, is a rampant climber, with good green foliage but quite dull flowers, smallish, dull white, unscented. But that form is not worth keeping now that the fine forms of the species, such as adorn the famous garden at La Mortola (on the Riviera), are in commerce here. The leaves of the good form are handsome, long, pointed, polished, and coppery when young. The large flowers in March–April have four to six rounded sepals, pure white or flushed, often with a scent of almond: they are carried in large bunches at the leaf-axils; in some forms the flowers are extra large and comparatively few, in others they are of medium size but very numerous. The plant can be grown up a warm wall, but it is apt to run up to the top unless carefully trained in zigzags. It is excellent for a pergola, as may be seen at La Mortola; and in a cold greenhouse or as a pot-plant it can be most effective. Best of all, I think, is to let it grow through a tree—a yew for instance—where it can freely hang out its splendid ropes of flower and leaf.

Good forms, propagated by grafting or by cuttings, are "Snowdrift," a white one with large flowers, and "Apple Blossom," pink in bud, with flowers that open (at least in some soils) pale pink. *C. Armandii* crosses readily with *C. Meyeniana*. A seedling, apparently from this cross, with rose-pink flowers, originated at La Mortola before the war, but was lost in the war years.

C. Meyeniana is another fine evergreen, which should not be ousted even by *Armandii*. The leaves are smaller and narrower; the flowers too are rather smaller, with five to seven pointed sepals, creamy-white, with a sweeter scent, suggesting orange-blossom. The plant flowers earlier, often beginning in February.

‡C. indivisa, more tender than these, is another plant which must rank amongst the most beautiful climbers we can grow. The white stars are like a glorified *C. montana*, wonderfully profuse in April. This plant, a New Zealander, common amongst the wild *leptospermum* bushes there, is hardy enough for mild maritime gardens here; but it is tender when young and may well be grown on till it has made some hard wood before it is planted out. In several Cornish gardens (Lanarth, Bosahan) it has climbed 50 ft. into tall trees; but it shows its beauty much better lower down. A huge plant of this over a summer-house at Pendrea, Penzance, used to be one of the outstanding flower-sights in Cornwall.

‡*C. aristata*, from Australia and Tasmania, is another of these evergreens, with profuse white stars, four-petalled, an inch across, followed by a silvery "traveller's joy" of seeds. Young plants were killed in Cornwall by the abnormal 1938 frost.

C. montana and *C. Spooneri*, with their varieties and hybrids, all deciduous, are as beautiful in their way as any of the evergreen species and much more reliable.

The typical white *montana* needs no recommendation. Don't

treat it only as a wall plant: let it ramp as a wild plant, like our native traveller's joy.

Wilsonii is a fine form, with scented flowers 3 inches across in July–August instead of April–May.

*montana rubens, the pink one, is perhaps the best of all clematises for general cultivation here; a most lovely plant. Get a good form if possible, preferably one with a purplish leaf. And if it must be on a wall, train it with some care, for it is fast-growing and may make a tangled lump of growth.

*montana lilacina is another first-rate form, with large lilac flowers. One who grows clematises in quantity reports that this is "with me the best of all the *montana* lot, a tremendous grower, and very free flowering, wind or no wind."

Spooneri (*C. montana* var. *sericea*, Franch), closely akin to *montana*, has finer more solid flowers, 3 inches across.

*C. vedrariensis, Vilm. (syn. *C. Spooneri rosea*, Vilm.), is a very beautiful pink hybrid (*C. montana rubens* × *chrysocoma*), with cool pink flowers of perfect shape. I find this thrives even in very acid soil and in a very windy and draughty position. If grown on a windy wall, it needs some tying in, when making its soft young growths in May, so that these do not blow about.

Other climbing species include:

*C. alpina. A good form of this species, with nodding clear-blue flowers in spring, is one of the best of blue-flowered climbing plants; pretty too when covered with its fluff of traveller's joy seeds.

C. balearica (syn. *C. calycina*) is not a showy flower, but the evergreen foliage, cut in a ferny pattern and bronzed in winter, is decorative, and the yellowish-white four-sepalled bell flowers, downy outside and speckled inside with reddish purple, are welcome in mid-winter. Oddly enough, it proves wind-hardy: even close to the cliff edge at Newquay, on the north coast of Cornwall, it thrives and flowers profusely in January.

C. campaniflora is another excellent plant for wild planting, with small saucer-shaped flowers which, in a mass, give the effect of a lilac haze in July–August.

C. cirrhosa is similar to *balearica*, but hardier and dwarfer. Its evergreen leaves, ovate or three-lobed, lack the fine-cut beauty of those of *balearica*: it bears its unspotted whitish flowers rather later and less freely.

A General Planting List

C. Flammula, with leaden-green leaves and small milk-white flowers from July to September, has a pleasant pervasive scent, and is one of the most wind-hardy of climbers. It thrives even in severe exposure in the Scilly Isles. The plant looks well up a gatepost or along a terrace wall, or rambling through a bush such as sea buckthorn.

C. rubro-marginata, a hybrid between *C. Flammula* and *C. Viticella*, has violet, white-centred flowers as fragrant as *Flammula's*.

C. glauca akebioides, with small yellow flowers and elegant glaucous foliage, is a good late sort for wild planting.

C. macropetala is a light trailer, a delightful plant flowering in May, with azure-blue, smoke-blue, or pink flowers (*C. Markhamii*). It looks well with rosemary or lavender.

C. paniculata, with a cloud of small white, scented flowers, is another familiar ramper, later than *Flammula*.

C. Rehderiana (Craib) (miscalled *nutans*) resembles *Veitchiana*; its pale primrose-yellow bells have a fresh cowslip smell in autumn.

C. tangutica obtusiuscula is a lovely sight, both when its yellow bells hang out from a bush or tree and when its silver seed-fluff follows. It flowers on the year's new growth, so if pruning is required, thin growths should be cut back to the ripe wood. "Gravetye variety" is a good form.

*C. Veitchiana (Craib). This rampant climber is a striking sight in autumn, e.g. growing along a fence. The leaves are doubly pinnate. The nodding bells are clear primrose-yellow, with the smell of cowslips, as in *C. Rehderiana*, but the plant is more vigorous.

C. Viticella. A slender, very graceful climber, most easily grown.

*C. v. kermesina, with small wine-crimson flowers, is a beautiful plant with many uses, e.g. climbing through a grey-leaved bush such as sea-buckthorn or through a *pyracantha*. Hybrids of *Viticella* include "Lady Betty Balfour," one of the best purples, and "Ville de Lyon," a crimson larger than *kermesina*.

Large-flowered Hybrid Clematises

These garden varieties, of which *Jackmanii* is the most familiar, include the most showy of hardy climbing plants. They like lime, and shade at the root with sun at the head. They must have plenty of water when making young growth. They often need protection against slugs, by a zinc collar at the base and by the use of "Meta." Plant them 2 inches deeper than they were when in pots. And note the differing requirements of the various sections as regards pruning. On the one hand, there are the varieties which flower on old wood in spring; on the other hand, those which flower on new wood in summer. The spring-flowerers include the *florida* varieties, such as "Duchess of Edinburgh," and the *patens* varieties, such as "Lasurstern." These should be pruned and thinned in winter, but not heavily, weak growths being removed and some strong ones shortened. In spring, before the flower-buds show, the growths may be trained to cover their space, and then left to run. The summer-flowerers include the *Jackmanii, lanuginosa,* and *Viticella* varieties. First, prune these to about a foot from the ground in February, just above a node. If the plant breaks from below ground, the old growth can safely be cut back severely each year thereafter, in February (except perhaps in the case of the weaker varieties of the *lanuginosa* type). If you want a low plant of a *Jackmanii* hybrid, such as "Perle d'azur," or of a *Viticella,* or of a vigorous *lanuginosa* such as "Henryi," prune it, when the growth buds show in spring, to about a foot from the ground or even lower; if you want a tall plant, prune it higher up; if you have let it ramp up a tree, you may be able to thin it.[1]

Get plants on their own roots, if possible. And allow for the probability that, no matter how careful you are (e.g. about shade at the root), some of the bought plants will die of clematis wilt. No sure remedy has yet been found. But one who grows a great number of clematises very well tells me that he finds "seedlings of the large-flowered kind are far more easy to establish than grafted plants, layers or cutings; all sorts of pretty colours result, and the plants live on for ever—no wilting or going off. I grow them from a sort with very large flowers such as 'Lasurstern.'"

These plants are commonly grown on walls; but they can be used, with little trouble and much effect, in flower borders. In particular, they are perfect in colour with the irises and lupins of May–June, and with some of the pink and purple border plants of late summer. Or they will grow up a tree—a hawthorn or an old apple tree, for instance. Any stiff-growing shrub, such as *pyracantha* or sea buckthorn, serves as support.

[1] For expert counsel on pruning these and other types, see "The Clematis as a Garden Plant," by R. Jackman, *R.H.S. Journal,* December 1946.

A General Planting List

The *patens* type, flowering in early summer from the old ripened growths, includes: *"Lasurstern," a large lavender-blue, excellent with *pallida* blue irises such as "Sierra Blue," "Aline," "Sirius," and pale-yellow irises such as "Pluie d'or" or "Sahara," and with lupins of clear colour (not those of mixed or coppery colours); "Mrs. G. Jackman" and "The Bride," whites; "Marcel Moser" and "Nelly Moser," very free-flowering, pale mauve with darker rays; *"The President," a large flower of fine pointed shape, deep purplish-blue, one of the best, often flowering twice; "E. Defosse," large violet.

The *Jackmanii* type, flowering in summer and autumn on growths made during the same summer, includes:
*"Comtesse de Bouchaud," mallow-pink, flowering very freely for a long season, a plant of good constitution, beautiful with *Lavatera olbia* and *Salvia virgata nemorosa, Echinops Ritro, Sidalcea* "Sussex Beauty," etc.; "Gipsy Queen," deep purple with wine-crimson in it, fine with buddleias, or with the purple-leaved *Rhus Cotinus*.
*"Huldine" is a beautiful translucent white, flowering very late (September–October).
Jackmanii superba, a broad-petalled, violet-purple form of the common *Jackmanii*, very free-flowering and vigorous, first-rate with buddleias and pink Anemone "Queen Charlotte."
*"Perle d'azur." A medium-sized lavender-blue of strong constitution, very free and long-flowering, perfect with *Ceanothus* "Gloire de Versailles." This is one of the best clematises.
C. rubella is a rich claret-purple.

The *lanuginosa* type, flowering in summer and autumn on lateral summer growths, includes: "Ernest Markham," a new crimson, superseding the earlier "Crimson King," which was a weak grower with flowers that faded from a lovely crimson when fresh to a bluer shade; *"Henryi," an old white but still unsurpassed; *"Lady Northcliffe," a magnificent powder-blue with white stamens, perhaps the finest of all in colour; *"Mrs. Cholmondeley," a light blue, early flowering and very free, good with blue June irises and lupins; "Beauty of Richmond," mauve; "W. Kennett," lavender.

The *Viticella* group, flowering in summer and autumn on summer growths, includes: "Lady Betty Balfour," one of the best purples, very late and vigorous; "Kermesina," crimson; *"Royal

Velours," deep purple, like velvet, not large-flowered but very free; and "Abundance," purple, very profuse.

The *texensis* group, with bell-shaped flowers on the summer's shoots, includes: "Countess of Onslow," purple with a scarlet band, very free; "Duchess of Albany," bright pink; "Sir Trevor Lawrence," carmine; and the new "Gravetye Beauty."

CLERODENDRON

C. fœtidum makes a thicket of strong shoots 5 ft. high, with large heart-shaped leaves which smell unpleasant when bruised, and large terminal umbels of purplish-pink flowers. It is a coarse plant, but can be very showy when grown in a hot place.

C. trichotomum, a tree-like spreading bush some 12 ft. high, has large leaves, fragrant white flowers in late summer, and blue seeds in a crimson calyx. A coarse plant, but pretty in the detail of its seeds, and easily grown. *C. Fargesii* makes a smaller bush and has a green calyx turning pink, and other differences; it may flower more freely when young and is hardy, whereas *trichotomum* may suffer from spring frosts.

CLETHRA

C. alnifolia, var. *paniculata*, pepper bush, is quite hardy, and makes a pleasant 6-ft. bush in a moisture-retaining soil, with white fuzzy flower-spikes, strongly scented, in August. The variety *paniculata*, with branching racemes and narrower leaves, is more effective than the type. There is a good pale-pink form.

C. barbinervis is similar, late-flowering, liable to injury by spring frosts. It will make a small spreading tree up to 30 ft. high.

*†*C. Delavayi* is a most beautiful West Chinese species with long white flower-sprays. It wants shelter and cannot stand drought or wind, but where it thrives it makes a large erect bush or small tree, covered with white plumes in late summer, and is one of the best late-flowering shrubs. The calyx is red; the petals are longer than the stamens.

C. monostachya is another plant of exceptional beauty, with very fragrant white flower-spikes 9 inches long, usually solitary. It comes from Central China, and is hardy enough for the milder counties.

For the outstanding but tender species *C. arborea* see page 323.

CLIANTHUS. PARROT'S BEAK.

*†‡*C. puniceus*, a magnificent wall plant which decorates many house walls in Penzance and other mild places, has light-green pinnate leaves in graceful fronds, and hanging branches of rose-scarlet flowers, pea-shaped, with long parrot's-beak keels; it reaches 10 ft. or more and a greater width, but can be pruned to fit a smaller space. It flowers very early and freely, sometimes repeating its show in the autumn; and the evergreen foliage is always beautiful. So it is one of the plants to consider if one has a mild climate, a south wall, and well-drained soil, preferably with some sand in it. It is a variable plant, with a white form inferior to the red, and a pink one very inferior in effect.

CONVOLVULUS

C. Cneorum is one of the most attractive of silver-leaved plants, silky all over; and the convolvulus flowers, white touched with pink, are pretty in May, and are freely sprinkled with flowers till September. It likes good drainage, e.g. where it droops down a rock; and it goes very well with such plants as woolly thyme (*Thymus lanuginosus*), *Teucrium fruticans*, *Olearia mollis*, and rose-red *helianthemums*.

*C. mauritanicus is another beautiful *convolvulus*, a rampant trailer, with lavender-blue flowers, borne for a long season with remarkable freedom. It makes a fine show on sunny rocks on St. Michael's Mount, together with *mesembryanthemums*. Excellent in dry walls.

C. floridus. See Chapter XIII.

COPROSMA

C. acerosa var. *brunnea*. A prostrate New Zealand shrub with translucent blue berries.

‡*C. Baueri*, with glazed light-green leaves, makes a bush up to 10 ft., a good plant for evergreen seaside hedges: it thrives at Tresco, but was killed on the mainland in 1938. There are many others, some with decorative berries, such as *C. Petriei*.

C. nitida is a dense low bush introduced by Comber from Tasmania, with orange or red berries; it needs cross-fertilisation.

CORDYLINE

§*C. australis*, dracæna. This palm-like New Zealander, now so familiar in the Cornish scene, can be a noble decoration in appropriate sites, and the scent spilt by its mop-heads of white flower makes one of the sweetest of Cornish airs in June. But it is often misplaced, for the sake of "tropical effect." May those who plant public gardens in Cornwall and Plymouth after the war refrain from overdoing the planting of "dracænas," remembering that so ambitious and gallant an enterprise as the planting of "Dracæna Avenue" at Falmouth cannot be counted a success. It should not be assumed that these palm-like shapes will create the "Riviera" effect suggested by pre-war posters in which ladies and gentlemen promenade in the shade of palms beside a sea for ever waveless and awfully blue. No plant looks more moth-eaten than a *cordyline* that has been damaged by frost and left untended. But the tree has remarkable powers of recovery, commonly bursting up again if cut by an abnormal frost. Some plants drop their dead leaves and so look much more trim than those which hold them. There is a form with bronze-red leaves—var. *lentiginosa*.

C. indivisa, with much broader bronze-coloured leaves, is an impressive plant, just hardy enough for mild gardens, but more tender than *australis*, and apparently much more shy-flowering. If cut to the ground by frost, it may break again. It is regarded in New Zealand as a much finer plant.

C. Banksii reaches 8 ft., with slender stems, often making a clump; it has long narrow leaves drooping at the tips, with lax branching flower-panicles sometimes 5 ft. long. There are many varieties, more or less ribbed with red.

Cornus. Cornel.

C. alba atrosanguinea is the best of the red-stemmed dogwoods.

*C. capitata (syn. *Benthamia fragifera*). Strawberry tree. This is one of the most decorative flowering trees for mild gardens. It is generally deciduous or sub-evergreen, but in sheltered gardens in Cornwall it is commonly quite evergreen. It generally grows to about 18 ft., but is sometimes much taller—up to 50 ft. Isolated trees are sometimes very decorative in shape. In June it is covered with conspicuous creamy flower-bracts, green-tinted, and these are followed (often but not always) by handsome red fruits rather like large hard strawberries. In Cornish woodland gardens this outstanding plant sows itself by the hundred. On the Cornish coast it has been found to be surprisingly wind-hardy.

A General Planting List

*C. florida and *C. florida rubra*. These white and pink dogwoods, which in the Eastern United States are the most beautiful of native shrubs, are very disappointing here in the Midlands or near London; for though the plant is extremely hardy, the flowering often suffers from spring frosts. But in many gardens in Southern England, e.g. in the Bournemouth area, and in at least one Cornish garden, the pink dogwood is a most lovely sight in spring. No small tree that is hardy here is more beautiful in colour than this: the pink has an unrivalled warmth and quality. In a suitable climate both forms, especially the pink one, have splendid autumn colour on the upper side of the leaf. Give it full sun at the head, but shade at the root, e.g. by planting low shrubs near it.

*C. Kousa makes a small tree or large bush with spreading branches in tiers, loaded with cream-white narrow-pointed bracts which flush pink in damp weather. A well-flowered plant of this is an arresting sight in June, when flowering shrubs are scarce. It makes a good foil to red *leptospermums*. In autumn, in climates less damp than Cornwall's, it puts on autumn scarlet.

The variety **chinensis* is a taller plant, with leaves paler and generally larger than the type's, and with larger but fewer bracts. It is reckoned an even finer plant, but this is questionable.

C. mas, the "cornelian cherry," with its smoke of small, fragrant, yellow flowers in February, will reach 20 ft. or even 30 ft. in southern gardens; the flowering branches are welcome for cutting at that flowerless time and last long in water, and the edible scarlet berries are decorative.

C. Nuttallii. In California and British Columbia this becomes a magnificent tree, brilliant for a long season with white bracts against the sky and brilliant again with autumn crimson. Sometimes it flowers freely in autumn as well as in spring. In this country it does quite well at Kew and elsewhere in the south, though, like *Arbutus Menziesii*, it seems unlikely to reach such a stature here as old trees have reached on the Pacific seaboard. (See, for instance, a photograph in *New Flora and Silva*, vol. viii, page 220.) It has the reputation of proving disappointing and short-lived here; but from such limited observation of it as I have been able to make, I believe gardeners in the milder counties who can give it well-drained, gritty, lime-free soil, in sun, should persist in trying this grand plant.

Corokia

§*C. Cotoneaster* is a very wind-hardy bush with sparse, small, grey-green leaves, spoon-shaped, white underneath, starred in May with small yellow flowers: fruits red. It is stiff and interlaced in habit and very wind-hardy. I have seen it well-used as a support through which *Mitraria coccinea* could hang out its scarlet flowers.

‡§*C. buddleoides* makes an erect bush which may reach 12 ft., grey-green, with white shoots and white undersides to the olive-green leaves, and small stars of light-yellow flower in profusion towards the ends of the growths. The berries change from yellow to orange red. The yellow and grey-green are beautifully related, and the bush is more effective in flower than the commoner *C. macrocarpa*.

‡§*C. macrocarpa* is similar but with broader leaves, flowers in the axils (not terminal, as in *buddleoides*) and taller growth. It comes from Chatham Island, and is a most useful and free-flowering wind-hardy plant. It goes well with *olearias* such as *Traversii*, *albida*, and *semi-dentata*. Killed in W. Cornwall in 1947.

§*C. Cheesemanii* is a natural hybrid between *C. Cotoneaster* and *C. buddleoides*, intermediate in characters.

§*C. virgata* is another small-leaved one, reaching 10 ft. or more, with leaves generally $\frac{3}{4}$ inch long, white underneath, and orange-yellow berries. Excellent for a hedge, and beautiful in colour against grey rocks or weatherboard.

Coronilla

C. glauca has glaucous pinnate leaves and yellow pea-flowers in clusters, fragrant in day-time, borne nearly all the year round, but notably from November till May. In a sunny spot this is excellent, even in exposed seaside gardens. Its perpetual flowering makes it suitable for such positions as the recess beside a cottage porch. It will reach 8 ft., but stands cutting back. There is a good dwarf form, *pygmæa*.

C. Valentina is similar to glauca but dwarfer: the flowers do not smell so sweet as *glauca's*.

C. Emerus, scorpion senna, with yellow pea-flowers streaked with rust-brown on the back of the standard, can at its best make quite a good show, but is generally hardly worth the space it takes.

CORREA. See Chapter XIII.

CORYLOPSIS. WITCH HAZEL.
C. glabrescens (syn. *Gotoana*), probably the best of the tribe, makes a large open bush, hung in March–April with primrose-yellow catkins of flower which scent the garden. This is perfect in colour with the violet-pink of heaths such as *Erica mediterranea superba* or *darleyensis*, and its smell is one of the pleasures of spring. It is the hardiest of the genus.
C. pauciflora, a much smaller grower, makes a twiggy bush 3–6 ft. high, with open primrose-yellow flowers hanging in short clusters from the bare twigs in March. In frosty sites the flowers may be nipped. Plant it up on a bank if possible, so that it can be seen from below. It looks well with blue flowers such as grape-hyacinths.

Other good species include *sinensis*, a 12-ft. bush; *spicata*, about 5 ft.; *Willmottiae*, 8 ft.; *Veitchiana*, 6 ft.; *platypetala*, 8 ft.

COTONEASTER
As noted in List B, cotoneasters include some of the best shrubs for rough conditions. Here are some further notes:

(a) TALL GROWERS
C. aldenhamensis, a seedling, is a fast-growing small tree, loaded with scarlet berries in autumn: a beautiful plant for the angle-recess of some outbuilding, or for a tall hedge.
C. frigida, especially its improved form **Vicarii*, is the well-known small tree with rather coarse leaves and unpolished red berries, lasting long on the tree. It shows its character best, I think, when grown as a tree with a single trunk rather than as a bush.
*"St. Monica," a natural hybrid found in a convent garden at Bristol, has very large, vividly scarlet berries, stands wind, and is certainly one of the very best. It will reach 30 ft.
*"Cornubia," which received the F.C.C. of the R.H.S., is very similar to "St. Monica," a very vigorous and effective plant. It would be hard to better these plants for a tall screen of shrubs.
**Watereri* is another small tree, very vigorous, and splendidly scarlet with berries on drooping branches.

C. salicifolia, and its varieties *floccosa* and *rugosa* (with intermediate forms), make a splendid tall hedge, red with berries late in the year.

(b) MEDIUM GROWERS
C. bullata, reaching 8–10 ft., makes a show of vermilion berries as early as September, sows itself and stands wind; excellent for naturalising or roadside planting.
C. buxifolia is good as an evergreen hedge, with scarlet berries.
C. divaricata, a spreading bush 5–6 ft. high, has, besides red berries, the most brilliant leaf scarlet in autumn (at least in climates where leaves colour well).
C. glaucophylla flowers later, has orange-red fruits, and is a very wind-hardy grey-leaved bush up to 9 ft. high.
C. Henryana has a beautiful arching habit, with evergreen leaves bronzed in winter and crimson berries in October. Give it room for horizontal spread.
*§*C. lactea*. This makes a large rounded evergreen bush in the open; or it can be trained as a small tree with upstanding trunk, or used as a hedge. In spring the pale young shoots along the arching sprays look like small Christmas Tree candles, and in autumn the plant is loaded with bunches of small red berries. In one form the leaves are yellow underneath. The plant thrives both on chalky and on peaty soils; and, as noted in Chapter II, it is extraordinarily wind-hardy. Undoubtedly this is one of the most useful all-round evergreens we have; and it is easily raised from seed. A plant known in America as *C. Parnayi* appears to be this species.
C. multiflora, white in May with bridal-wreath streamers of flowers, and reddened with fruits as early as August, should be more planted. The smell of its flowers is not attractive.
**C. pannosa*, with silver young growths, grey leaves, small dull-white flower clusters, and red berries, is a most graceful tall grower, remarkably wind-hardy. It looks well with white broom. It thrives without distortion of shape even amongst northward-facing rocks 600 ft. up on the Land's End moors, where very few other shrubs could stand the winds and draughts.
C. Franchetii is similar, equally wind-hardy, but a smaller plant.
C. rotundifolia is a stiff bush about 5 ft. high, sub-evergreen, brilliant in berry; and the berries, seldom touched by birds, are retained until well into the New Year.

A General Planting List

C. serotina is, like *lactea*, extremely wind-hardy. It makes a rounded evergreen mass up to 10 ft. high, and carries its orange-red berries very late.

C. Simonsii, a familiar plant, is scarlet with berries in October even when clipped. It makes a good hedge for small gardens, and is suitable for naturalising.

*C. Wardii, with grey-green leaves, and large orange-scarlet berries carried until the New Year, may be reckoned the best of all the *cotoneasters* for berry; a plant of good upright and arching habit, beautiful in colour in autumn. It should be widely planted, not only in wild gardens, but on roadsides. In the garden proper, it may seed itself too freely.

(c) Dwarf growers

C. adpressa is a very attractive plant for growing closely down a rock face or wall. There is an early variety, *præcox*.

*§C. conspicua, with small grey-green leaves and orange-scarlet berries, can make a brilliant show for a long time in winter, and its hawthorn-like flowers with pink anthers are faintly but pleasantly scented. It is a rampant spreader, generally not remaining low, but eventually reaching 5 ft. or more. A form which keeps down to $2\frac{1}{2}$ ft. was selected at Exbury.

C. Dammeri. A most valuable carpeter or trailer. It can make an evergreen weed-free covering for a steep bank or retaining wall, bronzed during all the winter months, and can serve as a carpet over bulbs such as grape-hyacinths.

*§C. horizontalis, with its flat fronds of leaf and berry, needs no commendation. It is never better than when self-sown amongst rocks, where it lays its fans close against the stone, or hangs them out over a space. Even when planted in pure sea-sand, it grows and fruits well. In many places the leaves, with the berries, turn so red in autumn that it becomes much the brightest plant in the garden. If grown on a wall, it fruits best if pruned so as to leave only the growth close to the wall. Bees love its inconspicuous flowers (indeed, *cotoneasters* in general are excellent bee plants); so that when summer is coming in, *C. horizontalis* makes more welcome noise than any other plant. Queen wasps love it too; if you want to slay wasps, preventive executions over this rendezvous in May will be far more effective than swatting ex-

peditions or bottles of wasp-liquor in days when plums are ripening. It is deciduous, but the period without leaves is short.

C. h. var. *perpusilla* is a good variety, sub-evergreen; and the variegated variety of horizontalis, much smaller in growth than the type, is better than most variegated shrubs.

§*C. microphylla*, another of the very familiar sorts, is a useful evergreen for covering banks, but blackish in general effect.

The variety *cochleata has brighter berries, and is a first-rate very dwarf plant. *C. m. thymæfolia* is another variety with minute leaves, a dense rampant grower which, like the type, will stand every wind unscorched.

CRATÆGUS. See page 69.

CYDONIA. JAPANESE QUINCE.

These, of course, are among the best-loved plants of our gardens in spring. The nomenclature of the family has lately been drastically revised, with results troublesome to most of us who have got used to calling *japonica* what is now to be called *lagenaria*.

Give them full sun, to ripen the wood, and good loamy soil. Don't grow them only on walls; they can make a fine show as bushes in the open. On walls they are generally pruned like pears, long shoots being shortened in late summer and then spurred back to a few buds in winter; but some growers do all the pruning in late summer. I think they are often over-pruned.

C. japonica. This is not the plant commonly known as "*Pyrus japonica*," but the one known as *Cydonia Maulei*. It makes a low dense bush with orange-scarlet flowers and large fruits which make excellent jelly (when sugar is obtainable). The colour is difficult to mix. Hybrids between this and *C. lagenaria* include *C. j. superba*, a large-flowered slow-growing form; and "Incendie," with brick-orange flowers.

*"Knap Hill Scarlet," which in its true form is a grand plant with globular orange-vermilion flowers $2\frac{1}{2}$ inches across, is probably one of such hybrids.

*Simonii, with substantial flowers of a magnificent deep blood-red colour, is often classed with these hybrids, but has a very distinct character. If planted in strong soil, it is not a weak grower, but it is slower, less rampant and dwarfer than the others—perfect for a position under a south window where other sorts would grow too high.

C. lagenaria (commonly known as *C. japonica* or *Pyrus japonica*). The typical plant sometimes begins to show its cheerful scarlet flowers before Christmas. It is not superseded by the garden varieties. Have you ever come in February or March from the dark skies of, say, Aberdeen or Glasgow, to a southern home and been cheered by the glow of good old "japonica's" flowers and breaking buds around the window?

Amongst the many varieties grown in Japanese and French nurseries, only a small proportion are familiar here: I think some of these would probably be worth importing, especially very early sorts. There is still need for a pure rose-red (not salmon-pink or brick-red) of good habit.

*"Rowallane seedling" is a very fine variety with deep-scarlet flowers (not as dark as those of *Simonii*), 2 inches or even 2½ inches across. *Cardinalis*, another red, is first-rate also; *rubra grandiflora* is a dark red, vigorous enough to reach the top of a house-wall if suitably pruned; *umbilicata* is a fresh pink; *nivalis* (which appears to be the same as "Snow Queen") is a free-flowering white, and *Moerloesii* is apple-blossom rose and white.

C. l. rosea flore-pleno is salmon-pink, not improved by having double or semi-double flowers, but bushy and free-flowering. "Phyllis Moore" has similar flowers, but is a straggly plant of poor habit.

C. cathayensis is a robust but ungainly Chinese species, with pink and white flowers rather small for the scale of the plant, followed by very large apple-like fruits. It is often an unsatisfactory plant, being liable to canker. But it has lately yielded a series of hybrids with *C. japonica*, which are said to be quick-growing, rigid in habit, wind-resisting, with flowers in shades of pink and red.

CYTISUS. BROOM.

C. albus, the tall white broom, quickly makes a fountain of white, beautiful amongst grey-leaved shrubs such as *Cotoneaster pannosa*. Easily raised from seed. "Johnson's crimson" is of this type, but crimson-flowered.

§*C. Battandieri*, a large shrub of spreading or lanky habit with silky silvery trefoil foliage and yellow or orange-yellow flowers in dense racemes. It is very frost-hardy, and should be very wind-hardy, since it comes from altitudes of from 5,000 to 7,000 ft. in the Atlas Mountains, where it grows as wind-swept scrub. Plant it from pots when two years old from seed, in full sun; being very difficult to raise from cuttings, it is sometimes grafted on laburnum.

†‡*C. proliferus* from Teneriffe is a very graceful small tree of showering habit, with greyish leaves and milk-white pea-flowers in long trails. A good form of this (sometimes distinguished as "Miss Wingfield's variety") used to be a lovely sight against dark trees in Miss S. Wingfield's garden at Pendrea, Penzance.

*‡*C. racemosus* (syn. *C. fragrans*) is one of the most fragrant and prolific flowers of spring and one of the first shrubs to choose for a mild garden. Given only such shelter as a recess in a house-front, it thrives in many a windy seaside garden; and whilst it may be killed by an abnormal frost, as in 1938, it is easily replaced and grows fast.

*‡*C. racemosus elegans* has larger, silvery leaves, and much larger, finer flower-spikes, equally fragrant; one of the best plants for a cold greenhouse and worth a good place, with ample head-room, out of doors in mild gardens.

*The Porlock broom, *C. monspessulanus* × *racemosus*, is a valuable hybrid, extremely long-flowering, much hardier than *racemosus* and with much of its beauty.

C. scoparius. This native broom makes as bright a show as any shrub that grows, and bushes self-sown in rocky ground become as tough and unshakable as gorse itself. Unfortunately, the beautiful garden varieties, at least the taller ones, are apt to get top-heavy and blow over in windy sites unless carefully staked and watched. But they are worth trouble, since they include some magnificent plants, and being quick growers they are very useful for new gardens. The hybrids, derived from *scoparius* and other species, include **Burkwoodii*, crimson (which supersedes the older "Dorothy Walpole"); "Geoffrey Skipwith"; *fulgens*, wallflower red; *"Cornish Cream," a plant of good habit, with flowers in two tones of light yellow; "Moonlight," pale yellow. Other brooms include the beautiful **præcox*, in pale yellow or in white; **kewensis*, a pale-yellow trailer, excellent with such plants

1. (L. to R.) *Olearia* x *haastii, Olearia* x *scilloniensis (Olearia stellulata), Olearia cheesmanii, Olearia* x *mollis* 'Zennorensis', not in flower. See pages 264, 267.

(Susanna Heron ©)

2. *Olearia albida* hort. *(Olearia 'Talbot de Malahide')*. See page 261.

(Susanna Heron ©)

3. *Senecio elaeagnifolius (Brachyglottis elaeagnifolia)* and *Senecio rotundifolius (Brachyglottis rotundifolia)* growing in full exposure. See pages 30–31. (Susanna Heron ©)

4. *Rhododendron 'Princess Alice'*. See page 304. (Susanna Heron ©)

5. *Rhododendron maddenii* subsp. *maddenii*, Polyandrum group. See page 305.

(Susanna Heron ©)

6. *Kerume azaleas* under rhododendron in late spring.

(Susanna Heron ©)

7. *Rhododendron sanguineum* with *Corokia.*
See pages 106, 291. (Susanna Heron ©)

8. *Eucryphia cordifolia.* See pages 126–7. (Susanna Heron ©)

9. *Rhododendron Cubittii (Rhododendron veitchianum Cubittii Group)*, see page 303. *Pieris Forrestii* in the background, see page 163.

(Susanna Heron ©)

10. *Rhododendron 'Loder's White'* and *Drimys winteri (Drimys winteri* var. *chilensis)*. See page 118. (Susanna Heron ©)

11. *Rhododendron 'Blue Tit'*. See pages 284–5.   (Susanna Heron ©)

12. Camellia oleifera. See pages 196–7. (Susanna Heron ©)

as *Rosmarinus corsicus;* and *decumbens,* a prostrate grey-green mat, yellow in May–June.
(See also *genista,* page 135, and *spartium,* page 73.

DAPHNE

Out of the many beautiful species, often difficult to grow, here are some, including those easiest to satisfy. All want good drainage; many like some lime; all should be planted when young, and then left without root disturbance.
D. arbuscula, a 6-inch bush with pink flowers in terminal heads. A scarce plant, but easily grown and very attractive.
D. aurantiaca. Flowers in pairs in the leaf axils, golden to orange-yellow, very profuse along the shoots. It seems capricious, generally difficult to keep, but has done well in some gardens, e.g. in a hole in a dry wall. In the wild it commonly grows on limestone cliffs.
D. Blagayana. A dwarf woodlander, evergreen, with milk-white flower-clusters in February, strongly scented like a lily. Many gardens find this beautiful plant recalcitrant, and varied recipes for its cultivation are offered. Generally, it must have some shade, but in the damp climate of West Cornwall I find it thrives in sun, in the peaty soil that suits dwarf rhododendrons. Layering is the usual prescription: the woody part of the lax shoots is covered, after the flowering season, with small stones and with a compost of loam-peat, leaf-mould and sand, so that the plant becomes a low mound in time. Others recommend only a light top-dressing with such compost in May and October. Others again suggest inter-planting, with *Erica carnea* as a companion, for a woodland carpet.
There is a vigorous, large-flowered form.
D. Burkwoodii, a hybrid between *D. Cneorum* and *caucasica,* makes a 2½-ft. bush, with scented pale-pink flowers for a long season. A good, easily grown plant. *D.* "Somerset" is from the same cross and appears to be the same plant.
D. Cneorum is one of the very best of dwarf shrubs but capricious. A low evergreen, 1–2 ft. high, several feet across, covered with most fragrant pink flower-heads in May. Top-dressing is often recommended for this, as for *D. Blagayana.* It likes some leaf-mould or peat. After ten or twenty years the plants seem to lose their vigour.

There are several forms, including *D. c. Verloti*, a looser grower, with acute narrow leaves and rose flowers, brilliant red in the bud, very fragrant.

D. Dauphinii (syn. *D. hybrida*) is a good erect plant, a hybrid between *D. odora* and *D. collina*, hardier than *D. odora*, with very fragrant flowers, purplish-pink at the back; it is easy to grow in the mild counties, and flowers for an extremely long season.

D. indica. See *D. odora*.

D. japonica forms an upright bush, about 3 ft. high, the leaves often narrowly margined with yellow. The flowers, pale lilac-pink with deep purplish-pink backs and buds, appear from the beginning of January till the end of March and are amongst the most deliciously scented of all the flowers we can grow. This is hardier than *D. odora* (see below) and more erect. It grows with remarkable vigour in some soils, e.g. at Lelant in Cornwall, where it makes bushes 9 ft. across or more in the open. It is hardy in the milder counties, but likes a fairly sheltered place.

*D. Mezereum. Where it thrives this is one of the best of winter-flowering plants, and none is more fragrant. In the typical plant, well grown, the leafless upright branchlets become solid cylinders of heather-pink in February–March: in autumn the berries are scarlet. It likes cool conditions and heavy soil with some lime in it; where it is really happy (e.g. in some Yorkshire gardens) it makes a solid rounded bush 3 ft. high or more, but even so it is apt to die off suddenly. It is said to resent being cut. Easily propagated from seed. Very good company for *Erica carnea* and its varieties.

D. m. autumnalis (syn. *grandiflora*) is (or was) a fine variety, now I fear unobtainable; it has rather larger flowers than the type, beginning in October and flowering through mid-winter. There is also a fine deep-coloured form of the pink type. **D. m. alba grandiflora* has very vigorous upright rods covered with large milk-white flowers; like the small-flowered *D. m. alba*, it bears yellow berries and comes true from seed. This handsome and distinct plant, more vigorous and long-lived than the red forms, may deserve to be classed as a species; at any rate, it should be widely grown.

D. collina var. *neapolitana*. An easily grown evergreen bush, 2–3 ft. high, with large flower-clusters, purplish-pink, fragrant in spring. It likes lime.

D. odora (syn. *D. indica*). This closely resembles *D. japonica*, but is a sprawling shrub when mature. Like *japonica*, its flowers are pale lilac-pink, darker at the back, wonderfully fragrant. It is often fastened up to a wall.

D. tangutica. This Chinese species is, like *retusa*, easily grown. It makes a rounded evergreen bush 3–5 ft. high, with flowers pale lilac-pink on the face and purplish-rose on the back, rather brighter than *retusa's*, early in May. The large berries are bright red and showy.

D. petræa grandiflora (syn. *D. rupestris* var. *grandiflora*). This minute bushlet with large rose-pink flowers is a rock-gardener's treasure. It wants well-drained soil, with lime and full sun.

D. retusa. A dense bush 1–2 ft. high, slow-growing, but quite easy so long as its roots are undisturbed, and very hardy. The flower-heads are like those of *D. odora*, pale lilac-pink with darker pink reverse, very fragrant; and the large berries are bright orange-scarlet.

DAVIDIA

D. Vilmoriniana and the closely similar *D. involucrata* make big trees like a lime, with large white flower-bracts hanging below its branches in May. Looking up into the green of an established tree, one sees these curious bracts like handkerchiefs suspended, each with a blob of black on it. The tree does very well in our milder counties and sows itself in at least one Cornish garden. It is recommended in Chapter III for planting in public places in towns and beside roads entering towns. It must be given time to show its character, for it will not flower for about twenty years from seed.

E. H. Wilson, one of the two introducers of *davidia*, gave an enthusiastic account of its remarkable beauty in the wild; but in this country, in a climate in which the leaves appear before the flowers, it is, I think, rather disappointing.

DENDROMECON

D. rigida. A lovely yellow tree poppy for the mild counties, with glaucous leaves on tall upright growths. The flowers, about 2 inches across, are borne from spring till November. It wants firm staking, so that it does not rock at the root, and is best against a wall. Like *romneya*, it can be propagated by root cuttings.

*Desfontainea

This magnificent Chilean shrub makes a large bush, with holly-like evergreen foliage and tubular flowers, scarlet and yellow (in one form all scarlet) for a long season from mid-summer till autumn. There are two forms, *spinosa* and *Hookeri*, the latter having darker, smaller leaves and a denser habit than the former, with fewer flowers.

The plant behaves erratically in gardens, perhaps because some secret of cultivation has not been discovered. In West Scotland and North-east Ireland it is an outstanding success: a North Irish garden has a plant 20 ft. across, and in Ayrshire it is used as a hedge. In Cornwall, on the other hand, I have not seen a big bush, and I am told from a very good garden near Penzance that it simply dies out there. Yet I hazard the prediction that this will prove to be one of the cases in which a plant has got a bad repute undeservedly; from what I have seen of *desfontainea* in my own garden and in Devon, I believe it can be grown well in such conditions as Cornwall offers. It comes from the dark rain forests of the coastal Cordilleras, where it grows, together with such plants as *Philesia magellanica*, in the shade of huge trees of the conifer, *Fitzroya patagonica*. It is presumably one of the plants which, like *eucryphia*, want constant shade at the root and top-dressings of leaf-mould.

Deutzias

These are outstanding for garden effect, and they will put up with poor soil and neglect, though they prefer good loam. Even *D. gracilis*, and *D. pulchra* from Formosa, prove remarkably hardy.

Among the best of the many species, and the hybrids which are largely due to the great work of Lemoine, here are some: Whites: *magnifica, or its varieties *erecta* and *latiflora*; *azaleæflora*; *staphylæoides*; *setchuenensis var. *corymbiflora*, with large corymbs of small flowers, very long-flowering and effective; *discolor major, which makes a waterfall of white; *kalmiæflora*, a very elegant bush some 5 ft. high with whippy growth and white flowers backed with pink; *pulchra, a bush with good foliage and, when well grown, beautiful flower-sprays 6 inches long with open white bells. The *magnifica* varieties (hybrids of *D. scabra*) and *Monbeigii* are effective in a border, e.g. with an *anchusa* such

A General Planting List

as "Morning Glory." Also *venusta, campanulata,* and the species, *D. Vilmorinæ.*

Pinks: *elegantissima*, an old hybrid seldom seen now but still first-rate, covered every summer with cool-pink stars in extraordinary profusion; "Magicien," rosy-mauve, with pale frilled margins, a fine hybrid of *D. longifolia;* "Contraste"; "Mont Rose"; *rosea carminea.* These mauve-pink *deutzias* go well with pinker forms of *Thalictrum aquilegifolium,* and with such plants as the purple-leaved *Rhus cotinus,* Iris "Betelgueuse," and cool-pink columbines.

DICKSONIA

D. antarctica is the species of tree fern most commonly grown in the mild counties here. In a good many sheltered gardens in Ireland and in Cornwall it makes magnificent specimens, and sows itself freely: its most beautiful stage is when it is only half-grown, still at ground-level, with croziers of young growth thrusting up from the midst of the enormous shuttlecock of fronds. Later, it carries its shuttlecock on top of a trunk 6–8 ft. high, still making a beautiful pattern, but apt to look a bit gloomy when grown in quantity.

Plants first came to this country at the time of the Great Exhibition nearly a century ago, when they were shipped as dry logs collected after bush fires from the hills of New South Wales.

DIERVILLA. See WEIGELA, page 186.

DIPELTA

D. floribunda. A deciduous bush reaching 10 ft. high or more, with fragrant flowers like those of a small *weigela,* silver-pink with yellow throat, in May and June. A good shrub.

D. ventricosa is similar but less effective.

DIPLACUS

D. glutinosus (Shrubby Musk) makes a small bush with large musk flowers, gentle orange in one form, wall-flower red in another. Suitable for the foot of a hot wall or rock, with good drainage; hardy enough to survive mild winters in the milder counties, and easily perpetuated by cuttings.

DRIMYS

D. andina is like a mountain form of *D. Winteri*. In the writer's exposed garden this promises to remain dwarf and to be free with its flower-clusters like those of *Winteri* in miniature; but in fully sheltered gardens it has, I understand, grown to 5–8 ft. with little or no flower. It is a scarce plant, very slow-growing.

D. aromatica. This is a pleasant dense evergreen, with dark narrow leaves, red stems, and small greenish flowers. The male form has redder stems than the female and rather more conspicuous flowers. It is excellent as a wind-break in woodland, forming a solid bush up to 10–15 ft. high.

*D. Winteri grows wild in the windy forest country west of the Straits of Magellan, together with *Nothofagus betuloides*. In the mild counties, especially in woodland gardens in such a climate as Cornwall's, it makes magnificent upright trees 40–50 ft. high, with large foliage, hung with clusters of slightly fragrant ivory-white flowers. The flowering lasts for about six months from the beginning of January. The plant grows fast, and despite the large size of its leaves, it can stand a good deal of wind. It makes a good wind-screen for magnolias. In the humid maritime counties this is a much more effective plant than one might suppose from seeing small plants in the drier South-eastern counties.

*D. Winteri var. *latifolia.* This is a distinct form of *Winteri*, with handsomer foliage, milky blue-green underneath, and larger flowers. A well-grown plant of this, full-sized, must be a noble sight. (I have not seen it more than about 10 ft. high yet.) It is more tender, unfortunately, than the type, but hardy in the mild South-west counties.

ECCREMOCARPUS

E. scaber. A Chilean climber, hardy here, running up a trellis like a clematis, with sprays of small orange-scarlet tubular flowers; very free-flowering in a hot exposure. It is short-lived, but easily raised from seed; common, but not to be despised.

§ECHIUM. See page 325.

ELÆAGNUS

E. angustifolia, Oleaster, makes a lovely silvery tree in the more extreme climate of Central Europe, e.g. beside the Danube bridges at Budapest; here I have never seen it so effective. Try it in full sun on a slope or by water, where it can show its streaming habit of growth. The small pale-yellow flowers spread a delightful smell.

E. macrophylla is evergreen, with large firm leaves, silvered all over when young as if washed with aluminium paint, and with silver lustre underneath when full-grown. The small flowers in October–November are very fragrant. A beautiful and hardy plant which can stand wind and full shade.

§*E. pungens*, see List A, page 14.

E. glabra is similar to *pungens*, but is not thorny, and its leaves are thinner, more pointed, and lustrous brown beneath instead of dull and whitish.

Elæocarpus

‡*E. dentatus*. An evergreen tree, 40–60 ft. in New Zealand but much less here, with sprays of small white flowers, fringed like the alpine *soldanella*. Fruits inky blue. Not a very showy plant (at least as grown here), but beautiful in detail.

Embothrium. Fire Bush.

E. coccineum (Forst.) provides the most vivid flower-sight that our milder counties can show. The catherine wheels of orange-vermilion shine with astonishing brilliance, especially in evening light.

Embothrium coccineum comprises several types, distinct from the gardener's standpoint, varying much in hardiness, and having a wide range of habitat in Chile.

The form most commonly grown in Cornwall, one which William Lobb introduced a century ago, is a tall evergreen, reaching 30 ft. or even 40 ft. when happy, with dark oblong leaves and flower-clusters on new wood near the end of the shoots. This was long regarded as too tender for any but the mild maritime gardens of South-west England and such places as Valentia. On Valentia Island it is naturalised, seeding itself freely. It now appears that this plant, the comparatively broad-leaved typical *E. coccineum*, has a wide range, from at least as far north as Temuco in latitude 38° down to the Straits of Magellan, and even to the island of Tierra del Fuego in latitude 54°, though not extending to Cape Horn. Plants raised from seed from Tierra del Fuego have withstood severe frosts here (*R.H.S. Journal*, Oct. 1945).

A form of *embothrium* which has long been grown at Rostrevor in Ireland is known in gardens as *E. coccineum* var. *longifolium* or *E. longifolium*. The classification as a separate species lacks scientific endorsement; but the plant is certainly a distinct variety from the gardener's point of view. It has been found by many gardeners here to be much more amenable to cultivation than the broader-leaved typical *E. coccineum* commonly grown. It is hardier than the forms of *E. coccineum* derived from Northern Chile, and some claim that it flowers earlier in life than the type. It is apt to produce suckers freely and can be propagated in this way. Suckering can be stimulated by scarring the root a few feet from the trunk. The plant is distinguished by its narrower, longer leaves and by its flowering, not only near the tips of the shoots (as the broader-leaved form does), but for some distance along the shoots.

A third type is *E. coccineum* var. *lanceolatum* (Ruiz and Pavon). This is still narrower in leaf and more deciduous. It comes from the Andes, and has a more northerly range than the broad-leaved *coccineum*. Mr. H. F. Comber, one of those who have collected this plant in the Chilean Andes, described it in his field notes in 1926 as a deciduous shrub up to 15 ft. or 18 ft. high, growing at altitudes from 2,800 ft. to 5,000 ft. on well-drained hillsides, and spreading freely by suckers. It flowers in clusters along the branches as well as at the tips. In this country this type has reached 20 ft. or sometimes 30 ft. A fine form has been exhibited under the name "Norquinco Form."

Lord Aberconway reports from North Wales that the narrow-leaved forms, even when young and newly planted, stand 32° or even 34° of frost unharmed.

As regards cultivation, all the forms need acid soil. Seedlings are very sensitive to root disturbance in spring, but can be handled more easily if left till autumn. Young plants should not be checked or allowed to become pot-bound: a plant 6 inches or 1 ft. high is generally big enough for planting out. One expert grower advocates planting *embothriums* carefully lifted from open ground rather than plants from pots. Suckers are not difficult to transplant successfully. Careful staking and watching of the

A General Planting List

stakes is required, since young plants shoot up very fast. As for placing, don't on any account plant an *embothrium* near a blue-pink rhododendron: its acid scarlet is a most jealous colour. And don't be astonished if an old plant dies or becomes scraggy: it may be that these plants are not long-lived because they spend so much strength in seeding.

Enkianthus

E. cernuus rubens. This scarce plant, the most effective *enkianthus* in flower, makes a bush up to 6 ft. high, hung with tassels of small translucent red flowers, almost as bright as red currants.

E. deflexus (syn. *himalaicus*, Hooker) has comparatively large cup-shaped flower-bells, ½ inch across, yellowish-red veined with red, in drooping clusters. It makes a large bush, sometimes a small tree, in the milder counties. *E. chinensis*, with salmon-red flowers, is akin to this.

E. perulatus (syn. *E. japonicus*), a dense bush, about 4 ft. high and as much wide, is one of the most brilliant shrubs in autumn, in climates favourable to autumn colouring. The small clustered flowers are white.

All these, and the other species of *enkianthus*, such as *campanulatus* and its red-flowered variety *Palibinii*, like lime-free soil with plenty of humus, and half-shade.

§Ercilla volubilis (syn. Bridgesia spicata)

An evergreen creeper, self-clinging if helped, with sprays of substantial leaves and racemes of whitish flowers. It stands wind remarkably well, thriving even on the east wall of the writer's house on Zennor Moor. Not exciting, but a useful wall-covering for an exposed place, needing no care beyond such cutting as will keep it out of roof-gutters and prevent too heavy a tangle.

Erica. Heath.

In windy gardens, as in sheltered ones, heaths can provide colour almost all the year round, including the winter months. And a lovely range of colour it is. (But don't mix the heather colours carelessly. They swear with the red of a bright camellia, and grey-green or dark green suits them better than a bright grass-green.)

I. Dwarfer Heaths of Winter and Spring

E. carnea. The best varieties of the alpine heath, and the hybrid *E. darleyensis*, contribute more colour over a long period than any other shrubs of winter and early spring; and none are easier to grow. The wild *E. carnea* is very variable; selected varieties are more effective than the type, but too many have been named. "Queen Mary" and "Winter Beauty" begin trimming their low mounds with heather-pink as early as November; the very compact *"King George" is at its best in January–February, with the snowflakes; the deep-coloured *atrorubra* is one of the best; *"Ruby Glow," flowering in March–April, is another richly coloured one, and *Vivellii*, glowing carmine with bronze foliage, in March–April, is perhaps the best of the lot. A new one, "Eileen Porter," is said to be the most vivid of this class.
*"Springwood" is an outstanding white, vigorous in habit; "Cecilia Beale," dwarfer and earlier, is worth growing in addition. "Springwood Pink" has the good qualities of the white form.

No shrubs better repay mass planting than these, whether in the open or in the half-shade of thin woodland. *Vivellii* is warm enough in colour to make a perfect foreground for the pink *camellia*, "J. C. Williams," though too blue a pink to be tolerably near red Camellias. This and others look well with *Daphne Mezereon* and with dwarf *rhododendrons* such as *ciliatum*, *cilpinense*, "Bric-à-brac," and *moupinense*. "Springwood" supplies a relief to the heather-pinks.

All these are easily grown, but repay an occasional dressing with soil and hop manure. All will thrive in sea-sand, even though it contains free lime. But a planting of them, especially the dwarfer sorts such as "King George," can soon be ruined by overgrowth of coarse grass. Don't plant until you are sure the ground is clear of such grasses.

E. darleyensis (*E. carnea* × *E. mediterranea*). Undoubtedly this famous hybrid is one of the most valuable of hardy shrubs for lime-free soils. Its mounded bushes, some 2 ft. high, grow together into a green weed-free carpet which begins to flush lilac-pink as early as the end of November. In March–April the plant is at its best, a mass of cool colour which accords perfectly with the colours of *Rhododendron præcox, R. emasculum, R. rubiginosum, Erica mediterranea superba*, and *E.* "Brightness." It stands wind very well. Mr. J. C. Williams, who rated it very high, advised cutting it very hard back once every three years after flowering, top-dressing it then with leaf-mould. Some growers cut it back annually.

*E. mediterranea "Brightness" is a very good form of *mediterranea*, with darker foliage than the type, deeper heather-pink flowers, and a compact upright growth up to 2–3 ft. high. Excellent in front of the taller *E. mediterranea superba*.

E. mediterranea "W. J. Rackliff" is a good white, 2 ft. high.

II. Larger Heaths of Winter and Spring

E. mediterranea superba, the best large-growing form of this species, makes a dense bush, 4–5 ft. high, wind-hardy enough to be useful as a wind-break in the garden, and smothered from March till the end of April in heather-pink. No shrub is more lavish. It is easily contented, and may succeed in sea-sand. Flowered shoots should be cut back in May.

E. australis. This, the most effective of the large hardy heaths, makes great plumes of deep heather-pink, darker than *E. mediterranea superba*, in April. Its one defect is that it is apt to get leggy and straggly; but this can be minimised by planting several together, with *mediterranea superba* to support and mask it, and by cutting back its flowered shoots immediately after flowering.

"Riverslea" is a good variety of this, with large flowers, very rich in colour.

"Mr. Robert" is the white form, now well known; a very clean white, but apt to be a gawky plant.

Four more white tree heaths are among the treasures of mild gardens in winter and spring:

E. arborea, the tree heath from whose roots brier pipes are (or were) made, normally reaches about 10 ft., but is sometimes 20 ft. or more. Its plumes of white flower—not a very bright white—are already whitening in January, and continue, greying as they age, till the end of April. On a damp mild morning the air of the garden is fresh with the scent. Top-dress the plant annually with leaf-mould.

E. arborea alpina makes a dwarfer bush, less apt to get bare at the base; its foliage is brilliantly moss-green, and the plant is very hardy.

E. lusitanica (syn. *codonodes*), with pink buds at the top of its plumes of white flowers, is a delightful very early-flowering species. It is one of the best for naturalising, reproducing itself freely from seed where it is happy; indeed, seedlings can be a nuisance, and in at least one garden it has invaded the lawn. This is the plant which has been naturalised with excellent effect along some miles of the G.W.R. main line near Doublebois, in Cornwall.

E. Veitchii is a beautiful bushy hybrid between *lusitanica* and *arborea*, very free-flowering, but rather more tender.

*†‡*Erica canaliculata* (see frontispiece). This is the finest heath that can be grown out of doors anywhere in Britain, and the most beautiful plant, I think, that I have seen in Cornwall. It makes great plumes of flowers, violet-pink, of a waxen quality, with black anthers, and may last in beauty for about three months. It stands a fair amount of wind, and can stand without injury at least 12° of frost. I have seen this 17 ft. high against a wall (in Canon Boscawen's garden at Ludgvan Rectory): 10 ft. is common; and it thrives in the open in gardens much colder and more exposed than Ludgvan. It is not difficult to propagate from cuttings and grows fast.

This is the plant formerly known as *E. melanthera*. The same plant (or is it an inferior form of it?) is much grown as a pot-plant, but under glass it comes white, not violet, and does not show its full character.

(For some other Cape Heaths, including *E. Pageana* and *Willmoreana*, see Chapter XIII.)

III. Summer and Autumn Heaths

Daboecia[1] *cantabrica* (syn. *D. polifolia*). Connemara Heath or St. Dabeoc's Heath.

*The white form of this, *D. c. alba*, is the most valuable of all the summer heaths, with large white bells very freely borne for at least four months. *D. p. purpurea*, the heather-crimson form, is much better than the typical purplish form.

Another species, *D. azorica*, has red-crimson flowers.

Erica cinerea, the common crimson-purple heather of the moors, has some varieties worth using, but others are poor growers.

---

[1] Daboecia is Linnæus's spelling; but the Irish saint whose name is used was St. Dabeoc.

Good ones include "Rose Queen," "C. D. Eason," and "P. S. Patrick." *E. Tetralix,* Bell Heather, has amongst its varieties "Pink Glow" and *Lawsoniana.*

E. ciliaris. Dorset Heath, like an enlarged Bell Heather, provides "Dawn," "Stoborough White," and "Mrs. C. H. Gill."

E. vagans, Cornish Heath, is invaluable, especially for the wilder type of garden and for naturalising. It multiplies by self-sown seedlings, and is easier to satisfy than the varieties of *E. cinerea.* *"St. Keverne" and *"Mrs. Maxwell," both with warm-pink flowers, are very effective and of good habit, but the colour does not mix well with blue pinks. *E. v. carnea* is a fairly compact pink, excellent with the dwarf *Polygonum vaccinifolium*: *E. v. rubra grandiflora,* a vigorous reddish one, goes well with *pernettya,* and *"Lyonesse" is a more effective white than the ordinary white form of the type.

The rust-brown of the dead flowers of these heaths is decorative, but the plants are much the better for being cut back after flowering. Give them plenty of room: they soon make wide rounded bushes. If you want a low mounded shape 2 ft. or 3 ft. high in a wild garden, few shrubs are better suited.

Calluna vulgaris. Ling.

The varieties of ling include some of the best autumn shrubs. *Alportii* is an old but still excellent crimson. *Searlei* is a first-rate tall white, and *Hammondii* is another good white. A good plant for the edge of a path is "Mullion," a dwarf bushy ling with deep heather-pink flowers.

Double varieties of singular beauty are now available: * "H.E. Beale" is still unsurpassed amongst these, with its little mauve rosettes on long spikes late in the season. The common double *calluna,* planted with this, flowers earlier, and so gives a long season. "County Wicklow," with pink flowers on a dense flat-growing mat, and "J. H. Hamilton," a wide plant about a foot high, are two more good doubles.

Elegantissima is a variety of outstanding grace, with slim spikes very late in the season; and *hiemalis* is another fine late one, little known as yet.

E. multiflora is a low bushy plant, with flowers of a glowing heather-pink, from the Mediterranean coast.

E. terminalis (syn. *stricta*), with upright growths, pink flowers in late summer and autumn, and conspicuous rust-brown dead flowers, can be quite effective and is very easily grown. It will stand limy soils.

E. umbellata, another Mediterranean plant, makes a wide low bush 1 ft. or 18 inches high, grey-green, with pink and white flowers for a long season.

ERYTHRINA

E. Crista-gallii (coral tree) is hardy enough in the mild counties for a sunny sheltered place, especially if given a little winter protection of its massive root-stock. It sends up powerful prickly growths topped with large deep-scarlet pea-flowers.

ESCALLONIA

A number of species and hybrids have been referred to in the chapter on Wind and Shelter, but others call for further mention here.

E. Iveyana, the handsomest white, has been mentioned; also "C. F. Ball," a bright red; "Donard Seedling" (*E. langleyensis* × *Philippiana*), which is first-rate for a drooping hedge; *langleyensis*, etc.

A recently introduced hybrid, *"Glory of Donard," with large red flowers, is perhaps the best of all these hybrids, though many are beautiful, free-flowering, and easy to grow. "Donard Beauty," a very hardy one, has a drooping habit, ample foliage, and profuse pink flowers. "Donard Gem," dwarfer in habit, with small starry flowers along slim sprays, is a charming plant. "Slieve Donard" is pink and white, better than the old *edinensis*. "Donard White" is a vigorous one of the small-leaved type, with white flowers, hardier than *Iveyi*. "Donard Scarlet" is very bright, but not a robust grower. *"Apple Blossom" is a bushy shrub of excellent habit, with exceptionally large flowers, rose and white; one of the best.

E. montevidensis, a species more tender than the others, has handsome white flower-clusters often a foot across, in late summer and autumn, on a bush that may reach 10 ft. It is one of the most effective late-flowering shrubs.

EUCALYPTUS. See Chapter VIII.

EUCRYPHIA

*§*E. cordifolia*. This superb tree is an upright-growing evergreen with stiff dark leaves of fine design, and pinkish shoots in spring.

A General Planting List

The white flowers in August–September are 2 inches across, like single white roses, with fluted petals and a ring of tawny anthers; they are so freely borne when the tree is well established that the whole plant is whitened. In some Cornish gardens, such as Caerhays and Tregrehan, the tree is now 50 ft. high; in Southern Chile, its home, it is a forest tree, often 70 ft. and sometimes 120 ft. high. Sometimes it makes rather open spreading growth, but it is generally a compact column of growth, which may be densely bushy right down to the ground. Bees and butterflies love its flowers, and in South Chile it is the chief source of real honey, besides furnishing timber for railway sleepers.

It stands a good deal of wind, and thrives (in a partly sheltered corner) even in so windy a garden as the writer's, where it has reached 25 ft. and is covered with flowers annually. It is used as a tall wind-breaking screen in woodland at Caerhays. One drawback is that it does not flower till some fifteen years after planting. But plant it. It is one of the most distinguished-looking of all the plants we can grow here. In a climate such as that of N.W.Wales, it generally needs shelter from a wall; in Cornwall it is hardy enough for the open, but suffered severely in the frosts of 1947.

*E. glutinosa (syn. E. pinnatifolia).

In all the year's pageant of flowering shrubs very few ever surpass this *eucryphia's* show, and in August, when it is in flower, no other equals it. Its flowers, like white St. John's wort, are $2\frac{1}{2}$ inches across, with a brush of stamens; and in autumn the deciduous leaves die off yellow and brownish-orange. It will grow to 35 ft. or 40 ft., but is generally not more than 20–25 ft. high.

It dislikes being moved. But get plants that have been grown in open ground: pot-bound ones are likely to be stunted and never recover freedom of growth. The roots should be kept cool (as in the case of *Embothrium coccineum*, which grows wild in the same jungle on Chiloe Island, in South Chile). Heaths are sometimes planted over the roots for this purpose, but mulching is a preferable method. The plant is easily raised from seed, but the seed capsules take a year to ripen. It needs lime-free soil, and appreciates some leaf-mould or peat and a little well-rotted manure. Don't expect it to flower for some years after planting.

It should be used much more extensively in public, as well as private, gardens; and large gardens might well raise it from seed and plant it in quantity in open woodland. The semi-double variety which comes only too often from seed is not an improvement on the type. Another variety, *camelliæflora*, has substantial reflexed petals.

*E. nymansensis is a superb hybrid between *cordifolia* and *glutinosa*; evergreen, upright, very free-flowering when established, not so slow to flower as *cordifolia*, and hardier. For a small garden which has sheltered room for a tree 30 ft. high, of columnar shape, this could not be bettered; and it is excellent in woodland. *E.* "Mount Usher," from the same cross, rather nearer to *cordifolia*, is not so good, the flower being generally marred by doubling.

*E. intermedia (syn. "Rostrevor"). I have put a star to three *eucryphias* already, but must star this one too. It is a hybrid between *E. glutinosa* and *E. lucida* (q.v.), evergreen and slender, with cup-shaped flowers like *lucida's*, but with the influence of *glutinosa* in its leaves, in its comparatively large flowers (1½–2 inches), and its hardiness. The plant is very free and graceful in growth, and a good evergreen. When better known it may come to be regarded as the best hybrid *eucryphia*.

*E. lucida (formerly *E. Billardieri*). Lovely in its distinguished way, with small leaves and small white flowers, perfectly cup-shaped, with anthers bright pink when fresh. It flowers for a longer season than any other *eucryphia*. It makes a substantial tree in time, and a good form of it is so free-flowering when well established as to discount the comparatively small size of its flowers. A Tasmanian, it is a variable tree, sometimes having much smaller leaves than the type commonly grown here. The variety called *E. Milliganii* is one of these forms of *lucida*, with very small leaves and flowers. It was supposed that this would remain a dwarf plant only a few feet high, suitable for a rock garden, but already, in at least one Cornish garden, it has become a dense upstanding bush many feet high. Not of much decorative value.

E. Moorei is another fine plant, an Australian, with evergreen leaves of most decorative pattern and flowers rather larger than those of *E. lucida*. Slow to flower, but worth waiting for. All these species are apt to intermarry, and some more hybrids of garden value are likely to appear.

EUGENIA APICULATA. See MYRTUS LUMA.

EUONYMUS

E. planipes and *E. alatus* are splendid in autumn colour.

Eupatorium

E. micranthum (syn. *E. weinmannianum*) is a valuable late-flowering shrub, making a large rounded evergreen, 5–8 ft. high, with a smoke of pinky-white flowers from August till November. It has a pleasant memorable scent; and butterflies flock to it as to *buddleia* or *Sedum spectabile*.

Euphorbia

§‡*E. mellifera* makes a large rounded bush here in mild gardens, covered with large pinkish-brown flower-heads powerfully scented of honey. Tender but wind-hardy. Not for a small garden.

E. Wulfenii, with robust blue-green growths and large heads of yellow-green flower, can look handsome if well-placed, and takes care of itself.

Exochorda. Pearl Bush.

*§*E. × macrantha*. This hybrid, the best of the *exochordas*, makes a big bush with sprays of round white buds and open flowers in April–May. Given plenty of room and a dark background, it is one of the best spring shrubs; and besides being perfectly easy to grow, it is remarkably wind-hardy. It responds to pruning after flowering.

E. Giraldii var. *Wilsonii* is another very good one. The bush is upright, reaching 10–12 ft., and the flowers are 2 inches across. One form of this is almond-scented. Also *E. Korolkowii*.

Fabiana

F. imbricata. In the mild counties this can be very effective with its quantities of tubular white flowers on strong heath-like plumes. It can reach 8 ft., sometimes considerably more. It likes a well-drained position in full sun, and should be cut back after flowering, since it may get too sprawling and untidy. Though generally grown in acid soil, it grows well also in a chalky one. There is a much smaller form, *F. minor*, suitable for a rock-garden.

F. violacea. This species, more recently introduced from the Andes, proves to be much hardier than *imbricata*. It is a more spreading plant, with shorter leaves and milk-blue or mauve flowers—apt to be washy in colour. In the wild it reaches 10–12 ft.

FEIJOA
F. Sellowiana is a vigorous evergreen with decorative grey-green foliage and curious flowers with a brush of red stamens which go well in colour with the leaves. In a hot exposure this flowers freely enough to make a considerable show. In Cornwall I have not seen it really effective as a flowering plant.

FENDLERA
F. rupicola. Against a hot wall, in a hot place, this hardy shrub from the dry south-west of the United States sometimes makes a decorative show with its four-petalled white flowers touched with pink. It grows to about 5 ft., and is rather sparse in habit.

FORSYTHIA
Forsythias, grown as single bushes, bring spring sunshine into countless suburban gardens; but the fact that they are familiar, hardy, and easily grown should not justify the neglect of such outstanding shrubs in country gardens, whether in mild climates or severe ones, especially where there is room for planting them in some quantity. Spend some imagination on the planning of a show of forsythia yellow, from February till April. Plant the several species, with some yellow daffodils, against a dark background, such as the camellia-leaved holly, on either side of a path.
F. intermedia var. *spectabilis*. *F. intermedia* is a hybrid between *F. suspensa* and *F. viridissima*, mentioned below, and its variety *spectabilis* is reckoned the most effective of the *forsythias*. A bushy plant of good habit, with flowers of a full "golden" yellow, very free-flowering, and as easy to propagate from cuttings as willow. *F.i.* "Lynwood Variety," a new variety with finer flowers than *spectabilis*, promises to prove even more effective.
F. suspensa, which flowers just before *spectabilis*, makes a fountain of a bush in the open, perhaps 10 ft. high: on a wall it will go much higher. *Fortunei* is a vigorous erect form of this; *Sieboldii*, a slender pendulous form with larger flowers than the others, which will trail down a bank, rooting as it goes: *atrocaulis* is a striking form with dark, purplish-brown, young shoots, but it is often less free-flowering. "Nymans variety" is an improved form of this.
F. viridissima, the other parent of *intermedia*, makes a bush some 6 ft. high, flowering a fortnight later. The variety *koreana* (Rehder) is a better form of this.

A General Planting List

F. ovata is worth growing also, since its flowers appear as early as February or the very beginning of March, even in bad weather. There are two forms, one golden yellow and the other sulphur. It has broader leaves than the others, and a dwarfer habit: full-grown plants seldom exceed 3 ft.

F. Giraldiana, introduced by Farrer, is even earlier than *ovata*; it makes a slender spreading bush 6 ft. high or more, valuable for its earliness.

Fothergilla

F. major is a deciduous bush of pyramidal habit, reaching 6 ft. or sometimes more, with cylindrical pincushion spikes of white stamens touched with pink in the stalk. The leaves, glaucous beneath and leathery, turn golden-orange in autumn in climates where autumn colouring is good.

F. monticola is a short-jointed twiggy bush, 6 ft. high or less, more open in habit than *F. major*, with rather wider milk-white flower-fuzzes than *major's*, and hazel-like leaves that die splendidly crimson. The leaves of *monticola* are green, not glaucous, underneath, and more markedly touched. Both species prefer light acid soil and some shade.

Fremontia

F. californica and *F. mexicana*. Very decorative bushes, 8 ft. or more, sometimes making small trees in their Californian home. Young shoots rust-brown: flowers with bright-yellow calyx 2 inches across, borne over a long period in the case of *F. californica*, but all at one season in *mexicana*. *Californica* is the hardier. Up-country they need a wall, but in mild counties they do better, perhaps, in the open, if well staked. They flower best in poor soil. They detest root disturbance, and are generally not long-lived.

Fuchsia

F. magellanica Lam. (syn. *F. macrostemma*, Ruiz and Pavon). Many invaluable shrubs for outdoor planting in the milder counties are forms or hybrids of this variable species, with red and purple hanging flowers, from Chile and Peru, introduced in 1800.

F. m. alba, a white-flowered form collected by Mr. Clarence Elliott, is pretty in its rather anæmic way, and very hardy.

F. m. conica (Lindley) is a stiff bush with small leaves and long red and purple flowers, not very effective.

F. m. globosa, with round buds, is a good red and purple one, near *Riccartonii*.

F. m. gracilis (Lindley) from Mexico is about as frost-hardy as *Riccartonii*, but rather less showy. It is more slender and soft in growth, with very thin stalks to the narrow flowers; but though it looks fragile, it proves to be one of the most wind-hardy shrubs we have, thriving in exposures where blackthorn is shorn to a hump 2 ft. high. Like *Riccartonii*, it is naturalised in some places here, generally beside streams. The form of *gracilis* which has purplish-red leaves is a very decorative plant, good with pink Japanese anemones.

*F. m. Riccartonii, said to be a hybrid raised near Edinburgh in about 1830, is to many of us in the milder counties the typical "fuchsia." This and the garden forms of hydrangea are the two most valuable flowering shrubs for the latter part of the year that the milder counties can grow. It is so familiar in our gardens, mild and not so mild, that we take its extraordinary qualities too much for granted—its hardiness, its very long flowering season, its freedom and its magnificent colour, its easy propagation, and, not least, its surprising tolerance of wind. It makes an excellent windbreak in gardens near the sea, and furnishes the most brilliant of hedges, especially if cut down annually. In Cork and Kerry, it is the common hedge-plant, even far up into the hills, and in the Isle of Man tall hedges of it shade the lanes. In Cornwall it can often be seen planted along the top of an earth-filled wall—a Cornish hedge; and, annually cut down, it is hardy enough for the colder counties.

*F. corallina (Porcher) is a very distinct shrub, first-rate for a whitewashed wall or for making a mound down a sunny slope. The arching growths have purplish-red stems, and the leaves have veins and stalks of the same colour; the large flowers are scarlet and purple. This is one of the hardier fuchsias.

F. pumila, a hardy dwarf form, is reckoned by some to be a worthless plant; but in Cornwall at any rate it is free-flowering, compact, and worth its place.

There is a series of fuchsias with small leaves and very small flowers, rose or scarlet, in which the names appear to be much confused.

F. microphylla, a dwarf Mexican species with small pink flowers, is one of these; but I understand that the pink-flowered plant

usually grown under this name is not the true species. *F. Cottinghamii* (syn. *F. thymifolia*?) is a charming plant in this section.
F. procumbens is a prostrate trailer or small climber, with curious little flowers, square in section, upright, not pendent: they are yellow and chocolate, with red stamens and blue anthers. The fruits are like small red cherries. This is hardy in mild gardens and pretty enough in detail to be worth growing in an odd corner. *F. triphylla*, a tender species with long scarlet flowers in small bunches, is thought to be lost to cultivation in England; but it has been the parent of many valued hybrids, such as "H. Henkel." At least one of these hybrids, with scarlet flowers and dark leaves, flowering in late autumn, has long survived in Cornish gardens.

The *triphylla* fuchsias are much more tender than the forms of *magellanica*, and will be killed out of doors in a hard winter, unless protected.

The garden hybrids, double and single, are very numerous. Some look too bloated, I think, to be attractive; but many, especially amongst the singles, are very effective and free-flowering, and fairly hardy. Many sorts, with names long lost, can be found in cottage gardens in the maritime counties, in places where they do not suffer from drought or severe frost.

"Mme Cornelissen," an old hybrid with small flowers, in the style of *F. Riccartonii* but scarlet and white, can certainly be recommended; it makes a very decorative bush, e.g. with Japanese anemones, and is hardy enough to be lasting in mild gardens.

I am indebted to the British Fuchsia Society for the following list of garden hybrids recommended for outdoor cultivation in the mild counties:
With purple corolla: "Charming," single; "Lena" or "Eva Boerg," very similar, double; "Lustre Improved," single; "Display," single; "Achievement," single; "Duke of York," single.
With corolla not purple: "Alice Hofmann," single; "Hapsburg," double; "Bella Forbes," double; "Fascination," double; "Pasteur," double; "Snowcap," double.

Varieties with white corollas are generally less hardy than those with red or purple ones.

The Fuchsia Society adds this note on cultivation:

"A couple or so shovelfuls of dry *weathered* ashes, with some dead dry leaves mixed in, placed round the collar and over the roots, should be protection enough. When new shoots start, or from late April onwards (depending on season and locality), scrape the ashes gently away. More plants are lost from drought than from any other cause; so, except during or just after frost, see that plants get attention in this respect."

I believe much could be done in raising fuchsias hardy enough for outdoor planting in the milder counties—plants with flowers of small or medium size, woody enough to carry their weight without flopping.

GARRYA. See page 18.

GAULTHERIA

G. *antipoda*, a dwarf New Zealand shrub, 1–2 ft., with ½-inch brownish leaves, profuse white flowers of lily-of-the-valley shape, and red berries (sometimes white).

G. *cuneata*, a 1-ft. evergreen carpet from China; white flowers and conspicuous white berries.

G. *depressa*, like a dwarf form of G. *antipoda*, with red berries large for the plant.

*G. *Forrestii* makes a rounded bush up to 5 ft. high, flowering profusely from March to May. The small, milk-white flowers, slightly fragrant, are close-packed along slim rods, some 3 inches in length, which grow from the leaf-axils. The flowers make a good show against, but rather underneath, the dark foliage. The berries are black, not blue. The true plant is rare, and seems difficult to propagate by cuttings.

G. *hispida* makes an upright bush about 2 ft. high, with dark evergreen leaves 1–2½ inches long, bronzed in winter; it has small white flowers in terminal clusters and white fruits conspicuous in late summer.

G. *fragrantissima*, from India and Ceylon, reaches 4 ft., with leathery leaves, drooping white flowers, and white or pale-blue berries.

G. *Hookeri*. A bush up to 3 ft. high, with large netted leaves, white flower-sprays, and effective grey-blue berries.

G. *oppositifolia*, a New Zealander, with 6-inch panicles of white flowers and showy white fruits. The last two are tenderer than the others.

G. *Shallon* is a well-known rampant bush, reaching 4 ft. or 5 ft., with upright panicles of pinkish-white flowers on red stems, and purple fruit (not bad cooked). This thrives under trees and is most easily grown. It may be undervalued, being common and easily satisfied, but in truth it is one of the most beautiful of its genus, and flowering sprays are excellent for cutting.

*G. tetramera. A low spreading bush about 1 ft. high (sometimes 2 ft.), with dark netted leaves, small racemes of small whitish flowers, and profuse fruits in clusters like brilliant blue beads in autumn. This is a very attractive plant, with enough blue berry to be conspicuous. It is sometimes supplied in place of the rare G. Forrestii. The parts of the flowers in *tetramera* are in fours, not in fives as is usual in *Gaultherias*.

G. tricophylla, a very dwarf Himalayan carpeter, is charming when covered with blue fruits like little hedge-sparrow eggs, but birds take them at once unless the plant is protected by net, and the plant is rather exacting.

G. Veitchiana, a 3-ft. bush with large leaves on arching sprays and pale-blue fruits, can be very decorative; but in many gardens it will not bear fruit. It resembles G. Hookeri, but is rather dwarfer, and paler green in leaf.

These are a few out of many. All prefer a cool, shady or half-shady position in peaty soil.

Gaulthettya

G. wisleyensis (syn. Gaulnettya "Wisley Pearl"), which is a hybrid between *Gaultheria Shallon* and *Pernettya mucronata*, makes a bush up to 3–4 ft. when established, with small white flowers, borne freely enough to make a show in June, followed by purplish-red berries. This is a delightful plant, easily grown in a cool place in lime-free soil. Another form of the cross has brown fruits and a dwarfer habit.

Gelsemium

G. sempervirens. Carolina Yellow Jasmine. An evergreen climber with polished dark foliage and flowers like a fine yellow jasmine, strongly scented, in spring. Much used in American gardens in such a climate as Virginia's, and should do well here, e.g. along a low south wall or over a porch.

Genista

*G. æthnensis, Etna broom, makes a cascade of small bright-yellow flowers, up to 15 ft. high, in July–August; a magnificent plant when given plenty of room. Apt to be bare at the base.

*G. *cinerea*, with slim silver-green drooping branches, and a load of scented yellow flower in June–July, is one of the very best brooms. It will reach 9 ft.

*G. *virgata* is similar but longer lived, easier to satisfy, stiffer and taller, very fragrant. In Edinburgh's Royal Botanic Garden it is used as a hedge, pruned twice a year.

**§G. *hispanica*, the well-known Spanish gorse, is most useful for covering banks of poor soil, quickly making a low carpet $1\frac{1}{2}$ ft. high, yellow in May. It thrives even in pure sand close to the sea in full exposure.

G. *lydia* makes a 2-ft. bush, pendulous in habit, brilliantly yellow in May–June.

§G. *pilosa* makes a tidy green mat, yellow in May.

The very fragrant Spanish species G. *monosperma*, a tall grey-green bush with showering little white flowers, is difficult here, but may be worth trying. It is a most beautiful plant in the climate of the Riviera.

§GERANIUM

No need to recommend the *pelargoniums* which (under the name of *geranium*) make so vivid and lasting a show on house-walls in the mild maritime counties. But there is one true *geranium*, sub-shrubby, which deserves to be better known.

§G. *anemonæfolium*, from Madeira, makes a short shrubby stem with a crown of very decorative cut leaves and a wide umbel of foxglove-pink flowers, 2 ft. or 3 ft. high. This makes a splendid show in June (at foxglove time), and is astonishingly wind-hardy. It sows itself when once established, and is one of the best plants for naturalising in mild climates.

GORDONIA. See page 330.

GREVILLEA

‡G. *alpina*. Small grey-green foliage and pinky-red flowers borne nearly all the year round. There are at least two forms of this: one, a bush 2–3 ft. high, a good rock-garden plant in full sun; another, hardier and considerably taller.

G. *rosmarinifolia*, the best-known species, has linear Rosemary-like leaves $\frac{1}{2}$–$1\frac{1}{2}$ inches long and small clusters of red flowers. It makes a bush 5 ft. high or more and considerably wider, quite showy at its best and seldom without flowers. It comes from New South Wales and is generally hardy in the mild counties.

G. *sulphurea* (syn. G. *juniperina*), with long juniper-like leaves and light-yellow flowers, is another hardy species; easy to grow and free-flowering.

G. *thyrsoides*, from West Australia, closely resembles *rosmarinifolia*, but is more upright and has longer leaves (2–4 inches).

For other *grevilleas* see Chapter XV.

HALESIA

*H. carolina. Snowdrop tree. A most beautiful spreading bush or small tree, generally about 10 ft. high but sometimes 30 ft.; hung with snowdrop bells in small clusters, just before the leaves come in May. It should be much more planted.

*H. monticola, the mountain snowdrop tree, is much bigger, reaching 80–100 ft. at home (in the mountains of South-east United States), with larger flowers than those of *carolina*, borne with the leaves. It flowers when still small, and is making a fine tree in this country, quickly reaching 30–40 ft. high, with a straight bole.

HALIMIUM and HALIMIOCISTUS. See under CISTUS.

HAMAMELIS

*H. mollis, the best of the witch hazels, makes a large wide bush, most welcome in December and the first weeks of the new year, when the bare branches are covered with spidery golden-yellow flowers which are sweet-scented and frost-resistant. In autumn the bush is conspicuous (even in mild damp climates), for the large deciduous leaves turn pale yellow. Woodland conditions suit it best.

H. japonica, which flowers in February, can be added where space allows, and its tree-like variety *arborea*, which some reckon the equal of *H. mollis*; also *H. Zuccariniana*, which has lemon-yellow flowers in March. The "Hiltingbury" form of Zuccariniana reddens splendidly in October.

HIBISCUS

H. syriacus (*Althea frutex*). Perhaps gardeners here underrate the bush hollyhocks. In a hot exposure they can certainly be very rewarding plants, flowering as they do in late summer; and some gardens do well with them in a damp climate, e.g. in North-west Wales. So far as my observation goes they do better in a hotter, drier summer than Cornwall's and are not fully satisfactory even in Dorset. They are good town plants, even in mid-London, and stand clipping. The single sorts are more beautiful than the doubles, e.g. "Snowdrift," or *totus albus*, white; "Hamabo," pale pink with crimson centre; "Woodbridge," pink with darker centre, and *cœleste*, lilac blue. Large-flowered hybrids raised at Fresno Nursery, Fresno, California, may be worth trying here, e.g. in such a climate as Suffolk's.

HOHERIA

This genus now comprises five New Zealand species, all of them of exceptional value for mild gardens.

§H. angustifolia is an upright evergreen, very elegant, with thin, narrow, polished leaves, sharply serrated. The smallish white stars of flower are very profuse, whitening the tree in July and August. It is remarkably wind-hardy, as I have found on Zennor Moor; a slower grower than *H. sexstylosa*, it can reach 30 ft. The flowers have five styles, not six like those of *sexstylosa*.

§H. Lyallii (Hooker) (formerly known as *Gaya*, or *Hoheria, Lyallii*, var. *ribifolia*). This is one of the finest flowering plants in the New Zealand flora. It is slow to get away, and in some places (e.g. I am told, in Northern Ireland) it does not thrive [1]; but in Cornwall, as at Kew, it does very well: it should be more planted here. It has lobed leaves, grey-green or even silvery, covered with fine down; and the flowers fit with this cool colour, being white, like cherry blossom, in great quantity. This tree often makes a distinct trunk, so that one looks up into the green in July and finds it full of whiteness. It stands wind well, and comes from the east of the main mountain ranges of the South Island, in drier places than the following. (Note that this plant and the following are deciduous, whilst the other three are evergreen.)

§H. glabrata (formerly known as *H. Lyallii glabrata*) is now, con-

---

[1] Canon Boscawen regarded it as better worth growing than *H. L. glabrata*, since it shows its flowers better. It was one of the finest sights at Kew in July 1945. But in Northern Ireland, on the contrary, so expert a gardener as Mr. Armytage Moore, of Rowallane, has discarded it as not worth growing in comparison with the other.

veniently, classed as a different species. Its leaves are much larger than those of *H. Lyallii* (3–5 inches long), of a yellowish-green (not grey), tapering to a "drip tip." The flowers in July are like those of *Lyallii*, wonderfully profuse but apt to be somewhat hidden by the terminal leaves, scented of honey, and much used by bees. The tree is vigorous and quicker growing than the other, leafy and branched almost to the ground. In the wild it often grows in water-courses, and it likes wetter places than the other. In the writer's garden it flourishes in a shady northern aspect, although it gets draught and winds so severe that common Ash near by has only reached 12 ft., with withered tops, after many years. Strongly recommended.

H. populnea is a tall evergreen, reaching 40 ft. in a favoured place, with long, polished, leathery leaves, boldly toothed at the edge, dark green. The starry white flowers are a lovely sight against this dark green, and they are specially welcome, since they come late—August or September. The plant is rather tender: many were killed or damaged in December 1938. But it is in the first rank of flowering trees here.

The variety *Osbornii* has light-blue stamens, and bluish-purple colouring on the undersides of its leaves.

*§*H. sexstylosa* (formerly *H. populnea lanceolata*) has very variable leaves when young; when mature the leaves are lanceolate, with tapering tips. The tree grows extraordinarily fast: plants put out here from pots at the beginning of the war had reached their full height of 25 ft. by the end of the war and were covered with flowers. The white flowers have six pink styles (hence the name). The tree varies very much in leaf-shape and in habit. When its showering sprays are whitened with flower in August, it rivals any white-flowered tree we can grow. It is recommended in Chapter III for town planting and tall hedges.

Self-sown seedlings come up under the tree in great numbers, and show much variety where the species grow together.[1]

---

[1] A seedling, probably a hybrid between *H. sexstylosa* and *H. glabrata*, found in the garden of the late Dr. Jones at Amlwch, Anglesey, has been selected and propagated by the Slieve Donard Nursery Co. under the name "Glory of Amlwch." It is a distinct and hardy plant, with toothed long-tipped leaves, and large, very effective flowers; it seems likely to prove an outstanding shrub.

HOLBŒLLIA

H. latifolia, Wallich (syn. *Stauntonia latifolia*). A rampant evergreen climber from the Himalayas, with leathery leaves divided into from three to seven leaflets. The small flowers clustered in the axils are not showy, the male ones being greenish-white, the female purplish; but they are intensely fragrant, spreading an unforgettable scent far from the plant. (Those who know Ludgvan Church, for instance, may remember the smell from the huge plant in the Rectory garden across the road, planted by Canon Boscawen.) If it must be on a wall, spur it back to encourage flowering; but it is really better suited for a rough place, where it can ramp.

H. coriacea is another, Chinese. *H. grandiflora* (Réaubourg), from West China, has very fragrant flowers, white, larger than in the other species. This is likely to be worth growing, but is not, so far as I know, in cultivation here.

Stauntonia hexaphylla resembles *H. latifolia*.

HONEYSUCKLE. See LONICERA.

HYDRANGEA

The garden forms of hydrangea, blue, pink, and white, contribute more than any other shrubs to the show of colour in the gardens of the milder counties from midsummer onwards. And few shrubs are so accommodating. They are frost-hardy enough to do quite well in London's suburbs and wind-hardy enough to thrive close to the sea's edge or in exposed positions 600 ft. up on Zennor Moor, where few other shrubs could survive. They stand full sunlight, but grow more lush and perfect in the shelter and chequered sunlight of open woodland. The pink and white ones, though not the blues, do well in chalk country, serving instead of rhododendrons in the loam and leaf-mould of woods. They are generally found to be perfectly at home in peaty soil, though this is not the case everywhere.[1] They make superb pot-plants. Planted

[1] In my own garden on a peat moor, and in the peaty soil of other gardens in this district, all these hydrangeas thrive. But so expert a grower as Mr. M. Haworth Booth has a quite different experience at Haslemere. "I find peat is quite fatal to both *H. macrophylla* and *H. serrata*: chlorosis, slug infestation, dwindling and death. When I had to move my hydrangeas to the wood-garden, where azaleas grow better than anywhere I know, I lost most of them."

A General Planting List

in towns, they make a long-lasting show with the minimum of attention, and no shrub is more easily and quickly propagated from cuttings.

H. hortensis is a wrong name. *H. Hortensia* (after Mme Hortense la Peaute) is nearer, but that too is incorrect. Rehder called the sterile garden form *H. macrophylla* var. *Hortensia*; but it now appears that the plant originally obtained from Japan by Thunberg in 1784 and named by him *Viburnum macrophyllum* was this sterile mop-headed form, not the plant with flat umbels of flowers from which Japanese gardeners derived the garden form. So the garden form should, it seems, be called *H. macrophylla*,[1] and the flat-headed type *H. macrophylla* var. *normalis*.

H. macrophylla.

Blues.—Good blues of the round-headed type include *cœrulea*, "Radiant," "Blue Prince," and *"General Vicomte de Vibraye." The last of these, often pink, is a magnificent blue when grown on some soils or when treated. *H. m. cyanoclada*, with blue stems, is apt to be a straggly grower, but worth a place. On some soils these keep blue naturally; but in many places they will only do so if treated with sulphate of aluminium or powdered alum. (Sprinkle an ounce or two over the roots every ten days from mid-May, till the flowers come, watering it in.)

Purple.—"Maréchal Foch," a plant of excellent habit, has purple flowers, with striking variations of colour between blue and crimson. It looks the better for a white sort near it.

Reddish-pink.—"Parsifal," another good grower, is bright carmine-pink, fringed; a vivid colour, but not easy to mix. "Rubis" is another.

Pink.—Amongst many good pinks, "Altona," "Etincelant," "Ami Pasquier," "Brightness," and "Munster" are included. The last of these, a deep pink, turns carmine and green in autumn.

Whites include "Mme E. Mouillière," with very large fringed flowers, excellent under glass, but too often stained with pink out of doors. "President Fallières" keeps its whiteness outside. It is said to be less hardy than "Mouillière," and is now seldom listed. "Neige Orléanaise" is good too. The plant sold as "Mme de Vries" is, I understand, the original *H. macrophylla*. It is a very vigorous tall plant with large shiny leaves and large heads of an

[1] See M. Haworth Booth, "Further Notes on the Garden Hydrangeas," *R.H.S. Journal*, July 1946.

undecided white, turning pinkish or bluish. It is wind-hardy and most easily satisfied, but a coarse plant, washy in colour; a great many gardens would do well to exchange it for a variety of decided colour, such as "General Vicomte de Vibraye," "Altona," or "Mme E. Mouillière."

H. macrophylla var. normalis. This, the wild plant, makes a flat umbel of small fertile white flowers, with large sterile flowers round the rim. It is often seen in Devon. *"Blue Wave" is a vigorous blue form of fine colour; "Mariesii" is a good pink; there is a white, var. macrosepala, in which the large sterile flowers have only three sepals, not four; and there is a very fine white, extremely floriferous and vigorous, which is provisionally called *"Lanarth White." These deserve a good place, as well as the sterile forms, especially as they flower rather later and are very vigorous.

Besides the macrophylla hydrangeas there are others very well worth growing, such as serrata and aspera.

H. arborescens grandiflora, the best form of a very hardy North American species, has sterile white flowers of good size on a bush some 4 ft. high. This stands cold climates and the air of towns. It is better left unpruned.

*H. aspera (Don), one of the best, has downy serrated leaves, whitish beneath, and large flower-heads, blue in the central fertile flowers, lilac-pink in the sterile flowers round the rim. It makes a decorative rounded bush in woodland, 7 ft. high and across: its cool pink goes well with pink Anemone japonica. It is liable to suffer from spring frosts. H. villosa (Rehd.) is nearly related to this; its fertile flowers are blue, the sterile ones lilac-pink. It is reputed to be hardy, and thrives on chalk as well as elsewhere. H. vestita and the tender H. strigosa are similar.

H. Bretschneideri is a very hardy white one, making a wide bush up to 9 ft., with corymbs pink in the centre, the ring of sterile flowers clean white. It flowers just after the white Viburnum tomentosum, var. Mariesii.

H. paniculata throws up vigorous stems ending in pyramidal heads, the central flowers surrounded by separate milk-white flowers like a ring of dancers. Better known but perhaps not better is the familiar H. p. var. grandiflora, with very large panicles of sterile flowers. Both forms are very hardy; in both, the white turns to pink as it ages. Don't prune grandiflora as is customary, or it will make flower-heads so heavy as to need support. The milky colour of these hydrangeas suits a damp, partly shaded green place—the sort of place in which willow gentians (*G. asclepiadea*) sow themselves, and ferns flourish.

H. petiolaris is a very hardy, self-clinging, fast-growing climber, suitable for a north wall or a tree or for a mound in the open. The large flower-corymbs, borne on the short laterals, are white, effective against the leaves, and the whole plant yellows in autumn. There is now a pink-flowered form.

H. Sargentiana is a remarkable plant with furry shoots, very large velvet-furred leaves, and flower-heads lilac-pink with whiter sterile flowers round the rim. It needs full shelter from wind, but is fairly hardy. It is generally a gawky plant in the open, and looks better if planted so that its legs are screened by shrubs.

**H. serrata* (De Candolle), syn. *H. Thunbergii* (Sieb). This species, with its varieties, is too seldom seen: it is a most valuable addition to the garden hydrangeas, being dwarfer than *macrophylla* and very hardy. The leaves have a duller surface than those of *macrophylla*. The flower-heads are flat, of medium size, generally a good blue in the acute-leaved variety *acuminata* (Wilson); pink in var. *rosalba*; flesh-pink and double in the dwarf var. *stellata* (Wilson).

A variety provisionally named *"Grayswood Variety" has white flowers which turn to a rich red, and may hold this colour till nearly Christmas.

HYPERICUM

**H. patulum* var. *Forrestii* is generally reckoned the best of the forms of *H. patulum*, and is a showy bush 4–5 ft. high, yellow for three to four months in the late summer with golden cups. The yellow bleaches in strong sun. The plant is much used by bees.

H. patulum grandiflorum is another good one, dwarfer than *Forrestii*, with flowers up to 3 inches across. And *patulum* was a parent of the common but excellent dwarf hybrid *Moserianum*; the other parent being *H. calycinum*, the familiar carpeter.

H. Leschenaultii, from Java, is a tender plant, hardy enough for the mild counties, with 3-inch flowers on upright growths. So far as I have seen, the flowers are not freely borne here.

H. Rogersii (or *H. Hookerianum* var. *Rogersii*), from Mt. Victoria, India, is a very fine plant, 5–10 ft. high, with solidly built deep-yellow cups, nodding, very free-flowering.

*H. "Rowallane Hybrid," a hybrid between the last two, is, I think, a better garden plant than either of them. It is hardy enough for the mild counties, bushy, extremely free-flowering, and so persistent that one may find perfect flowers open at Christmas or New Year's Day. The bowl-shaped flowers are of an intense golden-yellow which does not bleach much in sunlight, and are about 3 inches across, with remarkably firm petals. The flowering season varies according to pruning. It is a good plan to plant several together and to prune the alternate plants drastically each year. Cuttings strike easily.

JASMINUM. JASMINE.

*J. nudiflorum, the yellow winter-jasmine, needs no recommendation. Prune it immediately after flowering, shortening flowered shoots so as to leave only a few buds at the base. It likes to grow downwards; so if you can, plant it not only against walls, but also on top of rock slopes. Whilst it prefers full sun, it will also thrive in shade. It is one of the best of shrubs for cutting, if well pruned, since the long shoots set with buds open perfectly in water and last remarkably well. Indeed, this plant might well be grown commercially, I suggest, in Cornwall or another mild county, for the cut-flower market; in climates where there is little frost the flowers are unlikely to be spoilt.

*J. officinale grandiflorum (syn. J. officinale var. affine). This also is too familiar for description. The best form is the large-flowered one with pink buds. In the mild counties it does well as a bush in the open, pruned in spring; or it can be grown as a tangle on a house front or sprawling over an outhouse roof, where its scent can be enjoyed.

*‡J. primulinum. This magnificent plant has the finest flower of any of the yellow jasmines—much larger than nudiflorum, semidouble, of the same clear canary-yellow, for a long season in spring. The leaf, too, is larger and evergreen. On a hot south or west wall, well fed in summer and kept on the dry side in winter, it well earns its keep in southern gardens. But it is tender and not a plant for cold places.

J. revolutum, J. fruticans, and J. heterophyllum glabricymosum are showy yellow ones, summer flowering. J. Parkeri is a very dwarf yellow one, not more than a foot high, suitable for the rock-garden but often not free-flowering. J. Beesianum, a very rampant grower with carmine flowers, is not recommended, being shy-flowering and ineffective; *J. stephanense*, its pink hybrid, flowers freely, but the small flowers seldom make much show.

For other jasmines, especially *J. polyanthum*, see pages 334–5.

JUNIPERUS. JUNIPER.

This book has omitted conifers, except a few shelter-plants; but a word shall be said here about some of the junipers, since I think planters here have much to learn from the use made of these plants, especially the prostrate ones, in the severe climate of the United States and Canada. In that climate the range of evergreens is far more restricted than it is here. (In New York common ivy is a pot-plant in the flower shops.) That has led to the most careful and extensive use of junipers, dwarf yews, and (as at Washington) the small-leaved box. Prostrate junipers are massed with good effect on banks and beside drives, and Savin is among the dark evergreens that furnish narrow beds at the foot of the white wood-built houses.

J. horizontalis in its various forms is a most decorative prostrate grower, free (so far as I know) from the die-back which often disfigures *J. Sabina tamariscifolia*. On the coast of Maine one may find ancient plants of this pressed tight against rock-slabs just above high-water mark, gnarled and as full of character as the venerable specimens of *J. communis* which hug windy rocks on Snowdon. "Bar Harbour" is the most beautiful form of this. In the American climate (if not here) this turns plum-purple in winter. In the sand-dune country south of Lake Michigan a form of *horizontalis* covers wide stretches, with its main branches submerged in sand, its ascending branchlets showing as a green carpet. It might well be used in this way here, e.g. in gardens on the coastal sand of North Cornwall. *Douglasii* is a striking selected form of this, persistently steely-blue in colour. Yet another distinct form is *plumosa*, with horizontal flat-topped growths and bronzy-purple winter colour.

J. conferta (syn. *J. litoralis*). Another excellent plant for sandy shore-gardens, or other gardens, is this species from sandy places in Japan. It is of course extremely wind-hardy, and makes a mat.

J. squamata var. *prostrata* (Hornibrook) is perhaps the best form of *squamata*; better in habit than the type. Planted on a rocky hump, it makes an inverted saucer of trailing grey-green fronds, perfectly disposed. *J. s.* var. *Meyeri* (Rehder), a dense upright bush with leaves bluish-white on the back, is another beautiful plant, but not perhaps long-lived.

J. Sabina tamariscifolia, familiar in our gardens here, is superb when well placed and in perfect health; but as noted above, it is apt to have branchlets dead brown among the green.

Amongst larger junipers, the familiar *J. Sabina,* with its upward-flaring growth, is a fine distinctive plant; useful for banks where grass would be troublesome to keep tidy. *J. Pfitzeriana, J. rigida.* and the varieties of *J. scopulorum* are amongst the other large growers worth considering. The ordinary *J. communis,* in the bushy form common on Salisbury Downs, is worth considering as a wind-shelter.

KALMIA

*K. latifolia. This most beautiful pink-flowered bush, the pride of woodlands in the Eastern United States, is easy enough to grow in lime-free soils and is perfectly hardy. Why is it so seldom seen in Cornwall? In the severe climate of the Arnold Arboretum at Boston it flowers with astonishing lavishness; it thrives too in the mild climate of Virginia, and does perfectly well in this country. Plant kalmias. The variety *myrtifolia* is an excellent form of *latifolia,* making a dense bush not exceeding 3 ft., with flowers of a deeper pink than the type.

KERRIA

§*K. japonica.* The single sort, with flowers like small, golden, single roses, and the much more vigorous double one, *pleniflora,* are both welcome in spring. Whether against a paling, beside a cottage door, or throwing flowering shoots into the bronze-green of a Bay tree, the double one always looks at home; it is most easily grown even in bleak places, but soon makes a tall thicket that may need thinning.

KOLKWITZIA

K. amabilis. A wide deciduous bush some 6 ft. high, with greyish-rose buds set in white wool, and flowers in May–June, subtly fragrant, like small pale-pink yellow-throated *weigelas.* When well established in full sun this is free-flowering enough to be an effective garden decoration.

Laburnum

If both *L. Vossii* or *Watereri*, with long streamers, and **alpinum*, the late-flowering Scotch laburnum, are planted, the season is much prolonged. Laburnum-yellow does not mix well with other colours (e.g. with *Prunus Pissardii*, pink hawthorn, or lilac); but laburnums are too seldom planted in quantity by themselves, e.g. in a short avenue, or leaning out from the banks of a sunk lane. §*L. alpinum* in particular stands wind well.

Lapageria

*‡*L. rosea*. One of the most beautiful of climbers. It makes long shoots that twine round trunks or wires for support, reaching 20 ft. The evergreen leaves are thick and stiff, and the flowers, solid as if moulded in wax, are 3 inches long, shaped like hanging trumpet-lilies. *L. rosea*, the type, is deep shining rose-pink, stippled with whiter pink in the throat: its quality of pink is hardly equalled in any other flower except *philesia*. *L. superba* and "Nash Court" are very good varieties of this, but perhaps unobtainable now. There is also a white one, *albiflora*, as beautiful as the pink.

Lapageria is not difficult to grow, given a vigorous, unchecked plant to start with, shade, a damp air, lime-free soil, protection from slugs, and something for it to twine up—a trellis or rubber-covered wire on a north wall will do, as may be judged from page 144, illustrating a plant on a house in Kent. It is hardy in the mild counties and has a long-flowering season, flowering first on old wood and later on the current year's growth. It can be propagated from cuttings or from layers; and it comes readily from seed if the seeds are not dried off. (In the wild, the seeds germinate in the decaying fleshy seed-pods, never becoming dry.) One drawback is that the plant needs careful removal of dead stems if it is to flower with full freedom. Another is that slugs have a passion for eating it. Put an old lamp-chimney 6 inches high round the shoots when planting it, or a zinc collar.

Lavatera

‡*L. Olbia rosea* (tree mallow). Excellent for quick effect and one of the best shrubby plants for mixing with herbaceous plants. Flowers mallow-pink, July–October, on a 6-ft. bush. Needs

good staking in a windy garden. Goes well with *Ceanothus* "Gloire de Versailles," and with such herbaceous plants as blue *echinops, Sidalcea* "Sussex Beauty," catmint, *Aster Thomsonii, Sedum spectabile,* and clematises "Comtesse de Bouchard" and "Perle d'Azur." Or plant it with sea buckthorn (*Hippophæ rhamnoides*) and train *Clematis* "Comtesse de Bouchard," or *C. kermesina* into the buckthorn. Prune hard.

Leonotis

‡*L. Leonurus* is a shrubby sage from South Africa, suitable for a hot place in poor or sandy soil. Its stems, 5-6 ft. high, are ringed with whorls of tawny-orange hooded flowers with long upper lip. Long-flowering and easily raised from seed.

Leptodermis pilosa

This deciduous shrub, 6-10 ft. high, is valuable chiefly for its late flowering. It has dark grey-green foliage, and flowers like small lilac-flowers, white or pale lavender, towards the end of the shoots. The general effect is something like that of *Osmanthus Delavayi*; but the bush is more erect and the flowering continues for a long period from late summer till autumn. It is one of the two shrubs that make a show so late as October (e.g. at the Botanic Garden, Glasnevin). Other species are *L. oblonga*, a bush only 3-4 ft. high, with smaller leaves, and flowers like a small Persian lilac; and *L. Purdomii,* a very graceful shrub with panicles of pink flowers like lilac, borne on arching growths in August-September.

Leptospermum

These shrubs from New Zealand, Tasmania and Australia include some of the finest plants for mild gardens, especially near the sea. They are extremely free-flowering, and are easily raised from seed. They are soil-robbers, with a wide root system, and should be planted when small; they can stand a good deal of wind, but not full exposure.

L. baccatum, an Australian, has small dark leaves, whitish underneath, and white hawthorn-like flowers touched at the base with carmine.

**L. ericoides.* This New Zealander is one of the best, for though the flowers are small, they are so freely borne that the bush is as white as the bravest hawthorn in May. In the wild it varies from

a prostrate shrub to a tree 50–60 ft. high with shredding papery bark; here I have not seen it more than 15 ft. The leaves are narrow, rather heath-like; the flowers, carried on short stalks, are white, not more than ¼ inch across. The plant is of good upright habit, and stands some wind. Like other *leptospermums* it was killed in my garden in 1947, but never suffered in previous winters.
L. flavescens. A form of this, var. *obovutum*, growing in a Cornish garden, is illustrated here. It is a bush of excellent habit, very profuse in flower, and hardier than most *leptospermums*.
L. lævigatum is a white-flowered Australian species, with glossy leaves larger than those of *L. scoparium*.
‡*L. Liversidgei* (syn. *thymifolia*), another Australian, is a bush about 3–4 ft. high, with slender arching shoots close-set with minute leaves; the small greenish-white flowers are not striking individually, but make graceful sprays when the bush is flowering well in a hot place.
L. pubescens (syn. *L. lanigerum*). This Australian, which is a good deal hardier than *L. scoparium*, is valuable chiefly for its beautiful silvery foliage, the pointed leaves being overlaid with silky down. The white flowers are not freely borne till the bush is well established. The typical *pubescens* has reached some 10 ft. in this country, but may reach tree-size in its home forests; its variety *montanum* grows to 60–80 ft. in sub-alpine forests in Tasmania.
L. Rodwayanum, a tender Tasmanian plant akin to *L. pubescens*, has greyish leaves and white flowers as large as 1 or 1¼ inches across.
L. scoparium. This variable shrub, native of New Zealand, Tasmania, and Australia, is the "manuka" or "tea tree" of the New Zealand bush; it covers miles of the North Island, in heavy hungry clay soil where the forest has been burnt.

The type makes a bush, generally about 9–10 ft. here, but reaching 15 ft. or even 25 ft. in the wild; the white flowers, almost stalkless on the twigs, are nearly ½ inch across and very freely borne. Old bushes become leggy at the base, with many dead twigs and masses of brown woody seed-capsules.
**L. s. eximium* is a particularly good form of this from Tasmania, bushy in habit, and extremely profuse with its large flowers, white with a green centre. The leaves are sharply pointed, broader than those of the type; indeed, the bush looks like quite a distinct species. It did very well in Cornwall till 1947, but at Nymans (Sussex) has been killed by a severe winter.

L. s. flore pleno is a double form, white or pink, the stamens being replaced by small petaloid growths in the centre.

L. s. grandiflorum is a fine large-flowered variety.

L. s. Nichollsii is the famous crimson one. A well-grown bush of this, with its bronzed leaves, covered in May with flowers of a red as fine as that of *Rosa Moyesii*, is one of the best flower-sights that our mild gardens can show. Many seedlings of this type are much inferior to the true plant (which was shown by Canon Boscawen at the International Flower Show in 1912 and won the prize for the finest new plant in the Show). But **Nichollsii grandiflorum* can claim to be an improvement, having larger flowers of the true colour; and *gloriosa*, with large flowers of a more carmine red[1], is a plant of excellent habit and very prolific. A form of *Nichollsii* in a Cornish garden regularly flowers in mid-winter.

The strong colour of these red forms looks the better for some relief, such as a white *escallonia* (e.g. *pterocladon*) or the white *Cornus kousa*.

*L. s. Chapmanii is a splendid upright bush, hardier than the other coloured forms and a glowing mass of pink in May-June. Seedlings give a range of pinks of varying quality. There is a double pink, *roseum multipetalum*. A winter-flowering New Zealand variety, *Keatleyi*, which I have not seen in flower, has pink flowers, said to be "often larger than a florin"; a friend in New Zealand who grows this describes it as a magnificent plant. Another winter-flowering one is *Sandersii*. *Boscawenii*, a fine plant but tender, has white flowers with deep pink-centre.

L. s. prostratum (syn. *rupestre*) is generally quite prostrate, but is sometimes a 5-ft. bush in the wild. It is the hardiest of the lot; but the form originally introduced bore its white flowers so sparsely as to be not worth growing. Rather more free-flowering forms are, I believe, now in cultivation, but none is of much effect.

L. stellatum is a good upright white one, an Australian.

There are a good many others, such as *L. nitidum* from Tasmania; and with fuller trial we may find that some of the species and varieties not yet well known here, especially the Tasmanians, are hardier than those we grow already.

LIGUSTRUM. PRIVET.

L. confusum is a large sub-evergreen bush, rather tender, weighed down when well established by huge bunches of small plum-

A General Planting List

black berries. It is one of the most striking shrubs for berry, given a sheltered site.

L. lucidum. Much the handsomest of the evergreen privets: a fine dark evergreen with big panicles of white flower in August–September. It makes a small tree.

L. sinense is a most floriferous sub-evergreen, making a large bush or small tree of half-weeping habit, with a cloud of white flowers followed by black-purple berries. That this can make a striking show can be seen from the plate in Bean's *Trees and Shrubs*, vol. II, page 28.

Lilac. See Syringa.

Lippia

L. citriodora, lemon verbena, needs no recommendation for the smell of its leaves. Given some shelter and full sun, it makes a decorative shrub with woody trunks in very mild gardens; but in most places it needs a warm wall.

Lithospermum

*L. prostratum, best of dwarf, blue-flowered, shrubby plants, is easy to grow if the roots are kept cool with the head in full sun, in lime-free soil: it does well, for instance, planted in a retaining wall facing south, where it will make a long hanging mat, blue all over in May. "Grace Ward" is by some considered even better than the well-known form "Heavenly Blue"; and *erectum*, a more upright grower, is for most purposes a still finer garden plant. Like many blue flowers, "Heavenly Blue" looks its best in the company of some cream, white, or pale-yellow flowers. Propagate by cuttings of the previous year's growth.

‡*L. rosmarinifolium*, a 1–2-ft. bush with leaves like rosemary's, has flowers in mid-winter of intense blue; but it is more tender than *prostratum*, and though its blue sparks are very welcome in their season, there are not enough of them in the Cornish climate (so far as my experience goes) to make much show. In drier maritime counties such as Dorset it is a cherished plant, very long-flowering. It wants all the heat it can get. Easily raised from seed.

Lomatia

L. ferruginea (*L. pinnatifolia*). A Chilean evergreen tree, up to 30 ft., erect in habit, with leaves mostly pinnate, most decorative in their firm pattern. The branchlets, leaf stalks, and young growths are brownish-crimson; the curious flowers, buff and red, not showy, are borne in racemes in the leaf axils. There are some fine trees of this in Cornish woodland gardens. It stands wind well, but is a plant for the mild counties only. William Lobb introduced the plant a century ago; in Chiloe Island it grows with *Eucryphia cordifolia*.

LONICERA.   HONEYSUCKLE.
CLIMBERS

*L. americana (syn. *grata*) is a hybrid between this and the early cream honeysuckle, *L. Caprifolium*, one of the very best climbing honeysuckles, flowering from May till autumn, fragrant, yellow and carmine.

L. etrusca is a very effective vigorous climber for a high wall or tree, with masses of smallish cream flowers deepening to yellow.

L. fragrantissima, and the very similar *L. Standishii*, are not showy, but very fragrant and worth a place on, say, an outhouse wall, since they flower in mid-winter. *L. Purpusii* is a hybrid between the two, considered to be a better plant.

‡*L. Hildebrandtiana* is a very vigorous climber, with large tough leaves and very large upstanding white flowers quickly darkening to deep yellow. Often this large-scale plant looks out of place, dwarfing its neighbours; often it is too shy-flowering to be worth its room; but on a hot wall (e.g. formerly on the south wall of the house at Trebah, on Helford Estuary) it can make a splendid show.

L. japonica Halliana is one of the forms of the evergreen Japanese honeysuckle; rampant, with most fragrant flowers deepening to yellow; excellent for a house-wall.

*§*L. Periclymenum belgica*, and *L. p. serotina*, the early and late Dutch honeysuckles, are two varieties of the wild honeysuckle, better for the garden than the lovely plant of the hedgerow. For early cultivation, profusion of flower and scent, these two common climbers are hard to beat.

L. sempervirens, the scarlet honeysuckle, is a lovely North American evergreen, with scarlet and yellow flowers, hardy here.

*L. Tellmanniana, a hybrid of *L. tragophylla*, lately introduced, is reckoned by some the choicest of all the hardy honeysuckles. Its flowers are 2 inches long, yellow tipped with red, in profuse

clusters from June onwards. Plant it where it can twine up a bush with its base shaded.

L. tragophylla, the Chinese golden honeysuckle, is another superb plant, hardy all over Britain, I believe. The flowers, of a beautiful yellow, unscented, are 4–6 inches long in the tube and wonderfully profuse when the plant is doing well on a west wall. The leaves are brown-purple, a fine foil to the flowers. The plant likes cool loam, shade on its root, little pruning and no moving.

BUSHES

Besides the climbers, there are the bushy honeysuckles (among which *fragrantissima* and *Standishii* may be included). *L. nitida* is the small-leaved evergreen often now used for hedges; it stands wind well even near the sea. *L. yunnanensis*, with translucent violet berries, is very similar but rather better in growth. *L. pileata* is a dwarf horizontal grower, useful for rough banks or covering drain-pipes, with inconspicuous but fragrant flowers. *L. syringantha* has small lilac-pink flowers, which smell just like the scented orchis (*Gymnadenia conopsea*), and is worth growing in a rough corner. If *Lonicera tatarica*, especially its variety "bella," would fruit in this country as it does in the Eastern United States, it would be among our finest berrying shrubs; but so far as I know it will not do this here. The same applies to *L. Korolkowi floribunda*, with grey-green leaves and orange berries.

LUPINUS

L. arboreus, tree lupin. This stands a surprising amount of wind. It is extremely fast-growing and showy, so that it is useful for new gardens; it is short-lived and apt to get straggly, but is most easily propagated and much improved by drastic pruning after flowering. The white variety is beautiful in colour and good in a border, e.g. with *Anchusa* "Morning Glory"; but it leaves a big gap when it goes.

The home of tree lupin in California is on wind-swept coastal sands, in which it sends down immensely long tap-roots; it grows also in the forests of *Pinus radiata*, in a mixture of pine needles and decomposed granite, i.e. just such a soil as can be provided in many places in Cornwall. It would be worth sowing seed in such places here, and using it to bind sand-dunes. (It is used so at

Dawlish Warren, as one may see from the train; and on a large scale at San Francisco.) There are some beautiful lilac-blue shrubby lupins with grey or silver leaves. *L. arboreus Paynei* has flowers ranging from blue through lavender and purple to pink and white, with a yellow blotch on the standard.

Plant in spring, and plant small.

MAGNOLIA. See Chapter X.

MALUS. CRAB APPLES. See PYRUS MALUS, Chapter VII.

MANDEVILLA

‡ *M. suaveolens*. A rampant climber, with white flowers like a much-enlarged jasmine, very fragrant. In mild gardens it thrives on sunny walls: at Lelant, in Cornwall, for instance, it covers a house wall facing east in full exposure. Perhaps hardier than is commonly supposed.

M. Tweedieana, not seen here, is stated to have more substantial flowers, of a still sweeter fragrance.

MELALEUCA

‡ *M. squarrosa*. A shrub or small tree with bottle-brush flowers of clear pale yellow; a beautiful plant for mild gardens. It comes from wet heaths in Tasmania and from Australia. Plants from Tasmanian seed appear to be hardy enough for coastal gardens here. For other *melaleucas* see Chapter XIV.

* § METROSIDEROS LUCIDA and M. ROBUSTA. See Chapter IX.

MITRARIA

M. coccinea, mitre flower. An evergreen creeper, rampant where it is happy, with pendent flowers of a shining vermilion, shaped like the Roman Catholic mitre. In the wet forests of Southern Chile it flowers high up on the trunk of forest trees such as *Fitzroya patagonica*. "Often we were aware of its presence overhead only by fallen petals at the foot of the tree which it had climbed."[1] Here it is usually grown where it can spread over shady rocks, through dry walls and up into bushes; but it shows its flowers best when clambering through a stiff bush into sunlight. If left to grow into a dense mass in full shade, it may be too

[1] *Plant-hunters in the Andes*, by T. H. Goodspeed.

shy-flowering to be effective. In the colder gardens of the mild counties it may prove tender.

MUTISIA

M. Clematis. A vigorous climber, suitable for a tall shrub-covered wall, with large, red, daisy-flowers, like a *gerbera*.
M. decurrens has orange flowers like marigolds, 5 inches across. This, the best known, will reach the top of the south wall of a house.
M. ilicifolia, with pink flowers, has holly-like leaves; and so has *oligodon,* a moderate grower.

All these are apt to look very untidy. They are sprawling plants, rambling over a hump of ground or through a deciduous bush, where the roots do not get sun-struck. Propagate by cuttings of half-ripened shoots: do not try to propagate by suckers, or you may kill the parent plant. Put stones over the roots if there is risk of sunstroke. Slugs too are a danger—so put a zinc collar round the stem.

MYRTUS. MYRTLE.

M. bullata, from New Zealand, makes an upright bush up to 15 ft. high, with crimson-brown leaves curiously puffed up as if blistered. The white myrtle flowers are pretty but seldom profusely borne, and they do not make much effect. Sprays of this, cut, make a good decoration indoors.

‡*M. chequen* is a Chilean tree myrtle, an upright grower with aromatic leaves and white myrtle-flowers. It appears to be fairly tolerant of wind. I believe it is not hardy in Dorset, but in Cornwall I have not known it to suffer from frost till 1947.

**M. communis,* common myrtle, is a great success in very many mild gardens, especially where it can be given the warmth of a south wall, say beside a door. In such a position one sees the clear-cut pattern of the leaves against the wall, sees the discreet beauty of the bursting buds and the flowers with their fuzz of stamens, and has the leaf close at hand to bruise and smell. In a bleak position this is apt to get shabby in winter. In some gardens, e.g. at Tresco, it reaches the size of a small tree. It has a small-leaved form, *microphylla.*

§*M. communis* var. *tarentina,* with still smaller leaves, is a better plant than *communis* for windy gardens, being remarkably wind-hardy. Its fine leaf pattern and rounded bushy shape make it one of the best shrubs for planting against a house, or beside steps, in full sun, in windy gardens near the sea.

*‡ M. Lechleriana. This is a tall bush or small tree, reaching 30 ft., rather like the tree myrtle (M. luma); a handsome upright evergreen, leafy down to the ground. In April the young growth colours the whole bush a striking golden-brown; and the small milk-white flowers, scented and very profuse, come in April, not August, in clusters at the leaf axils. The berries are at first scarlet. It is remarkably wind-hardy, and may even prove worth growing as a wind-break within the outer wind-defences. Like M. Luma it sows itself, so it should soon be better known. Unfortunately, it is a tender plant. I have not known it to suffer in Cornwall, but it may get cut or killed in Dorset.

*M. Luma (Eugenia apiculata), tree myrtle. This is one of the very best of large shrubs for mild gardens. Plant-hunters will go on scouring the world to find new plants for our gardens; they will find treasure indeed when they find one so beautiful and amenable as the tree myrtle which William Lobb brought from Chile a century ago.

The leaves are small, dark, decorative like a myrtle's, the buds round like water-drops, and the flowers white myrtle-flowers with pink-touched stamens, with a slight but pervasive scent, from July to October. A characteristic beauty of the plant is its trunk—smooth, bright cinnamon-brown, with pale patches where the bark has peeled off; in an old tree the trunk has a sinuous grace and power rivalled only by that of Madrona, the Californian *arbutus*. The plant stands a good deal of wind, though not extreme exposure, and is recommended in List "B"; but it flowers even better in the shelter of a wood or in a sheltered position in the open. What must be the largest tree of it in the country is at Scorrier House, near Redruth; a magnificent specimen which may well have been part of the first batch of plants raised when the tree myrtle was introduced by William Lobb, who worked in the Scorrier garden before he went to Chile.

A myrtle tree looks very well by itself, e.g. alone on a lawn against a dark background. But the most beautiful use of it I know is as a little grove in the woodland garden of Lanarth, where the orange trunks stand on either side of the path, with a snow of flowers overhead among the dark leaves.

A General Planting List

I know, too, a small garden in a hollow on the Land's End moors, with a stream beside it and trees around. In the midst of this, in a shadowed hollow, you come suddenly on a great myrtle tree with a venerable trunk. It is worth walking far across the moor to see that tree put on its white.

Tree myrtle is so much at home here that it sows itself by the thousand in many mild gardens—no longer a "foreigner." It should be used here in public planting schemes. In an abnormally hard winter it may lose all its leaves, even in West Cornwall, but it will generally recover if left alone.

§*M. Ugni* (*Eugenia Ugni*). The edible myrtle makes a bush 3–6 ft. high, with pretty but not showy, pinky-white, drooping flowers, and dark-red fruits in October. The fruits have an aromatic smell, and what little there is of them tastes like wild strawberry. They are sometimes used for jam or for flavouring puddings, and there is a cherished legend that they were Queen Victoria's favourite dessert. The plant stands wind well and makes quite a good low hedge.

Nandina

N. domestica. A 5-ft. shrub with elegant evergreen leaves and terminal spikes of small white flowers, sometimes followed by red berries. The leaves often colour in autumn.

Nerium. Oleander.

Anyone who has seen oleanders growing in tubs and pots in Southern or Central Europe, or—better still—in some stony sunlit river-bed in the Middle East, will agree that they are amongst the most decorative of shrubs. The tough evergreen leaves are beautiful in pattern, and the large flowers, profusely borne in branching sprays, range from white to pink, red, pale yellow, and copper. In some the flowers are double, in some they are fragrant. None is better than a good form of the single pink. The plant is quite hardy enough for outdoor culture in such climates as Cornwall's, at least near the sea, and it is very easy to grow, given sunlight and heavy loamy soil. But there is a snag. Unless special care is taken it is apt, in this climate, to produce quantities of buds which do not develop into flowers. Indeed, so little is the culture of oleanders understood here that I do not recall ever having seen a well-flowered specimen in Cornwall. In the Penzance district one may see large healthy bushes, covered with buds each summer, but always flowerless. But given some care, this is perhaps remediable. Mr. Osborn, in his *Shrubs and Trees for the Garden*, gives this advice: "The flowers on healthy young plants may fail to develop because young shoots grow just below the inflorescence and take much of the nutriment. The remedy is to remove these young growths as soon as their development is noticed." Give the plant lots of water at flowering time. It is apt to grow leggy and may require a little spring-pruning.

NOTHOFAGUS. SOUTHERN BEECH. See Chapter X.

NOTOSPARTIUM
N. Carmichæliæ. A New Zealand broom, with rush-like stems, almost leafless, and small lilac-pink flowers in short bunches near the ends of the shoots. It used to be very pretty at Ludgvan, hanging out over a hollow floored with the vivid magenta creeper, *Heeria elegans*. In South-west Eire it sometimes makes a small tree.

OLEARIA. See Chapter XI.

OSMANTHUS
O. Delavayi. Small dark-green leaves; flowers small, white, in quantity in April, very fragrant; makes a large bush in time. Best in half-shade, e.g. in open woodland, where it will make long arching growths flowered all along their length.
O. Aquifolium is a well-known holly-like evergreen bush, extremely useful for a large hedge (6–8 ft.) or for a dark background. Unlike holly, this moves quite well even when fairly large. Excellent for giving back-bone to a newly made garden.
O. Forrestii, with larger leaves, is a large evergreen making a good dark mass, useful for a wind-break in woodland; but it has not fulfilled the hopes raised when it was introduced.

OSMAREA BURKWOODII
O. Burkwoodii, a cross between *Osmanthus Delavayi* and *Phillyrea decora*, is another good dark-green evergreen, vigorous and always trim. It has small highly scented white flowers in May, not showy but pleasant. It does not stand full exposure to sea-wind, but makes an excellent evergreen hedge.

Osteomeles

O. Schweriniæ. A shrub with decorative grey pinnate foliage starred with white flowers in June. Prune after flowering.

Oxydendrum

O. arboreum. This handsome shrub makes a tall deciduous bush here, but a tree in North America. In July–August it has long drooping sprays of little white bells, and in autumn the leaves flare orange-red. It is of high value to bee-keepers for its nectar. Hardy and easily grown in lime-free soil. It should be more planted.

Palms

Several of the species of palm are hardy enough for the milder gardens here and came through the frost of 1938. These include: *Chamærops Fortunei* (syn. *Trachycarpus Fortunei*), Chusan palm, which is perfectly hardy, standing 30° of frost, when once it has outgrown its juvenile stage; *C. excelsa*, of which there is a big tree in Morrab Gardens, Penzance; *C. humilis*, fan palm, which is in numerous gardens.
Phœnix reclinata is 30 ft. high at Penzance: and *P. canariensis* has done well at Enys, Cornwall, in a hot place. All should have a sheltered site, well-drained.

Passiflora. Passion Flower

P. cœrulea and its white variety "Constance Elliott" are a great success on walls and summer-houses in sunny gardens in the mild counties. If untended, they grow luxuriantly, but flower and fruit little. Plant them in well-drained soil with a restricted root-run, and prune hard in February–March, shortening the shoots to half length and preventing a top-heavy smother of growth.

For others, see page 340.

Paulownia

*P. tomentosa (syn. *P. imperialis*), when flowering well, is as beautiful a flowering tree as can be grown in this country. Unfortunately, it is an uncertain flowerer in the English climate; it makes its buds in autumn, and is liable, up-country, to get them frosted before they can open in May. In mild counties it generally escapes this trouble, but it prefers a hotter summer than ours.

The flowers are like pale-lilac *streptocarpus*, with purple buds, borne on short spikes before the leaves come: a wonderful sight against the sky. In this climate the tree is apt to be gaunt in habit, and it is liable to get lichen-covered if exposed to sea-winds; but it thrives in various South-country gardens, sometimes reaching 50 ft., and flowering well in good seasons. It might well be planted in public gardens in the mild counties, e.g. at Penzance, Falmouth, Truro, where it would often be a fine sight, as it is in Paris. Tender when young.

P. Fargesii, a more recent introduction, has pale-lavender flowers with a yellow stain in the throat.

‡PELARGONIUM. GERANIUM.

The scarlet shrubby geranium needs no description or recommendation anywhere; and in mild places it is the most vivid and long-flowering of wall plants. At St. Ives I have seen a whole house front covered to the top with one scarlet sort. At Tresco Abbey several South African species grow in masses, giving to part of the garden a scent which will be remembered by many who have visited that lovely place.

PENTAPTERYGIUM. See page 340.

PERNETTYA

P. furiens, a dense very dark-leaved bush, 2–4 ft. high, has effective clusters of white lily-of-the-valley-shaped flowers in May. On a raised corner in a half-shady rockery, it used to be a feature of Canon Boscawen's garden at Ludgvan.

P. leucocarpa. A low-spreading shrublet, 6 inches high, with very small leaves and lilac-pink or white berries. Good in colour with *Gentiana sino-ornata*, but tiresomely invasive.

P. macrostigma (syn. *Gaultheria perplexa*). Another dwarf spreader, laden with pink berries which it holds for several months; a good plant.

*P. mucronata. Stiff bushes 2–4 ft. high, with prickly dark-green leaves, small white flowers, and masses of berries, white, lilac-pink, scarlet, carmine, and blood-red. "Bell's Seedling" is a very distinct one, with large leaves and large scarlet berries; most effective at its best. A well-berried *pernettya* is a very fine decoration in autumn, but where other food is scarce, birds are quick to eat the berries. It associates very well with Cornish heath (*Erica*

A General Planting List

vagans) and the creeping *Polygonum vaccinifolium*. It stands all the winds. But be careful about placing it where its running habit will not be a nuisance: it is so invasive that it is better suited for a wild heath garden than for a rock garden full of choice plants. And it easily escapes: seedlings find their way from garden to moor. It likes to be kept not too dry at the roots, but can stand full sun. It must have lime-free soil, and berries much better if planted in some quantity, with some male plants as well as female ones. (I am told that "Bell's Seedling" does not need this.) The berried sprays are first-rate for cutting in autumn and winter, and growers for the flower market might well consider building up a demand for *pernettya*, and growing it commercially.

Amongst other *pernettyas* there are some nice plants for the gardener who enjoys the small unspectacular beauty of such things as the lesser *gaultherias* and *vacciniums*; e.g. *P. pumila* (syn. *magellanica*), *P. nigra*, with striking black fruits; *P. rigida*, with vigorous upright growths, and toothed leaves larger than those of *mucronata*, a handsome plant; and *P. tasmanica*, a prostrate grower, with light red berries large for the plant.

Perovskia

*P. atriplicifolia makes an upright grey bush with thin spikes of small lavender-blue sage-flowers in late summer, very decorative if well grown in a hot position. If cut level to the ground in February, it will make quite massive plumes 5–6 ft. high, especially in chalky soil.

Philadelphus

Why is it that one so seldom sees a good "syringa," "mock orange," in Cornwall? Is it because, like lilacs, these lovely and easily grown plants need a more extreme climate, or better ripening of the wood, or more lime? Or is it chiefly because Cornish gardeners have concentrated their attention so largely on other plants, notably rhododendrons? The best sorts are so beautiful as to be worth any gardener's care.

All the *philadelphuses* like lime and need good soil which does not dry out. In lime-free gardens, they will be much better for some bone-meal. Pruning should be done immediately after flowering; thin and spent wood should be cut right out so as to let the rest ripen.

Here are four first-class species, and some hybrids:

P. Delavayi var. *calvescens*. A fountain of a bush, up to 15 ft., with cup-shaped 1-inch flowers early in June, in clusters, the calyx flushed with violet. The typical *Delavayi* is good enough for any garden if the variety cannot be obtained.

P. *pubescens* (formerly *latifolius*). Another tall one, reaching 20 ft. It has larger dark-green leaves, and flowers 1½ inches across.

P. *grandiflorus* is a 15-ft. bush, with scentless 2-inch flowers late in June; beautiful as a decoration for the house if the leaves are picked off. P. *microphyllus*, the parent of many hybrids, is a compact bush only 3–4 ft. high, with small leaves and 1-inch flowers, with a distinctive scent suggestive of pineapple.

"Atlas" and "Norma" are two tall hybrids, with flowers of beautiful shape 2 inches across.

Burfordensis is a fine one, with cup-shaped flowers 2 inches across; it makes an erect bush up to 10 ft. high, flowering, some might say, to excess.

P. *insignis* (Billardii), another tall bush, is one of the most effective. The well-known double one, "Virginal," is handsome when well grown, but the bush requires careful pruning if it is not to get gawky in habit; "Girandole," another double one, may be preferred, but the perfect shape of the *Philadelphus* flower always loses a good deal from doubling. "Belle Etoile" is of medium height, and the flowers have a purple splash at the centre, and a scent like orange. None has a better-shaped flower than "Coupe d'Argent"; and *"Voie Lactée," erectus, "Velleda," and "Favorite" are among the best.

Philesia

P. magellanica (G. F. Gmelin : syn. *P. buxifolia*, Lam). If you have once seen this lovely Chilean plant doing well, you will want to grow it. It makes a low spreading bush, 2–3 ft. high and reaching many feet across in time. Narrow, dark, evergreen leaves, pale on the underside, on brittle growths, with strong suckers. Hanging flowers, solid and waxen, similar in shape to those of *lapageria* but smaller, of a shining self-rose colour.

Philesia wants a cool root-run in lime-free soil. It is commonly grown in full shade, but may flower better if given a fair amount of direct sun so long as its roots are kept cool. It should be top-dressed. Canon Boscawen, who had an immense and cherished plant of it, gave it a load of leaf-mould annually. The form *rosea* has flowers of a paler pink, and a taller growth.

PHILLYRÆA. See page 24.

PHOTINIA

P. serrulata is one of the handsomest evergreens in leaf, with large, leathery, polished foliage; brilliant, coppery-red, young shoots in spring; 6-inch clusters of small white flowers, and red berries. It makes a massive bushy tree in mild gardens, sometimes reaching 40 ft. or more.

P. villosa makes a twiggy tree, brilliant in autumn leaf-colour and loaded for some time with scarlet berries like hawthorn.

PHYGELIUS

P. capensis var. *coccineus*. A sub-shrubby plant, 6 ft. high or more in the open, and reaching 25 ft. on a wall, with tawny-scarlet flowers like drooping pentstemons in August–September. It comes from the Cape, and likes a hot dry soil and full sun; it will thrive even in a sunbaked gravel path. One treatment is to cut it to the ground after flowering. The variety *coccineus* has a much brighter colour than the common *P. capensis*.

PIERIS

P. floribunda is a familiar and beautiful evergreen bush, 3–6 ft. high, with slender upright spikes of white urn-shaped flowers in March–April; good with heaths. *P. f.* var. *elongata* is a good form of it.

†*P. formosa* makes a very handsome tall bush in various Cornish woodland gardens, reaching 20 ft. or even more. The leaves are dark green, with pink young shoots and stiff 6-inch spikes of fine white flowers, with a slight scent something like lily-of-the-valley. There is a noted plant of this at Pentillie Castle, St. Mellion, Cornwall, still in perfect health and probably more than a century old. It is 20 ft. high and some 30 ft. across.

*†*P. Forrestii*. In a sheltered garden, well protected from draughts, this is a superb plant. It is a vigorous grower, making a solid dark bush with effective drooping panicles of large white flowers and young upright leaf-growths like flames of the clearest rose-scarlet, almost as bright as *poinsettia*.

P. japonica. Another familiar bush, slightly earlier than *P. floribunda*, with heavy clusters of drooping spikes of small white flowers in March–April, followed by coppery young shoots. Excellent for general planting, though less beautiful than *Forrestii* or *taiwanensis*.

*P. *taiwanensis*. E. H. Wilson, the great plant collector who introduced this, called it "probably the finest of a very worthy genus." I think it is probably the best *pieris* for general cultivation in mild gardens, being easier to satisfy than the superb but wind-tender *P. Forrestii* (which Wilson had not seen). It is, at any rate, one of the shrubs which "earns its keep" all the year round, for its sprays of ivory-white flowers, like little inverted urns, make the bush progressively whiter for many weeks from February till the end of April; then the young growth breaks out in red and copper, changing to light and dark green; and in September the sprays of brown-pink buds begin already to decorate the bush in readiness for spring. It will reach 10 ft. in time, and is certainly worth a good place in any mild garden which can give it a cool half-shady position in lime-free soil. To do it justice, do not plant it near any very showy competitor: a cold white, such as the flowers of *Rhododendron fragrantissimum*, would dull the whiteness of the *pieris*.

PILEOSTEGIA

P. viburnoides. A handsome self-clinging climber for a half-shady wall or rock, with leathery evergreen leaves rather like those of *laurustinus*, and umbels of cream-white flowers in August–September.

PIMELEA

‡*P. ferruginea*, a bushlet a foot or so high, with terminal heads of bright-pink flowers; seldom out of flower; hardy enough for mild gardens except in an abnormal season. *P. lævigata*, with narrow glaucous leaves and white flowers, is another worth growing; also *P. coarctata*, with white flowers on a grey mat.

PITTOSPORUM. See page 341.

POLYGALA

‡*P. myrtifolia* (syn. *P. Dalmaisiana*). A shrubby milkwort, making a bush some 5 ft. high, covered with brilliant purple flowers like a much-enlarged milkwort, with a white brush of anthers. Very effective, easily grown, tender but easily propagated. *P.*

A General Planting List

virgata, with vivid magenta-purple flowers, should also be tried; a brilliant plant, excellent at Tresco.

POTENTILLA

P. fruticosa varieties. The shrubby *potentillas* akin to *P. fruticosa* include some beautiful plants—bushes from 1 ft. to 4 ft. high, with green or silver leaves, and flowers from white to deep yellow. *P. f. Friedrichsenii*, light yellow, and its paler variety, *ochroleuca*, are solid bushes, very long-flowering, which can be used as a 3-ft. hedge. *P. Vilmoriniana*, with silver leaves and pale-yellow flowers, is beautiful but sometimes not a very good grower and not free enough. The late Reginald Farrer collected a wide range of forms in China, including some white and yellow forms which are extremely free-flowering. *P. Wardii* is a fine deep-yellow one.

PROSTANTHERA [1]

*‡*P. rotundifolia*. One of the outstanding shrubs for very mild gardens. It comes from Tasmania and Australia, and makes a bush 5 ft., rarely 10 ft., high, with small round leaves, powerfully aromatic; in April it is a mass of vivid purple flowers and almost black buds. It used to be a splendid sight at Ludgvan Rectory, Pendrea, Trebah, and other Cornish gardens before the frost of December 1938. It is tender and not very long-lived, but easily propagated from cuttings and easily grown in sandy peat in a hot sheltered spot.

P. cuneata, which is much hardier than *rotundifolia*, is a 2-ft. bush with small wedge-shaped leaves crowded on the short growths, and lilac-white flowers spotted with purple, fairly large, free enough to be showy on a well-established plant, borne in May and again in autumn. This, too, is aromatic. Give it a hot place. It does not mind some wind. Sometimes miscalled *P. thymifolia*.

For other *prostantheras*, see page 343.

PRUNUS. See Chapter XIII.

PUNICA. POMEGRANATE.

P. Granatum. Fairly often grown on walls, but not a rewarding plant here, as its handsome fruits are seldom produced and probably never ripened in this climate, and its beautiful orange-vermilion flowers are seldom borne freely enough to be effective.

[1] Note the spelling: not Prostranthera.

Pyracantha
  P. angustifolia. This Fire-thorn carries its orange-yellow berries till March, when those of the common sort (*P. coccinea Lalandii*) have long fallen; it has narrow leaves, grey felted underneath, and the berries are yellow in November, only turning orange in the New Year.
  *P. atalantioides (syn. *P. Gibbsii*) is a splendid bush with vigorous straight growths, which can be trained to make a tree 20 ft. high. The masses of scarlet berries with a black eye mature in November and last generally till spring.
  *P. coccinea, var. *Lalandii.* One of the best evergreen wall coverings, thriving even on exposed or shady walls, but excellent as a bush. No need to recommend it for its extraordinary profusion of orange-scarlet berries from October onwards. It has only one defect: birds take the berries. The plant must be transplanted when small. Get a good form: it is variable. It makes a good prickly hedge, 7 ft. or 8 ft. high.
  P. Rogersiana is another good one, with small, narrow, glossy leaves, masses of cream-white flowers, and orange-red, orange-yellow, or yellow berries. I have seen it very effective as a low bush in a bank, fronted by a mass of *Lithospermum* "Heavenly Blue."

Pyrus. See Chapter XIII.

Raphiolepis
  R. japonica (syn. *R. ovata*). A rounded bush with handsome evergreen leaves, tough and wind-hardy; white fragrant flowers in clusters. It wants a hot position if it is to flower freely; hardy.
  R. indica is similar but with narrower leaves.
  R. Delacouri is a hybrid with very pretty pink flowers; handsome in leaf, and really effective in flower when the growth is well enough ripened. In the Cornish climate it is hardy enough but erratic in flowering; very good at Bournemouth, or in the hotter climate of the Riviera.

Rhamnus
  §*R. Alaternus variegata.* One of the few really good variegated shrubs; leaves edged cream-white; wind-hardy.

Rhododendron. See Chapter XIV.

Rhus

R. cotinoides, a large bush, reaching 10–15 ft. in good soil, with large round leaves; one of the very best shrubs for autumn colour.

R. Cotinus, smoke bush or Venetian sumach, is the well-known bush completely covered in late summer with a pinkish smoke of inflorescence—flower and seed. Give this and *cotinoides* poor soil. It grows wild on stony hillsides.

R. Cotinus rubrifolius. This purple-leaved form of the smoke bush is, with the purple-leaved *Berberis vulgaris*, the best of purple-leaved shrubs. Very beautiful when light shines through its leaves, and valuable for bringing a dark tone into a flower-border. Try it with June irises such as "Betelgeux" and "Senlac," lupins such as "Pink Pearl" or "G. Russell," and *Aquilegia kashmiriana* and pink hybrids; or in the August border with clematises such as "Gipsy Queen," *Jackmani superba*, or "Comtesse de Bouchard"; *Salvia turkestanica* and *S. nemorosa*; *Lavatera Olbia*, and *Sidalcea* "Sussex Beauty"; phloxes such as "Daily Sketch," "Undine" or "Le Mahdi"; and *Thalictrum dipterocarpum*. It shows its best colour if drastically pruned in February or March, according to climate.

R. trichocarpa, a small deciduous tree, is one of the most beautiful shrubs for autumn colour: the pinnate leaves turn vivid orange-scarlet.

§*R. typhina*, stag's-horn sumach, has large pinnate leaves, big hairy panicles of flower and fruit, and scarlet autumn colours (here as well as up-country). This familiar plant is wind-hardy and very easy to grow: in New England it makes splashes of scarlet among the wild michaelmas daisies. Prune hard. Choose the female form.

Ribes

R. sanguineum splendens. This is a specially good form of the red flowering currant. "King Edward VII" is another richly coloured one, a fortnight later. It is remarkable how well *ribes* stands sea-wind; it is one of the most useful shrubs for quick show in an exposed garden. It makes an excellent hedge, e.g. for backing a flower-border in a kitchen garden.

R. speciosum, with small pendent blood-red flowers, is a distinctive shrub, and can make a considerable show of colour at its best.

ROMNEYA. CALIFORNIAN TREE POPPY.

R. Coulteri. One of the loveliest of flowers—a white poppy 5 inches across, with petals like thin crumpled silk, a mass of yellow stamens, and a pleasant scent. Leaves and buds are bluish-green. Normally it reaches about 6 ft., but at its best (e.g. at Caerhays and elsewhere in Cornwall) it may reach 12 ft. It flowers for several months from July onwards. It is hardy here, and grows very freely when once it gets started, but it detests root disturbance, and should be planted with the ball of the roots unbroken, if pot-grown. Give it full sun and good drainage, in a place where it can spread. Beautiful as it is, it cannot be recommended for a small garden, as it runs at the root. And it is a singularly capricious plant.

R. trichocalyx is very similar.[1] In some gardens this is found to be the better garden plant of the two: Bean's *Trees and Shrubs* says that "it is a better plant for colder-situated gardens, being of hardier constitution, not so gross in habit, and cultivated with less trouble." In California, on the contrary, *Coulteri* is preferred as a garden plant. "As a horticultural subject for outdoor planting and mass display *R. Coulteri*, with its heavy, vigorous, leafy stems and numerous large clusters of flowers, is by far superior to *R. trichocalyx*. But as a cut flower the latter is preferable, since the slender stems with their three to five closely clustered flowers are far more graceful." [2]

ROSE

No attempt will be made here to suggest an adequate selection from the immense wealth of roses, but here are a few plants, especially species, which are worth remembering when making a choice.

R. bracteata, Macartney rose. This is a distinguished-looking species, worth growing on a wall in the mild counties. The large white flowers have a distinctive smell, and the evergreen foliage is handsome.

[1] The differences between the two species are: *Coulteri's* flower buds are smooth and beaked at the top; in *trichocalyx* they are silky and nearly beakless. *Coulteri* has thicker leafier stems, with more numerous flowers borne on longer stalks. The lower leaves of *Coulteri* and many of its upper ones are larger, thicker, and more broadly divided. See the study by Dr. Carl Wolf, based on examination of the wild plants, in *California Plant Notes II. Rancho Santa Ana Botanic Gardens, Orange County, California.*

[2] *Ibid.*

*R. "Mermaid," a superb hybrid of R. *bracteata*, has decorative foliage and very large, single, yellow flowers with a crown of deeper yellow stamens, beautiful in every stage. No rose better deserves a place on a sunny wall.

R. *lævigata*, Cherokee rose. Where it flourishes, this is surely the most beautiful of wild roses—which is saying much. Its white cups, 5 inches across, stand up, perfectly spaced, all along the arching growths, so that the bush is a fountain of white. No other rose so combines distinction with profusion. Unfortunately, so far as I know it never makes such a show in this country as it does at La Mortola (on the Riviera) at the end of April. It needs a mild climate and plenty of sun.

*R. *anemonoides* (formerly called R. *sinica anemone*) is near *lævigata*, perhaps a hybrid of it. The large flowers are flatter than *lævigata*'s, and of a lovely rose-pink. The plant associates well with the white one, and must be classed with it amongst the most beautiful of roses. There is a variety with flowers much deeper in colour, almost carmine; it is worth growing with the type, but is less beautiful in itself. R. *anemonoides* does well in some gardens in this country and should be more grown; it is fairly hardy, but likes a hot wall. Bend the growths zigzag when fastening it to the wall, so as to encourage short flowering growths.

*R. *Moyesii*, with its single blood-red flowers in June, is unsurpassed in colour at its best; but it is a variable plant. The flagon-shaped red hips are effective too. It is a rampant grower, with shoots 10 ft. high, wind-hardy, very thorny.

*R. "Geranium," raised at Wisley, is an outstanding hybrid of *Moyesii*, with blood-red flowers and hips that ripen to the most vivid scarlet. The bush is more compact and manageable than *Moyesii*.

R. *Hillieri*, a cross between *Moyesii* and R. *Willmottiæ*, deep blood-red, flowers earlier than *Moyesii*, and often flowers sparsely again in autumn.

R. *highdownensis*, with rampant arching growths and carmine flowers, is not an improvement on *Moyesii*, but it can make a fine show in fruit. *Fargesii* is another.

R. *Hugonis*, with small leaves and small yellow flowers, makes a lovely brief show in May; and so does its hybrid, *cantabridgensis*, which has larger flowers and makes more show.

Other yellows include:

R. primula, a delightful bush with primrose-yellow flowers 1½ inches across, on red twigs. Its long flowering season begins as early as April.

R. hispida (syn. *spinosissima* var. *ochroleuca*) is pale yellow in May, good with yellow tulips such as "Mrs. Moon." Also *R. spinosissima lutea*, *R. xanthina spontanea* (yellow), and the lovely milk-white *R. spinosissima altaica*.

R. Banksiæ is at its best a superb bush or climber, especially in its single yellow form, and the widespread idea that it cannot be grown well in our cool climate is by no means fully justified. But the plant wants all the sunlight it can get and lots of room; and the strong growths require three years before flowering, since the flowers are borne, not on the laterals that spring direct from the main rods, but on the lateral twigs on these laterals. So to prune this rose in the conventional fashion is to make its flowering impossible. Generally it needs no pruning except removal of dead and spent wood; but like many other wild roses, it bursts up with renewed vigour if occasionally cut right down. The double yellow form is the one most often seen in this country: there is also an effective double white.

R. "Fortune's Yellow." Perhaps to see this beautiful rose at its best one must go to France or Italy; but it is too seldom seen here. Plant it by a pillar or pergola, in limy soil, in a hot place, where you can look up at masses of large, loosely-double flowers, yellow flushed with pink.

Amongst the many splendidly rampant white roses suitable for growing up trees, none excels *R. filipes*, with large trusses of small white flowers, yellow anthered, single or semi-double, very fragrant. And plants such as the old "Dundee Rambler" and "Bennett's Seedling" still hold their own. *R. moschata floribunda* and *R. m. grandiflora* make decorative large bushes for a wild place, but need cutting down periodically. Another beautiful species is *R. sino-Wilsoni*.

Amongst the many pink bush roses the species *R. Willmottiæ* is one of the best. It makes a large bush with elegant little leaves, pink flowers an inch across for a long season, and small red hips. Give it a hot place where its prickles will not be a nuisance.

R. multibracteata is another good pink, flowering from June till September. It has red hips and spines.

*R. rubrifolia has many uses, for besides its pleasant pink flowers and red hips it has foliage of outstanding beauty of colour. Try this glaucous, purple-flushed bush with purple flowers such as dark clematis and gladiolus or a lilac pentstemon, or with the pink of *Anemone* "Queen Charlotte," or with the muted pink of *Dictamnus fraxinella* or the common martagon lily.

As for the immense number of garden hybrids, I will only say here that few climbers make a better show for a long time than the now-familiar pink, *"Albertine." Other good pinks are "Mary Wallace," "Mrs. Rosalie Wrinch," and the old "Lady Waterlow." For long-sustained colour effect no shrubs in the garden excel the better sorts of "Poulsen" roses, such as the deep scarlet "Karen Poulsen" and its successors.

ROSMARINUS. ROSEMARY.

§*R. officinalis*, common rosemary, that familiar and cherished plant, has many uses, including the flavouring of potatoes. For its scent it is a delightful plant to grow beside a door or gateway. Its grey-green colour goes well with many flowers, including pink China roses. It stands wind well, even on the sea-front (e.g. at Falmouth); and it makes a good informal hedge, especially if its upright variety, *pyramidalis*, is used. There is a white-flowered form.

R. prostratus is a more tender prostrate variety, most effectively blue with flowers when streaming down the face of a retaining wall in full sun.

R. corsicus is hardier than *prostratus*, an excellent plant of trailing habit, very wind-hardy. Its bright-blue flowers are beautiful in colour with such plants as the prostrate blue phlox and *Cytisus kewensis*. Grown in severe exposure, it keeps down to about a foot high, but in shelter it may, I understand, reach 4 ft.

†*R.* "Tuscan Blue." In the absence of a specific name this name may serve to distinguish a very distinct plant which I brought from Tuscany. It has bright-green (not grey-green) leaves, flat, and much broader than those of the common sort, white beneath, with a different scent, very pungent and pleasant. The flowers are much larger than those of the common sort and bright blue;

in Tuscany, hedges of this plant are conspicuous from a distance owing to their ceanothus blue. The plant is hardy in the mild counties, but a good deal tenderer than the common sort; it only flowers freely if the yard-long spikes are topped. It prefers a very hot well-drained position such as the edge of a retaining wall facing south. This, like the common rosemary, is useful as a quick-growing nurse for other shrubs. It is worth growing for its smell, and in hotter drier gardens than mine may make some show of blue.

RUBUS

R. deliciosus, most beautiful of the brambles, makes a bush 3–5 ft. high, and is not one of the spreaders. The white flowers in May are like small single roses.

SALVIA

S. Grahamii, Black-currant sage. A 3-ft. bush with ovate leaves that smell just like black-currant leaves when crushed; flowers rosy-red, persistent but not very showy; fairly hardy.
‡*S. Greggii* is rather similar, but the leaves are narrowly oblong, on drooping growths, with a different smell; flowers carmine. A good deal less hardy than *Grahami* and only suitable for mild gardens.
S. rutilans, with scarlet flowers and foliage scented like pine-apple, is another good half-hardy sage; and there are others.

SANTOLINA

§*S. Chamæcyparissus*, the common lavender cotton, is the familiar aromatic white-leaved bush, good for bold edgings or dry walls; very wind-hardy; best on poor soil. The yellow flower-heads are a pity, but the plant is one of the best of grey-leaved shrubs, especially if pruned nearly to the ground each spring so that it does not sprawl.

SARCOCOCCA

S. humilis (1½ ft.), *S. ruscifolia* (2 ft.), and *S. Hookeriana* (3 ft.) are very neat evergreens, with polished dark-green foliage, and in-conspicuous but very fragrant flowers in winter. They can thrive in the shade and drip of trees; and walking in the garden in January you may stop and wonder where the scent comes from.

SCHIZANDRA

S. rubriflora, a rampant, deciduous, twining climber, has dark-crimson flowers hanging from the leaf-axils like fruits, and these are followed by hanging bunches of vivid red fruits like narrow grape-clusters. It makes a surprising show of fruit-clusters late in the year.

S. chinensis has inconspicuous pink flowers and showy scarlet fruits; and there are several others.

SCHIZOPHRAGMA

S. hydrangeoides. Like a climbing *hydrangea*, and often confused with *H. petiolaris*, a commoner plant. Flat flower-heads, with yellowish-white fertile flowers and some sterile flowers consisting of a single white sepal; deciduous leaves 5 inches long, generally heart-shaped. Good for growing up a tree in half-shade or on an east wall; self-clinging like ivy; very hardy.

**S. integrifolium*, a much more interesting plant, is a climber with large deciduous leaves (up to 7 inches long) tapering to a long point; the inflorescence, a foot across, consists of small fertile flowers, and each of the branchlets on which these are borne ends in one large drooping milk-white leaf. The plant has handsome foliage, and the white rings of the flower-heads make a striking effect up the trunk of a tree. It is self-clinging, growing on cliffs in China as tree-ivy does here. It is hardy, and thrives on an east wall even in the Cotswold climate.

SEMELE

‡*S. androgyna*. A rampant evergreen climber, with luxuriant pinnate foliage—flattened branches as in "Butcher's Broom." It makes a striking pattern in some Cornish gardens.

SENECIO

S. scandens, a free-growing scrambling climber, with panicles of yellow daisies in late autumn. Hardy in the mild counties, but may become a pest. For other *senecios* see pages 31 and 32.

SKIMMIA

S. Foremanii and *S. Fortunei* are good forms of this very useful evergreen. They grow 3 ft. high or more, with clusters of small white flowers, not conspicuous but fragrant, and showy scarlet fruits; with these hermaphrodite forms one can be sure of berries without having to trouble about planting both sexes. They stand much wind and shade; move well, but rob the soil.

SOLANUM

S. crispum. A rampant bush or wall shrub, with large heads of blue potato flowers. Given plenty of room, plenty of sun, and hard pruning each spring, it can be most effective. The variety *autumnalis, or "Glasnevin" variety, is more slender, with deeper-coloured flowers; it begins in May and continues till September; a very fine plant. Try this with flowers of a warm contrasting colour, such as the orange *Lilium croceum* or the scarlet *L. Heldreichii.*

S. jasminoides var. *album*. This ranks with *Clematis montana rubens* amongst the very best of rampant climbers. Its slender shoots will run up a tree very quickly, and its white stars, like wide-open jasmine flowers, are showered, when it is doing well, with extraordinary profusion from midsummer till late autumn. It will sprawl on an outhouse roof or over tree tops, remaining decorative even so late in the year as November. Plant it well away from the bush it is to climb up, so that it is not starved; for such a plant it may be worth taking the trouble to sink an old barrel in the ground, filling it with good soil so as to give the climber a good start without root-encroachment. There is a large-flowered form, and one, the wild type, with smoke-blue flowers.

SOPHORA

S. japonica. A very beautiful deciduous tree, Chinese. It has dark, ferny, pinnate foliage, exceptionally handsome, and quantities of small cream-white pea-flowers in bunches all over the tree in September. In our climate it may not flower until it reaches an age of thirty or forty years, but in the more extreme mid-European climate it flowers much sooner. There are two magnificent trees of this on the lawn at Kew (see illustration in Bean's *Trees and Shrubs*, vol. II). This is one of the trees that should be more planted here in sheltered spacious public places. It is most effectively used so in Zürich.

S. microphylla, from New Zealand and Chile, is very different. It begins as a shrub with wiry zigzag stems and few leaves, but on reaching about 10 ft. it assumes a tree-like shape with leafy top and straight branches. The leaves are pinnate, with very numerous leaflets not more than ⅛ inch long. The drooping flowers, rather tubular in shape, are yellow, showy, but not free from greenish tinge.

S. *macrocarpa*, a Chilean, is a shrub or a small tree with larger leaflets than *S. tetraptera*'s (¾–1½ inches long) and effective racemes of yellow flowers about an inch long.

*S. *tetraptera* (syn. *Edwardsia grandiflora*), from both Chile and New Zealand, makes a tree with upstanding trunk, about 20 ft. high here, but taller in the wild. In the mild counties it is evergreen; the pinnate leaves have oblong leaflets up to ¾ inch long, decorative in pattern, with tawny stalks and shoots; and the half-tubular flowers, 1–2 inches long in racemes, are bright yellow and very effective. In some South-coast gardens this makes a brilliant show against blue sky. New Zealanders value it much—their "Kowhai" tree.

‡S. *secundiflora*, with shiny evergreen leaves and violet flowers, from Texas and Mexico, is perhaps worth trying here in hot situations.

S. *viciifolia* makes an 8-ft. bush of arching growths, with deciduous pinnate leaves and quantities of small pea-flowers, violet-blue and white. In cold gardens it may need some shelter, but it is hardy in the milder counties.

SORBUS. See Chapter XIII. page 280.

SPARTIUM. See page 73.

SPIRÆA

*S. *arguta*. This well-known hybrid bush, covered with little white star-clusters in April–May, is one of the best spring shrubs for any garden; and S. *Thunbergii*, one of its parents, flowering in March–April, is very good too.

S. *bracteata*, S. "Vanhouttei," S. *prunifolia* and its double form, and *S. *trichocarpa*, are larger, loaded with white in summer; all first-class plants.

S. *japonica* "Anthony Waterer" is a familiar dwarf, with flat heads of rose-crimson, never failing from June till the end of September.

S. *decumbens*, a very dwarf white, will stand poor soil and drought.

Besides these there are the vigorous fern-leaved species, such as *S. Aitchisonii, Lindleyana, Veitchii,* and *sorbifolia,* with large plumes of creamy Meadow-sweet flowers in late summer, which look fine beside a pond.

Lastly, there is the well-known *S. discolor (ariæfolia),* which makes a big bush covered with cream-white at midsummer, quickly browned but lovely while it lasts, especially beside reflecting water.

STACHYURUS

S. chinensis. A spreading deciduous bush some 8 ft. high with stiff drooping catkins of pale-yellow flowers in February–March. A distinctive plant. *S. præcox,* its Japanese counterpart, flowers about a fortnight earlier.

STAPHYLEA

S. colchica, a deciduous bush some 10 ft. high, most easily grown, with bunches of small flowers, translucent white, scented rather like tuberose, followed by conspicuous inflated seed-capsules. This is better than *S. pinnata,* and can be really effective. *S. c. Coulombieri* is a good hybrid.

*S. *holocarpa* var. *rosea.* This small tree, 20–30 ft. high, has proved to be one of the treasures of our gardens. In April it is hung with drooping clusters of small palest-pink flowers with pink stalks— a lovely sight against a dark background. Coming from Hupeh, in Central China, it should be hardy.

STRANVÆSIA

§*S. Davidiana.* A handsome evergreen bush, spreading 20–30 ft., with white flower-heads and effective bunches of scarlet berries like hawthorn. Wind-hardy, and first-rate for a large windscreen. *S. D. undulata,* generally a lower bush up to 10 ft. high, has coral-red berries.

S. salicifolia is similar to *Davidiana,* but more erect; it has been strongly recommended in Chapter III as a wind-hardy shrub for seaside planting.

STEWARTIA

*S. *koreana,* from Korea, is a deciduous tree reaching 50 ft. at home, perhaps not more than 20 ft. here, with round buds and five-sepalled flowers, crimped at the edge, three inches across, with whitish filaments. Seeing this in the Arnold Arboretum before the war, I thought it was probably the best of the *stewartias*; at any rate, it is a very fine plant and perfectly hardy.

S. *Malacodendron* (syn. *virginica*). A deciduous bush reaching 15 ft. or more, from the South-eastern United States, hardy in the climate of Kew. The flowers are fully 3 inches across, five-petalled, like open silky single roses or *Eucryphia* flowers, sometimes streaked with crimson at the base, with showy purplish stamens and blue anthers. It is one of the finest shrubs flowering in July-August, but a scarce plant. It wants moist soil.

S. *monodelpha*, akin to S. *sinensis*, makes a tree 50-80 ft. high in Southern Japan. Its small flowers have violet anthers, and the seed-capsules are much smaller than those of *sinensis*—only $\frac{1}{3}$ inch across.

*S. *ovata* (syn. S. *pentagyna*). A deciduous shrub from the South-eastern United States, reaching 15-20 ft. In the wild it grows in thickets beside streams. The bright-green leaves colour orange and red in autumn. The flower-buds are pink-flushed, and the silky petals make a translucent white bowl, fringed at the edge, with yellow stamens. In the beautiful form, *grandiflora*, the stamens are purple and the flowers may be rather larger—up to $4\frac{1}{2}$ inches across. Both forms are hardy, and flower in July-August, when the show of flowering shrubs is falling off.

*S. *Pseudo-Camellia*. A deciduous tree, reaching 50 ft. in Japan, smaller as yet here. The thick leaves colour vividly before falling. The flowers, short-lived but quickly replaced and very free, are 2-3 inches across, hemispherical, with cupped petals, the stamens white with orange-yellow anthers. Give it wind-shelter, sun at the head, shade and damp at the root. This thrives in mild gardens here, a rewarding plant.

S. *serrata* is Japanese, reaching 30 ft., with cup-shaped flowers $2-2\frac{1}{2}$ inches across, flushed on the outside, in June.

*S. *sinensis* is a deciduous tree of graceful habit, from Central China, some 30 ft. high, with fragrant, cup-shaped, white flowers $1\frac{1}{2}$ inches across, at the leaf axils. The young growths are silvered with down, and the leaves colour most brilliantly before falling. The bark too is decorative. At Caerhays this is considered the finest of the *stewartias* grown there.

Styrax

*S. *japonica*. A tree some 25 ft. high, branching in horizontal tiers, each branch being whitened underneath in June with a vast number of hanging 5-petalled snowdrops. Plant this above a path, where you can look up at it from below. It is one of the most beautiful of hardy shrubs in its discreet way.

*S. Obassia. This, too, is a lovely plant; very different in appearance, since its leaves are very large, some 6 inches long. The white flowers, 20 or more together, are borne in racemes 7 inches long, in June. Like *japonica*, it is fragrant. It does well in various woodland gardens here, in damp soil.

S. Hemsleyanum has smaller leaves than *Obassia's*, and the white flowers, 20 or 30 together, are borne in upright panicles some 5 inches long. A very beautiful plant.

S. Wilsonii produces its little white hanging stars when only a few feet high; but the general opinion seems to be that it is proving a disappointing plant, short-lived perhaps because it flowers so freely when so young. Other species include *officinalis*, *Veitchiorum*, and *lankongense*.

SYRINGA. LILAC.

Few shrubs make a finer decoration than some of the more recent single-flowered lilacs, such as: *"Marshal Foch," violet; *"Vestale," a superb white; "Masséna," deep violet, and "Lamartine," an early hyacinth-flowered one. The *Rouen lilac is a grand plant, even better than the old Persian lilac. There are some good species, notably *Sweginzowii superba*, which is covered with light pinkish plumes in June; and some beautiful hybrids of these species have lately been introduced.

No attempt will be made here to review this grand series of shrubs. But it may be worth offering this warning. Do not expect lilacs to be such rewarding plants in the mild climate and acid soils of South-west England as they are in the Midlands and Eastern counties. In the Land's End peninsula, for instance, I have never seen a really good lilac bush. Remember also that the highly bred garden varieties need good soil, whereas the common one thrives even in the poorest stuff.

TAMARIX. See pages 32–33.

TECOMA. See CAMPSIS, page 91.

TEUCRIUM

T. fruticans. One of the best grey-leaved shrubs. The stems and the undersides of the leaves are white, the upper side of the leaf grey-green, the salvia flowers lavender-blue. The bush has many decorative uses. It can be used as an informal hedge. It goes well in colour with *Ceanothus thyrsiflorus griseus*, or with *Convolvulus cneorum* and the grey woolly thyme (*T. lanuginosus*), or with pale-yellow gladiolus. If grown in the open it may be cut down by frost, but it generally recovers.

There is a form of this from the Atlas Mountains with greener, more slender growth and flowers of much brighter powder-blue; a beautiful plant, but less vigorous and a good deal more tender.

TRACHELOSPERMUM

***T. jasminoides*. This is a very beautiful climber, with its dark, polished, evergreen leaves leathery in texture, and clusters of very fragrant white flowers like jasmine, an inch across, in summer. It is hardier than is generally recognised, and can be planted on a wall in the mild counties with little risk of its being killed. It will stand some shade.

The variety *Wilsoni* has decorative narrow leaves, bronzed and veined; it flowers well on a sunny wall at Rowallane, co. Down, but many growers find it reluctant to flower. There is also a form with white-variegated foliage, sometimes called *T. radicans variegata*, hardy and quite pretty in its way, but always flowerless, apparently.

***T. japonicum* (or *T. jasminoides* var. *japonicum*) is very similar to *jasminoides*, but more vigorous and probably hardier, with larger oval leaves, conspicuously veined, bronzy-crimson in winter. In France and Italy it covers whole house fronts with dark polished green, starred with white flowers. Grown up the pillars of a veranda, the two plants give a prolonged flowering season.

T. asiaticum (syns. *divaricatum* and *crocostemon*) is hardier than *jasminoides*, and on a hot wall makes a profuse show of yellowish-white flowers, without the scent of *jasminoides*.

TRICUSPIDARIA

*§*T. lanceolata*. One of the very best large shrubs for mild gardens. Dark-green evergreen leaves; hanging flowers of solid rose-crimson, in splendid profusion, in May–June. The bush reaches about 20 ft. in a sheltered position and good soil. It stands cutting back, making dense growth if clipped. Like other plants from the Chilean forest, it likes shade at the root; apart

from that, it is not particular. It will not stand the fullest blast of sea-wind, but endures a great deal, and makes a fine tall windbreak in woodland. (There is a tall hedge of it, 80 yards long, planted as a wind-screen in Caerhays wood.) It is easily propagated from seed or cuttings: seedlings perhaps make better plants. Generally it is hardy enough for the mild maritime counties, but in West Cornwall it was hard hit—in some cases killed—by the great frost of 1947.

In planting a small garden in the mild counties, this is one of the first plants I should choose. Put it, if possible, on the eastern side of the garden, so that evening light will brighten its rose to scarlet.

This is one of the plants that William Lobb introduced. It is time that we had an English name, a pet name, for it. Its alternative name, *Crinodendron Hookeri*, is hardly less cumbrous. Perhaps "lantern tree" would do.

T. dependens, another Chilean but of very different appearance, with hanging white flowers in August, is often shy-flowering, and is much less effective than the red *lanceolata*; but it is hardy and wind-resistant, and may be worth its place if it gets full sunlight. There is a huge bush of this at Fota, near Cork, and a small tree with upstanding trunks at Garinish Island, Kerry.

VACCINIUM

V. arctostaphylos. A deciduous bush reaching 5 ft. high and through, with comparatively large bell-shaped flowers, flushed crimson, in late summer, and foliage vividly scarlet in late autumn. The stems of young growths are bright red. Like other deciduous *vacciniums*, it does not, so far as I know, colour well in the mild Cornish climate. The true plant is Caucasian, much hardier than *V. padifolium* from Madeira, which often carries its name.

V. corymbosum. This American blueberry makes a bush 4 ft. or more, with pale-green foliage, small, pale-pink, urn-shaped flowers in May, blue-black berries, and most brilliant autumn colours in suitable climates.

V. Delavayi. A most attractive, dwarf, evergreen bush with small round leaves and drooping clusters of white flowers and pink bracts, followed by blue-purple fruits. Slow to reach the flowering stage. When established, it throws up some strong stems which send out long horizontal shoots.

V. glauco-album. A 5-ft. bush of graceful habit, with arching growths; the leaves milky-blue underneath, racemes of small pink flowers with bluish-white bracts, and black berries overlaid with conspicuous blue-white bloom. A distinguished-looking plant, for mild counties only.

**V. Mortinia.* Though it comes from the mountains of Ecuador, right on the Equator, this is quite hardy in the mild counties. Grown in an exposed site, it is the most decorative of the *vacciniums*, beautiful all the year round. It makes wide low fronds of small evergreen leaves, purplish-red in young growth, with small pink flowers hanging underneath and plum-purple fruits like bilberries. It looks well among rocks, especially with the coppery young growths of *Rhododendron oleifolium*.

V. ovatum is another very good one—an upright evergreen, reaching 8–10 ft. with red stems, decorative in pattern and coppery-red in spring, and small pinkish-white flowers. It needs shelter from cutting winds.

V. pennsylvanicum, a low compact bush with small pinkish-white flowers, bilberry fruits, and fine autumn colour.

V. stamineum, deerberry, with little, greenish, five-pointed, star flowers (unlike those of other *vacciniums*) is pretty in its discreet way.

V. virgatum (confused with *corymbosum*) is a 3–5-ft. bush, pretty when bearing its pink flowers, and most brilliant when the leaf colours in autumn.

V. Vitis-idæa is the charming, native, creeping evergreen, cowberry, with pink flowers and edible red fruits.

VERONICA[1]

A number of shrubby veronicas, specially good for windshelter or for standing wind, have been noted in Chapter II. Here are some others of decorative value.

V. "Aoira." A good white, very free-flowering, with narrow blue-grey foliage.

V. "Bowles Hybrid" is a delightful rounded bush 2 ft. high or less, completely covered with lilac flowers in May and often flowering a second time. It is rather tender.

‡*V. Headfortii.* This hybrid makes a rather loose-growing bush 2–3 ft. high, with light panicles of blue-purple flower, vivid and

[1] Now called "Hebe."

profuse. This is a most beautiful plant, but it wants shelter and is tender.

‡*V. Hulkeana*, the most beautiful of the veronicas, makes flower-panicles a foot long, composed of little drooping streamers of lilac flowers. In sheltered gardens up-country it is often grown very well, and it is excellent as a greenhouse plant; but apparently it cannot stand sea-winds. Many a Cornish gardener has tried it repeatedly without success. In the South Island of New Zealand, in the only locality where it grows, it lives in the perpendicular faces of gullies, as does *Pachystegia insignis* (see page 265).

V. lavaudiana is similar, but the leaf has a crimson edge-line. It is reputed to be easier to grow.

V. leiophylla and *V. parviflora*. *V. parviflora* is a well-known bushy species, sometimes reaching the stature of a small tree, with narrow leaves and profuse slender spikes of bushy-white flowers. *V. leiophylla* is very similar but hardier and with larger flower-spikes; very good.

V. speciosa. This species, with claret-crimson flower-spikes and broad thick leaves, grows on rocks near the sea's edge in New Zealand, within reach of the spray and even of the splash of the sea. It has yielded many extremely showy hybrids, mostly frost-tender, and apparently less wind-hardy than the type; but these are very easily propagated from cuttings, very fast-growing, and excellent for quick effect in a new garden. They include: *Veitchii* (syn. "Alicia Amherst"), hardier than the others, with fine purple-blue brushes of flower for many months; "F. W. Meyer" (syn. "La Séduisante"), wine-crimson with bronzed foliage; "Simon Deleaux," crimson; "Gloriosa," bright pink; *Cookiana*, white. The wine-coloured sorts look well with pink anemone "Queen Charlotte."

Viburnum

I will deal first with the viburnums grown for their flowers, and then with those grown chiefly for their berries.

Flowering Viburnums

*V. Carlesii shall come first, for it is one of the best of spring shrubs, and heads a group of related plants. The bush is deciduous, generally 3–5 ft. here; but I have seen a hedge of it 10 ft. high in the severe climate of Ann Arbor, Michigan. The large flower-clusters, pink-tipped in bud, open clean white, very sweet-

scented. This is a maritime plant, coming from the coast and islands of Korea; but its flowers are liable to get blasted by wind, so it is better for some shelter. It does well in woodland, if the shade is not dense. Plant it small, and do not be surprised if a branch or a whole bush dies off suddenly. It is often grafted on *V. Lantana*, and such plants commonly thrive if suckers of the stock are kept cut off; but the suckers are very persistent and troublesome, and it is no good just cutting them off at ground-level. Some maintain that plants grafted on *V. Lantana* flower more freely than plants on their own roots. Propagate it from seed if obtainable.

V. bitchiuense is a taller, more open-habited bush, reaching 9 ft. or more, and the flower-clusters, pink or pinkish-white, are smaller, making less of an umbel. In general effect a good bush of this is as beautiful in its way as *V. Carlesii*.

**V. Juddii* is a hybrid between *Carlesii* and *bitchiuense*, raised at the Arnold Arboretum, Boston. It has salmon-pink buds and white flower-heads like those of *Carlesii*, but rather more open. The scent recalls that of clove carnations. The bush is very free-flowering, and has an easy vigour of growth. From what I have seen of it so far, I feel confident that this will prove a first-class addition.

V. Burkwoodii (*V. Carlesii* × *V. utile*) has quickly become widely grown, being a vigorous, easily grown bush, with fragrant white flower-heads, some of which are often borne just after Christmas. The flowers are fragrant, and have much of the beauty of those of *Carlesii*. The bush quickly reaches 6–8 ft.; it is deciduous—partly evergreen, and can look well in an angle in a courtyard.

V. Carlcephalum is yet another good hybrid of *Carlesii* (*Carlesii* × *macrocephalum*, the wild form), with flower-heads larger than those of the other hybrids and almost too strongly scented.

**V. fragrans*. One of the few first-class winter-flowering shrubs. It grows to 10 ft. or more, deciduous for a short time only, since it makes its new leaf early. It flowers between November and February, being in full flower early in November under suitable conditions. But some forms regularly flower later in the winter. The flowers are white, touched with pink, or pure white, in small clusters, very fragrant and very freely borne if the wood is well-ripened by sunshine and if it is a good form of this variable plant (such as "Bowles variety"). The bush is easily grown, and easily propagated by layers; it thrives in diverse conditions; but some gardens find even the best forms of it very reluctant to flower. It does not like a very windy position; I think it prefers limy or neutral soil to a very acid one. In China it has long been used in palace courtyards.[1] Don't expect it to flower freely for some years. When it makes old wood with short spurs, cut them out, leaving the young growth.

V. grandiflorum, from Bhutan, is a large, sparsely branched bush with stiff growths, carrying terminal flower-clusters, red in bud and opening like those of *V. fragrans*, but larger, pink and white. It flowers mainly in mid-winter, but also intermittently over a long period. The bush is apt to be a gawky grower unless rank shoots are pinched. *V. bodnantense* is a new hybrid of this with *V. fragrans*; very vigorous, beautiful in flower, a valuable addition.

V. Opulus sterile, the familiar "Snowball," is easy, excellent for many purposes, quite good as a hedge.

*V. tomentosum plicatum, like a dwarfer version of the Snowball, is first-rate, when in full health: its masses of white and green-toned white look well with deep-blue irises. It can do with half-shade.

V. tomentosum Mariesii and **V. tomentosum* "Lanarth variety" are both very striking in May–June, making a very wide spread of branches in horizontal tiers, whitened all along the upper side with flat flower-trusses. These are at their best, perhaps, in the half-shade of a woodland, on a slope where they can be seen from above. When they are established, cut out strong upward-growing shoots, to encourage the horizontal growth.

V. t. "Rowallane variety" is another of this type.

V. macrocephalum grandiflorum has snowball flower-heads larger than those of the ordinary snowball bush. I have not seen this as beautiful as *V. tomentosum plicatum*; as usually grown, the bush hardly becomes big enough for the flowers to look well-proportioned. The wild type, *V. macrocephalum*, has large flat flower-heads ringed with sterile flowers.

*V. Tinus, laurustinus. Common as it is, this deserves a star of recommendation, for it is one of the best and most easily grown of winter-flowering shrubs, very wind-hardy in its common form,

---

[1] See *On the Eaves of the World*, by Reginald Farrer, who collected seed in China. (It was introduced rather earlier by Purdom.) He told me that for a long time he could not get the seeds to germinate: at last he tried standing an 8-ft. pipe full of snow over the seed pans, and then the seedlings "came up like cress."

A General Planting List

and useful for quick effect in a new garden since it can be moved when fairly big. The finest variety is *lucidum, with larger, polished leaves, and much larger flowers and flower-heads, brilliantly white, borne all together in March–April. This grows to 12 ft. or more and makes a magnificent show at its best, but it will not stand nearly so much wind as the common sort. Plant *laurustinus* early in autumn.

Berrying Viburnums

Besides the viburnums grown chiefly for their flower, there are those whose chief beauty is in berry, such as our native *V. Opulus* —a splendid plant for a roadside hedge in damp soil. A specially good form of this is "Notcutt's variety."

V. betulifolium. To see this at the end of October at Trewithen, in Cornwall, is to get a new idea of what berrying shrubs can contribute to a garden's decoration. Several plants are growing together as one bush 18 ft. high, the slender cascading branches heavy with translucent scarlet fruit like red currants. No flowering shrub makes such a flare of scarlet or could keep its colour for so long: this last for months. Most fortunately, birds do not take the berries. The plant is perfectly hardy, perfectly easy to grow, and very easy to propagate; but its leaves cannot stand full exposure to sea-winds, and a gale would whip off the berries. The only serious drawback is that it will not fruit freely for a good many years—eight at least, perhaps fifteen.

V. lobophyllum is another fine berrying shrub; it fruits earlier in life and has larger but fewer berries, but birds eat these berries and the bush is less effective than *betulifolium*. Others of this type include *V. hupehense*.

V. Henryi, with red berries darkening to black, makes a very decorative branching sub-evergreen bush, 10 ft. high and across.

Vitex

V. Agnus-castus. A large deciduous bush, aromatic, with narrow foliage, grey beneath, and slender 4–6-inch spikes of *ceanothus*-blue flowers in August–October. In Eastern Mediterranean countries this is a lovely sight in the alluvial silt beside dried riverbeds, each bush differing slightly from its neighbour in quality of blue or lavender. Here it is hardy on a wall up-country, hardy in the open in mild counties; but I have not seen it used with much effect. Flowering so late, it would be worth trying in a hot place, planted in quantity with *Caryopteris clandonensis* and some warm contrasting colour such as red-hot pokers.

WEIGELA (syn. *Diervilla*).

These, like the *deutzias*, are amongst the most familiar and effective of easily grown shrubs. *W. japonica* (syn. *Weigela rosea*) is the commonest species, with pink flowers in May–June; *præcox* is earlier. The hybrids between these, which are even more free-flowering, include the pink *"Avant-garde," "Bouquet Rose," "Fleur de Mai," "Abel Carrière," "styriaca," "Majestueux"; the white "Avalanche" and "Mont Blanc." The red "Eva Rathke" is a weak grower. Early pink sorts such as "Avant-garde" go well with *Pyrus floribunda*, and others with irises.

WESTRINGIA

‡ *W. rosmariniformis*, Australian rosemary. An evergreen bush, somewhat like rosemary in general appearance, 4 ft. or 5 ft., with small white flowers spotted purple; not showy, but easily propagated and grown. Coming from exposed coastal cliffs in New South Wales and Queensland, it is wind-hardy, but will not stand much frost. *W. rigida*, a Tasmanian, with effective white flowers, is likely to be hardier.

WISTERIA[1]

* *W. sinensis*. No need to recommend this, the most beautiful of hardy climbing plants and one of the most fragrant. It stands more wind than might be expected from the softness of its growths. Prune new growths to 2 or 3 buds from the old wood.
* *W. floribunda* (generally known in gardens as *W. multijuga*). This has much longer flower streamers than *sinensis*; better for a tree or pergola than for a wall. It is a variable plant; some forms have inflorescences $3\frac{1}{2}$ to 4 ft. long; there is a very beautiful white form, and a pink one, and double-flowered forms.

Other *wisterias* should be tried in mild gardens, including *W. japonica*, with pale-yellow flowers, and the white *W. venusta*, a scented species.

VINCA

V. difformis. This periwinkle is a most effective and long-flowering carpeter, with milk-blue flowers for months in winter and spring. In Southern Spain it flowers extraordinarily freely on

[1] *Wisteria*, not *wistaria*, is the original spelling. See *Standardised Plant Names* and Bailey's *Hortus*, page 8.

A General Planting List

dry, sunburnt, open ground in February–March; but it does very well also in shady ground, e.g. around the foot of *Laurustinus lucidum* and *Berberis Darwinii*. It is less likely than the other periwinkles to become a weed.

XANTHOCERAS

X. sorbifolia. A stiff bush or small tree, with deciduous pinnate leaves and erect panicles of white flowers, marked with carmine at the base, in May. A beautiful plant, which should be more often planted in the milder counties.

YUCCA

The dwarf sorts, *Y. filamentosa* and *Y. flaccida* and their varieties, are very handsome in flower and—in a good form—very free-flowering. These plants are much grown in the severe climate of the North-eastern United States, and I think the varieties grown there may be better than those commonly grown here. At any rate, they flower extraordinarily freely.

Y. gloriosa, with stiff leaves, is a magnificent plant in shape, but its noble flower-spike is seldom produced.

Y. recurvifolia, with lax leaves, is a more regular flowerer.

Y. Whipplei (now named *Hesperoyucca*) has the finest flowers of any species we can grow here. It makes a basal rosette of narrow very sharp-spined leaves, and eventually throws up a dense spike of cream-white flowers, 10 ft. or 14 ft. high, deliciously scented of lemon. Plant this on a sunny, stony, well-drained slope, with a dark background. The main plant dies after this colossal effort, but the show is worth much waiting for. This and other yuccas— "Candles of the Lord" as they are called in California—should be more planted here. Finest of all is *Y. vomerensis*, a hybrid with immense spikes, not yet, I think, in commerce.

For the "red *yucca*," *Hesperaloe parviflora*, see page 333.

ZENOBIA

Z. pulverulenta and *Z. p. nuda* (syn. *Z. speciosa*) are two of the most beautiful plants of their kind. They make long sprays of large white bells like an enlarged lily-of-the-valley; the type has the added beauty of white-dusted leaves. They are perfectly hardy, and easily grown in half-shade in lime-free soil. The green-leaved kind, *Z. nuda*, appears to be a variable plant, one form making a better bush than the other.

CHAPTER V

Acacias

FOR their outstanding beauty both of flower and of foliage, and for their flowering season, no shrubs better deserve sheltered space in mild gardens than some of the *acacias*.

"Mimosa": every Londoner remembers how the sunshine of its yellow appeared on flower-barrows in London streets in pre-war Januaries; and a good many gardeners in the mild maritime counties grow an *acacia* similar to the plants which furnished those cut flowers. The range of *acacias* is wide, and though all the species are near the margin of being too tender for this erratic climate, a fair number are worth trying in mild places. Even if the plants do eventually get cut down by frost, or broken off by wind, they can be replaced quickly if seed or young plants are obtainable, since they are easily raised from seed and grow exceptionally fast. Moreover, some species, notably *A. dealbata* and *A. melanoxylon*, show remarkable powers of recovery, breaking up again from the base or as suckers, if the main stem is cut down.

A. dealbata is hardy enough to succeed in mild gardens in Sussex (e.g. at East Grinstead) until a hard winter knocks it out, and in the counties milder than Sussex it is often grown very successfully. The variety grown in such climates as Cornwall's is considerable, as this chapter will indicate, and at Tresco in the Scillies *acacias* are among the bravest sights of the garden.

In estimating frost-hardiness we need not look backwards only; for there is still a considerable field for experiment, especially with species endemic to Tasmania and those which come both from Tasmania and from Australia. The Tasmanian climate, especially in the mountains, has bred a hardier strain of *acacias* (and of eucalypts) than the Australian strain which was used, generally, by previous generations of gardening pioneers in this country.

As for wind, some species stand a good deal. Several are plants of the foreshore and sand-dunes—*A. longifolia*, for instance, especially its Tasmanian variety *A. l. Sophoræ*. *A. verticillata* is accustomed to rough weather close to the sea, but needs close planting or some shelter if its heavy head is not to get snapped off.

In gardens where frost or wind would be too severe to allow of growing any acacias well out of doors, many can be grown in a cold greenhouse with the minimum of trouble. (And what a relief it would be to see a change from present-day conventions in the use of greenhouse space.) Planted out in a fairly high greenhouse, *A. Baileyana* is lovely in leaf and most welcome in flower just after Christmas, and few plants can endure more drought and neglect. *A. Drummondii* and a good many others less vigorous than *Baileyana* make excellent pot-plants.

The following selection is divided into three parts. The first groups together the species and hybrids with pinnate ferny leaves like those of the typical "mimosa." The second covers those which have "phyllodes"—leaf-like developments of the leaf-stalk—like normal "entire" leaves: *A. longifolia* is an example. The third covers those with spine-like phyllodes like the prickles of gorse: *A. verticillata* is an example.

Acacias with Feathered (Pinnate) Leaves

*A. *Baileyana*, Cootamundra wattle. A large bush, 10 ft. or 15 ft. high and eventually wider than its height, half-weeping in habit, with beautiful glaucous-blue foliage very finely cut, and sprays of yellow balls of fluff, just after Christmas (sometimes at Christmas). In favoured gardens it does well outside; but it is more tender than *A. dealbata*, and is better planted out in a cold greenhouse. In a greenhouse it stands much drought and neglect, but unless ruthlessly pruned immediately after flowering may push the roof off. Unfortunately the lasting of the flowers when cut is unreliable. It dislikes lime, and where grown on calcareous soil (as on the Riviera) has to be grafted on to *A. retinodes*, which tolerates lime.

*A. *dealbata*, silver wattle, from Tasmania, has feathery foliage powdered with white, greener than *Baileyana*, and light-yellow flowers. This is one of the hardiest, having survived the 1938 frost in many Cornish gardens. In a windy place its flowers are apt to get spoilt, and its trunk, though very tough, may get broken; but even if broken or cut down it often breaks again. It grows extremely fast, soon reaching 40 ft. I have seen it some 65 ft. high at Abbotsbury, near Weymouth.

A. decurrens var. *normalis* (the normal and best type of this species) is a beautiful upright tree, with foliage like *dealbata* and dense masses of yellow flowers. It comes from New South Wales, and should be tried here as well as *dealbata*. Several good forms of *decurrens*, such as *A. d. rustica*, are grown on the Riviera, and supply the "mimosa" that comes to London. Sprays should be stood in warm water after cutting, to encourage the opening of the flower-balls.

A. Farnesiana has large deep-yellow flowers, quite strongly scented.

*A. *Hanburyana* is a very beautiful hybrid between *A Baileyana* and *A. podalyriæfolia*. The foliage is very blue, some of it feathered like that of *Baileyana*, some in flat phyllodes like that of *podalyriæfolia*. The flowers are light yellow—large fluffy balls, well spaced in panicles often 2 ft. long; and the plant is a vigorous upright grower. I reckon this, with *A. cyanophylla*, the most decorative acacia I have seen.

A. pulchella has bright-green pinnate leaves, minutely divided, and small yellow flower-balls. It makes a good pot-plant, not taller than a few feet. At Tresco it does well in woodland.

A. hispidissima is similar.

†*A. terminalis* (formerly *A. elata*). A tree 60–80 ft., with handsome ash-like foliage, yellow-green when young, but dark when mature; large trusses of pale-lemon flowers. Good in woodland at Tresco, but perhaps too tender for the mainland.

ACACIAS WITH "PHYLLODES," NOT FEATHERY, BUT ENTIRE

A. armata has bright-green spine-tipped "leaves" and large bright-yellow flower-balls in spring. It makes a bush some 10 ft. high, and is one of the hardiest, doing very well in many Cornish gardens against a wall and sometimes in the open. In some gardens it survived the frost of December 1938. There are several forms.

*A. *cyanophylla*, certainly one of the most beautiful of the genus, makes a wide bush of weeping habit; the slender, downward-streaming branchlets are strung from top to bottom with bright-yellow flowers—a yellow waterfall. It is an outstanding plant, tolerant of lime.

A. cultriformis. Small foliage like a little knife-blade with a hooked point to one side, silver-grey in the best forms; large trusses of golden-yellow flower; a tall bush or small tree, hardy enough for a wall in mild gardens.

*A. *longifolia*, coast wattle or long-leaved golden wattle. A large bush 15–30 ft. high with long yellowish-green "leaves"; the flowers are in long cylindrical spikes growing from the leaf-axils. Very variable, some forms being very free-flowering, others very shy. It thrives in many Cornish gardens, though many plants were lost in 1938. At Tresco it makes one of the finest shows of the winter months, both in windy positions and in the pine wood, where it makes brakes of sunny yellow. It is worth experimenting with this on the mainland, as a mass in a windy position in sandy soil, e.g. on Hayle Towans. It is a coastal plant, often growing on sand-dunes. In Tasmania, a broad-leaved maritime form of this, *A. l. sophoræ*, makes wide bushes on the sand-dunes; seedlings from this should be hardier than the Australian form, and would serve here, as in Tasmania, to bind sand, if planted thickly.

A. floribunda (or *A. longifolia* var. *floribunda*) resembles *longifolia*, but has very narrow leaves and paler flowers.

**A. melanoxylon*, "blackwood," one of the hardiest, makes an upright dark-green tree, with yellowish-white fragrant flowers. In Tasmania, where it reaches 80–100 ft., this is one of the most valuable timber trees; and in Australia it is reckoned the best of *acacias* for panelling and furniture. Here it makes a very handsome woodland tree at Tresco; and in many mainland gardens, such as Lanarth, it does well. Trees which were cut to the ground by the 1938 frost are being replaced by new ones from suckers. The plant grows very fast, making a substantial upright tree in eight years.

A. myrtifolia. A dwarf bush from coastal sands and sandstone in Tasmania and Australia; lanceolate leaves, red stems, pale-yellow flower-balls which are fragrant. It can be used as a hedge.

A. podalyriæfolia, one of the best, has beautiful blue-green foliage. It is less vigorous than its hybrid, *Hanburyana*.

A. pycnantha, golden wattle, is perhaps the finest of all in flower. It makes a shrub or small tree with lance-shaped phyllodes up to 8 inches long, and very profuse scented flowers, balls of golden-yellow fluff. Native of Victoria and South Australia as well as New South Wales. It prefers dry conditions. At Rostrevor (near Carlingford Lough, in Ireland) it has reached 25 ft., so it can presumably succeed in other mild districts.

A. retinodes is narrow-leaved, with arching cascading habit, flowering when still young. Its scented balls of pale-yellow flower are borne in loose panicles at the ends of the young growths from late summer till winter. Hardy in the open in mild gardens, but it needs wind-shelter.

ACACIAS WITH SPINE-LIKE FOLIAGE

These are of a different type again, with the phyllodes reduced to spines.

A. juniperina, "prickly Moses," is a tall bush with short spines, deep grass green, covered in April with pale-yellow fluffy flower. It comes from Tasmania as well as from Victoria, New South Wales, and Queensland, and often grows on the coastal sands; so it would be worth trying it here on the dunes, thickly planted.

*A. verticillata (also called "prickly Moses") is similar. Both these are most satisfactory plants, fast-growing, very free-flowering, and accustomed to sea winds, needing only enough shelter to prevent their heavy heads being snapped off. Planted beside a walk, backed by evergreens, they make a lavish show of gentle colour, the lemon-yellow of *verticillata's* newly opened flowers keying up the whiter yellow of the older ones.

*A. Riceana is another very good one, a Tasmanian, and one of the hardiest. It makes a bush or small tree of arching habit like weeping willow, with spine-like foliage and pale-yellow fragrant flower-streamers in April. Mr. H. F. Comber has introduced a fine form of this with broader phyllodes and denser racemes of flower; it has done well in this country, but gets killed in severe winters except in the mild counties. *Riceana* looks well on top of a bank, with such plants as *Erica mediterranea superba*, or rosemary, or early blue *ceanothus*.

A. Veitchiana (formerly "Exeter Hybrid") in an excellent free-flowering hybrid between *Riceana* and *longifolia*, one of the best.

Other *acacias* worth trying include: *acinacea*, "gold-dust acacia," 8 ft., very free-flowering; *A. salicina*; *A. saligna*, which is used near Cape Town to bind loose sand-dunes—a plant with drooping willow-like habit and coppery-yellow flowers; *A. glaucescens*, with glaucous scimitar-shaped leaves and abundant yellow catkin-like flowers.

ALBIZZIA

Two species of *albizzia* may conveniently be included here with the acacias, which they somewhat resemble.

A. Julibrissin (*Acacia Julibrissin*), silk tree, or pink siris. This handsome tree, native over a wide range from Persia to Japan, is fairly hardy—hardy enough to be used as a street tree on the lakeside at Lugano in South Switzerland, hardy on a wall at Kew, hardy in the open, at least in sheltered places, in the mild maritime counties. It makes a wide-headed bushy tree, and can be used as an umbrella-shaped standard. A plant in California has reached a branch-spread of over 80 ft., leafy to the ground, with a height of 35 ft. The leaves are doubly pinnate, very decorative in effect by day; at night they fold up, so that the tree looks quite different. The clustered flowers, set on top of the leaf-clusters as chestnut-plumes are set, open as brushes of thin pink-flushed stamens, like a fuzz of silk.

A. lophantha (syn. *Acacia lophantha*), from Australia, is less satisfactory. It is a short-lived plant, untidy when old; but it grows extremely fast, flowering in about 18 months from seed, and the feathery pinnate foliage is very decorative. The flowers are greenish-cream in bottle-brush spikes. It made large bushes in mild gardens of the South-west before the frost of 1938, but was killed then, being less hardy than the Asiatic *A. Julibrissin*.

CHAPTER VI

Camellias

OF all the privileges enjoyed by gardeners in the milder counties none is more valuable than the opportunity of growing camellias perfectly—except only the opportunity of growing so great a range of rhododendrons. Not that camellias are in the main tender plants. On the contrary, *C. japonica* in its many varieties is generally hardy in Britain as an evergreen. But in the cold counties frosts are liable to spoil flowers that come so early, whereas here in the mild counties we have little of such trouble. In these counties, wherever there is good lime-free soil we can grow at least some camellias well out of doors. Some can stand full sun, though in general they like some shade; they are remarkably tolerant of drip from trees overhead, and they can stand a good deal of wind, though they dislike draught. And where there is no shade, no shelter, no lime-free soil—still camellias can be grown well enough to be a great pleasure, in pots, provided that the pots are not allowed to get frozen through. Even in places where the soil is calcareous they grow well enough if there is a depth of say $2\frac{1}{2}$ ft. of good loam over the chalk.

Few shrubs are as handsome in leaf, and none is more beautiful in flower than the finer sorts, especially the single and semi-double ones. The old double camellias, as formal as the rosette on the side of a Victorian coach'man's top-hat, have their precise charm. Some of the single sorts have a grand simplicity and firmness of shape. One (*C. reticulata semi-plena*) is as sumptuous a flower as can be grown out of doors in Britain. And now, through the recent introduction of a new species (*C. saluenensis*), we have a race of hybrids that is extraordinarily free-flowering and continuous, hardy and easily grown, and most graceful in flower and habit. A few kinds are scented. And—not least important—camellias flower in the least flowery months of the year: some are at their best between October and December, some start before the year ends and continue until the end of April, and many are not merely dotted with flowers but covered all over in April. Not every garden, even in Cornwall, provides the conditions for growing the grand *C. reticulata* perfectly, but many camellias are ideal plants for cottage gardens, flourishing year after year without attention. (I think of a huge bush of double red *C. japonica*, smothered with flowers every January, out in an open windy field above Penzance; and of a white camellia tree up the front of a cottage on the main street of Constantine village.)

For the present, after the war, camellias are scarce and expensive, but propagation of nearly all of them is easy, if rather slow, by cuttings. *C. reticulata semi-plena* is likely to remain expensive, being more difficult to propagate. The new *saluenensis* hybrids, such as the lovely "J. C. Williams," are very scarce at the moment, but should soon be available in some quantity, being easy to strike; and camellias of this type can be grown from seed. So camellias should be more plentiful before long. (For propagation, see Mr. Hanger's article, *R.H.S. Journal*, February 1947.)

I should like to think that this chapter would encourage the planting of ten thousand camellias, in small simple gardens as well as grand ones. For these are not simply plants for the rich man's greenhouse, as used to be supposed: they are plants for Everyman.

We will first review the species and then the hybrids.

Species

C. cuspidata, which comes from thin woodlands in Hupeh and elsewhere in China, makes a large bush, with narrow, glittering, long-pointed leaves, heavily infused when young with crimson or blackish purple. The white flowers, $1\frac{1}{2}$ inches across, are pretty but not very effective, being quick to fall off. It makes a trim bush, decorative in young growth, but in a small garden the plant is hardly worth the space it takes. For the beautiful hybrid between this and *C. saluenensis*, see "Cornish Snow," page 204.

C. hongkongensis is a tender species with large leaves, conspicuous red young growths, and deep-red cup-shaped flowers. Even under glass it is not an easy plant, and out of doors, even in mild gardens, it is generally reluctant to grow vigorously. It persists in making young growths during the frosty season, and will probably not survive an abnormal frost unless protected.

C. japonica. The wild type, which has been grown in this country since 1739, comes from the mountains of Japan and Korea. Its glossy evergreen foliage is exceptionally handsome, and the single red flowers, cup-shaped, are borne freely enough when the plant is mature. It may reach 30 ft. or more.

This is the parent of the great majority of the camellias of gardens, which are of course outstanding in March–April, some of them in January–February. In the mid-nineteenth century they were extremely popular, those most favoured being the double ones, very regular in the pattern of their petals. At first the *japonica* camellias were grown in the high temperature of the "stove," then in greenhouses; in the mildest counties they were planted out of doors, generally on walls, where they have now become grand veterans, worthy of every care, though often they have lost their names. It was not until fairly recently that it was realised how hardy the *japonica* type of camellia is. Bean's *Trees and Shrubs* says of it: "Whilst it is not adapted for exposed windy positions, it is perfectly hardy near London, in places where there is moderate shelter from North and East. At Kew it has withstood 31° of frost without suffering in the least. It is indeed one of the most satisfactory of evergreens...." It should be added, however, that frost may brown the open flowers and the outer petals of flowers still in bud. These camellias prefer some shade: the red and pink ones are apt to lose colour in full sun, and the leaves may lose chlorophyll, turning yellowish if exposed to too much light. Some of the varieties and hybrids are described below. Besides these, there is a form with variegated foliage, so clearly and freely marked with white that it might be mistaken at a glance for the variegated buckthorn (*Rhamnus alaternus variegatus*).

C. maliflora. This double-flowered plant, introduced from China in 1818, was classified by Lindley (1827) as a species, and still ranks as such in Mr. Sealy's list of *camellia* species in cultivation (*R.H.S. Journal*, August 1937). A single-flowered camellia collected in Hupeh by A. Henry and by E. H. Wilson may be the original plant from which this double form may have been evolved in cultivation in Chinese gardens. *C. maliflora* makes a small-leaved bush which looks to the layman like a form of *C. Sasanqua*; it has slim hairy twigs, leaves minutely serrated, and neat little blush-pink flowers, quite double, borne from January to March. It can be seen at Kew, and flowers well outside in the milder counties.

C. oleifera. The true *oleifera*, common in China, is a very scarce plant in cultivation here at present. It is commonly confused with the Japanese *C. Sasanqua*, which it closely resembles in some respects; but the leaf in particular is distinctive. True *oleifera* has a stiff leaf, perfectly matt and lustreless, whereas the leaf of *Sasanqua* is thinner and less stiff, more or less brilliantly polished; *oleifera's* leaf has a conspicuously saw-toothed edge, whereas the other is finely toothed; *oleifera's* is generally pointed at the apex, broadly wedge-shaped at the base, whereas *Sasanqua's* is generally blunt-ended; *oleifera's* leaf is generally larger, though *Sasanqua* in cultivation sometimes produces bigger ones. The outer flower-bud scales are silky in *oleifera*, smooth in *sasanqua*; the stamens are erect in *oleifera*, spreading in *Sasanqua*; fruits and seeds are bigger in *oleifera*.[1] The plant I grow under this name is very sensitive to wind.

The plant which is in commerce under the name of "*oleifera*" has polished leaves and is markedly different from this. I understand that it is now considered by botanists to be a form of *C. Sasanqua*, and it is so labelled at Kew. Whatever its origin, the *C. "oleifera"* of commerce is a distinct, fragrant, and most beautiful plant. The leaves are rather light green, about 2½ inches long, toothed, on vigorous upright growths. The flowers are about 4 inches across, like single white roses, touched with pink in the bud; they have a pleasant smell, less earthy, I think, than that of *Sasanqua*; they stay in good condition on the plant for a week after opening and last well in water; they are very freely borne in November (in Cornwall) or in January (in Hants). Nothing in the garden is more cheering in the flowerless season than a mature plant of "*oleifera*," whether on a sheltered wall or as a bush in a sheltered place.

I hope it will be used by the hybridist to bring scent into such varieties as "J. C. Williams."

C. Pitardii, which is perhaps not in cultivation yet, must be a very fine plant. According to Mr. Sealy's account, the true *Pitardii* is closely related to *C. reticulata*, but has a narrower leaf and smaller flowers, deep pink. The leaf is larger than that of *saluenensis*, and is distinguishable by an elongated tip.

C. reticulata. In 1820 and 1824 the semi-double pink camellia known as *reticulata* was brought to England, and till 1932 this was regarded as the original species. But in 1932 Mr. J. C. Williams sent to Kew a single-flowered camellia raised from seed sent by the collector Forrest from Yunnan in China, where it grows at altitudes of 5,000–9,000 ft.; and this was identified as the wild type, the true *C. reticulata*, from which the semi-double form has been evolved during centuries of cultivation in Chinese gardens. The leaves of

[1] I have drawn this comparison from the authoritative paper by Mr. J. R. Sealy, in *R.H.S. Journal*, vol. LXII, Part 8. I have not seen or smelt flowers of true *oleifera*.

the type are leathery and dull, not shiny as in *japonica*, with a visible network of veins (i.e. reticulate). The wavy petals are generally glowing rose-pink, lighted by an upstanding crown of yellow stamens and anthers; but one form has paler flowers, dog-rose pink, one is deep rose, and one—most beautiful of all—is salmon-pink. Often the flowers retain a half-tubular shape, measuring about 2⅓–3 inches across and the same in length; but some forms open widely. One such wide-open form, deep rose, has been selected at Caerhays and named "Mary Williams." The flowers of all these forms are remarkable for their firm substance; they last well when cut and the buds come out in water. The whole plant is sturdy, standing quite a lot of exposure. It grows rapidly when established, and can reach 35 ft. when full grown.

*C. *reticulata semi-plena*, the semi-double garden form, is the handsomest of all camellias, and certainly one of the finest plants that can be grown in the mild counties. The leaves, like those of the species, are dull, netted, and thick. The flowers, deep glowing rose with some scarlet in it, are 5–6 inches across, semi-double, with two rows (sometimes more) of waved petals: on a small plant flowers so large may look disproportionate, but on a mature one they appear perfectly related.

The plant is commonly grown here on a sheltered wall, in half-shade or sometimes facing west. But it need not be treated as a wall plant, at any rate in the milder gardens; it looks much better as a free bush in the open in a woodland clearing. Grown thus at Caerhays, in Cornwall, it makes bushes 20 ft. high, spouting up great shoots heavy with flowers and buds. Branches are there cut for house decoration 6 ft. high, and hold their flowers remarkably well, whereas many kinds of camellia drop their flowers quickly. Perhaps there is no need to commend *reticulata* to gardeners here: they will surely want to grow it if they think they can—and if they can get it. It is an easier plant to satisfy than is commonly supposed; indeed (so far as my experience goes), it is quite a tough and accommodating plant. Don't be put off from trying it simply because it looks so grand. As for getting plants, that is a difficulty at present, and will remain so till fresh stock can be imported from Portugal or France, or until propagators here can work up a stock. The plant is difficult to raise from cuttings, and is best propagated by layers.

I hope that means will be found to enable those who really enjoy flowers (and who respect the conditions necessary for such enjoyment by others) to see such plants as *C. reticulata* and *Rhododendron Griffithianum* growing at their best in a Cornish garden with woodland shelter. Such plants in flower are miracles which Cornwall can show as no other county of England can; yet most Cornishmen have never seen even a spray of the flowers unless as a sample at Truro Flower Show.

*C. saluenensis.[1] This species was found in 1917 by Forrest, the great plant-collector, at altitudes of 7,000–9,000 ft. in thickets and scrub on steep slopes and stony hillsides north of Tengyueh, in Yunnan, where the mountains divide the Salween River from the Shweli. So it can stand some hard weather.

Plants raised from Forrest's seed, at Caerhays and elsewhere, were at first misnamed *C. speciosa*, but later christened *C. saluenensis*, from their native place. In the wild the plant reaches 10–15 ft.: here, in cultivation, some are already about 9 ft. It is hardy in the mild counties, but less hardy than its hybrid, "J. C. Williams." The leaves are pointed, glossy, finely toothed; in the usual forms they are 1½–2½ inches long; but in one form, *C. s. macrophylla*, known only in cultivation, they are considerably bigger. As for the flowers, Forrest found pink, white, and crimson, some very freely borne, some sparsely. And here in cultivation the seedlings show great variety, roughly divisible into two types: there are the pale-pink ones, dog-rose colour, and the deeper-pink ones, generally smaller and more substantial, with bright-carmine buds. Some of these deeper pinks are too blue in colour to be satisfactory, and some of the pale pinks have a flower too flimsy and poor in shape. But the proportion of beautiful plants that will result from a sowing of good seed is high.

As one of the parents of *C.* "J. C. Williams" and other outstanding hybirds, this species proves to be the means of introducing a new range of beauty and ease of culture to camellias. But the species itself, as well as those hybrids which retain its dog-rose grace, will retain its place among the treasures of our milder gardens.

C. Sasanqua, a Japanese speries, is another very variable plant, and very early-flowering. Old plants, in specially favourable climates such as that of North Italy, may reach nearly 20 ft. in height and

---

[1] For a study of the nomenclature of *C. saluenensis*, *C. Pitardii*, and *C. speciosa* (afterwards classified as a *Gordonia*), see "Species of Camellia in Cultivation," by J. R. Sealy, *R.H.S. Journal*, August 1937.

width; here I have not seen any bigger than a large bush or tall wall-covering. (But they need time.) The leaves are generally 1½–3½ inches long, generally with rounded teeth at the edge, glittering and decorative. In some forms the shoots are stiff and erect, in others lax and drooping; there is also a climbing or trailing form.

The wild plant has white flowers 1½–2 inches across, with a slight earthy scent, welcome for appearing between October and December but too fugitive to make much effect. But in Japan, where this type is highly valued, many varieties have been raised, including crimsons, pinks and whites, double and single. "Fuji-no-mine," for instance, is a lovely double white, fully 5 inches across. One known in California as "White Doves" has small flowers, neat as a *Gordonia*, with petals rolled inwards at the edge. "Hiryo" is a double crimson of unusual shade, in cultivation here. There are some good pinks; but the single pink seen in English gardens, though good in colour, is poor in form and fugitive. Importations from Japan, California and Australia can, I believe, much enrich our milder gardens in the least flowery months.

C. taliensis has soft-looking leaves up to 5 inches long, round white flower-heads in the leaf axils, and white flowers 2 inches across, with two rings of petals, in September–December. Still very rare and of unproved hardiness.

Garden Varieties

Pink. (1) Hybrids of C. saluenensis

Camellia *"J. C. Williams."[1] The late Mr. J. C. Williams, of Caerhays, was among the first to cross the two species, *C. saluenensis* and *C. japonica*, which are the parents of this hybrid; and a form selected by him from a great number of seedlings from this cross was awarded the First Class Certificate of the Royal Horticultural Society, and was named "J. C. Williams" after his death.

Certainly, this is one of the most valuable shrubs that has been introduced for a long time. The plant is a robust grower and very easily satisfied, thriving in full sunlight as well as in shade, and standing a lot of rough weather (see illustration facing p. 209, showing a plant against a windy wall, facing south, in the writer's very exposed garden). It is extremely hardy. Lord Aberconway records

---

[1] The full name of this plant is *Camellia* (*C. japonica* × *C. saluenensis*) "J. C. Williams." See *R.H.S. Journal*, vol. LXX, page 210.

that at Bodnant it does not lose a leaf or a bud when the temperature falls to zero in the open. A considerable frost will spoil the open flowers, but the buds quickly replace these.

The leaf is about 3 inches long, minutely toothed at the edge, with a smoothness derived from *C. japonica*. In some of the other plants resulting from the same cross the leaf is hardly distinguishable from *japonica*. After seeing a great number of these hybrids, I cannot agree with the suggestion that "J. C. Williams" is simply a selected form of *C. saluenensis*, not a hybrid at all.

The flowers, full pink in bud, open widely, and reach about 4 inches across. The substantial petals, generally about eight, are of the freshest pale dog-rose pink, with a deeper flush on those which are outermost in the bud. In the centre the stamens stand up in a firm crown, yellow-tipped when fresh. The profusion of these flowers is extraordinary: the whole bush is splashed with them, for it tends to flower all up the branches, not simply at the ends. Look at the buds still unopened on the spray shown on the second of the illustrations following page 208 ; that plant had been flowering for three months already when the photograph was taken in April. The flowering begins soon after Christmas, generally, and continues for about 3½ months. Some forms of the cross begin as early as the end of November, and some bushes will be bright with flowers on Christmas Day.

The flowers are much more durable than those of *saluenensis*, or of *C. Sasanqua*, though they fall off sooner than one would wish; they fall complete when their time is up, leaving the plant unmarred by a lot of browned flowers.

The plant produces seed, which germinates well but slowly; of course, this does not come true. Cuttings are fairly easily struck.

Amongst the other plants resulting from the cross, a very high percentage are good enough for the garden. Some are pale pink, like the F.C.C. form; some are deep; some are solid in petal, some too slightly knit.

C. × "Mary Christian" [1] is another form selected at Caerhays and named after Mrs. J. C. Williams. The flower is a deeper pink than that of the F.C.C. form, and is more cup-shaped. The plant flowers rather earlier, and tends to bear even more flowers along the branches. It won the R.H.S. Award of Merit; so too, recently, did another pink one from Caerhays named "St. Ewe."

[1] Not to be confused with *C. reticulata* var. "Mary Williams."

C. × "C. Michael" has pink buds opening to white, faintly flushed, and flowers larger than those of the F.C.C. form, but not so regular in shape. Another Caerhays seedling, unnamed, has a scent, not strong but delicious, recalling cowslips.

C. × *Donation*, a cross between *C. saluenensis* and *C. japonica Donckelarii*, has cool rose-pink flowers, semi-double, 4–5 inches across, with the starry regularly built-up shape of *Donckelarii*.

C. × *Salutation*, raised by Col. Stephenson Clarke, is a seedling from the cross *C. saluenensis* × *C. reticulata*. The large blush-pink flowers, single or semi-double, have waved petals. This won the A.M. so early as March 1936.

Other fine hybrids of *saluenensis* will no doubt appear before long. They are likely to add a new range of beauty, more like that of wild flowers, to the formalised beauty of the double imbricated camellias which used to trim the corsage of "La Dame aux Camélias."

PINK. (2) FORMS OF JAPONICA

Campbellii is a form of *japonica* with excellent compact habit, and semi-double or single pink flowers of good shape.

*Chandleri elegans (commonly so-called) is an old sort, still one of the best growers, with spreading habit and quantities of semi-double pink flowers.

*"Gloire de Nantes" is not far short of the famous *C.* "Lady Clare" in the quality of its large, semi-double, pink flowers, but it is hardier and, for many gardens, a more satisfactory plant.

*"Lady Clare" is a magnificent plant of lax spreading habit, with distinctive foliage, large and very dark green. The flat semi-double flowers, not too formal in pattern, are translucent pink, very freely borne on an established plant. This will only show its full beauty if given rich soil, with mulches of dead leaves, and ample shade and shelter in a place where it can spread and trail horizontally. An illustration in *The Flowering Shrub Garden*, by M. Haworth Booth, shows what this plant can do.

magnoliæflora, pink form. This, with its smallish, shell-pink, starry flowers, frail but lovely in shape, is a beautiful plant in shelter.

"Preston Rose." One of the hardiest, and extraordinarily free with its formal double pink and white flowers. A first-rate plant for a cottage garden.

GARDEN VARIETIES
Red

*"Adolph Audusson" is an extremely vigorous, fast-growing, upright bush, which would make a noble hedge. The flowers, semi-double or full double, are of a mild crimson-scarlet, not over-formal, very freely borne. It needs to have the dead flowers shaken off if it is to look its best. Grow it in shade, for the flowers scorch in full sun.

*"Apollo" has glowing scarlet, double flowers, resembling those of a good carnation. The glazed foliage is handsome, and the flowers are so profuse that the bush makes a gorgeous show when grown in good soil. One of the best camellias for garden decoration.

"Arajishi." A distinct Japanese plant, with large foliage and flowers 4 inches across, blood-red, with two rows of waved petals.

"Compton's Brow Cherry." A strong grower with light-green foliage and profuse flowers, cherry-red, 4 inches across, with 2 or 3 rows of rounded petals. A very effective plant in March–April.

*_Donckelarii_.[1] This old plant is one of the hardiest, freest, and best for garden effect. It is not a very strong grower, and often has a half-drooping habit. The foliage is rather small; the flowers are 3–4 inches across, starry, semi-double or double, rosy-scarlet, sometimes splashed with white. The white flaking can be cured by doses of soot water, applied in damp weather.

"Fred Sander" has crimson-red flowers, with a central tuft of frilled petals in the centre, like a carnation.

*"Jupiter," an old sort now scarce in commerce, is the most beautiful red I know. The very substantial, perfectly shaped, single flowers, with an erect crown of stamens, are of bright shining rose-scarlet, 5 inches across, opening flat. Fine for garden and cutting.

*_Kelvingtonii_. This is the most effective red camellia I have seen for making a show in the garden. It has the freedom of _Donckelarii_, with flowers little inferior to those of "Adolph Audusson." The large thick leaves are conspicuously toothed; the flowers, opening flat, are rosy-scarlet, double, but not too formal. It makes a very vigorous wide bush in woodland shade, splendidly red in April. If

---

[1] Thus spelt in von Siebold's original description in _L'Horticulture Belge_, 1834. The plant, imported from the East, was named after Donckelar, gardener at Louvain Botanic Gardens.

the flower gets flaked with white, treat the plant with soot.

"Kimberley." I mention this only for a warning. Under glass at Kew it is a fine plant, with small single flowers of vivid scarlet, and conspicuous yellow anthers. But out of doors it is, so far as I have seen it, very disappointing; it takes many years to reach flowering age, and when it does flower, the flowers are too small and sparse to be effective. There are much better reds for outdoor cultivation. Perhaps a poor form has been propagated.

latifolia, a late-flowering hardy sort, makes a handsome spreading bush with broad dark leaves and red semi-double flowers. Branches of this are fine for indoor decoration. "Taroan" is perhaps better still.

Mathotiana rubra. The flowers of this old variety are perfectly symmetrical in pattern, very double, flat, often $5\frac{1}{2}$–6 inches across, of an unusual purplish-red. The plant may grow lanky and needs careful pruning.

"Nagasaki" has large dark foliage, recalling that of "Lady Clare," and plenty of crimson-red double flowers. Handsome beside a shady door.

"A. M. Hovey" (syn. "Colonel Firey") is a fine American variety, double, bright Turkey red, regular but not excessively formal.

"Taroan" is a vigorous plant with handsome dark foliage and semi-double scarlet-red flowers 5 inches across with yellow anthers.

WHITE

A trouble about white camellias of the *japonica* type is that, grown out of doors, their brilliant whiteness is so readily browned by rain, frost, or friction.

alba simplex, single white, makes a handsome bush, with dark glittering foliage, loaded with flat white flowers of fine shape in March and April. It needs good soil and shade: in soil that does not retain enough moisture its flowers fall very soon. The flower browns badly and the anthers turn black too soon, but at its best this is well worth growing. "White Swan" and "Simplicity" are of this type, and *Devoniensis*, described below, is similar.

alba grandiflora (syn. *Gauntlettii*) has a large semi-double flower, very beautiful under glass but very liable to browning out of doors.

*"Cornish Snow." Though small in flower, this is one of the most

decorative of white camellias for the garden. It is a hybrid (*C. cuspidata* and *C. saluenensis*), raised at Caerhays; hardly less fine a cross than "J. C. Williams." The growth is upright, slender but strong, so that the plant, with its narrow leaves, is very graceful in carriage. The flowers, about 2 inches across, are pure white, cupped, with yellow anthers when fresh, not subject to browning and not too fugitive; and they are borne with exceptional freedom for a long season in early spring. It is a joy, in February or March, to come upon a tall bush of this, its snow-flakes on every spray patterned white against the dark of a Cornish woodland.

"Devona" (or *devoniensis*). A compact sort with smallish light-green foliage and single or semi-double white flowers, which are perhaps less subject to browning than those of other white camellias.

*"Mme C. Biard" is one of the best double white camellias. The flower, always fully double, is shaped like a perfect pæony, and as brilliantly white as a *gardenia*, firmly held on the stem. The plant is shy-flowering until mature, but is then free enough to be effective in the garden as well as excellent for cutting. If there is much frost when the buds are maturing the outer petals will be browned.

magnoliæflora. The white form of this, with high-centred white stars, is a beautiful plant in shelter, too readily browned but extremely free-flowering.

Mathotiana alba is a large double white, like the red one in pattern; a very good flower of its formal kind.

nobilissima is another double white, early-flowering, very subject to browning.

The *japonica* hybrids mentioned above are but a small proportion of the number that have been named. McIntosh's "The Greenhouse" (1838) lists 294 camellias, nearly all of this type, then offered by Makoy of Liège. Many of these were not worth perpetuating, as Makoy recognised, but a good many are still in commerce, and others are still in cultivation, in Europe or Australia as well as England. Some survive, more than a century old, with names long lost, in Cornish gardens. Before the war, Guichard Soeurs of Nantes listed 270 varieties. In France, Portugal, Italy, Australia, Japan, Florida and California, English gardeners may find treasure of this kind, new and old. *Camellia Quest*, by E. G. Waterhouse, is a new book from Australia, and *Camellias in America*, by H. Hume, has lately come from Florida.

CHAPTER VII

Ceanothus

CEANOTHUSES commonly grown now in this country include some of the most treasured decorations of our gardens. We make very good use of the later-flowering ones, of which the invaluable deciduous hybrid "Gloire de Versailles" is an example. We make good use, too, of some of the spring-flowering evergreen sorts, such as the varieties of *C. dentatus*, as wall plants. But I think we have still a good deal to learn about what the spring-flowering evergreen species have to offer to mild gardens, especially in the way of low-growing bushes suitable for planting amongst boulders and large rocks.

The genus, with its hybrids, now comprises many very distinct plants. There are some fifty-five species, forty-four of which are native to California; and the number of good hybrids raised in France, England, and California is considerable. And a part of this wealth is as yet unknown or very little known in this country; for the war years have delayed the importation of new species and varieties of species that have been discovered in California during the past decade, and of several very promising new hybrids. Moreover, it is now possible to obtain a more comprehensive picture of what the genus has to offer, since the writings of Lester Rowntree, Willis Jepson, and others have been supplemented by the publication in 1942 of a finely illustrated monograph, *Ceanothus*, by Mr. M. van Rensselaer, Director of the Santa Barbara Botanic Garden, California, and Prof. H. McMinn. I have drawn freely on this book for the following pages, and gratefully acknowledge the help I have received from Mr. van Rensselaer.

So far back as 1713 the first *ceanothus*, *C. americanus*, a hardy but comparatively uninteresting white-flowered species, reached European gardens. In Waterloo year, 1815, we got the lovely blue *C. thyrsiflorus*, and during the nineteenth century various collectors, including the intrepid David Douglas and the extraordinarily observant William Lobb, found and sent other outstanding species. But some of the most valuable introductions are quite recent. It was not until 1908 that *C. arboreus*, one of the handsomest, was first cultivated in America; not till 1920 that *cyaneus*, most beautiful of all in flower, was discovered; not till 1934 that *C. impressus*, though previously known, first found its way into cultivation and began to win recognition as an excellent garden plant. Even since 1934 the distinct and attractive form of *C. papillosus* known as *C. Roweanus*, and several new species, have been discovered. So the field of choice is still widening. It may continue to do so, for some of the species are extremely local in habitat and may still await discovery in the Californian hills.

Season.—The flowering season which *ceanothuses* divide amongst them is a very long one. In California some begin in January–February; here not till March–April. And some of the hybrids, such as "Gloire de Versailles" and "Autumnal Blue," carry on the show till October. The spring-flowering evergreen sorts flower on growths of the previous year, whereas those which flower in late summer and autumn do so on growth made earlier in the same year.

Stature and Habit.—The species range in stature from absolutely prostrate alpines such as *C. prostratus* to tree-like bushes 30 ft. high or more, such as *thyrsiflorus* and *arboreus*. In between these are thick carpets, low-spreading bushes that shape themselves into the recess below a boulder, weeping bushes, upright bushes; plants from woodland shade, from arid hill-tops, from coastal sand-flats, from pasture-land, and from granitic hill-slopes.

In general, they are very impatient of root disturbance, and should be planted small. *C. cyaneus* in particular is very sensitive at the root.

In general, too, they are plants that need perfect drainage. Poor stony soil they thrive in, but they cannot stand one that gets water-logged. This is evident from the company they keep in the "chaparral"—the brush of the Californian foothills. I recall a characteristic valley in middle California, in which six or seven species of *ceanothus*—*spinosus, megacarpus, oliganthus,* and others—were intermixed. Their companions were an oak (*Quercus dumosa*), shrubs such as *arctostaphylos*, and on every sunny stony slope spiky tufts of *Yucca Whipplei*. Evidently that was a very well-drained soil.

Colour.—The colour range is chiefly notable of course for its inclusion of blue—too rare a colour in shrubs; it covers many qualities of blue—deep blue, bright pure blue, grey-blue, the faint blues of wood-smoke or chalcedony, purple-blues and clear lavender, pink, and various qualities of white.

The pure blues of *C. dentatus floribundus* or of *thyrsiflorus* are apt to look rather lightless in a mass unless relieved, and are helped by a touch of contrasting colour, such as the yellow and red of honeysuckle or the reds of *Vitis Henryana*. The greyer blue of *Ceanothus* "Gloire de Versailles" provides one of the most valuable elements in the colour of flower-borders in late summer, lending itself to many uses, and I know of no colour in the garden which (to those who enjoy such use of their eyes) offers a more interesting problem of finding an appropriate complement than the equivocal bluish-white of *C. thyrsiflorus griseus*.

Scent.—It is commonly supposed here that all *Ceanothuses* lack scent. But some are fragrant, notably *C. ramulosus fascicularis*; *C. arboreus, cordulatus, cuneatus,* and *gloriosus* are scented also, at least in California. *C. rigidus* is so regarded in California, but I confess I have not noticed its scent here.

Hardiness.—It is not safe to judge of a plant's hardiness here from its native habitat; but broadly one can say that, whilst all but a few of the species are too tender for open ground in the neighbourhood of London, none is too tender for this in our milder counties (except some unimportant ones from climates such as Mexico's). *C. rigidus* is perhaps more tender here than its habitat (Monterey) would lead one to expect; whereas *C. cyaneus, C. arboreus,* and *C. austromontanus* from Southern California prove hardier than might be expected.

Cultivation and Propagation.—That is not to say, however, that cultivation of all the species is easy, or even practicable, in our mild gardens. In a good many cases it has proved baffling or impossible, in lowland gardens of California, to grow those from the high Sierras, accustomed to a long winter sleep under a snow-blanket. Perhaps species such as *cordulatus* and *prostratus* will respond better under the conditions available in those gardens in this country which have a severe winter.

As for the germination of seeds, I expect others have found, like myself, surprisingly poor results. I did not realise that *ceanothus* seeds from California, like *eucalyptus* seeds from Australia, are adapted to conditions in a dry climate: they have an exceptionally hard outer coat. *Ceanothus* seeds will only germinate well if stratified or treated with hot water.

By the courtesy of the Santa Barbara Botanic Garden, I quote this description of the hot-water treatment as recommended by their gardener, Mr. Stewart:

13. *Abutilon vitifolium.* See pages 80–81. (John Packer ©)

14. *Embothrium coccineum* at Fox Rosehill Gardens, Falmouth. See pages 119–20. (John Packer ©)

15. *Gaultheria forrestii.* See page 134. (John Packer ©)

16. *Grevillea rosmarinifolia.* See pages 136–7. (John Packer ©)

17. *Clianthus puniceus*. See page 103. (John Packer ©)

18. *Leptospermum flavescens* var. *obovatum* (*Leptospermum obovatum*). See page 149. (Roger Phillips ©)

19. *Lapageria rosea 'Nash Court'* in an unheated vinery at Sellindge, Kent. See page 147.

(Roger Phillips ©)

20. *Sophora tetraptera* at Penlee Gardens, Penzance.
See page 175.

(John Packer ©)

21. *Camellia japonica 'Adolphe Audusson'.* See page 203.

(John Packer ©)

22. *Viburnum tomentosum 'Lanarth'* (*Viburnum plicatum 'Lanarth'*) at Fox Rosehill Gardens, Falmouth. See page 184.

(John Packer ©)

23. *Metrosideros tomentosa (Metrosideros excelsus)*.
See pages 252–3.

(John Packer ©)

24. *Camellia* 'J. C. Williams' *(Camellia J. C. Williams* var. *Williamsii)*. See page 200.

(James Hodge ©)

25. *Rhododendron johnstoneanum*. See page 304. (John Packer ©)

26. *Rhododendron 'Loderi Pink Diamond'*. See page 299.
(John Packer ©)

27. *Magnolia mollicomata* (*Magnolia campbellii* subsp. *mollicomata*) alongside *Butia capitata*. See pages 231–2. (John Packer ©)

28. *Rhododendron davidsonianum*. See page 292. (John Packer ©)

29. *Brugmansia sanguinea.* See page 320.

(John Packer ©)

"A small cloth bag containing the seeds is dropped into briskly boiling rain-water, which is then allowed to cool gradually. Some species need only a few hours' soaking, while others require as much as twenty-four hours. The length of the soaking period is determined by the time required for the seeds to 'plump' or swell."

When the seedlings are up, they are very liable to stem rot; damp soil should not be allowed to reach above the level of the root-crown.

As for pruning, gardeners in this country know well that deciduous hybrids such as "Gloire de Versailles" require drastic spring pruning; and we generally prune evergreen Ceanothuses on walls, such as *C. Veitchianus*, immediately after flowering, to a couple of buds from a main branch. But as regards the pruning of many species, gardeners both here and in California have, it seems, a good deal to learn yet. The book *Ceanothus* referred to above recommends that cutting back into hard wood should be avoided if possible, since it may lead to the dying back of whole branches; in general, pruning should be limited to branches not thicker than a lead pencil. But, as many of us have found from experience, a large branch of *C. thyrsiflorus* which gets in the way can be removed without injury; and this applies to some other species. The *Ceanothus* book, and an article by Mr. L. Edmunds in the *Journal of the California Horticultural Society*, April 1947, show that *C. spinosus, incanus, leucodermis, cordulatus, integerrimus*, and *Palmeri* sprout well from the stump if cut down; and others which, it is believed, may be relied upon to sprout include *C. gloriosus, thyrsiflorus* var. *repens*, and probably their hybrids and *C. foliosus* var. *vineatus* and *griseus* var. *horizontalis*.

In general, however, it is safe to say that the *Ceanothus* species respond far better to persistent pinching back—persuasion by thumb and finger—than to any sudden coercion with secateurs.

Now for a list. I will deal first with some of the species, then with the hybrids.

SPECIES

C. arboreus. This is the largest grower, making a bushy tree up to 25 ft. high. It is one of the tender species, coming from the islands off the Southern Californian coast (the home also of *Lyonothamnus*); but Mr. Bean has reported it to be hardy against a wall at Kew (see *Trees and Shrubs*, vol. III, page 79), and it is doing well elsewhere. The leaves are large, 2–3 inches long, whitened underneath. In early spring—as early as February in its home—it produces an extraordinary profusion of large flower-panicles, light or deep blue, scented. In some forms the colour is washy. "Treasure Island," a shrub about 8 ft. high with flowers of a good blue, is a very handsome hybrid of this, which succeeds around San Francisco, where the climate is cooler and often foggy; so this is worth trying in our climate.

C. austromontanus, a tender plant from the mountains of Southern California, is half-prostrate, broader than its height, generally not exceeding 1½ ft. in the wild. It has glossy waved leaves, red-brown stems, and small light-blue flowers in spring. It grows wild on slopes of decomposed granite soil. A plant under this name, considerably taller, is doing well in this country. Prof. McMinn does not recognise *austromontanus* as a species, but regards it as a variant of *C. foliosus*.

C. cœruleus (syn. *azureus*) from Mexico and Guatemala is one of the parents of the splendid "Gloire de Versailles" and other hybrids; a tender plant.

C. cordulatus, a low-spreading thorny kind with very fragrant white flowers, must be a lovely sight at high altitudes in the Sierra Nevada and elsewhere; but though absolutely hardy, it is probably one of the plants that will not thrive at lower altitudes, where winter is much less severe.

C. crassifolius, from hot hillsides in Southern California, may be worth trying. It has grey foliage and small white flower-clusters.

C. cuneatus, with wedge-shaped leaves and white fragrant flowers, is not one of the best, but is easily raised, very drought-resistant, and firm in habit.

**C. cyaneus* is certainly one of the finest in flower; it may present difficulties in cultivation. Growing wild in Southern California, it makes a rounded bush 6–8 ft. high; but Mr. Bean records (*Trees and Shrubs*, vol. III) that on an east wall at Kew it reached the surprising height of 20 ft. in six years. It has shiny leaves up to 2 inches long, and flower-plumes sometimes 10 inches long, deep blue in bud and brilliant blue when open. It blooms in May–June, with sporadic flower-sprays for months thereafter.

Coming from Southern California, this is one of the more tender species, but hardy enough for the mild counties. It should be given plenty of room, since it grows very fast; but it also needs shelter from wind, being particularly sensitive to root disturbance. (This is well known in California, and experience here confirms it.) At Santa Barbara Botanic Garden *cyaneus* has been inarched on to the sturdy-rooted *C. griseus*, with good results; and a garden hybrid, "La Primavera," has been noted as having an easier constitution.

C. dentatus. The true species, which comes chiefly from the Monterey district (home of *Pinus radiata* and "Monterey" cypress), is a dense bush, reaching 4 ft. or 5 ft., but often dwarfed and in one form prostrate. The crowded alternate leaves, generally less than ½ inch long, have pinnate veining and glands along their margins; most of them look square tipped, being rolled under at the point and along the edges. The flowers are in roundish heads about an inch long, bright blue.

C. d. microphyllus (McMinn) is a trailing form, growing on sand-flats, with minute narrow leaves, usually without the glands at the margin.

C. d. floribundus, familiar in English gardens as a wall plant, has finer flower-clusters and leaves larger and less inrolled than those of the type. (This apparently is not the true *C. floribundus*, probably another form of *dentatus*, which W. Lobb found in about 1850 and of which survivors have been found in Devon.)

C. d. Russellianus is another gardenform, looser in habit, and more decorative than the type.

*C. d. "Brilliant," with very large, very blue, flower-heads, is, I think, the best of this series; a grand plant for a wall in cold gardens or for the open in mild ones.

C. dentatus is mainly a coastal species, and stands some wind; it prefers light porous soil, and the form *microphyllus* is a sand plant.

C. foliosus is a low spreader, wider than its height, with small, dark, wavy-edged leaves and small dark-blue flower-heads. It succeeds against a wall at Kew, but is not among the best.

C. gloriosus is a neat plant with toothed leaves up to an inch long, and fragrant lavender-blue flowers. This comes from the coast of Northern California, and does well in Victoria, B.C.; evidently one of the hardier species and well worth importing.

C. griseus. This splendid species has been confused with *C. thyrsiflorus*. It is, I think, distinct from the plant known in our gardens as *C. thyrsiflorus griseus*. It is generally an upright bush, but sometimes low and wide-spreading, with trim, glossy, oval leaves 1–2 inches long, silky grey underneath (hence the specific name). The flowers are deep blue, in clusters about 2 inches long at the end of a stalk of about the same length. There is a very good prostrate form, *C. g. horizontalis.*

It is probable that *griseus* is one of the parents of *C. Lobbianus* and *C. Veitchianus.*

C. impressus. A dense wide bush, up to about 5 ft. high, of excellent habit, with small, dark, hairy, furrowed leaves along stiff growths, pink buds, and 1-inch heads of bright-blue flowers. It comes from near Santa Barbara, half-way down the Californian coast, but appears to be hardier than *C. Veitchianus* commonly grown here. It is fast-growing and easily contented, but apparently not long-lived. As with *griseus* and many other species, severe pruning should be avoided. It appears to want a hotter climate than West Cornwall's if it is to flower with full freedom.

C. i. nipomensis is a vigorous form of this with arching growths, larger light-green leaves, and earlier flowering.

C. integerrimus, familiar in our gardens, is most beautiful in the wild, with a wide range of colour from blue to white and even salmon-pink. Since it comes from cold places in Washington and Oregon, as well as California, one might expect it to be hardier than is commonly supposed here. It is half deciduous, and the fluffy flower-plumes, up to 4 inches long, recall those of "Gloire de Versailles."

C. Lobbianus, found by W. Lobb, is believed to be a natural hybrid between *C. griseus* and *dentatus.* In this country it is a familiar wall plant, often confused with *C. Veitchianus*, which it closely resembles.

C. megacarpus (syn. *C. macrocarpus*). This makes a big bush, often tree-like, with a mass of white flowers and large reddish seed-pods. It has a very striking variety, *C. m. pendulus*, much handsomer than the type, with long drooping growths, white all along their length. This should be tried here, even though we want blue much more than white.

C. oliganthus speciosus. This is a selected strain of *C. oliganthus*, raised at the Santa Barbara Botanic Garden, with much finer flower-clusters than the type. It makes a flowery mass of blue, with flower-plumes 3–5 inches long on a large spreading bush. Very well worth importing when available.

C. papillosus. A bush up to 6 ft. high in the wild, twice as high in cultivation, with long arching branches. The leaves are narrow, 1–2 inches long, generally with little sticky warts on the upper surface (papillæ); and the flower-heads, an inch long, are blue or blue-purple. This grows in quantity, together with the blue *C. thyrsiflorus*, in the wooded Santa Cruz mountains south of San Francisco, where it enjoys a good deal of shade from redwood, *arbutus*, and other trees; it stands some shade in cultivation. The species has long been valued in our gardens. *C. papillosus* var. *Roweanus* is a beautiful and distinct variety of *papillosus*, discovered in 1935, and now popular in Californian gardens under the name *C. Roweanus*. It is a low-spreading bush, usually not more than 3 ft. high, with very narrow, elongated, deeply channelled, sticky leaves, unlike those of any other species; the flowers are deep blue. This is certainly a plant that should be introduced here, and is likely to be of special value in very dry sites.

C. prostratus. This very distinct alpine carpeter makes quite prostrate growths, with dark, spiny, leathery leaves, lavender-blue flowers in flat clusters, and reddish seed-pods. It is a beautiful plant in the wild, but has proved unrewarding in lowland gardens in California; I have not seen it good in this country. It can be propagated by layering. *C. p. occidentalis* is a variety which is thought likely to respond better to cultivation, at least in gardens with fairly severe winter climate.

C. purpureus, the holly-leaf ceanothus, makes a bush 2-4 ft. high, with rigid growths, dark holly-like leaves about ¾ inch long, red-purple buds, and bright lavender-purple flowers in small heads. A very attractive plant but, to judge from Californian experience, not easy to keep in good health.

C. ramulosus fascicularis. This is a local variety of the species *ramulosus*. It is a spreading bush usually 3-6 ft. tall, broader than its height, with arching growths, long narrow leaves in clusters, and lavender flowers, extraordinarily profuse and strongly scented of honey. I think it may be found that this is one of the best ceanothuses for our gardens. It is stated to be very difficult to strike, but comes true from seeds. It should certainly be imported.

C. rigidus, long familiar here, comes from the Monterey district, often growing on sand flats along with *C. griseus*, and thriving in windswept exposures overlooking the sea. In England it has been found frost-tender up-country, but it is hardy enough in the milder counties. The leaves are very small and crowded, the flowers blue-purple in small clusters along the stiff branchlets. On a wall here it may reach 12 ft., but in the open it is a low-spreading bush, about 4 ft. In California it is described as fragrant, but I have not noticed the scent in England. There is a white form; and a pale one, *C. r. pallidus*, which is perhaps preferable to the type.

C. sonomensis is a promising species discovered in 1933. It is a stiff grey-barked bush, 4 ft. high or more, with small holly-like leaves, blue flowers, and red seed-pods.

C. sorediatus, closely akin to *oliganthus*, is a very free-flowering bush, pale or deep blue. Worth trying here.

C. spinosus. This sturdy species, which in California makes a 20-ft. tree with a considerable trunk, can be a lovely sight against the sky, though its fluffy masses of flowers are only occasionally blue, generally pale grey-blue or white. Its vigorous root system shows itself in the hybrid "Theodore Payne" (*C. spinosus* × *arboreus*).

**C. thyrsiflorus*. No ceanothus is more valuable for our gardens than this old friend, introduced here in 1815. It is hardy enough to have made a group of trees 20 ft. high in the open at Kew, and will grow taller than that in milder places. It has handsome glossy leaves, oval, up to 1½ inches (sometimes 2 inches) long, not silky grey beneath as in *griseus*; and roundish compound flower-clusters, up to 3 inches long, light or deep blue. It often grows wild with the white azalea (*Rhododendron occidentalis*), or with the Pacific Coast rhododendron. I should like to see it planted in quantity here amongst *occidentalis* hybrid azaleas.

C. thyrsiflorus repens is a prostrate form from windy headlands overlooking the sea; one of the plants worth importing.

**C. thyrsiflorus griseus* (not to be confused with *C. griseus*) is a vigorous form with larger leaves; rather more tender, but a most beautiful and fast-growing wall plant. It will stand a good deal of shade, e.g. on an east wall, but needs room. Its elusive colour, which carries on the colour of rosemary and *Teucrium fruticans*, is even more welcome if it is offset by some deeper colour, such as the crimson of the rose "Cramoisie superieure."

An outstanding hybrid, "Treasure Island" (*C. arboreus* × *thyrsiflorus*), raised in California, is described below; also "Autumnal Blue," a valuable late-flowerer, raised in England.

**C. Veitchianus*. This is another of the plants introduced (and in this case found) by W. Lobb nearly a century ago. It is probably a natural hybrid between *C. griseus* and *C. rigidus*. It is one of the best as a wall plant, fast-growing and very blue, but less hardy than *C. dentatus floribundus*.

C. verrucosus. Our gardens have many white-flowered shrubs,

CEANOTHUS

few blue ones; but this is a white ceanothus good enough to earn its keep in the garden. For one thing, it does not get shabby after flowering, as some species, including *cyaneus*, are apt to do. The small leaves are dark, round, and shiny; the stems have corky warts on them; the flowers, white with dark centre, are slightly fragrant and profuse enough to whiten the bush. It is a compact bushy grower, native of Southern California; one of the least hardy, but hardy enough, presumably, for our milder counties.

HYBRIDS

*C. "Gloire de Versailles." This old plant (*C. americanus* × *cœruleus*) is still the finest of the deciduous ceanothuses, and the most useful for cold gardens. No need to describe its smoke of blue, with flower-plumes 4–6 inches long; but a word on its uses in the garden may be added.

Note that this type of ceanothus flowers in late summer and autumn on the growths of the *current* year, whereas the species we have just been describing, e.g. *thyrsiflorus*, flower in spring on growths of the previous year.

As a wall plant, with breast-wood severely pruned and the main branches regularly pruned and laid in, it makes a beautiful show, especially if it has with it some enlivening colour such as a blue-purple *clematis* or claret-leaved vine, or a yellow honeysuckle. But in mild gardens the wall space will commonly be wanted for other less hardy plants.

In the open, hard-pruned, it has many uses. No other shrub, I think, better earns a place in the English mixed border of late summer flowers. The colour, compounded of the blue of the florets and the violet of their stems, is one of the key colours in the restricted palette which the gardener has to paint with. It can be used to cool down hot reds and yellows. Or it can be a main element in a sequence of harmonising colours which includes many clematises (e.g. "Perle d'azur," *Jackmanii superba*, "Gipsy Queen"), *echinops*, *Nepeta macrantha*, *Salvia virgata nemorosa*, the cooler pink phloxes, *Lavatera Olbia*, early blue michaelmas daisies such as *Thomsonii*, *Potentilla Friedrichsenii ochroleuca*.

Others of this type include:
"Topaze," a good blue; "Indigo," the deepest blue; "Henri Defosse," deep blue with red young stems; "Marie Simon," pink; "Perle Rose," carmine-pink; "Pinquet Guindon," lavender pink.

All these are less vigorous than "G. de Versailles"; all, like it, are deciduous.

Evergreen hybrids include:

"A. T. Johnson," with Wedgwood-blue flowers borne in two bursts in summer and autumn.

"Autumnal Blue," a hardy *thyrsiflorus* hybrid, is light blue, very persistent in flowering.

"Burkwoodii" (*C. floribundus* × "Indigo") marries the spring-flowering and autumn-flowering types. It is a slightly evergreen bush about 6 ft. high, with rich blue flowers in 2½-inch spikes from July onwards.

*"Delight" is an evergreen spring-flowering one, with glossy foliage and intense blue flowers; hardy and quick-growing, one of the best for this climate.

"La Primavera," a garden hybrid of *C. cyaneus* which originated at the Santa Barbara Botanic Garden, flowers earlier than that species and has a better root system.

"La Purisima" is a garden hybrid between *C. Roweanus* and *C. impressus*; a compact dwarf shrub with such excellent parents that it should be worth a trial here.

"Theodore Payne" (*C. arboreus* × *spinosus*) is described as combining the beauty of *arboreus* with the drought-resisting quality of *spinosus*—a species of excellent constitution. It is a large bush, deep blue in flower.

"Treasure Island." This cross between *arboreus* and *thyrsiflorus* combines the foliage of *arboreus* with the rich blue of the other parent. Judging from photographs, it must be a magnificent sight in flower, with an astonishing mass of flower. It does well in the comparatively cool climate of San Francisco, and deserves high priority, I think, in the list of desired importations for mild gardens here.

CHAPTER VIII

Eucalyptus

FOR gardeners in Cornwall and other exceptionally mild counties the planting of eucalypts offers both a lure and a hazard.

The lure is strong. For this large genus comprises some of the most beautiful flowering trees in the world, some of the most decorative in foliage, some of the most wind-hardy and most drought-resistant, some of the fastest growers, and some valuable sources of timber, fuel, and honey.

But the hazards are considerable too. All the species, except a few, are near the margin of hardiness for such counties; and though a fair number have been grown successfully here for a time, not many out of those which have been tried have proved able to withstand so abnormal a frost as that of 1938.

Consider first what the eucalypts have to offer.

Beauty of Flower.—First, there is the outstanding beauty of some species as flowering trees. Of all flowering trees *E. ficifolia* must be among the most brilliant when at its best. There is a grand specimen in the Botanic Gardens at Melbourne which has been photographed in colour: a huge mound of vermilion. Would such a mass of scarlet look too fierce, I wonder, under the Australian sky? I have only seen that marvellous cinnabar-scarlet compounded with gold-dust in a few sprays of flowers on a November evening in the dark wood at Tresco. Up against a serene light-blue sky there were buds just throwing off the caps that keep their stamens "well-covered"[1] and open flowers showing as scarlet brushes amongst the reddened leaves. A memorable sight.

E. ficifolia is far from being the only eucalypt with outstanding beauty of flowers; nor is scarlet the only colour that *E. ficifolia* can offer. At Perth, Western Australia, one may see roadside avenues in which this tree shows many colours, including reddish-purple. *E. calophylla rosea*, which makes a tall tree, has large flowers, shell-pink, coral, or dark red. *E. leucoxylon*, which flowers in three or four years from seed and is more brittle than the others, has pink,

[1] The word *eucalyptus*, derived from *eu* = well, and *kalyptein* = to cover, refers to the lid on the flower-bud, which keeps the flower "well covered" till it is ready to appear.

crimson, and scarlet varieties, including *macrocarpa rosea*; and *sideroxylon*, one of the hardier species, has a crimson-flowered form. *E. torquata*, which has a graceful habit, and is recommended in Australia as a decorative tree for lawns, has red flowers, as has *E. erythronema*; and *E. macrocarpa*, the desert gum, has deep-pink flowers 5 inches across, with very glaucous leaves. *E. miniata* is vermilion or orange, and *E. Preissiana's* flowers are large, lemon-yellow. Most of the rest have milk-white flowers, some of them very beautiful in pattern, such as *radiata*; even the ordinary *E. coccifera*, in the writer's garden on Zennor Moor, makes quite a decorative show of white fuzzes against its blue-green leaves.

Economic Value.—Many species are of very high value for timber, notably *E. marginata* and *E. diversicolor*; they provide some beautiful woods for furniture and panelling as well as for posts, shipbuilding and general contraction, and for firewood. A single tall tree of *E. regnans* provides timber enough to build a large wooden country house in Australia. Numerous other species are valued as a source of honey, or for various oils and stains, and for tanning bark.

Beauty of Leaf.—Even if there were no beauty of flower, there would remain much beauty of leaf and of carriage and of bark. Few trees that we can grow here exceed in beauty of leaf *E. coccifera* or *E. Gunnii*. I recall, for instance, a group of *coccifera* on a slope at Killerton, near Exeter, making a lovely pattern of cascading sprays, palest blue-green against a dark background.

Wind-hardiness.—Some of the species cannot stand much wind; but others, including *coccifera*, are amongst the most wind-hardy trees we have.

Speed of Growth.—Many of the species grow extraordinarily fast, so that even if they do get knocked out by frost, they can be replaced quickly if seed is obtainable. In California it has been found that *E. globulus* has reached a height of 42 ft. 6 inches in three years and two months from the date of sowing[1]; that eucalypts twenty-five years old are as large as native oaks which have lived for two or three centuries; and that if *globulus* is cut down, it shoots up to 75 or 100 ft. in six or eight years in that climate, and can repeat the renewal indefinitely. In Brazil, where a law requires replacement of each tree felled, *E. citriodora* is found to be the fastest grower for replacements.

[1] Ellwood Cooper, quoted by McClatchie in *Eucalypts Cultivated in the United States*, page 18.

EUCALYPTUS

Economic Value.—Many species are of high value for timber—and for firewood; they furnish posts, piles, telegraph poles, paving, shipbuilding-timber, and furniture woods. Such species as *polyanthemos, sideroxylon, hemiphloia, rostrata,* and *corynocalyx* (the sugar-gum) are valued as a source of honey.

Smell.—Lastly, there is the smell. *E. citriodora,* one of the more tender species, has a leaf with a fragrance just like that of lemon verbena. And the other species have their characteristic cordial smell—a smell which some may associate only with cold in the head, but which recalls sunlit places to many a traveller and home to many an exile. (One golden afternoon in May 1940, before we got the news of Dunkirk, the Emperor of Ethiopia visited a famous Cornish garden, which was arrayed just then in its utmost pride of rhododendrons, crimson and rose and white. He was walking down a sun-chequered path—a small distinguished figure with a cloak at his shoulders, enjoying the spectacle but rather aloof. Just four years before, on that day in May, he had been driven from his capital. Suddenly, his face lit up and he asked for one thing from that rich garden; not any great scarlet rhododendron, but a small grey sprig of eucalyptus. He bruised a leaf, sniffed it, and murmured, "C'est mon jardin." That smell had carried the exile back for a happy moment to the eucalyptus-shadowed garden of his palace at Addis Ababa—to which he has since returned.)

With all these qualities to offer, the eucalypts have spread far from their original homes. The species, numbering over 600, are natives of Australia and Tasmania, New Guinea, Timor, one of the Moluccas, and other Australasian islands. But some of them, notably *E. globulus,* have spread into some part of every continent save the Arctic regions. In Southern Europe they are much grown, and they have changed the face of the French Côte d'Azur within the past century. They are much planted in North Africa, South Africa, and parts of India, e.g. the Nilgiri Hills. They thrive in parts of South America; and in the south and west of North America they are an outstanding feature. Referring to California, an American writer says: "The landscape of many parts of the state has been completely changed by the growth of these trees. Over much of the state they are the principal wind-break, shade, and fuel trees, and the number of useful purposes they serve is continually increasing. Without the eucalypts California would be a very different state, and their value to the Commonwealth is beyond calculation."[1] Here in Britain we certainly do not want our long-matured landscape "completely changed by the growth of these trees." But it is evident from the foregoing review that we do want much that eucalypts could provide. The only question is—are they hardy enough for this climate?

I do not claim that the following notes are adequate as a description, or as an estimate of the hardiness of the species dealt with. I have had almost no opportunity for growing eucalypts myself, and war-time restrictions on travel have prevented an ample review of the condition of the trees which have survived the great frosts during the years from 1938 to 1947. Mr. Bean, in his *Trees and Shrubs Hardy in the British Isles*, has pointed out the need for a thorough trial of eucalypts here; but, so far as I know, no such trial has been made, except by Mr. Robert Birkbeck, of Kinloch Hourn, on the West Coast of Scotland, whose experience with forty or fifty species is summarised in Elwes and Henry's *Trees of Great Britain and Ireland*, page 1019. Mr. E. H. Walpole, of Mount Usher, County Wicklow, has been good enough to help me with notes on the species tried there; I have had advice from California; and Mr. D. Martin of the Australian Scientific Research Liaison Office has sent me a valuable classification of Tasmanian eucalypts according to hardiness.

Some of the Hardiest Species

The following list includes a few species which, I believe, are so hardy that they can be planted with confidence in the mild counties and with fair hope of success in many of the less cold parts of the colder counties, especially in well-drained light soil. These include E. *coccifera*, *Gunnii* (especially its variety *montana* and its hybrid, *Whittingehamensis*), *urnigera*, *subcrenulata* (*Muelleri*).

The following are probably nearly as hardy as those just mentioned: E. *Beauchampiana*, *gigantea*, *cordata*, *Perriniana*, *pauciflora*, *Dalrympleana*, *rubida*, *Macarthuri*, *pulverulenta*. Slightly less hardy are *viminalis*, *radiata*, *virgata*, with *globulus* more tender still.

E. *acervula* (Miguel), from Tasmania as well as Australia, has peeling bark, smooth trunks, leaves larger than those of *Gunnii* and more glaucous. It has done well, at least for a time, in Cornwall.

E. *amygdalina* (Lab.). See E. *salicifolia*.

E. *Beauchampiana*. Plants of this are now about 120 ft. high at

[1] McClatchie, Eucalypts *Cultivated in the United States*.

EUCALYPTUS

Mt. Usher, and seed themselves. Mr. Walpole reckons the plant "hardy" there. It has succeeded too in Cornwall.

E. cinerea. See *E. pulverulenta* var. *lanceolata*, page 224.

**E. coccifera* (Hooker). This is one of the species most likely to succeed. It is one of the most frost-hardy, and remarkably wind-hardy too. It comes from high altitudes (about 4,000 ft.) in the Tasmanian mountains, where it may be stunted and blasted by wind, and where frost is severe. At Mt. Usher it has stood 26° of frost without apparent injury, and so far as my observation goes, it survived the 1938 frost in Cornwall better than any other species. It is wind-hardy enough to thrive even in the writer's very exposed garden on Zennor Moor.

The tree is commonly 20–30 ft. high, but it may reach 60–70 ft. in shelter, e.g. in some Cornish woodlands; at Powderham Castle, near Exeter, a famous specimen is (or was) 75–80 ft. high.

On young trees the leaves are blue-green whitened with bloom, opposite, roundish, only 1 inch or 1½ inches long; but when the trees reach flowering age the leaves become grey-green, alternate, and lance-shaped. The flowers, little crowns of milk-white stamens, in clusters, are sometimes borne freely enough to make some show. The pale trunks and leaves, and the showering habit of growth, make a beautiful effect when the tree is planted in a group against a dark background, as at Killerton, near Exeter. It would, I suggest, be worth experimenting with this eucalyptus in windy seaside towns in the mild counties, e.g. where the pattern of its quivering leaf-shadows falls upon some plain colour-washed wall.

E. cordata (Lab.), from southern uplands of Tasmania, is fairly frost-hardy. It makes a shrub or a small erect tree 30–50 ft. high. The leaves on mature trees are opposite; they are stemless, clasping the twig at their base; round or heart-shaped, usually with a short point, with waved edge; green, overlaid with blue-white bloom, reddened at the margin. The flowers are borne in threes. The bark peels in ribbons. This has done well in many places, notably at Tregrehan, near Par, in Cornwall.

E. Dalrympleana. The juvenile leaf is like *Gunnii's*, but in the adult form it may reach 10 inches long, 2 inches wide, hanging down. The peeling trunk is silvery. A good tree of this decorative species has survived even the 1947 frosts at Winchester, and plants have thrived for the past six years in an exposed site at Willaston, Cheshire.

E. Deanei survived the 1938 frost in Cornwall, and is a handsome tree at Bosahan (Helford).

E. delegatensis. A tree under this name has proved hardy at Mt. Usher, and produces its white flowers fairly freely there.

E. gigantea. This does very well at Rowallane, near Belfast, at Mt. Usher, and Menabilly, Cornwall. It makes a beautiful tree, some 90 ft. high, with narrow leaves and cream-white flowers.

E. globulus, blue gum. This is not one of the hardiest eucalypts, though it is now the most widely distributed throughout the world. At Mt. Usher it is reckoned quite hardy. In Cornwall immense trees of it have been grown, and some of these, left alone, have recovered completely from the 1938 frost, though others were killed. Simmonds, a New Zealand writer, in his *Trees from Other Lands for Shelter and Timber in New Zealand*, classes *E. globulus* amongst species "adapted to localities where there are light falls of snow some years, where hard frosts occur in winter and early spring, but where summer and autumn are usually warm and without extremes. Estimated range in mean annual temperature for successful cultivation 52°–57° Fahr. Probable limit of vigorous resistance to cold for seedlings and young saplings between 16° and 22°." It is an extraordinarily quick grower, with great powers of renewal after being cut down. It is one of the best for chalky soils.

In a suitable place this can look magnificent; on the steep, dry hillside behind Berkeley, California, for instance, or beside the road from Gibraltar to Malaga. But it is often misplaced, and then looks coarse, ragged, dusty. For a small garden it is the most unneighbourly of plants, littering the ground with large scimitar blades of dead leaf and with flakes of bark, and robbing all the ground with hungry roots.

A form of this species, *E. globulus compacta*, is recommended from California for trial in this climate. I have not seen it. As for the typical *globulus*, it is certainly worth planting (or replanting) in suitable sites, where it will have plenty of room. It is worth trying to get seed from trees grown in a cool climate. The frost resistance of eucalypts depends much on the source of the seed.

*E. Gunnii (Hooker), the cider gum, is generally regarded as the hardiest eucalyptus hitherto tried here, especially in its mountain form, *montana*. The type, which is extremely variable, is usually a small tree 20–30 ft. high, but sometimes reaches 60–80 ft. in shelter.

EUCALYPTUS

In young plants the leaves are opposite or nearly so, round, about 2½ inches wide, glaucous blue-green, with short stalks or none; but in adult plants the leaves become alternate, narrow, and pointed, with longer stalks, and when the tree reaches flowering age they are 2½-4 inches long, ¾ inch wide, with inch-long stalks. The flowers, seldom produced here, are pale-yellow fuzzes. The hybrid, *E. Whittingehamensis* (*E. Gunnii* × *urnigera?*), which has long flourished at Whittingehame, in Scotland, has slightly narrower leaves, longer in proportion than *Gunnii's*, never ovate, and less glaucous when the plant is adult. It is said to flower earlier.

In the mountain form the tree is smaller, often only a shrub, and the leaves are generally smaller.

Gunnii has survived many hard winters at Kew, as has the Whittingehame variety in Scotland. In the cold climate of the Cotswolds trees thirty-five years old were 60-70 ft. high in 1937. In the fairly severe climate of Seattle, up at the extreme northern end of the Pacific seaboard of the United States, *Gunnii* is the only species which has so far proved reliably hardy. It thrives both at high altitudes in the North Island of New Zealand and at low ones in the cool parts of South Island. . Simmonds, in his *Trees from Other Lands*, estimates this as one of six species [1] which have "a probable limit of vigorous resistance to cold for seedlings and young saplings between 8° Fahr. and 14°." He classes these six species as "adapted to localities where there are heavy falls of snow, where severe and prolonged frosts occur from late autumn to middle spring, and where the summer season is variable." He estimates the range in mean annual temperature for successful cultivation as 48°-53°.

It would be worth planting this beautiful tree in seaside towns in the mild counties. It might well be tried as a plantation in moisture-retaining soil, but needs protection from rabbits.

E. Macarthuri, a handsome species with long narrow leaves, is worth a trial in the mildest gardens. In the New Forest it has done well, at least for a time; at Mt. Usher it was growing well till it succumbed to 26° of frost in the 1939-40 winter.

*E. *Muelleri*. See *E. subcrenulata*.

E. pauciflora, Sieb. (syn. *E. coriacea*, Cunn). This too is worth a trial, having long survived in an exposed site in the cold climate of Winchester, where it is now (1947) a beautiful tree. Mr. Birkbeck,

---

[1] The other five species referred to are *coccifera, cordata, Muelleri* (syn. *subcrenulata*), *unialata,* and *urnigera*.

in his trial at Kinloch Hourn, found it less hardy than *E. globulus*. It comes from Tasmania as well as Australia. The juvenile leaf is round, the mature one alternate, long and sickle-shaped, of thick leathery texture. The trunk is silvery.

E. Perriniana, with silvery perfoliate leaves in its juvenile stage, is probably not far short of *E. Gunnii* in hardiness. (See *R.H.S. Journal*, November 1947, page 454).

E. pulverulenta, which resembles *cordata*, is fairly hardy and is one of the most beautiful in effect. In the typical form the foliage is round and vividly blue-white. The variety *lanceolata* (syn. *E. cinerea*) has narrow leaves. At Mt. Usher this is about 90 ft. high: though severely cut in 1939–40, it has now recovered. It does well at Winchester.

E. regnans (Mueller), king of Tasmanian forests, is a noble, very tall tree, but not one of the hardiest. At Mt. Usher it gets badly cut by frost, except where well sheltered by trees. It was killed there in 1939–40, and is unlikely to stand more than about 20° of frost.

E. radiata has long, light-green leaves showering downwards on an upright graceful tree, and very decorative flower-clusters. Near Penzance this stood December 1938, but was killed in 1947.

E. salicifolia (syn. *E. amygdalina*, Lab.). In Mr. Birkbeck's trial this was reckoned about equal in hardiness to *E. globulus*, and able to stand 15° of frost. At Mt. Usher it is reckoned as not hardy enough: "It gets killed to the ground whenever we have over 10° of frost, but shoots up again from the base. It forms a shrub about 6 ft. high [under these conditions] and has never flowered." On the Riviera and in North Italy it is reckoned one of the most serviceable eucalypts.

*E. subcrenulata (syn. *E. Muelleri*, Moore), mountain red gum, is certainly one of the hardiest. Simmonds called it as hardy as *E. coccifera*, and it has lately been cited as "probably more cold-resistant than *E. Gunnii*" (*R.H.S. Journal*, November 1947). At Mt. Usher it is now 100–120 ft. high; though cut by the 1939–40 frosts, it recovered fully, showing no permanent damage. It commonly grows on bleak uplands in Tasmania, and may reach 200 ft. in some places there. The dark lanceolate leaves, 3–4 inches long and ¾ inch wide, are blunt pointed.

E. unialata (probably *E. globulus* × *viminalis*) is recommended by Simmonds as being as hardy as *coccifera*.

E. urnigera (Hooker). This tree resembles *E. Gunnii*, differing in having a longer main flower-stalk, well-developed secondary flower-stalks, urn-shaped instead of funnel-shaped calyx-tubes, and light-green leaves, not grey ones. At Menabilly, Cornwall, it has done well. At Mt. Usher it is regarded as "perhaps the most satisfactory eucalypt with the exception of *E. Muelleri*. It showed no visible sign of damage with 26° of frost, but since then in some cases part of the bark near the base of the tree has come off, leaving the wood exposed, which may eventually rot the tree. This damage may be due to the severe frost. The trees flower and seed freely, and several of them stand 120 ft. high."

E. vernicosa is probably the hardiest of the lot, being an alpine form of *E. coccifera* from the Tasmanian mountains, where it grows in full exposure. It is generally a dense bushy shrub with flowers hidden in the leaves. Not likely to prove of decorative value.

E. viminalis (Lab.) is Tasmanian as well as Australian, and is among the moderately hardy species. It makes a tall tree, sometimes as high as 200 ft. in the wild. The leaves on adult trees are narrow, 5–6 inches long, and only $\frac{1}{2}$–$\frac{3}{4}$ inch wide, sickle-shaped, with a long fine point; they are light-green, not glaucous. At Kinloch Hourn Mr. Birkbeck found this less hardy than *E. globulus*. But at Mt. Usher Mr. Walpole has two trees about 120 ft. high, one of them apparently hardier than the other, though they grow in similar positions. The tree, he says, "gets defoliated in bad frosts, but shoots again and grows well." It has done well in some Cornish gardens.

E. virgata. Mr. Walpole records that at Mt. Usher this was "cut to the ground in 1939–40, but has since grown again and has not been damaged by 10° of frost."

Amongst the species omitted from this list, *E. citriodora, pulchella,* and *resinifera* are noted in Thurston's *Trees and Shrubs in Cornwall* as growing there (before the frost of December 1938).

Some Tender Species

Here are a few species which are of high value, but too tender for any but the mildest gardens.

E. calophylla rosea. This tree, with beautiful pink or red flowers, is probably a hybrid between the brilliant *E. ficifolia* and the large tree *E. calophylla.* In habit it is like a more vigorous *ficifolia.* It does well at Tresco in woodland shelter, and has been recorded as succeeding on the mainland.

E. ficifolia, scarlet gum. This is an outstanding plant worthy of every care, but it must be regarded as a border-line case even for the most favoured of mainland gardens. It makes a smallish tree, usually not more than 30 ft. high, with large leaves often flushed with red, and flowers which in some forms are red-purple, in others pink, and in the most striking form a dazzling vermilion. As mentioned above, this does well in the wood at Tresco. It has been flowered out of doors on the mainland, e.g. in Miss Wingfield's garden, "Pendrea," Penzance. Many plants under this name are natural hybrids.

E. leucoxylon, in its scarlet-flowered form, is hardier than *E. ficifolia* and is used instead of it at La Mortola, It will survive 20°–25° Fahr. This might well be tried here, in a place sheltered from wind; it is more brittle than others.

E. calophylla is like a more vigorous *ficifolia* in habit. At Tresco, it does well in woodland, and it has been grown on the mainland.

E. citriodora has, for chief attraction, leaves deliciously scented of Lemon verbena. It has succeeded for a time in some Cornish gardens, but is sure to succumb to a severe frost. It can easily and quickly be grown in a cold greenhouse, as a young plant.

Others Worth Trial

What other species are worth trying here, besides those mentioned above?

On this question I consulted Dr. van Rensselaer, Director of the Santa Barbara Botanic Garden, California, having seen how much use was made of these trees in California. I am much indebted to him for the following replies, gathered from authorities up and down the Californian coast and from his own wide experience.

Mr. Hanley, then Director of the University of Washington Arboretum, reported in October 1944 that, so far as he knew, *E. Gunnii* was the only species "thoroughly hardy in the comparatively cold region near Seattle." Forty-six species were then being grown for trial in the Arboretum, but very few of these survived the war years.

Professor Woodbridge Metcalf, of the Department of Forestry, University of California, reports that he has found the following

EUCALYPTUS

species to be most hardy in various parts of California: *E. crebra, viminalis, rostrata, tereticornis, rudis, polyanthemos.*

Mr. Eric Walther, of Golden Gate Park, San Francisco, stated that the commonest species in the region of San Francisco Bay are: *E. globulus, ficifolia, viminalis, obliqua, polyanthemos, amplifolia, cinerea, sideroxylon.* (Of these, *polyanthemos*, as well as *ficifolia* and *obliqua*, have proved too tender for the climate of Mt. Usher.)

Farther south down the Californian coast, at Santa Barbara, Mr. Van Rensselaer finds that the following species withstand the colder temperatures:

E. crebra, hemiphloia, leucoxylon and its variety *rosea, melliodora* (honey-scented and good for bees), *obliqua, polyanthemos* (a medium-sized tree with grey egg-shaped leaves, a good street tree), *rudis* (a medium-sized tree with drooping branches), *sideroxylon*, with white flowers, and its variety *rosea, Stuartiana, tereticornis,* with grey flaking bark.

He recommends for trial in Cornwall:

E. cæsia, which is a small tree with drooping branches of silver leaves and pink flowers.

E. Forrestiana, a small tree with distinctive red square buds.

E. globulus compacta.

E. Lehmannii, a small tree with seed-cases united in large horned masses, and pale-green flowers. It will survive 20°–25° Fahr.

E. Preissiana, a small thin tree with stiff leaves and large lemon flowers, one of the best.

E. torquata, a small slender tree with coral-pink buds and flowers. (Like *cæsia, Forrestiana, Preissiana*, this is severely cut by 25° Fahr.)

Also *E. cinerea, erythronema,* and *punctata.*

Finally, here is a valuable classification of Tasmanian eucalypts, based on their natural distribution with altitude, which I owe to Mr. D. Martin, of Tasmania, Senior Research Officer with the Australian Scientific Research Liaison Office:

Very hardy, *E. vernicosa, coccifera, subcrenulata, urnigera, Archeri, Gunnii*; hardy, *E. pauciflora, cordata, Dalrympleana, Johnstoni, gigantea, rubida, Perriniana, aggregata*; fairly hardy, *E. viminalis, regnans, orata, salicifolia*; tender, *E. globulus, Risdonii, Sieberiana, Tasmanica, obliqua, linearis.*

CHAPTER IX

Magnolias

(*with special reference to Cornish gardens*)

By G. H. Johnstone

NO apology is needed for allotting a separate chapter to magnolias, for these beautiful trees are indeed princes in the realm of gardening. This chapter refers especially to magnolias in Cornish gardens; they grow well elsewhere, but both the soil and the climate of Cornwall, excepting the wind, are very suited to their requirements.

Unfortunate it is that magnolias are for the most part somewhat slow in reaching the maturity required for flowering, and that when they do flower they are, generally speaking, so big that only the larger gardens can afford adequate space for their display. Something can be done to keep them in bounds by judicious pruning, pinching the growth-buds, and cutting back when the leaves have fallen (early spring in the case of evergreens); but magnolias so treated can never reward the eye with the same delight as those of unimpeded growth.

If camellias can substantiate the claim to flower over a period extending from November to May, the magnolias can offer an even longer one; for, if hybrids as well as species be included, they cover the months from late February to early November; only the rhododendrons doing better than this.

Magnolias are not for group planting, a single specimen being sufficiently satisfying; and, although certainly not plants for the migratory gardener, they will provide a memorial for those who plant them which will outlast the originators, and surely a happy memorial, provided they are planted with foresight.

It is to be hoped that local authorities who have public gardens under their care will, as the finer species become available, make the beauty of some of these magnolias available to all who pass that way. What could better appeal than the stately magnificence of a well-grown specimen of *M. Campbellii*, in a setting where the children play or the old folks rest, raising to the blue sky its offering of hundreds of crimson goblets; or, if earlier reward is asked, what could excel *M. mollicomata*, which will attain flowering size when twelve years old.

How precious are the plantings which have been done by those who have gone before. Times have changed, and are yet changing, and it may well be that gardens where space could be provided for such plants as these are passing too; and it may not be unsuited to this chapter, which treats of long-lived plants, to plead that those who gave them to us deserve our appreciation in the maintenance of the beauty in the places that they once loved and tended.

This country, especially Cornwall, has many magnolias, besides other garden treasures, which may well be regarded as "County," if not "National," plants, for all that they are most of them today in private gardens. Surely it may be argued that, where such gardens are at times made available to enjoyment by the public, the owners should be entitled to include those employed in them in their maintenance claim; for the upkeep of such gardens becomes a duty where it can no longer be afforded as a labour of love.

In any attempt to give an account of magnolias, one is faced with the need for decision as to how they may best be grouped for the purpose: whether in order of botanical classification, or by the several parts of the world from whence they came to us, or by the gardens in which they are now growing, or alphabetically, or in order of preference. Any sequence based on personal predilection is unlikely to be shared by all, but for the purpose of these notes it may be the most helpful; it must not be forgotten, however, that the appeal which a plant such as the magnolia makes to us depends upon the setting in which it is placed, the light in which one sees it, as well, of course, as the health and well-being of the plant itself.

I

Magnolia Sargentiana robusta. Well does the writer remember the receipt of a telegram from the late Mr. J. C. Williams, asking him to come to Caerhays because there was something which the sender wished him to see. At first Mr. Williams occupied much time in showing other plants until the light was, in his judgment, right, when he led his unsuspecting guest to a magnificent plant of *Magnolia Sargentiana robusta* flowering for the first time. The sight was an unforgettable one, and the following note was made by the writer the same evening.

"13.4.31. I was privileged today to see *Magnolia Sargentiana robusta* flowering at Caerhays for the first time in this country. I do not hesitate to say that it is the most beautiful of all the magnolias I have yet seen in flower. The flowers, formed with twelve tepals, are semi-pendulous at the ends of the spreading branches, and in size appear to be about 8–12 inches in diameter, in colour pale rose-purple shading to pale pink at the tips. Looking up into the blooms, they appeared like opening parachutes of coloured paper, their beauty accentuated by black scales of unopened or partly opened buds."

The flowers of this beautiful species are followed by obovate leaves which, by their rather long, blunted, emarginate (i.e. notched) shape, make this tree easily distinguishable from the type (*Sargentiana*). It is still a difficult plant to come by, although seeds have been raised from the Caerhays plant. It appears to be quite hardy in Cornwall, although, as with most of the early-flowering magnolias, the flowers are spoilt by spring frost in some years.

There is a good specimen of this species (for species it may ultimately prove to be) at Lanarth, where, however, the site is too restricted to afford the best display, and another at Trengwainton (Col. E. H. W. Bolitho) 25 ft. high and measuring 85 ft. round the ground it covers.

This is one of the drawbacks of the magnolia as a garden plant—that it demands considerable space in which to spread itself. In the forests of China, where this magnolia was found and collected by E. H. Wilson, it is said to grow 60–80 ft. high; but it is better seen, as are all the magnolias, as a large spreading bush such as can only be accommodated in the larger gardens. Nor is this all, for the magnolias generally are intolerant of disturbance of their rather "fleshy" surface roots, and the subsequent removal of other plants which have been put in close to them when the magnolias were first planted has led to the death of many good specimens. Space and foresight are demanded of those who plant magnolias, as well as the quality of patience, since many of them are slow to attain flowering age; sometimes so long a delay as twenty-five years has to be endured before the patience of the planter is rewarded by the first instalment of rent. But if these magnificent trees are well sited, he who plants them can feel that, even if he goes unrewarded, his successors will some day reap where he has sown.

M. Sargentiana. It must not be assumed from this praise of *M.*

Sargentiana robusta that *M. Sargentiana*, of which *robusta* is at present regarded as a variety, should be rated as an inferior plant. Indeed, where mature trees can be compared, some competent judges regard *Sargentiana* as superior.

Sargentiana blooms at a fairly early age, and the flowers then appear rather thin and scattered; but as the tree develops, the flowers increase in size as well as in number, and certainly make a very beautiful effect. The number of tepals is normally less than the twelve to fourteen which *robusta* carries; whereas one may often count as many as sixteen tepals on a flower of *robusta*, twelve is normal and fourteen exceptional in *Sargentiana*. The poise of these flowers varies considerably, even on the same tree; some are upright when they open, others horizontal, and the latter often hang vertically down when past their best.

The leaf of *Sargentiana* differs from that of *robusta*, being smaller, rounder, abruptly pointed at the apex, and lighter in colour. In habit too this magnolia differs from *robusta*; it is tree-like, whereas the latter is best described as making a gigantic bush in our gardens.

M. Campbellii. Having started with what is perhaps the finest of them all, it may be well to refer next to those magnolias which some will say can claim equal rank, or are even superior to it. Of these *Campbellii* is entitled to stand next in order, for the large flowers 8–10 inches across, warm rose on the outer side of the tepals and paler within, can provide an astonishing sight in early spring, whether seen against a background of blue sky or perhaps better in a setting of dark evergreen trees.

With the exception of *mollicomata*, this is the first of the big magnolias to come into bloom, and the risk of flower damage by frost is correspondingly greater; but once the tree has reached flowering age, it will continue to provide an annual feast for all who see it unless a hard frost intervenes. If frost does spoil the season's flowering, the owner must console himself with the thought that any plant that is as prodigal of flower as this one will benefit by an occasional compulsory rest from the strain of full development.

The cup-shaped flowers are upright on the tree, which will attain a height, if encouraged to do so, of 50 ft.

Good specimens of this in Cornwall are to be seen at Bosahan and Killiow as well as at Caerhays, though perhaps the finest plant of it in the county is growing at Rosehill, Penzance, a tree which is probably more than 50 ft. high and girths 6 ft. 2 inches at 3 ft.

above the ground. When last seen by the writer in March 1945, this tree carried over 500 flowers in full bloom—an unforgettable sight. This tree was planted early in the present century by the late Dr. Howell, who certainly has conferred a benefit on all of us who have the opportunity to see this wonderful sight.

There is said to be a white form of this species, and it may be that there is an example of it at Caerhays, where Mr. Charles Williams' description of a flower which appeared there in 1943 accords with the claim; but unfortunately the plant on which the flower appeared has since been badly frosted, and has been cut back to enable it to develop again from the base.

M. mollicomata. *M. Campbellii* is a native of the Himalayas and of China, where it is found in company with *M. mollicomata*—a close relative, if it be not in fact a variety of the same species. This magnolia is also one of the earliest to bloom, sometimes preceding *Campbellii*; and the rose-tinted flowers, sometimes as much as 8 inches across, are freely produced, and make a wonderful display at a time when the eye, starved by the winter, is hungry for colour in February or early March. But it is certainly not to be compared with its relative for warmth of colour, unless it be a form of *mollicomata* growing at Lanarth and Werrington Park, the rose-purple flowers of which undoubtedly challenge even the beauty of *Campbellii*. This variety or form of *M. mollicomata* has only lately reached flowering maturity and has at present no varietal name, so that it must be designated by the collector's number, Forrest 25655. It can be distinguished from the typical *mollicomata* not only by the darker colour of its flowers but also by its leaf.

The best examples of the type in Cornwall may be seen at Caerhays. (One of these is here illustrated.) One of the Caerhays plants is fastigiate in habit. At Werrington Park Commander A. M. Williams has a plant with white or nearly white flowers. Plentiful supplies of seed of *M. mollicomata* have been sent from China in recent years by Mr. George Forrest, and other collectors, and it may be that, as plants from this seed reach flowering maturity, we shall find other variants from the type, possibly even some new species hitherto ascribed to *mollicomata.*

At Caerhays there are two or three magnificent examples of this species, including one which is fastigiate in form. Comdr. A. M. Williams has at Werrington a form of this species with flowers of a much darker colour than the type, approaching the purple of

M. Soulangeana nigra, and another which is said to have white flowers.

Plentiful supplies of seed of *M. mollicomata* have been sent from China by Forrest and other collectors of recent years, and it may be that, as flowering plants become available, it will prove that variants from type have been grown, or even possibly new species which have been included as being this one.

M. Dawsoniana. If we are to give preference to the most beautiful, or spectacular, species (and this system of personal preference will assuredly provoke both difficulty now and controversy presently), *M. mollicomata*, according to some, should not have taken precedence over *M. Dawsoniana*.

M. Dawsoniana forms a spreading bush or small tree. At Lanarth, where it may best be seen, it is about 35 ft. high and, though rather tightly enclosed by other plants, has a spread of some 30 ft. and girths 3 ft. 2 inches (1945). Another specimen may be seen at Caerhays, but not quite such a large one. The flower is more slender than any of those yet mentioned; the tepals, which number nine, sometimes more, some 6 inches long and 2 inches wide, bend over on their axis at an early stage of flowering, somewhat as do those of *M. stellata*: they are white inside and suffused with rosy-violet on the exterior; and when this tree is seen in full bloom it presents a striking sight, bedecked, as it appears at a distance, with slender strips of white and coloured paper.

The leaf of this species is darker green than that of most of the deciduous magnolias, and its mid-rib is reddish at the base. It is pleasantly aromatic when bruised. It measures $5\frac{1}{2}$ by $2\frac{1}{4}$ inches, and reaches its broadest part at about 4 inches from the pedicel, to which it narrows rather abruptly, so that it has a pronouncedly elliptic-obovate shape.

Certainly this is a welcome introduction to our gardens, even though it is one of those that takes many years before it first bears flowers. Small plants raised from home-saved seed are in some gardens, while plants of flowering size may be seen at, for instance, Werrington, Trewithen, Caerhays, and Rowallane.

M. Sprengeri diva. One other species must be mentioned in order to complete what forms the section of Chinese deciduous magnolias with coloured flowers, and that is the almost unique example of *M. Sprengeri diva* (*denudata purpurascens*) at Caerhays which, in the colour of its flower, is as rich as all but the very best forms of

M. Campbellii. This plant was bought by Mr. J. C. Williams at the sale of Messrs. Veitch's stock at Coombe Wood in 1910, and has now grown to a plant of some 40 ft. high, girth of 4 ft. 4 inches, and with a spread of 39 ft., although a large branch was blown off it a few years ago. The flowers are rather smaller than those of *M. Campbellii,* but are beaker-shaped rather than cup-shaped. It follows *Campbellii* closely in date of flowering. It is perhaps more closely allied to *M. denudata (conspicua)* than any other species.

Sprengeri diva is one of the gems amongst magnolias, and it is to be regretted that it is not in wider cultivation. This is not due to any lack of effort on the part of Mr. J. C. Williams, who raised a number of seedlings from his plant. Some of these, with his well-known generosity, he distributed amongst his friends; others he grew to flowering age in his own garden, but all the latter that up to date have flowered have produced white flowers more or less heavily tinged with violet instead of the crimson of the seed parent. Maybe they are hybrids with a form of *denudata* or *Soulangeana* growing near by. (The flowers of some of these seedlings have sepals, which is consistent with *M. liliflora* and its hybrids, but not with *Sprengeri.*) The writer knows only two of these Caerhays seedlings which have flowered true to type, one being at Kew Gardens and the other at Trewithen, which latter is a small grafted plant—all that remains from the original seedling from the Caerhays plant, for it died after attaining flowering age.

In addition to *M. Sprengeri diva* and *M. Sprengeri* which, so far as is known, is not in cultivation, a third variety of *Sprengeri* is recognised under the name of *M. Sprengeri elongata.* This, however, has a white, not a coloured, flower, and is in all respects less desirable than either *Sprengeri* or *S. diva*; indeed, it is possible that *elongata* will ultimately be removed from this subsection and be accepted as a separate species, or be linked with another.

M. liliflora should perhaps be mentioned here, because it is a Chinese deciduous species with coloured flowers. Whilst this is said to form a tree sometimes, it is generally a bush, which increases in size by the rooting of its outer branches and by suckers. The flowers are formed of six rather slender petals, and are a dark rosy-purple—so dark in fact that they tone in with the dark-green leaves and thus lose much of their effect. None the less, the flowers are very handsome in themselves; and they have the merit of affording a longer flowering period than any other deciduous magnolia, from

April till July. *M. liliflora* is undoubtedly the origin of a whole race of hybrids, including one named *Soulangeana nigra*, with which it is sometimes confused.

II

M. parviflora. The section which seems to fit in here as next to be dealt with is that of deciduous Chinese or Japanese *magnolias* with white flowers, which section can be subdivided into upright and pendent, or "nodding," flowers—and of the latter, mention must first be made of *M. parviflora*, which, being of smaller growth than many, and of bush rather than tree habit, demands less space and so offers itself for inclusion in more restricted gardens, although it requires as much as 30 ft. of ground space to admit of full display.

This species is a native of Japan and Korea. Its correct name is *M. Sieboldii*; but it is said to have been described previously under the horrible name of *M. pentapeta*, from which it seems to have had a fortunate escape. It is said to have been introduced into this country as early as 1865, and again in 1882, but the oldest plants in Cornwall are of much later date—the oldest probably being that planted by the late Mr. J. C. Williams at Caerhays about 1912.

In Cornwall this may be regarded as a hardy plant. Its beauty justifies its inclusion in every garden that can provide the space it requires. The flowers, which are about 4 inches across, are generally white with purple anthers (though occasionally these are nearer scarlet), and they are suspended at the terminals of the branches at an angle at which their interior can be seen without the need, as in *Wilsoni* and some others, to look at them from below. This species can always be depended upon to flower well, and when later in the year the bright-orange seeds ripen on the pendent gynandrophores, it provides a second display which never fails to attract. Large plants of *M. parviflora* can be seen in several Cornish gardens besides Caerhays.

M. Wilsonii. Related to this is the larger-growing *Wilsonii*, introduced by E. H. Wilson from China in 1908; a hardy plant which, as in the case of others of this section, given good drainage, does not seem particular as to conditions. The leaves are pointed and narrower than most of this section (elliptic-lanceolate), about 5 by 3 inches where broadest; and the flowers (as in all this section) appear with the leaves, and measure about 5 inches in diameter. They are white with red or crimson anthers, and hang suspended like saucers at the ends of the branches in May or June, being followed later by a September display of ripened orange-coloured seeds produced in such quantity that the constitution of the plant is apt to suffer unless the flower-stools are removed soon after the petals fall.

M. sinensis. Larger than the foregoing both in leaf and flower but of the same group is *M. sinensis.* Typical plants of this are readily distinguishable from *M. Wilsonii* by the obovate leaves, which are more densely pubescent on the underside than those of *Wilsonii* (or of *parviflora*), darker and more shiny on the upper surface, and rounded at the apex to an abrupt point. Unfortunately this distinguishing characteristic is not wholly reliable, since plants raised from home-saved seed often develop leaves which are ovate-lanceolate and invite the contention that they are hybrids between *sinensis* and *Wilsonii*, since they appear intermediate between the two; but seedlings raised from plants of *sinensis* growing at a considerable distance from *Wilsonii* carry leaves of both types, though never on the same plant. Perhaps the variation in character is in part responsible for the confusion of name, for *sinensis* was introduced to this country (via France) as *Nicholsoniana*, under which name it is still sometimes found, and was also introduced (from America) as "*globosa* near *sinensis*," being considered as a form of *globosa*, the next to be mentioned.

The flower of *sinensis* is larger than that of *Wilsonii*, which in other respects it resembles both in colour and character; and *sinensis* has the additional recommendation that, although it may be said to bloom in May or June, it will often produce late flowers in July and August. It is certainly a magnificent species. The type plant was at Lanarth, and is now unfortunately dead, but there is a very large specimen of it at Caerhays, where it appears as a low-growing spreading bush some 16 ft. high and covering 34 ft. across the centre. At Trewithen there is a plant of this species which is more upright in form, being about 17 ft. high (1944); but this, although raised from the type plant at Lanarth, is the form with pointed, and not the characteristic, leaves.

M. globosa is less often met with in Cornish gardens, and probably the largest plant of it in the county is at Trewithen. It is readily recognisable by the dense tawny fur (pubescence) which clothes the pedicels and leaves in a young state and remains persistent to some extent until the leaves fall off.

The flowers, which are the same in colour as in the rest of this section, open in June and are less pendent than those of *sinensis* or *Wilsonii*. They measure about 5 inches across, are slightly tinted with pink, and are scented when they first open. They are at their best just before fully opening, when they are egg-shaped, horizontal or nearly so, and still carrying the crimson bud scale which protects the bud until it has developed sufficiently to push the scale off.

Unfortunately, the flower of this species is very susceptible to damp, and buds which promise to open on the morrow will be turned brown by an evening mist before the promise can be fulfilled. Nevertheless, it is a remarkable plant for foliage alone, the leaves when fully developed measuring as much as 9 inches long and $3\frac{3}{4}$ inches across the broadest part.

M. globosa was introduced from China under the name of *M. tsarongensis*, but it has since been recognised as identical with the Himalayan *globosa* with which it is now included and from which it appears to differ only in habit of growth; but as there are only young plants of the latter at present available for comparison, no claim for the Chinese *globosa* as a separate species can be maintained against the herbarium material. It may be worth recording, however, that the two plants—Indian and Chinese—growing side by side in the writer's garden are easily distinguished, since the former lacks the dark-brown coating of hairs which makes the Chinese plant so remarkable. We must await the flowering of the Indian introduction.

M. Watsonii. Perhaps *M. Watsonii* should be next in order to be mentioned, since it may form the bridge which links the upright-flowering type with this section, if it is—as sometimes claimed—a hybrid between the two Japanese species *parviflora* and *hypoleuca* (obovata).

As to whether it is or is not a hybrid, this is not the ring in which to contend; and, as there are available some plants raised from seeds of *Watsonii*, it may be that its specific origin will, before many years, be established. But, accepting the supposed hybrid parentage as correct, whence does this variety obtain the heavy scent which characterises it? The flowers are saucer-shaped, with eight petals, and remain upright upon the tree, gradually opening flat before finally falling.

This is a hardy plant, and the astonishing scent of the flowers might alone have secured for it more recognition in British gardens. The flowers are creamy white with crimson anthers. It develops its flowers in June, later in the summer than most *magnolias*, and does not demand the best place in one's garden. Certainly it does not stage the display of *parviflora* in flower, or of *obovata* in leaf, but as a back-row plant, where it will fill the vicinity with its rich perfume, it will make its contribution to the garden.

M. denudata, which, until the pundits intervened, we have known as *conspicua*, is a more popular species, which seldom fails with its abundant display of white flowers to add its note to the chorus of spring; although the note would be more emphatic if the leaf of this species did not develop almost at the same time as the flower. Still, it offers a very lovely sight, year after year, besides being one of the parents of a number of valuable hybrids raised originally by Soulange Bodin, some of which are referred to later.

M. denudata forms a small and usually rather untidy tree of 15 to 35 ft. which, if allowed to do so, will occupy a considerable spread, but the reward for those who can afford to give it room is assured.

Perhaps the best Cornish example of this species is to be seen at Killigordon, near Truro. The flowers of this plant are flushed with rose, and it is possible that it is one of the Soulange hybrids already mentioned, but whether true to type or not it is certainly a "county plant." The height of this tree, which consists of four main branches springing from the base, from which four smaller branches extend, is about 45 ft. (1945), with a spread of 38 ft. and a girth of 6 ft. 9 inches. It is reputed to be more than fifty years old.

M. obovata (hypoleuca), which is one of the larger-leaved species, is a valuable Japanese contribution to our gardens, and although the creamy-white flowers are rendered less conspicuous by the fact that they come in June or July after the large leaves are fully developed, they are of large size and are scented.

This magnolia has the upright habit, and will form a tall tree if encouraged to do so, which means, of course, that the flowers are out of reach, and often out of sight too. There are several good plants of this species in Cornwall, notably at Caerhays, where the largest measures some 40 ft. high. There was a magnificent plant of it at Lanarth which unhappily fell victim to the wind; the bole, still lying on the ground (1945), girths 6 ft. at 4 ft. from the base. In Japan this magnolia is said to attain 100 ft. in height. It is quite hardy, and the lovely sea-green tone of the leaves is followed in the autumn by a rich bronze which offers value to those who seek for autumn colour.

M. officinalis. Of late years *M. officinalis*, which is the Chinese counterpart of *obovata*, has been introduced. The leaves of this may be slightly larger than those of the latter, but except for the colour of the bark it is indistinguishable to all but the expert—and he is not always right, although his opinion can be confirmed by the fruit, which differs somewhat from the Japanese species.

M. officinalis is to be seen at Lanarth and at Caerhays, where the best tree measures about 60 ft., but is unfortunately showing definite symptoms of decay.

M. rostrata. Larger in the leaf than either of the last two mentioned is the Chinese *M. rostrata*, so called because of the curiously beaked seed-vessels. This is worth a place in the garden on account of its magnificent leaves, which measure as much as 19 inches long and $10\frac{1}{2}$ inches across, providing an almost tropical effect when they can be seen undamaged by the wind; but it is essentially a plant for a sheltered place, for it hates a wind, and it is not as resistant to frost as are most of the cultivated magnolias. It demands a large space in which to be seen at its best, and the flowers, which appear in June, are not its strong point—certainly they are not proportionate to the size of the leaves; they are ivory white, rather creamy, stiff in substance, and heavily scented.

It is surprising that this, the giant of the race, should produce the smallest seeds of all magnolias. Seedlings of this species have been raised from plants grown at Caerhays and elsewhere. There is a good specimen grown from Chinese seed at Trewithen, where, however, the top having reached the weather, it is growing outwards rather than upwards. A plant for the specialist's garden rather than for general planting.

M. Kobus. More floriferous, but with a less spectacular leaf is *M. Kobus* from Japan, another of the spring-flowering species. At Caerhays there were two magnificent specimens of this rather unusual species, now reduced to one, and anyone who has seen this in flower would at once go home and endeavour to obtain a plant of it. Or instead he might obtain the sub-species of it, *Kobus borealis*, a native of the Northern Island of Japan, which has smaller leaves and which flowers at a younger stage; but it may be as well to add here that plants raised from seed collected in Japan and sent to this country as authentic *borealis* have not yet flowered (1945) either at Werrington or Trewithen or indeed elsewhere since they were planted in 1926. This plant has a larger and more lanceolate leaf than the type *borealis*, and what it is must remain a garden mystery for the present.

Of the two plants of *Kobus* at Caerhays, referred to above, one was heavily scented while the other was without scent. There is a magnificent specimen of this magnolia also at Penjerrick, although, alas, it was blown over in the autumn of 1943. It continues to flourish, although much of the root is exposed. As it lies, it measures 30 ft. in length and 4 ft. 3 inches round the base of the main stem (1945).

M. salicifolia. Related perhaps to *Kobus* is *M. salicifolia*, introduced from Japan in 1906. This is a species that every garden should include if possible. The flowers are smaller than in most of the species, but there are many of them and they come early in the year. It is a hardy plant, and flowers in a young stage, so that one does not have, as with many, to wait for years before seeing the flowers. Moreover, *salicifolia* makes a neat little tree, and the white flowers, about 4–5 inches, at the ends of the slender branches, coming before the leaves, give a pleasing effect. It is a hardy species and does not cover a lot of ground. The leaves are about 3–4 inches long, and differ in shape from other magnolias, being tapered at both ends and lanceolate. Both the bark and the leaves when crushed give off a strong scent similar to the lemon-scented verbena. There are two forms of it, one of which grows as a tree, the other being fastigiate. There are several good specimens at Caerhays, one measured (1945) about 45 ft. high, with a spread of 43 ft. 6 inches and girth 3 ft. 4 inches. This species is easy to raise from seed.

M. stellata. Another Japanese species is *M. stellata*, which ought perhaps to be called *Halleana*, but the "star" magnolia is much more descriptive and suits the flower so well that one hopes, despite Vienna conventions past or future, this charming species will retain its popular instead of its correct name.

This species is probably more generally grown in our gardens than any other, and sufficiently well known not to call for any description, except perhaps to mention that there is a pink form, although the pink loses its colour for white at so early a stage of the development of the flower as to make the claim that it is a pink form illusory.

There is a good specimen of this magnolia at Lis Escop, the residence of the Bishop of Truro, which measures 14 ft. high and 12 ft. spread (1945). At Enys there is a rather starved plant of the same species 15 ft. high and 20 ft. spread, and at Lanarth Mr. Williams has one which is some 18 ft. high and covers about 30 ft.; but this specimen is not true to type, and it may be a poor form of *Kobus* or a hybrid.

III

Reference may conveniently be made here to the hybrid magnolias which have enriched our gardens.

The chief credit for these is due to Soulange Bodin, said to have been an officer in the French army who, after the defeat of Napoleon, exchanged the art of war for that of horticulture.

However that may be, Soulange Bodin had by 1840 attained great eminence in French horticultural circles; and he was thus addressed in the dedication to him of a monograph on camellias by L'abbé Berlese: "Soulange Bodin, Secretary-General of the Royal Society of Horticulture in Paris; member of many learned societies and Chevalier of many Orders; to you, the Founder of the very rich Horticultural Establishment of France; to you, who grow in your huge greenhouses at Froment the most precious offerings of Nature; to you who, by your writing, your learning and your example, have given such a powerful example for the progress of Horticulture; to you I dedicate this essay."

Certainly Soulange Bodin set up a lasting memorial to himself when, by crossing *Magnolia liliflora* with *M. denudata (conspicua)*, he gave us the range of magnolias which may be grouped as *Soulangeana* hybrids.

It is fair to assume that others besides Bodin, especially Dutchmen amongst whom he worked, are responsible for some of the hybrids with which he is credited; but we have no proof of this, and even if he cannot claim to have raised the whole range of *conspicua* hybrids, Soulange Bodin must be regarded as the father of hybrid garden magnolias.

M. Soulangeana bears the name of the raiser, and is a plant of great garden merit, producing each year a beautiful crop of large cup-shaped white flowers so heavily stained with rosy purple that they might be described as being this colour. Nor is the beauty of the flowers lessened by their opening coinciding with the incipient unfolding of the young leaves, although it should perhaps be added that while this applies in Cornwall and other parts of the country similarly favoured as regards climate, elsewhere the full beauty of the later flowers is to some extent obscured by the leaf.

It is quite hardy, but should be planted where some shelter is afforded from the prevalent winds of early spring; for it is distressing to see so lovely a sight as this ravaged by a hostile wind. Unless kept in order, this *magnolia* is apt to form a wide-spreading bush, but where space can be afforded to allow it to grow untutored by the saw and the secateurs, it is better so.

While there are numerous larger and older specimens of *M. Soulangeana* to be seen, it may be helpful to mention that a small plant introduced into the writer's garden in 1908 and left to grow as it liked, is now (1945) nearly 40 ft. across and some 14 ft. high.

M. rustica rubra probably originated from the same parentage as *Soulangeana*, being similar in most respects, but coming into flower a little later, when the leaf is more fully developed. Its large goblet-shaped flowers have a rather pinker shade than those of *Soulangeana*; indeed, in volume I of *Flora and Silva* there is a coloured illustration of this flower, showing it as a pink lovely enough to place it amongst the best for colour.

The plant hunter can only be sure of getting the best forms if he is certain when buying a plant that it is from one seen in flower. This is not easy to do with magnolias; but instead of ordering a plant of a species or hybrid without seeing it, one should if possible visit the nursery at a time when at least the older-established stocks can be seen in flower, and should there mark the particular form one fancies.

Perhaps it may be mentioned, too, although rather beside the point when dealing with *magnolias*, that the gardener (apart from the plant hunter), when buying three or more of a particular plant, should specify that they shall differ in size, thus breaking the line which is formed by a batch all of one height.

M. Soulangeana nigra is the darkest-coloured flower of any *magnolia*, the base of the rather narrow petals being so dark a purple as to approach black, and the whole being a port-wine colour outside and somewhat lighter within.

Flowering in May and June when the leaves are fully developed, the blooms fail as a display, and the straggly habit adds nothing to recommend it. This variety is said to have been introduced into this country from Japan about the middle of the nineteenth century.

M. Lennei, which has flowers almost as dark in colour as the foregoing, is certainly the better to plant. It has larger flowers and a better habit, besides flowering earlier. This hybrid is said to have originated in Italy. Certainly it is a worth-while plant, but is often confused with *M. Soulangeana nigra*; and it is advisable to be sure that one is getting the right thing before purchase.

M. Brozzonii. In addition to the coloured hybrids already mentioned, there are several with white flowers, and white with more or less purple markings. The best of them is *M. Brozzonii*, both in size and character of flower. It blooms later than the white *Soulangeana* hybrids, and the conspicuous white flowers 10 inches across, sometimes with a trace of purple at the base, are not "swamped" by the foliage as in the case of *nigra* mentioned above. Unfortunately, *M. Brozzonii* is a difficult variety to obtain, though another called *Soulangeana spectabilis* is so like it as to suggest that it is of the same parentage.

M. Alexandrina may be placed next in order of merit amongst the so-called *Soulangeana* group of hybrids, while another worthy of mention is *M. alba superba*. This list might be lengthened; for there are others attributed to the same parentage—*Norbirtii*, *triumphans*, etc.; but mention has been made of the pick of them; and when one has slightly more colour than another on the rib or at the base of the white petals, it is hardly sufficient reason for according a separate name.

M. Veitchii. Before closing this reference to hybrids, mention should be made of *M. Veitchii*, which is certainly one of the best of them; although here again a warning is advisable regarding the space required to accommodate it, for this hybrid between *M. Campbellii* and *M. denudata* (*conspicua*) is (for magnolias) fast-growing and soon covers a lot of ground. A specimen at Trewithen has in twenty years attained 40 ft. in height and has claimed 45 ft. of ground across the spread, and is still growing apace. It seems that this hybrid is particularly brittle and so subject to damage by wind, the sappy branches being twisted off when they appear large enough to withstand attack. However, beyond disfigurement, little harm seems to result from this drastic pruning if the wounds are painted after paring clean, so as to keep out the wet.

This hybrid was raised by Mr. Peter Veitch, of Exeter, and the forms obtainable vary in the amount of pink which stains the otherwise white flowers. The so-called "best pink form" is certainly not pink but rather white suffused with pink marking on the outside tepals. A large plant bearing many hundreds of blooms before the leaf develops is certainly a very lovely sight; and, although flowering early in the year, and so somewhat subject to weather which in some years causes the flowers to be disfigured by "spotting," it can be depended upon to pay a good rent for the ground it occupies.

IV

M. Delavayi. If the deciduous species of *magnolia* merit all the space we can give them in our gardens, it must certainly not be to the exclusion of at any rate one or two of the evergreen species. *M. Delavayi* is certainly the most spectacular of these, and for planting in open ground is preferable to the American *M. grandiflora*, which is deservedly popular for covering the walls of a house. For while the latter does well for this purpose, it does not seem to respond to open planting, while *Delavayi* is too strong a grower for a wall plant and, in Cornwall at any rate, does not require this aid for ripening the flowers. If it can be afforded space, *Delavayi* will make one of the finest examples of an evergreen tree that is to be seen in our Cornish gardens, and no one who has seen the two specimens of this species planted in generous space at Caerhays is likely to fail to have carried away a lasting impression of these magnificent plants.

In flower, *M. Delavayi* is no "fife and drum" plant, for, although the flowers are of good size and measure as much as 8 inches across, creamy-white in colour, and heavily scented, they are very fugitive, and last only about twenty-four hours before they begin to fade; indeed, they seem almost to prefer to open at night. Nevertheless, a mature tree can be depended upon to produce a succession of blooms over a long period in late summer. But if ungenerous in floral display, this does not dispossess it from the claim to provide one of the greatest contributions which China has made to our gardens, although in return it demands space which only the larger woodland gardens can provide. Introduced in 1900, the Caerhays specimens already referred to have reached a height of 35 ft. and together cover some 45 yards of ground. *M. Delavayi* forms a gigantic shrub rather than a tree, being flat topped and well furnished to the ground, with leaves about a foot in length and 8–10 inches across. For those who would propagate *Delavayi*, the best method is by layering; for this species takes root readily round the skirt of the plant. This is more than can be said of most *magnolias*, which are increased with difficulty either by this means or by cuttings, although the writer once succeeded in rooting a branch of *M. rostrata* which had been cut off near the base of the main stem and, without further preparation, pushed into the adjoining ground which was then firmed by stamping round it; but many attempts to repeat the process with this and other species have failed.

If layering is attempted, it is advisable when possible to pick out a branch so situated that it will not become overgrown by others before it has had time to root, and it seems helpful to scrape the underside of the layered branch, or to notch it, and later to remove the bark from about one-third of the circumference of the layered branch behind the layered portion, removing another one-third the following year, and completing the process the third year, if the layer has not already rooted, so that it is now completely ringed.

M. nitida. If the praises of *M. Delavayi* as an evergreen plant have been loudly sung, those of *M. nitida* must surely be pitched in yet higher key, for the brilliantly polished green of the mature leaves of this plant is only equalled by the lovely shining bronze of the immature foliage. The writer knows of no evergreen which compares with this for shiny polish, and it is a remarkable plant even without flowers.

Another recommendation for this species, and one eagerly accepted by any of us, is that it does not demand half the garden in which to display its beauty. Even so, it is still a scarce one to meet, although it appears to be hardy in Cornwall. Its scarcity may be due to the difficulty experienced in propagation by layers or from cuttings. Reginald Farrer in his field notes records that this species in its own country "attains an enormous stature"; but it is slow-growing. For the most part it seems to form a pyramid densely covered with the lovely shining leaves already mentioned; but other specimens can be seen which are sparser in leaf and more tree-like in habit. One of the latter is to be seen at Trewithen, being one of the original plants introduced by seed from China in 1918, and is now some 20 ft. high. The bush forms are best seen at Caerhays, where some have attained a height of 16 ft. and measure as much as 45 ft. round the skirt.

The white flowers, which, like the leaves, are smaller than those of the majority of magnolias, appear in April and May, and are scented, a pale primrose when they first open. The outermost of the 10-12 petals of which the flower is composed are heavily stained on the outer side with crimson-purple. The flowers are upright in habit, and about 3-4 inches long, the leaves being about the same length.

Plants have been raised from the seed of plants at Caerhays and Trewithen, which suggests that in time this hardy species will be more commonly seen in gardens in the milder counties. The seeds are a brilliant orange colour and, set off by the equally brilliant apple-green of the carpels, are very decorative.

M. grandiflora and varieties. Reference has already been made to *M. grandiflora*, which is by far the most commonly planted of evergreen *magnolias*, but nearly always as a wall plant, where it gets the warmth it requires to ripen the wood and so to develop its flowers; and though "standard" plants are to be found in Cornwall, they are not numerous, and do not make such good woodland plants as do other species; neither are they generous in the number of blooms they produce at one time, although to be depended upon to provide a succession of magnificent flowers, measuring as much as a foot across, over a long period, sometimes from July to November; but in this respect variety has some influence, for of the several varieties some appear to produce their flowers more freely than others.

Best of all is *M.* "Goliath," which produces larger flowers and more of them than most. This variety, too, offers the advantage that it is easily distinguished from others by the leaf, so that when obtaining a young plant one can be sure that in this instance one is not making an investment which will pay no dividend so far as flowers are concerned.

The leaf of *M.* "Goliath" is glossy green on the upper surface and green also beneath, but, unlike other varieties of *grandiflora*, it is rounded and blunt instead of acute at the apex and is shorter than others. This has been planted as a standard plant in a few of our gardens, but without good drainage and the admission of full sunlight the large flowers are apt to "miff off" before they open.

The most commonly planted varieties are *exoniensis*, which is a form of *lanceolata*, and *ferruginea*, which is probably another form of the same variety. Both these have a rusty-brown underside to the leaves, and are thus distinguishable from some other forms of *grandiflora* which, as in the case of *angustifolia*, have no brown felt on the undersides of the leaves.

Perhaps the most remarkable example of *M. grandiflora* in Cornwall is to be seen in the garden of the "Chaplaincy" of the Old Prison at Bodmin. It was evidently originally planted as a wall plant, but a merciful neglect has left it to grow as a standard, and it has now reached a height of 38 ft. 10 inches and measures 4 ft. 3 inches round the bole at 3 ft. from the ground.

Another remarkable plant of this *magnolia* can be seen by those who are observant growing on the south side of a small house standing a little back on the north side of the main road at Devoran Hill, on the main Truro–Falmouth road. Remarkable if only for the storms which this old warrior must have weathered. Fancy would tempt one to hope that Loudon, who lived in Devoran, was responsible for the planting of this *magnolia*, but it was probably put in long after his day. This plant flowers fairly freely, as may be seen by those who are on the lookout for it, towards the close of summer or the entry of autumn.

All varieties and forms of this American magnolia root readily if layered, and so those who would plant it have a means at hand to avoid forms which are stingy about flowers. *M. grandiflora* has been raised from seed ripened in this country, but the writer is unsure of seed having ripened on Cornish plants.

V

M. macrophylla. This note on *M. grandiflora* leads the way to the mention of other species of magnolia introduced from America, though these do not appear to have attracted the notice of Cornish gardeners—or should they not rather be styled Cornish plant hunters?

No large specimen is known in Cornwall of *M. macrophylla*, for instance, and yet this must surely rank amongst the finest of flowering trees, with its magnificent light-green leaves sometimes as much as 3 ft. in length and auriculate at the base, and huge white flowers 10-15 inches across, the inner petals of which are splashed with purple at the base. The reason why this *magnolia* has received such scanty recognition in Cornwall may well be because it is brittle and apt to be broken by the wind, if indeed it be not blown out of the ground altogether. This brittleness is a characteristic common to all deciduous magnolias, but *macrophylla* appears to be more "sappy" than most, and requires much sunshine to ripen and toughen the wood; so that the more sheltered the site selected for it, the less chance there is for the sunshine to do its work. This sappy growth, moreover, is very pronounced in immature plants, which are very apt to be cut by frost or cold winds, and for this reason young plants seem to take years before they will "catch hold" and start to develop. Nevertheless it is hardy enough, as indicated by the remarkable example of it which used to grow in Claremont Gardens, at Esher, which was more than 40 ft. high, with a trunk circumference of 5 ft. at 5 ft. from the ground.

M. Fraseri, which has smaller leaves and flowers than *macrophylla*, is an easier subject to grow. This, with its pronounced auriculation of the leaves (a characteristic which varies somewhat with different plants), forms a striking garden feature. As in *macrophylla*, the petals number six, the flowers measuring 8–10 inches across when fully opened. Mr. J. C. Williams introduced several plants of this species into his garden at Caerhays where they are growing well, the largest having reached 24 ft.

M. virginiana. There, too, can be seen a good specimen of *M. virginiana*, another American plant well worth a place in our gardens, although, alas, again a brittle subject. The leaves are shiny green above and bluey-green below, and are some 5–6 inches in length. The flowers, which are yellowy-white, are 2–3 inches and sweetly scented; occasionally a specimen can be seen of which the flowers are almost a canary-yellow, but the writer of these notes knows no example of this in Cornwall.

M. Thompsoniana. There is a hybrid, said to be between this species and *tripetala*, which, though not so attractive as *virginiana* when in flower, is certainly more pleasing both in form and in scent than *tripetala*. *M. Thompsoniana* is the name of this hybrid, and though it does not merit the best place in our gardens, it will grow well and form a slender and rather untidy bush or bushy tree without causing anxiety that it will be blasted out of the ground or chopped into an ill-balanced or unsightly specimen by the wind.

CHAPTER X

Metrosideros

THE genus *metrosideros* includes several of the most decorative and wind-hardy of all the trees and shrubs that can be grown in the temperate zone; but, unfortunately, frost sets narrow limits to their use on the mainland.

Canon Boscawen, of Ludgvan, who was keenly interested in these plants, summarised his experience thus:

"Of the eleven species of *metrosideros* growing in New Zealand, only two or three, as far as I have experienced, are hardy in Cornwall. The best of these are *M. lucida* and *M. robusta*. Considering their beauty, I wonder they are not more often grown; of all New Zealand shrubs, I know of none more desirable. They will stand wind well; they are not affected by wind or the salt spray near the coast; they are beautiful in habit and growth." [1]

But that estimate needs some qualification now, since the abnormal frosts of 1938 and 1947.

*§*Metrosideros lucida*, the "Southern rata." [2] This, the hardiest species, has polished evergreen leaves, like a myrtle's but more solid. In June, when the leaf-buds break into new leaves, the plant is flushed with coppery red, and in July the shoots that have not borne new leaves end in cymes of scarlet flowers—a scarlet with more crimson in it than that of *M. robusta*—each flower having a brush of long red stamens round a central saucer glittering with honey.

The plant is extremely wind-hardy. In the South Island of New Zealand, which is its principal home, it makes strange dark forests of clustered trunks. But it also stands a much windier climate than that, in Stewart Island, in the Snares Islands, and especially in the Lord Auckland Islands 190 miles south-west of the South Cape of Stewart Island (which is the southernmost extremity of New Zealand proper). In these sub-antarctic islands, *M. lucida* is the

[1] *R.H.S. Journal*, January 1923.
[2] The name "Southern rata," commonly used in New Zealand, to distinguish this plant from *M. robusta*, is rather misleading, for both grow in both islands. *M. lucida* is more common in the South than North, but *robusta*, the "Northern rata," is common in both.

chief tree of the forest, but under the continual pressure of antarctic gales its trunks lie almost prostrate, with branches turning up to make a close canopy of dark glittering green. Even above the forest level in the Aucklands, in the dense scrub 3–8 ft. high, *lucida* manages to survive. Thus, one would expect it to be one of the most wind-hardy of all plants in such a climate as Cornwall's; and so it proves. Six hundred feet up on Zennor Moor, it stands up to salty gales without a leaf being seared and without any distortion of its trim rounded shape. In the Scillies, though equally wind-hardy, it is less at home, conditions there being too dry. As for frost-hardiness, *lucida* is hardy enough, so far as my experience goes, for any Cornish garden near the sea, and is worth trying in any favoured garden in the mildest counties. In the frost of December 1938, when *M. robusta*, the North Island "rata," was killed at Ludgvan, Zennor, Penzance, and other places (though not everywhere), *M. lucida*, from the colder climate of South Island, survived without substantial injury. At Zennor, I have never known it suffer more than the brief loss of some soft young growths. (Since this was written, the large bushes here, over twenty years old, have been killed or almost killed by the great frosts of January–February 1947. But those frosts, so severe that common gorse appeared to be killed in all except sheltered positions here, and ilex lost every leaf, were so abnormal that I do not feel it necessary to amend the foregoing estimate.)

The plant has one serious drawback: it does not flower at all freely (at least in the form in which it is grown here) till it has been established twenty years or more. I do not know of any very long-matured plant in this country, so cannot yet say with certainty whether *lucida* will ever make so brilliant a show here as the more tender *robusta*; but my conviction is that it will. New Zealanders describe it as one of the finest flower sights of their country, where it flares red in such places as Otira Gorge. Here, plants at Ludgvan, Lanarth, Caerhays, and Zennor are, or were, mature enough, after some twenty years, to make a good show in patches. I remember Canon Boscawen looking over his bush, finding a few flower-heads one year and a few more the next, but never the lavish reddening that he confidently expected. But in 1944, after his death, one whole side of the bush, then some 15 ft. high, was covered with little explosions of scarlet. I recall, too, seeing a bush of it against a wall at Caerhays in 1924, which Mr. J. C. Williams said he would cut down because it did not "earn its keep" by flowering. He was induced to spare it, and now, being mature enough, it makes a splendid show each summer and survived the 1947 frosts.

The plants in this country are all, or nearly all, derived, I believe, from a bushy form of the plant, not a tree form. They keep the shape of a round bush at present, leafy almost to the ground. It is most desirable that the tree-like form should be imported from New Zealand.

*§‡ *M. robusta*, "Northern rata." Here is another magnificent plant, one of the finest of all trees that can be grown in our mildest gardens. It flowers much earlier in life than *lucida*, but unfortunately it is more tender, so that, whereas *lucida* survived the frost of 1938, most of the plants of *robusta* were killed. In its juvenile form *robusta* has narrow pointed leaves, thin and light green, about 1¼ inches long, set along conspicuously red stems (not green as the young shoots of *lucida* are). In the mature stage the leaves are darker green, thicker, and tougher; one form has leaves dark-green and rounded, the other a pointed leaf of brighter green.

The flowers are coppery-scarlet in June–July, with a curious distinctive smell; and in July–August they are followed by coppery-red young shoots, hardly less glowing than the flowers.

I recall one July evening with Canon Boscawen. When he looked up at his great tree of *M. robusta*, some 45 ft. high, against its background of dark pines, evening light was adding a fiery glow to the vermilion on the sunny side of the mass of flowers. Half-way round towards the shadow, light caught the edges of the flower-heads; and farther round still, the redness of the flowers and the green of the pines were muted by full shadow. Few flowering trees in England can have given a braver show. I like to think that that grand old man of Cornish gardening, who for forty-seven years replenished the well-spring of his life in cultivating Ludgvan garden, had the happiness of seeing his old tree in such glory before it was struck down by frost, and he by paralysis.

In New Zealand the plant generally grows as an epiphyte, starting life as a seedling on top of another tree [1]; and in such

---

[1] The fine seed often germinates on top of a "rimu" (*Dacrydium cupressinum*, "Red pine"). From there it quickly sends down roots through the moss on the tree's bark, and in time these bonds of "iron wood" (i.e. *metrosideros*) choke the supporting tree. Only the "puriri" tree, *Vitex lucens*, is tough enough to withstand this stranglehold. Thus, when the Maoris came to New Zealand, they

conditions it may reach 100 ft. in height; but when growing independently from the ground upwards, it reaches a much lesser height. Having the epiphytic habit, it can grow with little soil to start with, in a crevice of rock or even in a chink of wall, sending out long surface roots to find more nourishment.

The plant grows fast; and it often flowers when quite small. Plants from cuttings may flower a little when only 2 ft. high, and I have seen a bush 4 ft. high covered with flowers. It will stand lots of sea-wind, thriving in severe exposure on Tresco Island or up on Zennor Moor.

In short, it is an outstanding plant. But there are two drawbacks. Firstly, like others of its kind, it is a soil robber, sending out long surface roots. Secondly, it is sufficiently frost-tender to have succumbed in many Cornish gardens, though not in all, in the 1938 frost. It survived at St. Michael's Mount, Gorran Haven, and probably elsewhere; but at Ludgvan, Zennor, and Penzance it was killed.

Nevertheless, I have no hesitation in recommending it to gardeners in mild places near the sea. The disaster of 1938 was so abnormal. This is a plant sufficiently hardy and quick to be worth taking a risk on. I hope, too, that public authorities in, say, Penzance and Falmouth will plant it, and that nurserymen will raise a stock of substantial plants. I suggest, too, that a hybrid between *lucida* and *robusta* would be worth trying for: it might combine the good qualities of both.

‡*M. tomentosa* (Rich), "pohutukawa" (which means in Maori, "splashed by the spray"). This, the "Christmas Tree" of the North Island of New Zealand, is the finest *metrosideros*; Kirk, the New Zealand botanist, described it as "perhaps the most magnificent plant in the New Zealand flora"; and of all the flowering trees that can be grown outside the tropics there can hardly be any more beautiful than this.

Unhappily, whilst it is perfectly at home in the Scillies, it has hitherto proved just too tender for effective cultivation on the English mainland. (Apparently it is not grown in South-west Ireland.)

found, it is said, fallen trunks of "rimu" all ready for their canoe-making, hollow within and bound with iron-wood roots.

In this connection it is interesting to note that the wide distribution of the genus *metrosideros* shows, according to some authorities, some correlation with the distribution of the seafaring peoples who were pioneers in the use of the outrigger canoe.

From a distance the tree looks rather like a massive round-headed ilex; but the leaves are much thicker, very tough, dark grey-green with silvered undersides, and the young shoots are greenish-white, very conspicuous against the darker colour of the leaves and flowers. The flowers are carmine-scarlet—a colour not far from that of old cramoisie velvet, lovely in relation to the grey-green leaf; they are borne in umbels like huge pincushions, so freely that in a good season they completely cover most of the tree. The illustration, showing a single spray, gives a faint idea of this lavishness of flowering. In the Scillies one may see trees glowing red in gorgeous masses up against the sky early in July; in a year when the trees in Tresco Abbey garden are flowering well, the colour can be seen from far out in Crow Sound.

In the North Island of New Zealand, especially around Auckland, the tree grows on cliffs overlooking the sea, often with its branches almost brushing the water. In some places where it grows right down on the shore, it flowers when only a foot or two high. Elsewhere it is the principal tree of forests, growing 70 ft. high or more, with hanging masses of aerial roots. It is very wind-hardy, and does not mind being swept by salty spray.

As to frost-hardiness, *M. tomentosa* is evidently safe in the Scillies when once it is well established, having exchanged the thin light-green leaves of its juvenile form for the thick grey-green leaf of the mature plant, and having made some hard wood. But the seedlings, very common in the Tresco woodland, are often killed by frost; those which survive are commonly the ones which find lodgment against the stump or trunk of a tree (such as *Pinus radiata*).

On the mainland, the plant has often been tried without success. It grows well enough for some years, but then gets knocked out by a hard frost,[1] or, if not quite killed by one winter, gets too weakened to be able to withstand a second blow. Nevertheless, I think it may be worth while for those who have very favoured gardens near the sea to persist in trying to grow so outstanding a plant. Probably some forms are hardier than others. (Messrs. Duncan and Davies, New Plymouth, offer for sale a form so described.) Cuttings from the adult form can be struck, though not easily, and these will be

[1] I know of one plant, in the angle of a wall on the south side of St. Michael's Mount, which survived the frost of 1938, though very severely damaged. This flowered a little in 1944. At Ludgvan Canon Boscawen got it to flower once, at 12 ft. high, before losing it.

much hardier than seedlings. There is a form with greener, waved leaves which is probably a hybrid between *M. tomentosa* and *M. robusta*, and is likely therefore to be rather hardier; but it was killed in my garden by the frosts of February 1946. It is worth growing the plant for a good many years in a large pot or box so that it can be wintered under shelter until it has formed hard wood and has completed the change of leaf from the juvenile to the adult form. If once you can get this plant thoroughly hard, and if you can plant it where it will not get much more than 8° of frost, you may succeed. And this is a plant worth much trouble.

M. villosa (Sm.) is similar to *tomentosa*, but smaller in all its parts, with grey leaves waved at the edge. It is probably not worth bothering about, for it comes from the sub-tropical Kermadec Islands, 600 miles to the north-east of the North Island. Oddly enough, I did have a measure of success with it, since I started with an old hardened plant; it flowered here a little in 1938, and would have flowered freely in 1939 if the frost of December 1938 had not killed it when about 18 ft. high.

M. Parkinsonii (Buch), the only other tree *metrosideros* of New Zealand, makes a small tree or straggling shrub, often prostrate, and has crimson flowers generally borne on the branches below the leaves; despite this habit, which must tend to hide the flowers, it is said to be very handsome. Coming chiefly from the north-west and west of the South Island, from sea-level up to 3,000 ft., it is likely to prove hardy enough for mild gardens here, and should be well worth importing for shady places in mild gardens.

The other six New Zealand species are all climbers.

M. diffusa (Sm.). Much the best of these climbers is *diffusa*; and I know of few shrubs which I should more like to grow well than this. In its immature form it has tiny round leaves, quite thin; but in the mature form these are different, being thick and about an inch long. The flowers are umbels of carmine-scarlet stamen-clusters, each flower with a shining cup of honey at the centre, and each stamen tipped with a speck of yellow pollen. The plant makes a low bush among mossy stones in shade, or climbs up a tree or shady rock face. It does very well at Tresco Abbey in full shade, and is one of the loveliest plants grown there. On the mainland it flowered very well at Ludgvan and Penberth in 1938, before being knocked out by the frost of that winter: in the writer's garden it survived the frosts of 1946 but not of 1947. It is well worth trying in the mildest gardens, but only plants grown from cuttings of the mature form are worth bothering about. (Canon Boscawen grew the immature form for some twenty years on a shady wall without a sign of a mature leaf or a flower.) Plant it where it will never have to face direct sunlight, and try putting it on a mossy tree, to grow as an epiphyte, as it commonly does in the wild.

M. perforata (formerly *M. florida*, Sm.),[1] Scarlet climbing rata. This is the biggest of the climbing species, reaching the tops of tall trees and making stems like great cables, with loose flaky bark. In the forest on the western side of the Southern Alps (South Island) it is at home, and coming from that climate it should prove hardy enough for the mildest gardens here. Bushy plants with the mature leaf flower very freely when only 2 ft. high. The plant has flowered in the open for several years in my garden at Zennor. It will be worth making persistent efforts to get this splendid plant established. Evidently, the scarlet-flowered form is the one to get; the rare yellowish-orange one, *M. perforata*, var. *aurata*, has flowers too weak in colour, so far as I have seen them, to be very effective.

M. florida (formerly *M. scandens*, Solander: what tiresome changes of name!). This clinging rata has small leaves, ¼ inch long, and small heads of white flowers. It climbs to the tops of tall trees in South Island and grows also on scree down by the coast west of the Southern Alps; so it should be hardy enough for the milder gardens. A bushy plant has done well outside for some years with me, but has not yet flowered. (It was killed in 1947.)

M. albiflora (Sol.), white climbing rata, is a very handsome plant, with larger leaves than the other climbing sorts and large branching panicles of flowers of a clear white. Coming from the northern part of North Island, it probably cannot be relied on here in a severe winter; but for the past four years it has flowered against a shady rock at Zennor, and only suffered minor injury from the frosts of spring 1946. So it is well worth trying in sheltered shady places in mild gardens. (Killed in 1947.)

M. hypericifolia (Cunn), the common climbing rata, is widely spread in New Zealand, from the North Cape down to Stewart Island in the extreme south; so it is pretty hardy. But from what I have seen of it at Ludgvan and Tresco, I do not recommend it as a

[1] See Laing and Blackwell, *Plants of New Zealand*, 3rd Edition, 1937, page 281, for the change of names of *M. perforata* and *M. florida*.

garden plant: the flowers, produced on the old wood, are small and ineffective, pinkish-white.

M. Colensoi (Hook) is similar but more slender, with little pinkish-white flowers. Probably not worth troubling about.

So much for the eleven species of *metrosideros* which are native to New Zealand. As for the others, I will not attempt to deal with them here, one reason being that there is little chance of any of them proving hardy enough to be worth trying out of doors in even the mildest of British gardens. The genus comprises about 100 species, with a range from Madagascar to Hawaii. The distribution extends to India and Malaya, but not to Australia, Tasmania, or South America. In Hawaii the widely spread species, or group of species, known as *M. polymorpha*, is an outstanding feature, being almost the only plant which brings a mass of brilliant colour into the green of the tropic forest. It is a tree some 20 ft. high, very variable in leaf, with flower-heads of crimson-scarlet (like that of *M. tomentosa*) rather than coppery-scarlet like *M. robusta*.

CHAPTER XI

Nothofagus—Southern Beeches

THIS book deals little with trees; but the southern beeches, still too little known here, are of such exceptional promise for planters in the mild counties that they must have a chapter to themselves.

A number of the species are of outstanding beauty, combining the stature of a big tree with an extreme elegance due to the smallness of their leaves. Many provide excellent timber; and some may prove commercially valuable here, as in New Zealand and Chile. Broadly speaking, all thrive in sheltered places in Cornwall and other mild counties, and some thrive in the cold ones, too; and whilst many are trees of the forest, unable to stand much wind in isolated positions, several come from extremely windy climates, and at least one, the mountain beech, *N. cliffortioides*, appears likely to stand some exposure.

Our native beech, *Fagus sylvatica*, is a gregarious plant, making whole woods of one tree, with few or no competitors. The same is true of the southern beeches in New Zealand: they make large beech forests—the hard beech, *N. truncata*, growing with the black beech, *N. Solandri*, the red beech, *N. fusca*, with the silver one, *N. Menziesii*. In the South Island, a mountain forest-belt stretching for several hundreds of miles is completely dominated by one species, the mountain beech, *N. cliffortioides*. This suggests that southern beeches should be planted here, not only as isolated specimens in the shelter of mixed woodlands, but as beech-woods, sheltering themselves, when propagation here makes mass planting practicable.

The few, fairly long-matured trees in Cornwall are evidence both of their unique combination of massiveness with grace and of their contentment with the Cornish climate; and young trees are shooting up in Cornish and other woodlands with a speed and vigour that should satisfy the forester as well as the gardener. The evidence grows that planters in such climates as Cornwall's have in the southern beeches a very rich and far too little used means of adding to our wealth of trees.

All the southern beeches come either from South America—

the Cape Horn country and the Chilean coast—or from Australasia—New Zealand, Australia, and Tasmania. Most of them are evergreens, including all but one of the Australasians; but most of the South Americans are deciduous.

Here is a list. I wish that difficulties of travel had not prevented a more adequate study of existing plantings for these notes. It would be useful to have an expert up-to-date study of our opportunity for growing these trees, based on a survey of what has been achieved already, and taking into account the experience of New Zealand and Chilean foresters.

Nothofagus antarctica, Antarctic beech, a large *deciduous* tree, with small leaves $\frac{1}{2}$–$1\frac{1}{4}$ inches long, crumpled on the surface. The leaf may colour here before falling, as it does at home. It comes from Tierra del Fuego and the coast of South Chile. As a young plant it is growing with great speed in Cornwall; a most elegant tree. It comes from a climate which Darwin described as "equable, humid, and windy"—just such words as might be chosen to describe West Cornwall's or Western Ireland's climate; and the soil of Tierra del Fuego's coast is granitic like that of the Land's End peninsula. So it should thrive here.

N. betuloides. This, too, comes from Tierra del Fuego, and from the Chilean coast (where it grows with *Drimys Winteri*). But this is *evergreen*, making a large dense tree, with leaves $\frac{1}{2}$–1 inch long. It is doing very well in Southern England, including Cornwall.

N. Blairii is a New Zealand evergreen tree, reaching 40–60 ft., similar to *N. cliffortioides* and *N. Solandri*, but larger in leaf, the leaves being toothless, $1\frac{2}{3}$/$\frac{3}{4}$ inch long. Perhaps not yet in cultivation here.

N. cliffortioides, mountain beech. A New Zealand evergreen tree, usually 20–40 ft., but dwarfed to a bush in alpine exposures. It has heart-shaped leaves, only $\frac{1}{4}$–$\frac{1}{2}$ inch long, smooth and not toothed, but entire. In parts of New Zealand this grows near sea-level, but it is chiefly a mountain plant, dominating hundreds of miles of forest, above the level where other forest trees thrive, and surviving as bushy scrub, above the timber level, up to an altitude of 4,500 ft. Encouraged by these facts, I have tried it in severe exposure on Zennor Moor; I cannot say that it has done at all well, but the ordeal is an extreme one, and it may prove wind-hardy enough to thrive in more normally windy sites. It is not, so far as I have seen it, one of the most beautiful species.

N. Cunninghamii. This may be reckoned the most beautiful of all the southern beeches. It is an evergreen, from Tasmania and Victoria, reaching over 100 ft., sometimes 200 ft., in the lowland forests there, but reduced to a shrub at high altitudes. In Tasmania, it is commonly found in damp gullies in the mountainous country, together with the tree fern, *Dicksonia antarctica*. Though the tree can be so large, the tooth-edged leaf is only ¼–1 inch long; so that the plant has the elegance of a fine-cut fern. The tree is still scarce here, but thrives in various Cornish woodlands and promises to be one of the finest additions to our trees. In fairly open sites, e.g. at Ludgvan Rectory, it is doing well, but it cannot be expected to show its beauty in exposed places, or to stand much frost.

N. Dombeyi. A magnificent timber tree from Chile and Argentina, evergreen or nearly so, reaching a great size. It commonly grows with *N. obliqua*, one of the deciduous species, and with that tree provides Chile with its chief timber supply. *Eucryphia cordifolia* and *Desfontainea spinosa* are amongst its other associates. The leaf, finely toothed, is ¾–1½ inches long. It is very free and graceful in growth, and has already made a fine tree at Caerhays.

N. fusca, red beech, is another very fine one, from New Zealand, reaching 80–100 ft., with a buttressed trunk and blackish or dark-brown bark; leaves coarsely toothed, 1–1½ inches long. It grows up to altitudes of 3,500 ft., liking ample rainfall and wetter situations than the other New Zealand species. Its timber is red, and its leaves, here as in New Zealand, often colour to the crimson of a copper beech in autumn. In sheltered Cornish woodland the tree is growing at a great pace; and a plantation of it is doing well in moderate exposure at Tregrehan (near Par).

N. truncata, hard beech, is very similar to *fusca*, perhaps only a variety, but its leaves are smaller, paler, and thicker, and its timber pink instead of red. (Sometimes called *N. fusca* var. *Colensoi*.)

N. Gunnii, a Tasmanian, is the Australasian counterpart of the South American *N. antarctica*; a deciduous tree from altitudes of 4,000 ft. in the Tasmanian mountains.

N. Menziesii, silver beech, is one of the most beautiful, and should, I think, be extensively planted here, where wind-shelter is adequate. It is a New Zealander; similar to the Tasmanian *Cunninghamii*, but not so tall, reaching 60–100 ft. in mountain forests but becoming a shrub on the heights. The toothed leaves are only ½ inch long, making ferny sprays. The trunk is often buttressed, and the bark is silvery, with horizontal streaks like a cherry tree, especially when young. The tree has reached 40 ft. or more in some Cornish gardens (e.g. Lanarth and Caerhays). So far as my experience goes, it cannot stand any severe maritime exposure.

N. Moorei, from mountain slopes on the southern coast of New South Wales and from mountains in Queensland, has larger leaves than the other evergreen species, sometimes as long as 4 inches but generally about 2 inches; they are dark and polished, with a toothed edge, and very decorative. It makes a tree sometimes over 100 ft. high, with a clean trunk. It is doing well at Trewithen, Caerhays, and other Cornish woodland gardens, and is evidently a first-rate evergreen tree in sheltered gardens here. Coming from New South Wales, it is presumably more frost-tender than the other species, but appears to be quite hardy enough for our mild counties; it is not likely to be able to stand much wind. Easily raised from cuttings.

N. obliqua, a *deciduous* beech from Chile, is proving a most satisfactory and beautiful tree, tender when young, but quite hardy when mature, up-country as well as in Cornwall. It thrives in East Scotland and in the severe climate of Whipsnade, has already reached about 80 ft. at Kew, and does splendidly in Cornish woodlands, e.g. at Caerhays, Lanarth, and Trengwainton (though oddly enough a mature tree at Trengwainton was killed by bark-splitting after the frost of 1938). It was first introduced by William Lobb, but for some reason was lost, and was reintroduced in 1902 by J. C. Elwes.

N. procera is another fast-growing deciduous species from Chile; a beautiful tree, succeeding in the eastern counties as well as here. The leaves yellow in autumn.

N. *pumilio* is yet another deciduous Andean beech, reaching 100 ft. in the rain forest, but dwarfed to a bush at high altitudes.

N. *Solandri*, black beech, an evergreen New Zealander, is similar to N. *cliffortioides*. It grows 40–70 ft. high, making forests on dry hillsides, up to an altitude of 2,500 ft. The leaves are $\frac{1}{4}-\frac{3}{4}$ inch long, not toothed but entire, sometimes bronze-coloured not green; and the bark is rough and black. Not one of the more beautiful species, but I think fairly wind-hardy.

N. *truncata*, hard beech. See above under N. *fusca*.

CHAPTER XII

Olearias

NO genus has more to offer for windy maritime gardens than this. *Olearias* can provide some of the best of shelter-plants for such climates, and a few of them rank among the most beautiful flowering shrubs we can grow.

If you happen to be starting a garden in one of the windier coastal parts of the mild counties after gardening in serener air up-country, you may be inclined at first to be scornful of these daisy-bushes; you will remember perhaps that hardy but dowdy plant, *O. Haastii*, and probably you will not have seen such plants as *O. semidentata* and *O. Colensoi* at their best. I felt like that once. Now, after twenty-five years of trying to grow plants in one of the windiest gardens in Britain, I can only counsel you, if you do scorn *olearias*, to take extra trouble to learn what they can offer; and if, after that, you still find them a bit dull—respectable but unloved—well, I can only say that you had better be thankful for what will grow so heartily as *O. macrodonta* in a wind so often unkind. And by the time that the coastal scene is familiar to you—when the colour of bracken beginning to rust in August beside a glittering grey-blue sea seems homely to you—then, maybe, you will feel that *O. albida*, with its off-white flower-heads and grey-green leaf, fits singularly well into the picture.

*§*O. albida* (*oleifolia* in some catalogues). One of the half-dozen best shrubs for wind-shelter in exposed coastal gardens (see Chapter III). Besides being useful for shelter, it has a pleasantly scented flower, and though its white tarnishes all too quickly, it makes an effective decoration for the garden in August, e.g. as a background to the splendid but unmixable colour of tiger lilies. It looks more at home in gardens that are wild and wind-swept than in sheltered ones, and is one of the best plants for massing amongst large rocks in full exposure.

O. angustifolia. A splendid shrub in the style of *O. semi-dentata*, but bigger, sometimes reaching 20 ft. in the wild. The leaves are long and very thick, deep-green above and silvered beneath; the flowers are 2 inches across, white with purple centre, fragrant, in clusters of four to ten, set in a crown of leaves. It grows in full exposure on rocky headlands, often washed by spray, in front of *O. Colensoi*. It is still very rare here; an effort should be made to propagate it from seed, or from cuttings when available. It is a slower grower than *O. demi-dentata*, and seems less easy to satisfy; the tips of the leaves often die off brown.[1] (Killed in my cold garden in 1947.)

§*O. arborescens* (commonly known as *O. nitida*). This well-known plant is very useful for exposed positions and as a fast-growing nurse for other plants. Leaf dark-green above, silvered below with a satin sheen; flowers in loose drooping plumes all over the bush, white with darker centres, very profuse and showy, though not very white in effect. It makes a bush 12 ft. high in time, and very wide. §*O.* "Rowallane hybrid," a cross between *O. arborescens* and *O. macrodonta*, is a good, free-flowering, wind-hardy plant, with the toothed holly-like leaf of *macrodonta* and flower-panicles hanging out like those of *arborescens*.

O. argophylla, Australian musk tree. Leaves silver beneath, flowers yellowish-white; musk-scented. It makes a small tree in the Scillies. Not effective in flower and less useful than the next; a plant for moist shady places.

§*O. avicenniæfolia*. This is similar to *O. albida*, but less rigid and rather later flowering. It makes a rounded bush completely covered with flower-heads even in the severest exposure; but the flowers lose their whiteness very quickly. Occasionally a whole branch dies, but the bush quickly recovers when cut back. Inferior to *albida*.

§*O. chathamica*. Rather like *O. semi-dentata*, but with much broader, greener leaves, white beneath; flowers pale violet, quickly fading to white, with purple centres. A very handsome plant even when not in flower.

§*O. Colensoi* is a grand foliage plant, making a large round bush, 10–15 ft. here, up to 30 ft. in the wild. The leaves are very large and leathery, of splendid design, especially fine when newly expanded in June, when they look like grey-green velvet. The young shoots, brilliantly silvered, are decorative in April. The flowers,

[1] Somewhat similar to *angustifolia*, but not yet (I think) in cultivation here, are *O. Traillii* and *O. operina*. Both appear to be fine plants worth importing. *Traillii* has erect branching racemes of from three to eight flowers, white with purple centres. *Operina* comes from the south-west coast of South Island, where it makes coastal scrub, together with such plants (well-tried here) as *Senecio rotundifolius* and *Veronica elliptica* and *salicifolia*. It grows 6–12 ft. high, with thick narrow leaves 2–4 inches long, and white yellow-centred daisies.

purplish-red with yellow stamens, have no ray-florets and make no show. Nearly all my plants were killed in 1947.

There are two forms of this scarce plant, one greener than the other; choose the grey one. Cuttings are slow to strike. This is a plant for massing in such a place as the south-east side of St. Michael's Mount, amongst grey granite rocks.

‡O. dentata makes a pretty little bush, 2–3 ft. high, with rough toothed leaves, with rust-coloured hairs when young; purplish buds and solitary flowers 1–2 inches across, pale lilac or white, with yellow centre. This comes from Victoria and New South Wales, and is tenderer than the others.

O. erubescens makes a large rather sprawling shrub with reddish shoots and small, dull white, starry flowers; not first-rate.

§O. excorticata has handsome dark-green foliage, glittering above, with a conspicuous mid-rib, rust-brown beneath; small flower-heads of a dull white. It has some of the character of O. lacunosa, but is a much less striking plant, with much shorter, broader leaves. Unlike lacunosa, it is easily propagated by cuttings. It may be useful as a hedge.

§O. Forsteri (syn. Shawia paniculata). This plant, well known in mild seaside gardens, makes one of the best wind-hardy hedges. It is a large bush or small tree, with brown stems; rounded leaves wavy at the edge, light green above and dull white beneath; flowers in November–December, inconspicuous but fragrant. The variety O. F. robusta, a stronger grower with larger leaves, is a handsome plant. There is also a purplish-leaved form.

§O. furfuracea. One of the toughest. It is rather like arborescens in leaf, grey-green and leathery, with silvered underside. The large white flower-heads come in August. This, and O. pachyphylla which resembles it, should prove valuable in the windiest coastal gardens. It reaches 20 ft. in New Zealand.

O. glutinosa. An 8-ft. bush with long dark-green leaves and rather effective corymbs of cream-white flowers. An Australian, more tender than the New Zealanders.

O. Gunniana (Hooker). This is one of a large group of species which have been much confused, often renamed, and lumped together by some authorities under such names as O. Gunniana, O. stellulata, and O. lyrata. The descriptions here given follow the revision of this group of species by Dr. Hutchinson, of Kew (Gardener's Chronicle, January 6, 1917).

The plant common in gardens under the name O. *Gunniana* is not really that species, but O. *subrepanda* (Hutchinson), which is described below. *Subrepanda* is one of the hardiest species, coming from altitudes of 3,000 ft. in Tasmania; whereas the true *Gunniana* comes from lower altitudes and is only hardy enough for our milder counties.

Gunniana makes an evergreen bush 5–10 ft. high, with narrow leaves about 1¼ inches long, smooth and dark grey-green above, lighter with greyish tomentum below. The flowers, very freely borne in April–May, are carried in corymbs on very slender stalks, well above the leaves.

Varieties are O. *Gunniana* var. *brevipes*, with very short flower-stalks; var. *phlogopappa*, with broader leaves and short flower-stalks; var. *microcephala*, with very small flower-heads; var. *angustifolia*, narrow-leaved; and var. *salicifolia*, with longer willow-like foliage. But probably none of these is in cultivation.

O. *flavescens* (Hutchinson), with larger leaves and stouter flower-stalks, is a closely related species.

*O. *Gunniana splendens*. Mr. H. F. Comber, on his Tasmanian expeditions of 1929–30, introduced a series of coloured forms of O. *Gunniana* which are of high garden value. The colours range from pink to mauve, purple, and blue. Selected forms are excellent in colour; and all the seedlings, resembling michaelmas daisies in shrub form, flowering in April–May, are effective in a mass, e.g. under the blue-pink of Judas trees. These forms are frost-hardy enough to have been an outstanding success at Nymans (Sussex) and many other up-country gardens, but they are, so far as my experience goes, not wind-hardy enough to be easy to use in exposed seaside gardens.

O. *Haastii*. This familiar plant—the only *Olearia* generally hardy in Britain—makes a dense round bush, generally 3–4 ft. high, much wider than that in time, with small, tough, grey-green leaves on stiff growths, whitened in August with flower-heads that quickly brown, and a mass of fluffy pale-brown seed. A dull plant, but extremely hardy and wind-resistant, and useful for seaside gardens.

§O. *ilicifolia*. This resembles *macrodonta*, but has long narrow leaves; very wind-hardy, and pleasantly musk-scented.

§O. *ilicifolia* × *lacunosa* is a beautiful hybrid with long narrow leaves, toothed like those of *ilicifolia*. It is extremely tough, and should make a first-rate hedge when plentiful. Like *lacunosa*, it is slow to reach the flowering stage; but, unlike *lacunosa*, it strikes fairly easily. It is scarce in this country at present, but deserves propagation, and is worth trial in the colder counties.

Pachystegia (Olearia) insignis. A low-spreading shrub with stems lying along the ground; large very thick leaves, white-felted below, and white young growths; flowers like 3-inch ox-eye daisies. In the wild, it grows in clefts and ledges of sun-baked schistose rocks (together with *Veronica Hulkeana*), and is there, according to those who have seen it, a very handsome plant. Evidently it should be treated as a saxatile plant, with plenty of stone about its roots. As grown here, it commonly looks rather coarse and out of scale; but by itself, amongst large grey rocks, it can be very decorative.

O. lacunosa. This is one of the most distinctive of foliage plants, very handsome and strange. The leaves are $\frac{7}{8}$ inch wide, but up to 7 inches long, dark green above, with a conspicuous pale mid-rib that looks as if it were inlaid, and pale rust-brown underside. In June the young shoots are bright rust-coloured, and the leaves are covered when young with rusty tomentum which soon rubs off. The flowers, not seen here, are white, in corymbs up to 8 inches across. The plant is extraordinarily strong and hard, with clear-cut design, and the firmness of a thing fashioned in metal. It needs damp soil. In the wild, it grows by streams, and drought may have been the cause of the death of some of the few plants grown here, e.g. at Ludgvan Rectory. A plant in the writer's garden, which came from Ludgvan, is now over 10 ft. across; it grows in damp soil in a shady position facing north, and after nearly twenty years has not yet flowered, but perhaps it would have done so earlier in life if it got more sun. Judging from illustrations in Cheeseman's *Illustrations of the New Zealand Flora* and Cockayne's *Cultivation of New Zealand Plants*, the flower-heads should be effective. Unfortunately the plant is very difficult to propagate from cuttings. It is very hardy.

O. lineata makes a bush 10 ft. high or more, with wire-thin twigs, dark green, with very small leaves; it is a tall plant but pendulous in habit. The flowers are very small, at the base of the leaves. The plant is graceful in growth, but like *O. virgata*, which closely resembles this except for its erect habit, *O. lineata* is hardly worth a place.

O. Lyallii closely resembles *O. Colensoi*, but is more open and even more robust in habit, sometimes reaching 30 ft., and it has even larger leaves, 4–8 inches long, woolly on top as well as beneath. The young shoots, as in *Colensoi*, are white, very conspicuous against the dark grey-green leaves. It grows in dense masses in the Snares and Auckland Islands, and would be very handsome here, planted in some quantity in exposed sites on the Cornish coast. But it is a very rare plant here, if indeed it is in cultivation.

O. *lyrata* (Hutchinson) is a very distinct species, with large untoothed (or very slightly toothed) tapering leaves up to 7 inches long, mealy underneath. The flower-heads, in dense bunches at the ends of lateral branchlets, are freely borne, but not showy. In good soil it will reach 7–10 ft. The outstanding hybrid, O. *scilloniensis*, described below, is believed to have *lyrata* as one of its parents.

*O *macrodonta* has been described on page 22.

O. *mollis*.[1] A dense rounded bush, 3–4 ft. high (so far as I have seen it, but perhaps more eventually); the whole plant light silver-grey, as silvery as *Convolvulus cneorum* in effect. The leaves are 1¾ inch long, waved at the edge, slightly toothed, rather sticky, musk-scented. The corymbs of small white flowers are very profuse when the bush is well-established in a sunny place. This is an excellent plant for a windy seaside garden, and looks well in front of *Olearia semidentata* or O. *scilloniensis*.

O. *moschata*. Another dense rounded bush, similar in general appearance to the last; said to reach 4–12 ft., but not more than 6 ft., so far as I know, here. Leaves not more than ¾ inch long, without teeth, sticky, musk-scented, closely set on the stiff twigs. Flowers small, white, in corymbs, very free when the bush is established. It is less decorative than O. *mollis*, but a pleasant plant.

O. *nitida*. See O. *arborescens*.

O. *oleifolia* (true). A dense bush, similar to O. *Haastii*, but more upright, with longer narrower leaves; white flower-heads. It is one of the duller species, but neat and useful for a windy place, being as wind-hardy as O. *albida* (which often passes under this name).

§O. *pachyphylla*. This is like a more robust, large-leafed form of O. *furfuracea*, with conspicuous flower-heads in July 4–5 inches

---

[1] The plant here described is the one grown under this name at Kew. O. *mollis* (Cockayne), as described in Cheeseman's *Manual of the New Zealand Flora*, is stated to have "size and habit of growth entirely that of O. *ilicifolia*," but differs in having white or yellowish-white tomentum. The plant I describe has a size and habit apparently quite unlike that of *ilicifolia*, but shares its musky smell.

across. It makes a small tree at Tresco, and should prove excellent for wind-shelter on the mainland, being extremely tough.

‡*O. ramulosa*, Tasmania. A beautiful small shrub with slender sprays whitened with starry flowers. The Australian plant hitherto grown here under this name, now identified, I understand, as *O. microphylla*, is very tender—too tender, perhaps, for the mainland; but the Tasmanian form collected by H. F. Comber should be tried again in favoured gardens if lost.

O. Rossii. A fairly good hybrid between *macrodonta* and *argophylla*, with soft grey-green leaves.

*§*O. scilloniensis* (*O. stellulata* × *lyrata*). This is much the most effective white *olearia*, and is one of the best of all *olearias* for general garden decoration in the milder counties. It makes a solid rounded bush 5 ft. high or more, grey-green; and every shoot becomes so covered with white daisies in May that the leaf almost disappears. It is wind-hardy, strikes readily, grows fast, and requires no attention except the removal of flowered shoots after flowering. This fine plant, valuable wherever a cold-white flowering bush would be in place, originated by chance at Tresco, and has how been named *scilloniensis* by Major Dorrien Smith.

*‡*O. semi-dentata*. This is, I think, the best of all the *olearias*, and one of the finest shrubs we can grow in the mild maritime counties. Leaf thick and tough, elongated, toothed, grey-green above, silver-green below, and the young shoots brilliantly white; each flower hangs out on a separate stalk like a lilac ox-eye daisy with purple centre. The flowers open small and deep lilac, becoming larger and paler, so that the bush shows a play of colours. I know of no foliage more decorative for cutting.

In Chatham Island, from which it was brought by Major Dorrien Smith, it grows in boggy soil in full exposure. Cheeseman, the New Zealand botanist, refers to it as "a beautiful little plant," but here 6 ft. or 7 ft. is a normal height, and 9 ft. is not uncommon.

Don't coddle it: if you put it in a dell in full shade and shelter, it will grow lank and floppy, losing both its compact habit and its remarkable floweriness. The finest plants I have seen were in full sun amongst boulders on a southward slope.

The grey-leaved *Banksia integrifolia*, and *olearias* such as *Colensoi* and *ilicifolia* × *lacunosa*, are good company for it, and the grey of granite rocks makes a good background. It is a fast grower and very easily propagated from cuttings. But it has one defect: a whole plant, or a branch, may suddenly die, unaccountably. It may be that the remedy is to plant it so that its roots never get sun-struck. In my garden old plants were killed by the frost of 1947, but not young ones.

O. *Solandri* makes a dense bush of twigs with small linear leaves, all yellowish in effect like *Cassinia fulvida*, extremely wind-hardy and wind-proof. It often grows wild on sand-dunes, and is very useful in sandy seaside gardens as a wind-breaking hedge.

O. *speciosa* has dark thick leaves, tawny below, and ineffective white flowers. It is wind-hardy, but not beautiful enough to deserve its name.

O. *stellulata* (De Candolle). This species is probably not in cultivation, but several other plants are grown here under this name. The true plant comes from low altitudes in Tasmania, and from New South Wales; Mr. H. F. Comber saw it in Tasmania as a very straggly grower. It has lanceolate leaves, coarsely toothed, up to 4 inches long, shining above, with yellowish tomentum below. The flowers are on slender stalks, in panicles at the ends of the shoots.

O. *subrepanda* (Hutchinson) is the plant commonly grown in the Home Counties under the name O. *Gunniana*. It has small, obovate leaves, shorter and rounder than those of O. *Gunniana*, hairy on the upper surface as well as the lower. The flowers are less effective than those of *Gunniana*; but the bush is much hardier.

O. *Traversii*. Invaluable for wind-shelter, especially in sand. See page 23.

Amongst the species not mentioned above some are likely to prove well worth getting. In particular, O. *Cunninghamii*, a large bush or small tree from both islands of New Zealand, is likely to be very effective. The whole bush is covered with white or buff tomentum, and the flower-heads are said to be handsomer than those of O. *macrodonta*. O. *floribunda*, a Tasmanian bush from damp ground, is very floriferous, with spiræa-like plumes. The growths when not in flower recall *Fabiana*, the stems being closely set with very small leaves. The plant seems very sensitive to any sudden change, and may (like *Erica Pageana*, for instance) be killed by a shock. A compact hybrid between this species and O. *subrepanda* has originated at Muckross Abbey, Killarney. Another Tasmanian is O. *persoonioides*, a very tidy little bush, wind-hardy.

CHAPTER XIII

Prunus, Pyrus and Sorbus

(*including Cherries, Crabs, Rowans and Whitebeams*)

TWO great families of plants, *prunus* and *pyrus*, contribute more than any others to the decoration of the majority of gardens in this country. Think what we owe to almonds, cherries, plums, and apricots, to the pears and apples, for beauty as well as for our dinner. To millions of town-dwellers as well as country people, the keenest realisation that spring is here comes with the sight of an almond's pink—that pink which goes as well with the smoke-darkened red of brickwork as with the dusky green of an ilex tree. How much one would miss in the woodlands of the chalk country if one never came suddenly upon the whiteness of a wild cherry tree; how much duller a London spring would be if no clean white tassels of double cherry hung out over the black and green gardens of the Squares. Those who go to work by suburban roads, suburban trains, and who can receive joy through their eyes, would be much impoverished if there were no crabs and cherries in the front gardens, no white and rose of pear and apple blossom in the back gardens. Not even the Vale of Evesham can show a beauty more lavish than that of its plum blossom; and even hawthorn hardly excels the blackthorn, whether growing in tall brakes in Savernake Forest, or in low thickets shorn by wind and whiskered with grey lichen, close by the Cornish sea.

Prunus comprises the almonds (*Amygdalus*), peaches (*persica*), cherries (*cerasus*), plums (*prunus* proper), apricots (*Armeniaca*), bird cherries (*Padus*), and the cherry laurels (*laurocerasus*).

Under *pyrus* may be grouped the apples (*malus*) and pears (*pyrus* proper); and with them the whitebeams (*Sorbus Aria*, etc.), rowan and service tree (*Sorbus Aucuparia*), and the chokeberries (*aronia*).

As regards cultivation, it is safe enough as a generalisation to say that *prunus* and *pyrus* grow to greater perfection and live longer in soil containing free lime, or in neutral soil, than in acid soil. In Japan there is no free lime, and certainly the Japanese cherries, hybrids of *Prunus serrulata*, grow quite well without it. To judge from their behaviour in West Cornwall, they can make good trees in very acid soil; but they are not so long-lived in such conditions as elsewhere, partly perhaps because of the acid soil, partly no doubt because of the shortness of the season of dormancy in so equable a climate. In particular, one may often notice in West Cornwall that *Prunus subhirtella* is not a success, being very liable to "Witches Broom" growths. Crab apples, such as *Malus floribunda, purpurea,* and *hupehensis,* thrive both in acid and limy soils.

Whitebeams, and the native gean (*P. avium*) manage to thrive in very thin soil over solid chalk; but generally the cherries, pears, and crabs want a good deep soil if grown over chalk. As for the plums, they want lime, like other stone fruits, but the blackthorns can put up with acid peaty soil.

Here is a selection from this wide range.

PRUNUS
A. Almonds and Peaches

*ized *Prunus Amygdalus,* common almond. No need to recommend this for its beauty. But it does not thrive everywhere. It wants warm soil and a ripening sun. I have never seen it so good in Cornwall as in the suburbs of London. *P. A. macrocarpa* is a large-flowered form, fine where it thrives, with nearly white flowers and edible almonds.

**P. Pollardii,* a cross between almond and peach, is a magnificent plant, with substantial flowers 2 inches across, brighter pink than those of common almond.

P. tenella (Rehder, syn. *Amygdalus nana*) is the dwarf almond, a delightful bush 2–4 ft. high, with slim growths and small pink flowers in March–April. Get it on its own roots and give it, say, aubrietia or blue anemone for a carpet. If branches wilt, cut them to the ground. *Gessleriana* is a better form with larger flowers.

P. Persica sanguinea plana, double peach. Lovely where it thrives, with double carmine-pink flowers. Give it a warm place with a background that will be dark in April. "Cambridge Carmine" is a more robust and hardy hybrid between this and *P. Persica* "Clara Meyer," with flowers of brilliant carmine-red. "Russell's Red" is another, very brilliant in colour.

P. triloba multiplex, with its small pink rosettes set all along the previous summer's shoots, makes a great show for a short time as a wall plant; as a bush it is hardy, but not always satisfactory, being very liable to wilting of branches, especially in acid soils. Prune immediately after flowering.

B. PLUMS

P. cerasifera, cherry plum, myrobalan. A round-headed tree of this, 20 ft. high, whitening at the end of February, is a sight as welcome in its way as the more spectacular cherries of April. Its smoke of small white flowers, greening as the first leaves break, fits perfectly into a woodland scene, where the purple-leaved form *P. c. Pissardii* would look much too sophisticated.

P. c. Pissardii, with its pink-flushed flowers and brown-purple leaf, is in every garden: an excellent garden plant where well placed and well treated. Don't put it with laburnum. The leaf-colour can be useful as a dark tone behind a large informal flower border. It flowers and colours better if cut hard back after flowering. Bullfinches sometimes ruin the flower-buds.

P. c. nigra (syn. *Woodii*) is an improved form with pinker flowers and more consistently purple leaves.

P. c. Blireana, hybrid between *P. Pissardii* and *P. Mume*, a Japanese apricot, is less vigorous than *Pissardii*; but if planted in good loam, in full sun, it is not shy-flowering or a poor grower, and can be very effective with its double pink flowers and purple foliage.

C. APRICOTS

P. Armeniaca, "Ansu," var. *flore pleno*, is a beautiful semi-double pink apricot, much better in constitution than the difficult *P. Mume*.

D. CHERRIES

P. avium, gean. For a wild place, in a wood or at the garden's edge, the native single cherry is incomparable as a flowering tree. It does best on limy soils such as the chalk downs at Whipsnade; it does well also on neutral and rather acid soils, but is never very healthy or long-lived on very acid soils. I have never seen a really good one in West Cornwall.

**P. avium plena*, the double gean, is a better garden plant than the single form, being more lasting in flower, whiter in effect, and not so tall. For a garden with a good depth of soil containing free lime, or for a fairly rich neutral soil, where there is room for a wide deciduous flowering tree 40–50 ft. high, this might well be first choice. (Do you remember the trees of this near the Victoria Gate at Kew, at the end of April?)

P. Conradinæ. A tree of light graceful habit up to 30 ft. high, with pale-pink flowers, notched at the petal's edge, as early as February or early March. *Semi-plena,* the semi-double form, is rather less vigorous, but more lasting and more effective.

**P. Hillieri* is a hybrid between *P. incisa* and *P. Sargentii* which originated by chance in Messrs. Hillier's nursery at Winchester. It is a beautiful free-growing tree—one of the cherries which looks at home in a wild place as well as in a garden. In April the whole tree is covered with light-pink flowers of good shape and lasting quality, intermediate between the flowers of its parents; and in autumn the foliage is superbly coloured. (Similar crosses have occurred elsewhere, and one received the A.M. of the R.H.S. I have not seen these, to compare them with *Hillieri*, but they are not likely to excel it.)

**P. incisa.* An invaluable plant for many uses, smothered in March–April with small white flowers with notched petals, and red calyx and stamens which give the bush a flush of colour. The leaves have a long point and are doubly toothed. Left to itself on a bank it commonly makes a wide spread, but it lends itself exceptionally well to shaping as a hedge or as a bush. This is a cherry for small gardens as well as large ones.

**P. mahaleb pendula,* St. Lucie cherry, weeping form. This should not be ousted by the more spectacular double cherries: it is one of the most lovely of its tribe for a half-wild place, e.g. at the entrance to a wood, making a smoke of small white flowers, with a fresh sweet smell, at the end of April. The form *pendula* is not "weeping" like a weeping ash, but the tree has a showering habit more graceful even than that of the type. If you doubt whether this neglected plant is worth bothering about, go and see it near the Temperate House at Kew. If a flowering tree is wanted for the churchyard, near a big yew tree, this is one of the trees worth considering.

P. Rhexii (syn. *P. Cerasus flore pleno*). The double white form of *P. Cerasus* is like a late-flowering, less vigorous, form of the double gean (*P. avium fl. pl.*); so it can be used in town gardens where the other would get too big.

The wild *P. Cerasus,* less decorative than *P. avium,* is one of the parents of the fruiting cherries, including the Morello.

The single Morello cherry is most beautiful in flower, and so, of course, are the edible cherries of Kentish cherry orchards. Indeed, the most beautiful cherry tree I remember is (or was) a huge

Morello growing out of the stone steps leading up to the forecourt of an old house in Tuscany. White against a blue sky, or white and blurred grey on a misty morning, that was as lovely a sight of cherry blossom as any Japanese hybrid could provide; and the jam we made from its black cherries was incomparable.

*P. Sargentii,[1] Sargent's cherry. (*P. Sargentii* of Rehder; *P. sachalinensis* of Schmitt; *Cerasus Lannesiana* of Carrière.) This is the outstanding tree of which E. H. Wilson said that "if only one kind [of Japanese cherry] can be planted, it should be this." The rose-pink single flowers come in March–April, together with the beginnings of the foliage, then coppery-red. In autumn the leaves turn splendidly orange and red. In good soil, not too dry and hungry, it makes a tree 30 ft. high or more—much more in Japanese woods; in stodgy clay or in very shallow soil over chalk it will not thrive. Do not be surprised if, in your garden, it does not make a first-rate plant.

P. serrulata var. *spontanea* (syn. *P. mutabilis*), hill cherry, and *P. serrulata* var. *pubescens*. This variable species is a tall tree, reaching 50 ft. It has been much planted in Japan, near Kyoto, and trees still flourish there which date from the eighteenth century. *Spontanea* has coppery-red young leaves like *Sargentii*, flushed white flowers, and hairless leaves, oblong-obovate in shape. A good form of this may even be preferred to *Bargentii*. The other has greener young foliage, leaves somewhat hairy, and flowers a week later. Both flower freely when mature, but not till then, and both colour well in autumn. *P. serrulata* var. *hupehensis* (not to be confused with *Malus hupehensis*) is another form, closely related to *P. serrulata* var. *spontanea*, with pink flowers and good autumn leaf-colour.

P. SERRULATA, JAPANESE VARIETIES

"Amanogawa" (syn. *P. s. erecta*). This is the perfectly upright cherry with single or semi-double pale-pink flowers; a stiff-looking plant, but decorative when well placed.

"Fugenzo" (syn. "J. H. Veitch"). A moderate grower which makes a wide tree; at the beginning of May the interlaced branches are hung with double flowers, deep pink—a pink with a good deal of blue in it; the flowers are generally a good deal hidden by the coppery young leaves.

[1] See Captain Collingwood Ingram's account of this plant in *R.H.S. Journal,* vol. L, Part I; vol. LIV, Part I, and vol. LXX, Part I.

*"Hokusai" (syn. *roseo-pleno*). This familiar tree is a good grower, reaching 20 ft. high or more, with a spread often greater than its height. The semi-double flowers, borne with exceptional freedom even for a cherry, are light cool pink, and the young leaves bronze. Flowering at the end of April, this makes a striking background for the crab, *Malus purpurea*, which is a deeper pink in the same colour sequence.

*"Jonioi" (syn. *affinis*) makes a well-shaped small tree some 10 ft. high, and stands a good deal of wind even near the sea. The young leaf is light golden-brown; the white flowers are single, not very large, recalling those of the Morello cherry, and make the air fragrant for some distance around the tree. This is one of the best cherries for half-wild places, and can be used where the double pink sorts would be wrong in colour. Try it on either side of a gateway.

"Kiku Shidare" (syn. *rosea*, or "Shidare-sakura," or "Cheal's Weeping Cherry"). A tree of weeping habit with clusters of deep-pink double flowers along the long drooping branches. Best as a standard or at the edge of a steep bank.

"Kirin." This and the well-known "Kwanzan" (or "Kanzan") are similar, but "Kirin" flowers rather earlier, has flowers of a softer pink, and makes a lower but broader tree than the other.

*"Kwanzan" (syn. "Seki-yama"; also miscalled "Hisakura," which is really a single cherry).

This, the most-often planted of the Japanese cherries, grown now in thousands along suburban roadways, is a hearty grower even in light soil, quickly making strong upward-slanting rods, loaded with dark-pink flowers, redder in the bud, amongst coppery opening leaves. The tree generally has the defect of making straight rank growths, unbranched; so, while these cherries should not be pruned more than is absolutely necessary, the long growths of "Kwanzan" may need to be tipped, to encourage more branching growth. The colour of the flower is much more pronounced than that of "Hokusai," and the pink has much blue in it; so care should be taken in mixing it with other colours, especially when the tree is used in quantity as an avenue. Its upright habit makes it more suitable than most of the Japanese cherries for street planting.

Longipes and "Oku-miyako." See "Shimidsu Sakura."

"Ojochin." A vigorous grower with large crinkled flowers, pink in bud, pale pink or white when open, generally single.

"Shirofugen" (syn. *albo-rosea*). A fast-growing, spreading tree, flowering later than most of these cherries. The pink buds open into large double white flowers, hanging under bronzed young leaves. The plant is often grown as a standard tree, but I think this (and *P. s. Wasinowo*) is at its best when grown in bush form on an ample bank with dark evergreens such as yew as a background.

*"Shirotae" (synonymous with or close to "Kojima" and "Mt. Fuji"). The paper-white flowers, bell-shaped, single or semi-double, hang under long horizontal branches. Beautiful to look up to when well placed. "Tai-Haku," described below, is a finer plant for most purposes, but "Shirotae" flowers earlier, and is so beautiful that both should be grown, if possible.

*"Shimidsu sakura" (syn. "Oku Miyako" of gardens, or *longipes*). This is the new name of the plant commonly known in gardens under one of the other names given above.[1] None of the cherries makes so brilliant a whiteness in the garden as this one. Late in the season the pink buds, hung on long stems, open to large double or semi-double flowers, notched at the edge, with twin green carpels in the centre. The leaves open bronzy-green.

*"Tai-haku." This outstanding tree is certainly the best single white Japanese cherry. The flowers are exceptionally large, pure white, contrasting with the reddish-copper of the young leaves. It makes a vigorous, fast-growing, upright tree. A short avenue of this cherry (which has not long been in commerce here) can be seen near the restaurant at Whipsnade. Excellent for street planting.

*"Ukon" (syn. *grandiflora*). The best of the yellow cherries, with large semi-double flowers, sulphur-white, contrasting with bronzed leaves. The colour is weak, but lovely when well placed, either by itself against a dark background or hanging, say, over a red rhododendron (such as "J. G. Millais"). The tree is often rather gaunt, with too few branches and leaves; it wants good loam.

P. SUBHIRTELLA, SPRING CHERRY
and its varieties and hybrids

The spring cherry of Japan, "Higan Sakura," includes among its varieties some of the most beautiful flowering trees we can grow. It is a very long-lived tree, and very variable. In Japan very ancient trees exist; the height of one famous specimen is given (by Miyoshi) as 90 ft., and many trees over 40 ft. high, with massive trunks, exist. Some have the habit of an upright bushy tree, others are weeping

[1] See Collingwood Ingram, *R.H.S. Journal*, vol. LXX, Part I, page 14.

in growth. Some have deep-pink flowers, some pale-pink, some white; most forms have small flowers, but some are fairly large; most are single, but some are double. They flower from the end of March till about the third week of April; but the variety *autumnalis* flowers in mid-winter. Coming before the leaves are out, the flowers of the spring cherry make their full effect.

Here are the principal varieties cultivated in this country:

var. *ascendens* (Wilson), "Shiro Higan Zakura," is probably the wild species; it makes an upright bushy plant, flowering early, with pinkish-white flowers which, in some gardens, are not very freely borne.

*var. *autumnalis* (Makins), "Jugatsu-Sakura," is the well-known variety treasured for its habit of flowering in winter. It begins to flower sometimes in October, but generally in November–December, when the leaves have fallen; it may continue intermittently till spring if the weather allows, or flower again in a burst in early spring when the new leaves are coming. The flowers, faintly flushed white, are semi-double, stemless in autumn but with stems in spring. It will make a small tree 20–30 ft. high, of spreading habit. Give it a dark background to show up its pale flakes of flower.

*var. "Fukubana" (Makins). This variety, which Captain Collingwood Ingram has described as "without question the most striking variety [of spring cherry] in cultivation," is a vigorous grower, not weeping, with semi-double or double flowers, carmine in bud and deep pink when open. The petals—12–14—are deeply notched, so that the flower looks frilled. It blooms a week or so later than the singles. A plant in commerce under this name is, I understand, the variety referred to below as *pendula plena rosea*—"Yae Beni-shidare."

var. *grandiflora* (Ingram), "Otsuna Higan Zakura," is a seedling raised by Captain Collingwood Ingram with large almost white flowers.

var. *pendula* (Tanaka), "Ito Sakura," the form of weeping spring cherry most commonly seen here, has a weeping habit and profuse pale-pink flowers.

*var. *pendula lanceolata* (Ingram), "Ibara-shidare," is the brightest coloured of the weeping forms. (It may be a hybrid of the carmine Formosa cherry, *Prunus campanulata*.) Its bright-pink flowers are borne in loose, long-stalked clusters, and the leaves are comparatively large, with a distinctive lanceolate shape.

var. *pendula plena rosea* (Miyoshi), "Yae Beni-shidare," has deep-pink double flowers on trailing growths. This is the weeping spring cherry of Sendai; it has been confused with "Fukubana" (q.v.), which is not of weeping habit.

*var. *rosea* (Ingram), "Beni Higan Zakura." This lovely tree has pale-pink flowers of good shape, with red calyces, and is extremely free-flowering, beginning at the end of March.

Hybrids include:

P. × *Pandora* (*subhirtella* var. "Beni Higan" × *P. yedoensis*), which is a beautiful early-flowering hybrid, raised by Messrs. Waterer Sons and Crisp, with profuse flushed-white flowers of good shape.

P. *subhirtella* × *campanulata*. Captain Collingwood Ingram has raised hybrids between these two species which are, I believe, delightful plants, very free-flowering, and of rich pink colour.

Other forms of *subhirtella* or a closely related species, from the Kurile Islands, are now in cultivation in this country.

*P. *yedoensis* (syn. "Yoshino"). If, by my recommendation, I could increase the planting of one flowering tree, this is the tree I should choose—the cherry of Tokyo. It is a fast-grower, making a wide-headed tree of excellent habit—a tree that looks at home in an English wood. The flowers, blush-pink fading to white, make a cloud of flushed white in March–April, before the leaves appear. There is a pendulous form, var. *pendula*. Plant *yedoensis* in English villages, e.g. as a war memorial. I know a small Hampshire village where it grows in some quantity: every spring, travellers by the road through that village stop and enjoy the sight. I think, too, of the avenue at Whipsnade and the planting around the lake at Washington. In Tokyo, the Japanese of a past generation planted 50,000 of this tree.

E. Bird Cherries

Prunus padus Watereri (syn. *grandiflora*). This, the best form of bird cherry, makes a bushy tree some 20 ft. high and through, surprisingly white in the green of a wood or hedge in May. The flower-spikes may be 8 inches long. *Albertii* is another good form.

F. Cherry Laurels

P. *Laurocerasus*. Common laurel, unpruned, can make a very handsome tree besides serving as a tall wind-screen in woodland.

So, too, can Portugal laurel, *P. lusitanica*. *P. Zabeliana*, with its dwarf spreading habit and narrow leaves, is a decorative evergreen for a large-scale edging.

PYRUS

I. MALUS. APPLES

Malus coronaria. This, and its semi-double form, *Charlottae*, makes a large bush or small tree, covered with flowers like a large pink apple-blossom, scented like violets, in May–June. The leaves colour in autumn. Very hardy.

**M. floribunda*. No small tree is more flowery in April–May, none is fresher in colour when the carmine buds are opening to pale pink. The tree is apt to be lumpy in shape. It looks well as a group on a bank with a few plants of *M. atrosanguinea* adding a deeper pink.

PINK HYBRIDS

M. Hartwigii (*Halliana* × *baccata*) is a good grower (unlike *Halliana*), with large apple flowers, rose outside, white within.

M. magdeburgensis (*spectabilis* × *pumila*) is first-rate—a crab of very erect habit, with bright-pink semi-double flowers in May.

M. micromalus ("Kaido" of gardens), a hybrid of the species *M. spectabilis*, is an upright-growing tree with a lovely show of apple-blossom pink—pinker than *spectabilis*. Both of these are excellent for a large hedge or screen.

**M. Hillieri* is later flowering than *floribunda*, as effective as *M. Scheideckeri*, but with a much better constitution.

M. Scheideckeri (*floribunda* × *prunifolia*) has a bad repute, being a poor grower if not well fed, and liable to canker. When well grown it is one of the most beautiful of the crabs, a mass of semi-double rose and white apple-blossom. But the double pink form of *spectabilis*, *M. spectabilis flore roseo pleno*, may supersede it, being a better grower, with larger flowers.

WINE-RED HYBRIDS

**M. Lemoinei*, *M. purpurea*, and *M. aldenhamensis* are, in that order, the three best crabs with purplish-carmine or wine-red flowers. All three are wonderfully free-flowering and very easily grown.

Purpurea flowers first. The strong colour looks much better with some white near by, to temper it; and it swears with bright-red brick.

M. Eleyi is (so far as my experience goes) less effective than these.

CRAB APPLES

**M. pumila* "John Downie" is still the best of red-fruited crabs, white in spring, and loaded in autumn with scarlet-flushed crab-apples. "Dartmouth," with purple fruits, and "Veitch's Scarlet" are among the others.

M. "Cheal's Golden Gem" is one of the names of the best yellow-fruited crab. (Another is "Gibbs Golden Gage.") It has neat flushed-white flowers and a profusion of small yellow apples, brilliant against the sky. It is a variety of *M. prunifolia*, the typical red-fruited form of which is also worth growing.

**M. hupehensis* (syn.*M. theifera*). This vigorous wide-headed tree is one of the best flowering trees for half-wild places. It flowers late (May–June), the cup-shaped flowers making an effect like a single cherry. In the type they open white, but in the beautiful form *M. h. rosea* they are light pink. *M. hupehensis* deserves to be used freely, not just as an isolated specimen; like *Prunus yedoensis*, it would make a lovely informal avenue, backed by dark trees; like *Prunus mahaleb* it has the quality of a wild plant, and fits perfectly into the scene if planted in a tall hedge or at the edge of an English wood. It thrives in acid or chalky soil.

M. Sargentii (not to be confused with *Prunus Sargentii*) is best used as a dense bush 5–8 ft. high, but can be grown as a standard. White with flowers in May, and very effective when planted in some quantity in a wild place. It will stand exposure, e.g. on an open chalk down. In autumn the small red fruits make some show.

M. spectabilis and varieties. See above under *Pink Hybrids*.

II. PYRUS. PEARS

Pyrus salicifolia pendula. The silver-leafed pear, especially in the form *pendula* which is more weeping than the type, is one of the most effective of silvery trees. The trails of willowlike leaves, white in the young growth, with white flowers, are a lovely sight, especially when hanging over water. Silver poplar goes well with this.

SORBUS

1. AUCUPARIA. ROWANS

The rowans are distinguished from the whitebeams by their pinnate, or partly pinnate, leaves. They include:

Sorbus Aucuparia, rowan or mountain ash, which is lovely whether in a wild place, naturally grouped, or in a street. Its chief drawback is that birds eat its berries (scarlet or in one form yellow) so quickly. It will reach 40–50 ft., but is generally not more than 30 ft., and it is very suitable for suburban street planting or for country roadsides.

*S. *commixta* is another excellent tree, especially for street-planting, being columnar in habit when young. Its leaf is like that of common rowan, the berries and autumn foliage red.

S. *discolor* (syn. S. *pekinensis*) is in many autumns one of the most brilliantly coloured of trees. The tree is of open habit, up to 30 ft. high. S. *hupehensis* is allied to this.

S. *domestica* (syn. *Pyrus Sorbus*), service tree, makes a fine tree, sometimes 60 ft. high or more, but generally 30–50 ft., with pinnate leaves, white flowers, fruits greenish. Suitable for country roadsides.

*S. *Esserteauiana* and the very similar S. *Conradinæ*, are among the finest in this section. The dark leaves are whitish beneath, coloured in autumn; the white flower-clusters make some show; and the huge clusters of scarlet fruit are vivid among the falling leaves. *Conradinæ*, which is stiffer in habit, with broader leaflets, whiter beneath, is perhaps the better garden plant.

*S. *hupehensis* (syn. S. *oligodonta*). This, I understand, is the correct name of the fine white-berried *sorbus* often seen under the name S. *Wilsoniana*, which is really a red-berried species. S. *hupehensis* has grey-blue pinnate leaves, whiter beneath, turning orange and red in autumn; and the conspicuous clusters of berries are white, with a pink star, lasting on the tree after the coloured leaves have fallen.

S. *hybrida* L. (syn. *Pyrus pinnatifida*). This hybrid between S. *Aucuparia* and *intermedia* is a handsome tree, suitable for country roads; and its more erect form, *fastigiata*, might well be used for suburban street-planting. The leaves show the hybrid origin; the red berries are effective.

S. *thuringiaca* (syn. S. *decurrens*) is a similar hybrid between rowan and whitebeam, as brilliant as any in autumn colour.

S. Prattii subarachnoidea (*Koehne*). A shrub or small tree 10–20 ft. high with most elegant foliage, with rust-brown cobwebs of down under the leaves, and pearl-white berries.

**S. Sargentiana*, not long in commerce here, is proving a magnificent mountain ash. The strong growths end in big buds, sticky like those of Horse Chestnut; the pinnate leaves colour in autumn; and the huge flower-corymbs turn to masses of scarlet berry.

**S. scalaris* is a lovely greyish-leaved rowan, with brownish-red fruit-clusters and brilliant autumn colour. This and *discolor* are excellent for roadside planting.

S. Vilmorinii is a distinguished-looking bush or bushy tree, with decorative pinnate foliage and pink berries that pale to white.

II. ARIA. WHITEBEAMS

*Sorbus Aria. The whitebeam's flash of silver as the wind lifts its leaves is characteristic both of the tree and of the chalk country. The shoots are silvered; the leaves green above, white beneath, russet or yellow in autumn; the berries red and showy till birds clear them. The tree thrives in windy sites, and though it does not require lime, it succeeds even on poor shallow soil over solid chalk. It is recommended in Chapter III for roadsides and streets.

S. A. Decaisneana, better known as *S. A. majestica*, with larger leaves and berries, and a stiffer habit, is generally rated as handsomer than **S. Aria*; but the latter shows better the whitebeam's silver in a wind.

S. A. lutescens, with leaves cheerfully yellow in spring, is worth planting also; and so is *S. intermedia* (*Ehrh*), Swedish whitebeam, with lobed leaves and orange-red fruits, which makes a large, grey-green tree.

III. ARONIA. CHOKEBERRY

A. arbutifolia. A bush 5 ft. high or more, with white flower-corymbs, scarlet berries, and most brilliant scarlet autumn foliage. *A. melanocarpa* has black fruits, with the scarlet autumn leaf. Try planting these on a foreshore with blue michaelmas daisies, and sumach (*Rhus typhina*).

CHAPTER XIV

Rhododendrons and Azaleas

IN the British Isles more than anywhere else in the world rhododendrons have been the joy and study of gardeners; and nowhere in these islands can gardeners grow so wide a range of rhododendrons as in Cornwall, and in favoured places in Ireland and West Scotland. Here there grows now an array of these flowers which is not paralleled anywhere this side of the Himalayas. The South of France and California can grow many plants that Britain cannot grow; but in this field they cannot compete, for their climate is too dry for rhododendrons. Of all Cornwall's plant treasures, rhododendrons provide the largest and most unique part. Indeed, those who have planted the woodland gardens of Cornwall may perhaps be criticised for having lavished care and garden space too exclusively on this one genus of plants—*Rhododendron*.

In a brief chapter it is, of course, impossible to give more than a slight indication of the wealth of rhododendrons from which gardeners in the mild counties can choose. For the range is enormous. Some rhododendrons are creeping alpine plants a few inches high, coming from an altitude about equal to that of the top of Mont Blanc; some are moorland plants, growing together, densely interlaced, and forming wide masses of wind-shorn scrub; others again are fragile woodland azaleas; some are trees from dripping windless forests, with massive leaves 2 ft. long. Some can stand all the sun and wind of a Cornish moor, whilst others endure no wind and only tempered sunshine.

All I can hope to do is to give a selection, divided into categories and annotated, so as to indicate approximately the character and requirements of each kind. As regards the character of the plants, you will find in the following lists rhododendrons small enough for the smallest garden. If your garden is wind-swept, here are some plants which will stand as much wind as heather does on Cornish moors. If the garden is fully exposed to the sun, some rhododendrons will stand that; but most of them prefer some shade as well as some shelter. And if you are fortunate enough to be able to plant in woodland or elsewhere, in a place that is shaded but not dark or draughty, then you can grow some of the finest of all rhododendrons—some of the most beautiful shrubs in the world.

As for their requirements, no rhododendron (except *R. hirsutum* and to some extent *rubiginosum* and perhaps a few others) can stand free lime. Fortunately for those who want to grow rhododendrons, only a very small fraction of all the milder counties of the British Isles has calcareous soil; nearly all is neutral or more or less acid. In Cornwall, for instance, the only calcareous soil in the whole county consists of a few small areas of blown coastal sand. Briefly, then, if your garden is in one of the mild parts, you are not likely to be prevented from growing rhododendrons or other ericaceous plants owing to the presence of lime, unless the soil has been artificially limed. Be careful, of course, about that.

Peat is not indispensable; indeed, one of the finest gatherings of rhododendrons in the world, that at Caerhays, is in a place where there is no native peat whatever.

But rhododendrons do need humus. So wherever your garden is, be at pains to make an ample compost-heap. Save leaves and soft prunings; and lay logs of crumbling wood over the roots of the larger rhododendrons, for them to eat. If you can get bracken, cut fern at the end of June and use it as a mulch.

I

THE WIND-BREAKER: RHODODENDRON PONTICUM

The common purplish-pink *Rhododendron ponticum* was recommended in Chapter II as one of the very best shrubs for giving shelter. Amongst rhododendrons it is unique in this respect. So tough is it that even on the high open moor it thrives and sows itself; and in woodland or elsewhere it makes a wind-proof screen, invaluable for protecting other plants.

It is variable in colour. In the chequered shadows of a wood the typical purplish *ponticum* can be beautiful; and on the moor (on Madron Carn, near Penzance, for instance) the blue-pink of *ponticum* and of foxgloves, too often despised, provides just the right complement to the blues and greens of an English June. But these are colours that swear violently with warmer pinks and with scarlet, so that the use of *ponticum* in company with other rhododendrons has to be carefully managed. If wind-shelter is needed in a wood and *ponticum* cannot well be used because of its colour, some other species with flowers of neutral colour, such as *crassum, Maddenii, discolor* or *decorum*, or some of the vigorous garden hybrids, are useful. But for the outposts *ponticum* remains unrivalled.

II

Dwarf Species and Hybrids

All the following plants grow to a height of not more than 4 ft., and some of them do not normally rise so high as 4 inches. Some are marked § to signify that they will stand severe exposure. Most of the rest stand as much exposure as they are likely to get in normal gardens; but many prefer some shade, and the notes recommend wind-shelter for some kinds, especially those which bloom very early and are therefore specially liable to encounter rough weather at flowering-time. Most of them are readily increased by cuttings of half-matured shoots, $\frac{3}{4}$–$1\frac{1}{2}$ inches long, taken in July, inserted in peat and sand in shade.

Lilac-blue and Purple

*R. impeditum makes a flat wide bush, less than a foot high (at least in an exposed site), with dark bluish-green foliage and small purplish flowers: a good sight when well established amongst silvery rocks. In one form, var. "Indigo," the colour is deep purplish-blue. In another form, var. *pygmæum*, the habit is very dwarf.

R. *fastigiatum*, rather more upright and greyer in leaf, covers itself with flat lavender flowers.

R. *intricatum*, slightly taller, with grey-green leaves and blue-lavender flowers, is a lovely plant, especially in a good blue form. It commonly flowers again in August.

Other species in this group include *Edgarianum*, pale purple; *orthocladum*, mauve; *drumonium*, mauve, and *telmateium*, lilac with white centre.

These species have given rise to some hybrids of outstanding garden value, notably the following:

*"Blue Diamond" (R. *Augustinii* × *intrifast*). This has large blue-lavender flowers of fine colour. There are many forms of the cross; the selected one which won the F.C.C. of the R.H.S. should be obtained, if possible.

*"Blue Tit" (R. *Augustinii* × *impeditum*). This outstanding plant, more plentiful and cheaper than "Blue Diamond," makes a dense low bush, not exceeding 2 ft. in full exposure, but reaching

4 ft. or more in shelter. When mature it is completely covered with flowers of clear lilac-blue, slightly smaller than those of "Blue Diamond." It stands wind as well as common heather (even here on Land's End Moor). Plant a number so that they will grow together into a weed-free mound. Cuttings strike easily.

"Blue Bird" (R. *Augustinii* × *intricatum*) is intermediate between "Blue Diamond" and "Blue Tit." Yet another is "Sapphire," dwarfer than the others.

Impeanum (R. *Hanceanum* × *impeditum*) is another excellent dwarf blue.

prostigiatum (R. *prostratum* × *fastigiatum*) is about 1 ft. high, blue-green in leaf, with violet-purple flowers, often borne afresh in autumn.

*R. *hippophæoides*. Coming now to the rather taller species, we have two first-rate plants in *hippophæoides* and *scintillans*. Both will reach 3–4 ft. in shelter, but in exposure, or when regularly pruned, they keep down to 1½–2 ft. A good blue form of *hippophæoides* is a plant of rare quality, the clear lavender-blue perfectly related to the grey-green of the leaves.

*R. *scintillans* is similar, and is even more apt to flower again in autumn. Pinch back lanky projecting shoots. (Some growers annually shear the tops off *scintillans*.) And plant these species in a mass, near enough to shade each other's roots. All these purple-blues look the better for some shade, and for some contrasting pale yellow or white.

*R. *russatum*, *R. *cantabile*. These are very much alike, if not forms of one species; *cantabile* is rather dwarfer than the other. In full exposure, *russatum* grows to about 2 ft., a very stocky firm shrub; but in shelter it may be 3–4 ft. It stands wind as well as heather or dwarf gorse. The dark leaves are rust-yellow underneath, and the flowers are bright blue-purple or wine-purple. There is a white form.

R. *rupicolum* is similar, with smaller leaves and flowers, rich purple.

R. *prunifolium*, a stiff 2-ft. bush, has drooping bell-shaped flowers, plum-purple in a good form, but often washy. Most of these dwarfs have a very pleasant aromatic smell when bruised, but this one smells unpleasantly.

Magenta and Pink

R. *radicans* makes a wide mat only 2 inches high, with nodding purplish-rose flowers. Excellent for a rocky garden.

R. prostratum is another prostrate one with small leaves and flat foxglove-pink flowers.

**R. imperator.* Only one wild plant of this has been found. Kingdon Ward discovered it on an exposed granite ledge in North Burma. It is quite prostrate and extremely free-flowering, with purplish-rose flowers on red stems, an inch across. It seems to prefer a good deal of shade.

R. myrtilloides, a slow grower 3–6 inches high, with polished leaves bronzed in winter, has little nodding flower-bells, red-brown or purple, with a bloom like a plum. Like *imperator,* it was found by Kingdon Ward, and only one wild plant is known. It is variable in colour and in freedom of flowering. I have had plants for nearly twenty years which have not flowered yet, whilst a new plant alongside them flowers profusely.

R. keleticum, a cushion about 6 inches high, has flowers of a good heather-crimson.

R. pemakoense is a tidy-looking plant a few inches high, with the habit, unique amongst rhododendrons, of spreading by suckers. The flowers, early and very freely borne and large for the plant, are pale lilac-pink—rather washy in colour, but good in company with a stronger colour such as Primula "Wanda."

**R. crebreflorum.* Another very low bush, with leathery foliage and shell-pink flowers, exceptionally beautiful in colour. (An illustration of this, growing on a rock in North Burma, appeared in the *R.H.S. Journal,* November 1946.)

R. saluenense may reach a foot or more in time. It has bristly shoots and large purplish-rose flowers.

**R. calostrotum.* A first-rate garden plant. It makes a wide bush, generally less than 1 ft. high. The summer leaves are dark green, russet underneath, edged with hairs; in winter they darken to russet, and the young growths are conspicuously blue-green. The flowers, large for the plant, are like foxglove-pink cistuses, borne in pairs; sometimes pale, sometimes deep-coloured, almost heather-crimson. The plant flowers very freely in May and often again in autumn. Farrer, who collected it at about 12,000 ft. in the granite mountains of Upper Burma, wrote that it "covers the barest open braes and tops of moorland in a close flat carpet of dark foliage"; on a granite moorland in Cornwall it will do the same, so long as it does not get sun-struck at the root. Top-dress it with peat moss; and plant a number, if possible, close enough to grow together into a single cushion.

It goes well in colour with the similar but rather taller *R. riparium*, and with plants such as the dwarfer *R. keleticum* and the taller *R. ravum*.

R. ravum makes a sturdy upright bush 3–4 ft. high, the leaves brown underneath, the flowers blue-pink or in some forms magenta. A good plant.

**R. tephropeplum* is, for the fairly mild counties, one of the best. It makes a bush 2–4 ft. high, with narrow bright-green foliage, and a remarkable profusion of bell-shaped flowers of a pure cool pink, darker outside. It stands wind but prefers some shade. Close to this is the very beautiful

**R. deleiense*, with larger broader leaves up to 4 inches long, and larger flowers, cool pink in the best form, magenta in others. This, too, is very free-flowering, and it is hardier than *tephropeplum*. It should prove a good parent for hybrids; a cross with *R. Johnstoneanum* is a showy plant.

**R. racemosum*, a species with many forms, is one of the standbys. It flowers from leaf axils all up the shoots as well as at the ends. In some forms the buds are apt to get frosted if grown in an exposed place. Some show their warm rose and white very early. Some are deep rose (such as F 19404); others pale or white. Some are low, almost trailing, others upright bushes, reaching perhaps 4 ft. Close to this is

**R. oleifolium*, which has leaves silver-white underneath, and flowers of a warm pink, free from blue. This stands full exposure, and looks well with the dwarf *Vaccinium mortinia*, which has red shoots. Yet another in this series is

R. mollicomum, looser in growth than *racemosum*.

**R. ledoides* and *R. sphæranthum* are closely allied to each other (? one species), with white and pink daphne-like flowers in small dome-shaped heads. The plants are more aromatic than bog-myrtle. It is customary to grow these in damp ground, but I find that (at least in the humid air of West Cornwall) they grow more compact, and flower with remarkable freedom, in full exposure along with such tough species as *R. russatum*. None of the dwarf species is more attractive.

R. radinum is very similar; and

R. chamætortum is a very dwarf pink.

R. glaucum, known to our gardens for nearly a century, is generally about 2 ft. high; the leaves are blue-white underneath and have a strong gummy scent; the bell-shaped nodding flowers show (in a good form) graduated tones of an unusual warm pink—a colour which goes well with that of "London Pride." It is not a plant for an exposed site.

*R. charitopes, with clear rose-pink flowers speckled with darker colour, recalls a dwarf *glaucum*, but is a finer flower, and performs its miracle in autumn as well as spring.

R. Tsangpoense is similar, but with flowers of a more aggressive pink.

*R. Williamsianum. A low wide-spreading bush with small egg-shaped leaves and open bell-shaped flowers, pure rose-pink. It is often slow to reach the flowering stage and prefers some shelter. A beautiful plant, and easily propagated from cuttings. Hybrids include: *Williamsanum* × *orbiculare*, a very good pink; "Cowslip," pale yellow and pink; "Kingfisher," pink flushed scarlet, which makes a large rounded bush, free-flowering and excellent.

*§R. præcox. This hybrid (*ciliatum* × *dauricum*) is still one of the best early-flowering shrubs, unfailing in mild climates, and surprisingly wind-hardy. In an exposed site it keeps to about 3 ft., but old plants in shelter will reach 6 ft. or more. The profuse heather-pink flowers in February–March are perfect in colour with the early heath, *Erica darleyensis*. If the plant gets leggy or unhealthy, cut it back ruthlessly; it will generally recover.

*§R. emasculum is similar to *præcox*, but comes into flower just as the other fades. It is rather more beautiful in colour and equally wind-hardy. For a small garden there could hardly be a better investment than some bushes of *præcox* and *emasculum* with *Erica darleyensis* or a late form of *E. carnea*.

White

*§R. leucaspis. A bush 1 ft. or 1½ ft. high, a yard or two across, with hairy leaves, and large, milk-white, saucer-shaped flowers with brown anthers in February–March. Even in full sunlight and exposure this flowers very freely; but perhaps it likes some shade, and it flowers so early that some shelter is preferable. In the complete shelter of a wood the plant loses something of its character.

There is a distinct form with pink buds.

*R. moupinense. A delightful early species, often beginning to flower in the first days of January. It makes a bush some 2½ ft. high, with large flowers, white, or apple-blossom pink and white. There is a very beautiful form with flowers of a full warm pink. The flowers are easily spoilt by bad weather, and the growths are easily broken; so give it some shelter.

*§R. "Bric-à-brac." This hybrid between *leucaspis* and *moupinense* proves to be an even better garden plant than either parent. Its large white flowers in March are remarkably weatherproof, and it goes very well with dwarf *carnea* heaths. First-rate.

*§R. *ciliatum* is one of the first rhododendrons to plant in the mild counties—one of the unfailing sorts. It makes a bush 1½–3 ft. high normally, but some old plants in Cornish gardens are as big as 6 ft. The leaves are hairy; the flowers flushed white, covering the plant. It flowers so regularly and freely that it may damage itself unless promptly relieved of its seed-capsules after flowering. Whilst it stands exposure well, its flowers, coming so early, get a better chance in some shelter. It is very effective as a bold edging in front of some tall red rhododendron which flowers at the same time, or with the dark-pink heath, *Erica Vivellii*.

*R. *cilpinense* is a good hybrid between *ciliatum* and *moupinense*, a white-flowered bush of 2–3 ft.

*R. *yakusimanum*. Lately introduced from Japan, is one of the most beautiful dwarf species, very free-flowering, with pink buds and trusses of white bells.

Yellow

*R. *Sargentianum*. This very dwarf slow-growing shrub is one of the treasures. It has small hairy leaves, and small heads of primrose-yellow flowers, very pure in colour.

R. *Hanceanum*, var. *pygmæum* is a remarkable form, very dwarf and compact, of a species which is generally much taller. It is exceptionally free-flowering, with light yellow flowers.

R. *megeratum* has hairy leaves like those of R. *leucaspis*, but the flowers are not white but pale yellow.

R. *muliense* and R. *chryseum* are two good yellows of the *lapponicum* series, good company for the purples. They make bushes some 2 ft. high, with flowers pale yellow in *muliense*, pale or deeper yellow in *chryseum*.

R. *flavidum* (syn. *primulinum*) grows to 2–3 ft., and when well grown makes a good show of light primrose-yellow flowers. But it seems more fastidious than the purple-blues which associate so well with it, and prefers a fair amount of shelter.

R. *Valentinianum* is a 2–3-ft. bush, with hairy leaves and flowers like a pale-yellow *ciliatum*. It needs a sheltered place.

Red

R. *repens*. This famous plant, with scarlet flowers very large for the plant, is seldom seen flowering freely enough to make any show. But, as has been proved at Caerhays, it can be a rewarding plant, and it has been a parent of a series of outstanding hybrids.

The plant is prostrate, with deep-scarlet trumpet flowers of great substance. It has a habit of growing downhill, and success at Caerhays was achieved by planting it where its branchlets can grow vertically down the face of a low, mossy retaining wall in woodland half-shade. There are several forms of the type.

The hybrids are extremely free-flowering and much more effective for the ordinary garden. They include:

*"Elisabeth" (*Griersonianum* × *repens*), a low bush with deep-red flowers and small dark leaves.

*"Ethel" ("F. C. Puddle" × *repens*), very dwarf, light rose-scarlet.

"Little Bert" (*repens* × *euchaites*), a dwarf plant with the freedom and vivid scarlet of *euchaites*.

"Jaipur" (*repens* × *Meddianum*), of which there are two forms, one dwarf, with the downward growth of *repens*, the other less useful, being erect like *Meddianum*.

*"Venapens" (*venator* × *repens*), very dwarf, with large scarlet flowers.

R. *didymum*. A low bush, slow-growing, with very dark-red flowers of firm substance, freely produced. The flowers are too dark to make a brilliant show, but lovely with the light through them, port-wine coloured. This plant is much more easily contented than most of its kin. Its hybrids include the outstanding *"Red Cap" (*didymum* × *eriogynum*), a low bush, very slow-growing and late-flowering, and most profuse with its blood-red flowers. This is generally in full flower in mid-July, and can be grouped effectively with the white-flowered *Hoherea glabrata*.

"Carmen" (*didymum* × *repens*) is very dwarf, with blackish-crimson flowers.

"Exburiense" (*didymum* × *Kyawi*) has effective foliage and dark-red flowers, very late.

R. *hæmatodes* is a wide compact bush, generally not more than 3-4 ft. high, with leaves rust-felted beneath, and glazed flowers, deep crimson-scarlet, with a distinctive calyx. It is slow to reach flowering stage, and often not free-flowering enough to make much effect in the garden. It likes fairly heavy soil and some shade.

It is a parent of some very fine hybrids of medium height, such as *"May Day," "Humming Bird," "Choremia," which are free-flowering. See page 294.

Other dwarf red-flowered species include R. *sanguineum*, blood-red; R. *hæmaleum*, blackish-red. These are generally fastidious plants and not free-flowering; but some very good hybrids have been raised from them.

III

Plants of Medium Height, generally with Small Leaves

(A) Blue, Lavender, Lilac-mauve

*R. *Augustinii*. A good form of this variable plant is one of the best of all Rhododendrons. Eventually a 10-ft. bush, with flowers lavender-blue of various tones, or lilac-white, or in the best form clear horizon-blue with a splash of exactly the right yellow-green. The colour looks best in half-shade, and the plant needs wind-shelter.

Parent of "Blue Tit," "Blue Diamond" and other dwarfs; also of *russautinii* (× *russatum*), an excellent purple-blue of medium size; and "Electra" (*chasmanthum* × *Augustinii*), with fine nearly-blue flowers.

But a good *Augustinii* cannot be improved on.

*R. *chasmanthum*. An 8-ft. bush; flowers lavender to mauve, a little later than *Augustinii*. R. *chasmanthoides* is similar. Both very good.

R. *cæruleum* (syn. *eriandrum*). 3-5 ft., with rose-lavender flowers; also a fine white form.

R. desquamatum, good mauve flowers, spotted. This can be very showy.

R. exquisitum has clear-lavender flowers, unspotted, a beautiful colour.

**R. oreotrephes*, a dense 7-ft. bush with beautiful glaucous-blue foliage on violet-tinted shoots, and clear-mauve flowers, generally spotted; a very decorative plant, especially in half-shade.

R. timeteum is another good one, in the style of *oreotrephes*, extremely free with its lavender flowers.

R. zaleucum, a tall bush, eventually a 30-ft. tree, with narrow leaves, glaucous white underneath; flowers mauve-lilac or nearly white. This cannot stand wind.

(B) HEATHER-PINK

**R. Davidsonianum*. In the style of *yunnanense* (see below), but with flowers cool pink in the best form; very good with *Erica darleyensis*, *E. mediterranea superba*, *E. australis*, and excellent for massing. The rank shoots can be cut back to keep the bush compact, but it is naturally a tall-grower, and looks well in woodland left unpruned.

R. emasculum. See page 288.

**R. mucronulatum* has bright foxglove-pink flowers on bare twigs in January, sometimes as early as Christmas. A bush of this covered with flowers, 8 ft. high, is one of the most cheering signs of New Year. Easily grown and very hardy; but give it some shelter, since it flowers so early. Apt to get lichen-covered in mild maritime gardens.

§*R. præcox.* See page 288.

§*R. rubiginosum.* A big bush, eventually a 30-ft. tree, very wind-hardy, with good foliage and a mass of heather-pink flowers in April. Excellent with *Erica darleyensis*. It stands calcareous soil if the seedlings are raised in such soil. Very easily grown.

§*R. villosum*, intense heather-crimson or magenta, most floriferous; fine with *Erica australis*; stands weather well.

(C) WHITE AND PURE PINK

R. callimorphum, a bush 4–8 ft., small round leaves, pink flowers, open bell-shaped, with deeper pink buds. A lovely plant.

**R. chartophyllum* is like *yunnanense*, but generally deciduous; its flowers are most profuse, pinkish-white or white, spotted rust-red.

R. *Davidsonianum* is similar. See page 292.

*R. *orbiculare*. A large symmetrical pudding of a bush, with round leaves, and large, nodding, pink flowers, open bell-shaped. It is rather exacting and needs shelter and space; it may grow very wide in time. Hybrids include *orbiculare* × *Williamsianum* (syn. "Temple Belle"), a beautiful and easy plant, and "Humming Bird."

R. *oreodoxa*, an early-flowering bush or small tree with pinky-white flowers.

*R. *Souliei*. A lovely flower, varying from rose to white, saucer-shaped, on a bush some 10 ft. high. Like *campylocarpum*, it prefers a drier climate than Cornwall's.

R. *Stewartianum*. A bush 3–7 ft., with flowers white or rose or crimson or pale yellow, in February–March.

*R. *yunnanense*. No Rhododendron better deserves to be more widely known and grown. A tall bush, with narrow dark leaves, evergreen (unlike the similar *chartophyllum*, which is sub-evergreen); flowers white or lilac-flushed, with spots or a splash of rust-red. Most free-flowering, and with a lightness of habit which makes it look at home in woodland. It stands some wind and makes a decorative hedge or mass; an isolated plant or group in a wood shows up every May as a plume of tinted white. It is a variable plant; none is better than a white form with a marked red blotch. Strongly recommended for small gardens as well as large.

(D) Yellow and Orange

R. *ambiguum*. A 5-ft. bush with flat pale-yellow flowers, weak in colour, but quite effective on a well-flowered plant.

R. *caloxanthum*. A 4-ft. bush with sulphur flowers, orange tipped, and scarlet in bud, earlier than *campylocarpum*. Orange forms exist.

R. *cinnabarinum*, yellow form. See page 296.

R. *concatenans* has lovely glaucous foliage, as blue as that of *oreotrephes* or *Roylei* at their best, and bell-shaped flowers, apricot-orange, often slightly shaded purple outside. Parent of "Alison Johnstone" (*yunnanense* × *concatenans*), a fine new hybrid, clear amber, or yellow and pink: also "Lemon Bill," with waxy white bells.

R. *croceum* has nodding saucer-shaped flowers, clear yellow, sometimes with a crimson blotch. R. *litiense* is similar, but unspotted.

R. *dichroanthum*. A low dense bush, eventually 6 ft. Flowers orange to pink: clear orange in the best form. Parent of "Fabia" (× *Griersonianum*), pinkish-orange, or orange-scarlet in the variety "Tangerine," and other good hybrids.

R. *lutescens*, a light-growing bush, with narrow leaves, red-brown in young growth; flowers pale primrose; pretty and rather effective in a mass in woodland, especially in damp ground.

(E) Red

R. *catacosmum*. A bush 6–9 ft., with thick leaves cinnamon-felted underneath; crimson flowers in a large cup-like calyx.

R. *chætomallum*, 4–5 ft., leaves tawny beneath, flowers brilliant crimson, in the style of *hæmatodes*.

*R. *euchaites*. A bush in the open or small tree in woodland; leaves smooth, white underneath, flowers bright scarlet, like *neriiflorum*, but finer. This and *neriiflorum* cannot stand wind, the attachment of the leaves being fragile.

R. *fulgens*, a round bush, 4–8 ft.; leaves with tawny wool underneath, flowers blood-red in February–March. Slow to flower.

R. *Hookeri*. A 12-ft. bush, with characteristic tufts of hairs on the veins of the underside of the leaves; flowers intense blood-red. A scarce plant.

R. *Meddianum*. The Chinese form of R. *Thomsonii*, 6 ft. or more, with flowers deep crimson, or in one form scarlet. A parent of "Jaipur" (× *repens*).

R. *neriiflorum*, a bush of about 8 ft.; leaves light green, very white underneath; flowers scarlet, most freely borne. It must have shelter, since the leaf-attachments are weak. A good form of this in full flower is an astonishing splash of vivid colour.

R. *pocophorum*. A bush 4–10 ft. (not more than 4 ft. as yet in gardens here), with thick dark leaves, densely felted beneath, and dense flower-heads, brick-crimson.

R. *sperabile*. A bush 3–6 ft., with narrow leaves deeply veined, with pale-brownish wool underneath; flowers rose-scarlet. Var. *weihsiense* is similar, with narrow leaves. Both forms are less showy than *neriiflorum*, but better for a windy garden.

R. *sperabiloides* is similar, but with smaller leaves, less woolly, and with smaller flowers, crimson; it is dwarfer, keeping down to 2–4 ft.

III

Larger Species and Hybrids requiring Shelter

R. arboreum, the Himalayan tree rhododendron, was introduced about 1810, and first flowered in this country in 1825. It makes an upright conical tree, hardy in the mild counties, flowering in March–April; large lanceolate leaves, silvery beneath in the typical plant, russet in the form *cinnamomeum*; flowers red, pink or white. Parent of many fine hybrids.

Forms and hybrids include: *arboreum, "blood-red"; *Bodartianum*, white, spotted, in April; *"Cornubia," round heads of vivid crimson-scarlet in April, a grand plant; "Red Admiral"; *"Sir Charles Lemon," a noble white with dark anthers, and dark foliage brilliantly russet underneath [1]; *arboreum Werei*, and "Mrs. Henry Shilson."

R. Delavayi is the Chinese counterpart of the Indian *arboreum*, but a good deal tenderer. A crimson-scarlet form of this is very fine.

R. auriculatum. A wide bush, up to 15 ft. high, with very large leaves, crimsoned when young; flowers large white, sometimes pink, scented, as late as July–August. A plant for large sheltered gardens. Parent of good late hybrids, notably the very fine white *"Polar Bear" (*diaprepes* × *auriculatum*), which flowers in August.

R. barbatum. A tree about 20 ft. high here. Leaves dark green with bristly stalks; trunk a beautiful chocolate-crimson; flowers scarlet, in March. Slow to reach maturing age. *Shilsonii* is a grand scarlet hybrid, raised at Tremough; "Redwing" (*Shilsonii* × *Barclayi*) is like an improved *Shilsonii*. "Duchess of Portland" is a good early white, unspotted, compact.

R. calophytum. A tree with rosettes of long leaves, whitish when unfolding, then light green; flowers white or flushed, with a dark basal blotch, set on a wide platter of radiating leaves. Unfortunately this noble plant remains shy-flowering.

**R. campanulatum*. A variable plant, with clear-lilac flowers in its best form, with darker buds; the leaves have a bright rust-brown

[1] The original specimen of this grand variety long survives at Carclew in good health, on the spot where Sir Charles Lemon's notable garden was. It originated as a seedling from Hooker's Himalayan seed, and is believed to be a natural hybrid, white *arboreum* × *campanulatum*. The plant, over 30 ft. high, one of the monuments of Cornish gardening, has now disappeared, having presumably been inadvertently destroyed.

felt underneath. A good *campanulatum* is one of the most beautiful rhododendrons. It looks best in half-shade. "Susan" is a good hybrid of it.

*R. *campylocarpum.* One of the most outstanding species, but not often seen at its best in Cornwall. Round leaves, blue-white underneath; flowers light canary-yellow, open bell-shaped. The form *elatum* may reach 8 ft., and has orange buds and a touch of crimson on the open flowers. Hooker's form reaches about 8 ft. and lacks the crimson. Kingdon Ward's 5853 is dwarfer. This species is most floriferous, and makes a wonderful effect of shining yellow when in full flower; but it should be disbudded and well fed, especially in the Cornish climate, or it may die of exhaustion after an excessive effort of flowering.

Hybrids include some of the very best shrubs we can grow, e.g.:

*"Penjerrick" (*campylocarpum elatum* × *Griffithianum*). This most distinguished of rhododendron hybrids has large translucent bells, pale yellow in one form, pale pink in the other, very free-flowering. It was raised by the late Mr. S. Smith, formerly gardener at Penjerrick. The yellow form, with coral-red buds and flower-stalk, and five spots of carmine at the bottom of its flower-bell, is, I think, the most beautiful rhododendron I have seen. The plant needs shelter.

*"Damaris" (Dr. Stocker × *campylocarpum elatum*) is a first-rate pale yellow. Also "Marcia," "Lady Bessborough," "Butterfly," *Unique, "Letty Edwards," all lovely pale yellows of good constitution.

R. *cinnabarinum.* A bush, up to 10 ft., with blue-green foliage, glaucous blue when young; flowers in one type (*Blandfordiæflorum*) yellow with red shading, tubular in shape; flowers in another type, *Roylei,* translucent port-wine red with a bloom like a plum, shaped like a *lapageria* flower. *Roylei is one of the most beautiful and distinguished-looking of all; and it is easy to grow, standing a good deal of sun and weather, and flowering very freely when well-established. The two types are sometimes found on one plant.

The hybrids are outstanding.

*"Royal Flush" (*Roylei* × a special form of *R. Maddenii*) was raised by Mr. J. C. Williams, and is the finest version of this notable cross: one form is apricot, the other pink. Visitors to the Truro Flower Show before the war may remember amazing branches of this hybrid, loaded with hundreds of flower-bells. The Caerhays plant is hardy enough for Cornwall, but too tender for most up-country gardens. Hardy forms of the cross have been produced, notably by the late Mr. L. de Rothschild, who recrossed "Royal Flush" in its two forms with *Roylei*; the resulting plants include *"Lady Chamberlain," apricot, and *"Lady Rosebery," pink, both of which are very free-flowering and easy to grow, and very beautiful (notably in the forms which received the F.C.C. of the R.H.S.).

Mr. Mangles, who was probably the first to try the *cinnabarinum—Maddenii* cross, raised "Rose Mangles," but that has been far surpassed by later introductions: "Bodnant Yellow" from Lord Aberconway's garden, with flushed orange-yellow flowers, is a fine recent example.

R. *decorum* is a tall spreading bush with thick grey-green leaves, and flattish seven-lobed flowers, scented, white or pink-flushed, in May or later. This and *discolor* are useful for dividing bright-coloured rhododendrons in a wood. Parent of many hybrids.

R. *diaprepes* is somewhat similar; the finest of this type, but more tender and unfortunately very subject to bark-splitting; its white flowers are about 5 inches across, shaded green at the base.

R. *discolor* is similar to *decorum*, with long leaves tapering at both ends (whereas those of *decorum* are round at the apex), and large flowers, white or flushed, in June or July. This stands apart, with *auriculatum*, for its late flowering. It has been parent of many good hybrids, specially valuable for flowering in June.

R. *Fortunei*, which is very similar, but pale lilac-pink and scented, is a parent of the famous "Loderi" and other hybrids.

*R. *Elliottii*. This small tree, in the form originally introduced, has rose-purple flowers; but Kingdon Ward's form (7725) has magnificent scarlet flowers, with darker speckles on the scarlet and darker honey-glands at the base of the trumpet. The trusses are borne with exceptional freedom and have a glowing quality of colour not excelled by any other red-flowered species. This, with *eriogynum*, *Kyawi*, and especially *Griersonianum*, is bringing a new range of scarlet rhododendrons into gardens both in Cornwall and up-country; the hybrids are proving hardier than the parents.

Hybrids include *"Fusilier" (*Elliottii* × *Griersonianum*), which has magnificent flowers, on a loose-growing bush. The well-shaped flower-trusses, 9 inches across, are very freely borne; the flowers, open bells 3 inches across, are very firm in substance, glowing scarlet, faintly speckled inside, so rich in colour that they make the leaves look blue-green by contrast. Like other *Griersonianum* hybrids, it can be kept compact by pruning after flowering.

Another fine hybrid is "Grenadier" ("Moser's Maroon" × *Elliottii*), blood-red, in close trusses.

R. eriogynum, another magnificent scarlet species, has most beautiful large foliage, silver-washed when young, and pure scarlet flowers in June. It is a tender plant in most if not all the forms introduced; its home is the rain-forest, and it needs woodland shelter here, and such a climate as Cornwall's. It is a great success in such gardens as Trewithen, Trengwainton, and Caerhays. The hybrids, which are much hardier, include:

*"Tally Ho" (*Griersonianum* × *eriogynum*), huntsman's scarlet, rather later than "Fusilier"; *"Redcap" (*didymum* × *eriogynum*), a low, slow-growing, wind-hardy bush with deep-red flowers in July, *"Romany Chal" (Moser's Maroon × *eriogynum*), bright red, spotted black, in June–July.

R. Falconeri is one of the great tree rhododendrons, reaching about 30 ft. in Cornish woods, with rigid leaves a foot long, felted brown beneath, and close trusses of milk-white or pale-lemon flowers with a basal blot of crimson-purple. Where it has space enough this is a most stately plant. At Lanarth it sows itself.

R. *eximium* is similar to *Falconeri*, but the flowers are flushed pink, and the orange felt on the young foliage is very striking.

R. *Fargesii*. A large bush with bell-shaped pink flowers, so freely borne that it may flower its head off unless disbudded and well fed. A showy plant, but rather harsh in colour.

R. *fictolacteum*. A tree akin to *Falconeri*, with long felted leaves and big heads of ivory-white flowers blotched crimson; a stately and hardy plant, but some forms are bud-tender.

R. *grande* (syn. *argenteum*), a large bush or small tree, with magnificent foliage, generally silvered underneath and brilliantly silver in the young growth; flowers in March (earlier in one form), ivory-white, blotched red at the base. It is a tender plant, requiring full shelter, but does splendidly in mild Cornish gardens.

R. Griersonianum. A very distinct species, beautiful itself, and invaluable as the parent of hardy red hybrids. It makes a spreading bush about 7 ft. high if left to itself, apt to sprawl, but easily kept compact by drastic cutting back immediately after flowering; leaves long and pointed, pale buff underneath, with bristly stems; large wide-open flowers, downy on the outside, of a gentle azalea scarlet unlike that of any other rhododendron—a red with no blue in it.

Up-country the plant is on the edge of hardiness, but it is hardy in the mild counties, and its hybrids are proving quite hardy—considerably hardier than their parents—and are free from the purplish tinge that often comes out in hybrids of *Elliottii*.

These include:

"C. P. Raffill" ("Britannia" × *Griersonianum*), bright red.

*"Laura Aberconway" (*Griersonianum* × *Barclayi*), dark leaves, flowers crimson-scarlet: the best of the outstanding red hybrids raised at Bodnant, which is saying much.

"Sunrise" (*Griersonianum* × *Griffithianum*).

"Romarez" (*Griersonianum* × *Kyawi*), unspotted scarlet, mid-June.

*"Matador" (*Griersonianum* × *strigillosum*), brilliant dark scarlet. ("Fusilier" and "Tally Ho" have been noted above.)

Also, amongst plants of medium height:

"F. C. Puddle" (*neriiflorum* × *Griersonianum*), orange-vermilion.

*"May Day" (*hæmatodes* × *Griersonianum*), scarlet, a very effective bush of fine colour.

"Vanguard" (*Griersonianum* × *venator*), scarlet, spotted black.

See also "Elisabeth," under *R. repens*.

*R. *Griffithianum* (syn. *Aucklandii*) is king of all the species, and one of the outstanding sights of sheltered woodland gardens in the mildest counties, where it thrives as it seldom does up-country. It makes a large rounded bush, with peeling bark; long narrow leaves, rather pale green, with glaucous undersides; flowers in loose trusses of five to six—wide-open bells 5 or 6 inches across, translucent white. There is a pink form, not more beautiful than the white. Bracts like strips of ribbon hang from the stems of the young growths, red in one form, sea-green in the other.

Its hybrids are outstanding. They include:

*Loderi (*Griffithianum* × *Fortunei*), which has huge trusses of flowers each 5½–6½ inches across, white or in some forms pink. "King George" is pure white, at least when grown in some shade; "Pink Diamond" (true) is pale pink. This magnificent plant makes a wide spread and needs shelter, so it is better suited for large gardens than small ones.

*"Cornish Cross" (*Thomsonii* × *Griffithianum*), a most beautiful translucent warm pink, with varying tones of pink on the bush at the same time. Old plants have beautifully coloured trunks. It needs full shelter.

*"Loders White." Probably the best white for the average

garden of medium size; a most beautiful and reliable plant. It makes a large mounded bush, covered at the beginning of May with large trusses of white flowers with pink buds; it does this almost unfailingly each year. It stands a good deal of weather, but the flowers flag in hot sun.

"*Kewense*" is another very good *Griffithianum* hybrid; also *Manglesii*. "Pink Pearl" is too well known to need description; it has the defect of ageing to too blue a pink. "Alice" is a better garden plant, more compact and able to stand sun. Better still is *"Mother of Pearl," which might well supersede "Pink Pearl." It can stand a good deal of sun. "Snow Queen" is a fine pure white (*halopeanum* × *Loderi*); *"Beauty of Littleworth" is another.

R. *Kyawi* is another rain-forest species, with different forms varying in degree of tenderness. Flowers vivid scarlet, larger than those of *eriogynum*, late. Parent of "Romarez" (*Griersonianum* × *Kyawi*), unspotted scarlet in mid-June.

R. *lacteum*. A tall shrub or small tree with dark foliage, tawny beneath, and compact round trusses of clear-yellow flowers, yellower than *campylocarpum*. This is a most beautiful plant, but very difficult to keep in good health. Parent of "Mariloo" ("Dr. Stocker" × *lacteum*) with pale-yellow flowers.

*R. *Macabeanum*. A wide bush, eventually a tree 40 ft. high, with very striking large leathery foliage, felted underneath, and a huge truss of pale-yellow flowers, spotted purple, with a striking red tip to the pistil, set on a wide platter of radiating leaves. It is valuable in mild places for flowering so early as March.

R. *mallotum* (syn. *æmulorum*) makes a tall shrub or small tree. It has tough leaves, with conspicuous rust-red wool underneath and flowers in round trusses, crimson-scarlet. A very handsome plant which will stand rough weather.

*R. *sino-grande*. A tree reaching 35 ft., with magnificent foliage, grey when young, then shining dark green, deeply veined, grey underneath, generally some 15 inches long, but sometimes $2\frac{1}{2}$ ft. long and a foot wide; the flower bells, in large trusses, are cream-white or palest yellow, with crimson smears at the base. This is one of the out-size rhododendrons that looks disproportioned when small but magnificent when full grown. It is an impressive sight in Cornish woodland gardens, such as Trewidden, Caerhays, and Trengwainton.

R. *sutchuenense*. A wide bush, up to 10 ft. high, with long, narrow, tapering leaves and pale-rose flowers with crimson markings, from January to March. R. *s. prævernum* is a kindred species, a dwarfer grower, with a crimson blotch at the base. Between these two is *Geraldii*, probably a natural hybrid, which in its best form is pale lilac with a deep-purple blotch.

*R. *Thomsonii*. One of the old champions. A large bush, 12 ft. high or more when full grown, with oval leaves not more than 4 inches long, blue-white beneath, and very blue-green when young; flowers in March, blood-red, very substantial, set on a conspicuous large calyx. It takes time to flower, and in some gardens remains shy-flowering; but where it thrives it is one of the best.

Its hybrids include:

*Barclayi, "Robert Fox," one of the finest reds; "Ascot Brilliant"; "Hecla" (*Griersonianum* × *Thomsonii*); "Chanticleer" (*Thomsonii* × *eriogynum*), vermilion. (*Shilsonii* and "Redwing" have been referred to above).

R. *venator*. A bush up to 12 ft., with huntsman's-scarlet flowers; parent of "Vanguard" (*Griersonianum* × *venator*), a scarlet-flowered bush of medium height, and *venapens* (*venator* × *repens*), dwarf, scarlet.

R. *Wardii*. A large bush with dark oval leaves, glaucous below; flowers in trusses of about seven, flat, saucer-shaped, clear unspotted yellow. A very beautiful plant, and parent of many of the best yellow hybrids.

Hybrids include:

*"Hawk" (*Wardii* × "Lady Bessborough"), a very good yellow; "Inamorata" (*Wardii* × *discolor*), with larger flowers than *Wardii*; "Cowslip" (*Wardii* × *Williamsianum*).

R. *zeylanicum* (syn. *Kingianum*). A small tree, akin to *arboreum*, with magnificent firm foliage, tawny underneath, and close flower-heads, scarlet or pink.

Other fine hybrids of various parentages include:

REDS. "Bagshot Ruby," ruby-red; *"Britannia," fine rose-scarlet; *"Earl of Athlone," deep red with some crimson in it in May; "Essex Scarlet," red in June; *"King George," a fine gentle scarlet in early May; *"Mars"; "Queen Wilhelmina," carmine-pink in April; *"J. G. Millais," a most effective large-flowered scarlet in

April; "B. de Bruin," late red. Most of these, notably "Earl of Athlone," need some shade.

PINKS. "Corona," a low bush in varying tones of warm pink, very good of its kind; "Mrs. G. W. Leak," with a very large tall truss, pale pink with dark markings; *"Betty Wormald"; *"Raoul Millais"; "Silberrad's Winter Flowering," which produces its fresh pink flowers in January. See also the selection on page 77.

Besides these, there is the outstanding old hybrid, *Nobleanum* (*arboreum* × *caucasicum*). The typical form is bright pink; *N. album*, "Gill's variety," is a beautiful white; *N. venustum* is pale pink, and *N. coccineum* is pinkish scarlet. In sheltered places the type, and the white one, often begin flowering in November, and they carry on intermittently till March; *venustum* comes a little later. In our milder counties the flowers are not likely to be spoilt by frost, so that the *Nobleanums* provide flowers in the garden and in the house at, and just after, Christmas, when there is very little else.

IV

SCENTED SPECIES AND HYBRIDS

Two series of rhododendron species, the *Edgeworthii* and the *Maddenii* series,[1] provide, with their hybrids, a range of very beautiful and very fragrant plants. Nearly all are white-flowered. All are more or less tender; but some, such as "Princess Alice" and some forms of *bullatum*, are hardier than is commonly supposed, and thrive in gardens outside the milder counties if planted against a shady wall. Many, such as *Sesterianum*, "Lady Alice Fitzwilliam," *Forsterianum* and *ciliicalyx* are magnificent pot-plants for a cold or occasionally heated greenhouse, and require much less labour than most of the more conventional greenhouse plants. Gardeners in chalk country can, with a little care in watering, enjoy year after year the wonderful show and scent that a pot-plant of "Lady A. Fitzwilliam" produces annually.

A few cultural points are worth noting. Firstly, whilst all the larger rhododendrons are the better for having their seed pods removed promptly, these scented ones need such care especially. Secondly, many of them are apt to become straggly. Some of these, such as

[1] These are not the only scented rhododendrons. In particular *R. Fortunei* and its hybrids, including *Loderi*, have a pleasant smell, though not a strong pervading sweetness such as many of these can offer.

Edgeworthii and *Lindleyi*, are incurable in this respect; they "belong to be like that" (as we say in Cornwall), commonly growing as epiphytes in the wild. But much can be done, in most cases, by pruning. Do not be afraid of cutting back ruthlessly leggy plants of "Lady Alice Fitzwilliam," for they will soon grow up again with fresh vigour. Thirdly, most of these flowers wilt quickly in hot sun, and prefer a good deal of shade.

*R. bullatum. One of the best of the scented species. Its thick leaves, felted underneath, are deeply channelled by a network of veins; the flowers are white, more or less flushed with pink, beautifully simple in their five-lobed shape, fragrant and more weatherproof than is usual in this type. There are several forms, varying considerably in hardiness, in pinkness, and in stature; generally, the plant becomes tall, with lank bare stems, unless carefully pruned; but one form is compact, with white flowers, and leaves with bright rust-brown felt. The species is one of those worth trying as an epiphyte in the crook of a tree or in a rock-crevice.

R. ciliatum, one of the *Maddenii* series, has been dealt with in the list of dwarf kinds, see page 289.

R. ciliicalyx, a partly deciduous bush, with flaky cinnamon bark, and large pink-flushed flowers, like a much-enlarged *ciliatum*, in March–April. It is tender, and the flowers are fragile, but it is excellent as a pot-plant, kept in a cool greenhouse during winter.

R. Cubittii, a rare plant, is like a fine *ciliicalyx*, with coppery-pink buds and a stain of the same colour on its open flowers. A most beautiful flower when freshly opened. The plant is tender, but does well outside on a sheltered wall in a very mild garden.

*"Countess of Haddington" (Dalhousiæ × ciliatum). A compact bush of good habit with somewhat tubular flowers, pearly white flushed salmon-pink, scented. This is tender, and may lose its flower-buds in a severe winter, but is hardy enough for very mild gardens out of doors, and for cold ones in a cool greenhouse. No rhododendron has a more subtle beauty of colour.

R. crassum. A tall bush with large firm leaves and waxen-white flowers in June, like lilies, scented. This, like the range of similar plants connecting it with *Maddenii*, stands a surprising amount of wind, and is useful as a wind-break in woodland. One of the hardiest.

R. Dalhousiæ. A tender plant and a weak grower; but a most beautiful flower, which looks as if it were moulded in wax, with hollows pressed by the moulder's thumb; sulphur or sulphur-white, with green shading, it suggests the green light of the Himalayan jungle that it comes from. It does well on a shady wall in mild gardens in Cornwall, or in a cold greenhouse.

R. *Edgeworthii*. A straggling shrub, with large white bells, fragrant; not so good a garden plant as its relative, *bullatum*, or as its hybrids.

R. *formosum* (syn. *Gibsonii*), a good scented white for outdoor planting.

R. *fragrantissimum* (*Edgeworthii* × *formosum*) has dead-white flowers touched with pink, very fragrant and freely borne.

R. *Forsterianum*. A splendid greenhouse plant with frilled white flowers 5 inches across, fragrant and free; rank shoots should be pruned.

R. *Johnstoneanum*. This species makes a compact bush with hairy leaves, and milk-white flowers of medium size, often marked with a flash of orange-yellow. It is very free-flowering and very decorative in a good form. A double form has originated in a Cornish garden, but the doubling spoils the shape. One of the hardiest of the *Maddenii* series. Its offspring include *Johnstoneanum* × *Dalhousiæ*, a tinted white of excellent form and substance; *Johnstoneanum* × *deleiense*, a showy and floriferous pink, etc.

*R. "Lady Alice Fitzwilliam." This is strongly recommended for mild gardens in the open, and for pot-culture elsewhere, being very easily grown, very fragrant, very free-flowering, and lovely, especially when the buds are opening. It makes a 4–5-ft. bush, with coppery buds and large white flowers stained orange-pink in the throat when first opened. The scent is delicious, something like that of honeysuckle, and pervades the garden at the end of April. The plant flowers with the utmost freedom every year, but like others of its class needs prompt removal of seed-pods after flowering. Its chief defect is that the petals are thin, so that the flowers quickly flag if exposed to hot sun. ("Princess Alice" and *bullatum* are better in this respect.) The bush will get leggy in time, but quickly grows again if cut back. In mild gardens it is quite hardy in the open, though flower-buds may be killed by an abnormal frost; and in colder gardens it will often thrive against a shaded wall. It is one of the most rewarding plants for a cold or cool greenhouse, flowering with extraordinary freedom year after year, and requiring far less attention than most of the plants commonly grown there.

It is easily propagated from cuttings. Inferior hybrids often pass under this name.

R. Lindleyi. A straggly shrub, which grows wild as an epiphyte on trees in the forest. Clusters of four to six large, funnel-shaped, scented flowers, as if modelled in white wax. A most beautiful flower; but the plant is scarce and tender and not easy to keep in health.

R. Lyi. Fine white flowers with a yellow stain.

R. Maddenii. A bush of about 8 ft., with large firm leaves, large buds formed nine months or so before the flowering, and solid white flowers, flushed pink on the outside, scented. This variable plant is hardy in mild counties, and (like *crassum*) stands wind and weather surprisingly well. It thrives, and produces its grand lily-like flowers very freely, even in considerable exposure and sunlight (e.g. on Zennor Moor). Hybrids include the outstanding series referred to under *cinnabarinum*.

R. megacalyx, a bush 10–15 ft. high, with white flowers, long, bell-shaped, with the lower petal ahead of the top ones. It has a distinctive scent which to some suggests nutmeg. At its best (as at Trewithen, in Cornwall) this is a beautiful and very free-flowering plant, but it is not often seen in perfect condition, and cannot be recommended as a species for the average garden.

*‡*R. Nuttallii.* A shrub, eventually a tree 30 ft. high, with big leaves strongly veined, crimsoned in young growth; flowers in clusters of about five, half-drooping, very fragrant waxen trumpets of great substance about 4 inches long, pale yellow like *Lilium sulphureum*. Like *Dalhousiæ, Lindleyi*, and some others, this flower is splendidly modelled, with hollows near the base, as if impressed by the potter's thumb. The plant is very tender, but has flowered well outside in some Cornish gardens, against a shady wall. It is a grand plant for the cold greenhouse. It was a parent of the magnificent *Tyermannii* (*Nuttallii* × *formosum*), which has enormous white flowers, and of *Victorianum* (*Dalhousiæ* × *Nuttallii*), which is cream-yellow; other hybrids, probably hardier than *Nuttallii*, may be expected. *R. sino-Nuttallii* is the Chinese counterpart, equally good.

*"Princess Alice" (*Edgeworthii* × *ciliatum*) is probably the best of the scented hybrids for general cultivation out of doors. It is remarkably hardy; at Bodnant, in North-west Wales, where winter temperatures sometimes fall below zero (Fahr.), this loses fewer

flower-buds in winter than any of the other plants in this series. Its capacity to tolerate sunlight without the flowers wilting may be inferred from the illustration of plants growing in full sun in a Cornish garden. It makes a large bush in time—9 ft. or more high and through—smothered each year with fragrant white flowers touched with pink.

R. *rhabdotum* makes a 12-ft. tree with large cream-white flowers streaked outside with red; a most striking flower. But the plant is tender and very slow to make growth outside; better suited, apparently, for a cold greenhouse.

R. *Scottianum*. A 12-ft. bush, with scented white flowers, blotched yellow. It comes from open rocky places.

R. *sesterianum*. One of the best of the *Edgeworthii* hybrids; smothered with white flowers, not so large as "Lady A. Fitzwilliam's." An excellent pot-plant, and a bushy grower outside.

R. *suave* is another excellent *Edgeworthii* hybrid, of dwarf bushy habit; white flowers flushed pink.

R. *supranubium* comes from altitudes of 10,000–12,000 ft. in Yunnan, where it grows in dry rocky positions and cliff ledges, and is likely to prove hardier than others of this series. It makes a 4-ft. bush, with white flowers, flushed outside, scented. Probably worth trying in positions more exposed than the others.

*R. *Taggianum*. A rather sparsely furnished upright bush with magnificent flowers in heads of from three to seven open bells, glistening white, often with a splash of yellow at the base, intensely fragrant. It comes from 10,000 ft. to 11,000 ft. on the edge of conifer forests and on rocky slopes. It is doing very well in Cornwall in sheltered gardens. Like *Lindleyi* and some others in this series, *Taggianum* should not be judged by its decorative value as a plant; its distinction lies in the marble beauty of its great flower-clusters.

(R. *Valentinianum*, a dwarf species, referred to in Section I, belongs to the same (*Maddenii*) series.)

R. *Veitchianum*. A 3-ft. bush, growing wild on rocks or trees in Burma and Siam, with white flowers frilled at the edge, washed with green outside. A fragrant greenhouse plant. Crossed with *Edgeworthii*, it produced *Forsterianum*, which has flowers 5 inches across, white marked with yellow, first-rate for the greenhouse.

VI

AZALEAS

Lastly there are the azaleas, all of which—the deciduous ones as well as the evergreens—are classed as members of the rhododendron family.

No shrubs are more beautiful than some of the azaleas. Most of them are extremely free-flowering, and most of them are easy to grow if the soil is lime-free and if some simple requirements can be met. Above all, don't suffocate them by deep planting.

Yet it is not often that one sees them making a satisfactory garden picture. Why is that?

A few kinds are easy to use. Given lime-free soil, one can hardly go wrong with the common yellow azalea, good old *Rhododendron luteum* (syn. *Azalea pontica*)—so fragrant a plant, so vigorous, so clear and congenial in colour, and so completely at home in the English climate, in shade or sun, that it sows itself freely (as does *Rhododendron ponticum*). Another species, *R. Vaseyi*, with the freshest of apple-blossom pink flowers, looks lovely wherever it is content to grow, provided that it is not mixed up with incongruous plants. These and some others are easy enough to place.

But think of the large-flowered sorts—those magnificent hybrids of *R. molle* and *sinense*, of which "Anthony Koster" and "Koster's Brilliant Red" are examples. No shrubs excel them in their range of yellow, orange, and flame. And yet to use them well in the garden is more difficult than is commonly recognised. Many a perfectly good English birch wood has been damaged—not improved but messed up—by a planting of lobster-pink azaleas which arrested the planter's notice at a flower show. Of course, this is not to say—don't plant these splendid shrubs; but be careful with the mixture: don't assume that "all the azalea colours go together," or that these sunset colours harmonise easily with the English scene. It is, I suggest, generally advisable to keep yellow as the preponderant colour in a mixed planting of azaleas of this type, letting the yellow shade into orange and into yellowish-white, and restricting the redder colours to a proportion of not more than, say, 10 to 15 per cent.

It should be noted, too, that most of the large-flowered sorts have a serious drawback: they are so frail in petal that they flag in full sunlight and can stand little rough weather. But this is being corrected to some extent; some of the newer large-flowered hybrids (such as those on which the Knaphill Nursery, Woking, has long been working) are more resistant. Some of the smaller-flowered sorts, such as the old Ghent hybrids, "Unique," *coccinea speciosa*, "Gloria Mundi," or *Daviesii*, commonly make more effect in the garden than the large-flowered but more fragile ones.

Another problem for the planter of azaleas concerns the brilliant dwarf sorts of such types as that called "Kurume." They are so brilliant and so free-flowering that they are apt—at least in my opinion—to look blatant in the garden. A slab of Azalea "Hinomayo," bright sugar-pink, all flowers without one relieving leaf, is a marvellous exhibit, but, frankly, it can look painfully crude in the garden; and a large planting of "Hinode-giri," all cerise-scarlet, bright enough to make one blink, may raise in one's mind a question —"Isn't this really, if truth be told, too much of a good thing?"

One more problem. In the damp air of our mild seaside counties, most of the azaleas, including sometimes the evergreen "Kurume" sorts, are liable to get a growth of grey lichen on their stems and twigs; and this does eventually damage the plants.

R. *alabamense* is one of the finest American species, flowering very freely before the leaves open, with small flowers, usually white, splashed yellow, strongly scented like lilies.

*R. *Albrechtii*. A deciduous bush 3–5 ft. high, with bright foxglove-pink flowers, very pure and beautiful in colour, especially good in the deeper-toned forms. It is a delightful plant where it thrives, one of the very best, but is not easy to satisfy and requires full shelter.

R. *amœnum*. See *obtusum*.

R. *arborescens*. A large, fast-growing, deciduous bush from the hills of the Eastern U.S., with very fragrant pinky-white flowers in June, when the plant is in leaf. Plant it in thin woodland shade, with plenty of space, for it will reach 10 ft. or more (even 18 ft. in the wild).

R. *atlanticum* makes a delightful low bush, with fragrant flowers, generally flushed white with pink tubes.

"*Azaleodendrons*" Hybrids between azaleas and rhododendrons include at least one first-class plant, *R. "Glory of Littleworth," pale yellow with a dark-yellow blotch, and handsome sub-evergreen foliage with a purplish lustre when young. Others are "Nellie," white with yellow eye; *Broughtonii* var. *aureum*, a good yellow; *gemmiferum*, magenta-pink; "Galloper Light," yellowish pink; "Jackie," deep pink, spotted; **odoratum* (syn. *azaleoides*), pale lilac-pink, fragrant.

**R. calendulaceum*. The flame azalea from the hills of Carolina is the most brilliant and one of the best of azalea species, well worth planting itself and parent of some of the best hybrids. It reaches 4–10 ft., sometimes more. The flowers are golden-orange to flame-scarlet, small individually but clustered, profuse, and more resistant to weather than the larger-flowered sorts; only faintly scented. Old hybrids, such as **coccinea speciosa* (orange-flame), *"Gloria Mundi" (orange-vermilion) and *"Unique" must owe their burning colours to this species; and large, long-established bushes of these are as cheerful a sight as any garden can show in May. *"Harvest Moon," with large pale self-yellow flowers, is of this parentage; perhaps also the red "H. H. Hunnewell."

R. *indicum*, a low evergreen with pink, red or orange-red flowers, is valuable for flowering in June and is very wind-hardy. Its double salmon-pink form, *balsaminse florum*, is less attractive.

"Ghent" azaleas. See under *luteum*.

R. *japonicum* (formerly called *molle*: a pity that the name is changed). This is a Japanese plant, a deciduous bush up to 6 ft. high, with large flowers, orange to brick-red, or in one form yellow. It is one of the parents of the *molle-sinense* hybrids, which include many of the most beautiful azaleas. A brief selection is: "Anthony Koster," yellow; "Clara Butt," pink; *"Dr. M. Oosthoek," deep orange-red; "Floradora," orange-red, spotted; *"Koster's Brilliant Red," orange red; *"Mrs. L. J. Endtz," yellow; "Mrs. O. Slocock," orange and yellow, spotted. Also, amongst similar types, *"Adriaan Koster," deep yellow; "Babeuff," salmon and orange; *"Knaphill White," palest shell pink on white, with a mark of orange-yellow; *"Marmion," pale yellow with amber splash; "Robespierre," flame; *"Satan," a noble red.

R. *Kæmpferi*, see under *obtusum*.

R. *ledifolium*, see under *mucronatum*.

R. *luteum* (syn. *Azalea pontica* or *Rhododendron flavum*). The common yellow azalea, with the characteristic azalea scent. It makes a vigorous bush, reaching about 12 ft. high and 15 ft. or more across, with leaves vividly coloured in autumn; sticky young growths; yellow flowers, not very large, but profuse, showy, and very fragrant. *Crippsii* is a fine form.

R. luteum has been used in providing the wide range of hardy "Ghent" azaleas, single and double, which flower a little later than the *molle* hybrids and are more weatherproof. These include, besides such orange varieties as *coccinea speciosa* mentioned above (under *calendulaceum*), such sorts as "Aida," dark pink; *"Altaclarense," orange-yellow; "Bouquet de Flore," salmon; "Corneille," double pink; *Daviesii*, white, flushed straw-yellow, good for cooling down the hot orange colours; "Dr. C. Baumann," deep red with orange flush; "Freya," nankeen yellow, double; *ignea nova*, carmine; *"Nancy Waterer," golden yellow; "Pallas," red; "R. de Smet," pink and white, double; "Sang de Gentbrugge," crimson.

R. molle (formerly called *sinense*). This Chinese species has golden-yellow flowers with a greenish blotch, velvety outside. Its winter buds are pubescent, not smooth like japonicums. With *japonicum*, it has been a parent of many hybrids. (See list under *japonicum*.)

R. mucronatum (syn. *R. ledifolium*, or *Azalea ledifolia*). A partly evergreen bush, eventually reaching 6 ft. or more, but generally about 3 ft., with large dead-white flowers, slightly fragrant. It is easily grown, and makes a most effective mound of white in May. Var. *Noordtianum* has larger flowers, and var. *ripense* is pale mauve, very free-flowering, and sweet-scented.

R. oblongifolium makes a low, glaucous-leaved bush, flowing after *alabamense*, white and fragrant.

R. obtusum and its forms *amœnum*, *japonicum*, and *Kœmpferi* are the source of many dwarf evergreen varieties of great value, many of them hardy throughout Britain, and all hardy in mild counties.

The typical *obtusum* only known in cultivation, is a low, partly evergreen bush, seldom more than 3 ft. high, with flowers ranging from white, through pink, to salmon, scarlet, and intense magenta.

R. obtusum var. *amœnum* is the familiar bush smothered with small flowers (often "hose in hose") of the brightest magenta; a grand show in chequered sunlight, kept to itself so that its intolerant colour does not fight with other bright colours.

R. obtusum var. *japonicum*, from Southern and Central Japan, is the origin of the "Kurume" azaleas, not long introduced, but now so well known for their brilliant show. A selection of these is: "Anny," orange-red; *"Adzuma-Kagami," deep pink, double; "Atalanta," a good lilac-pink; "Betty," salmon; "Fidelio," deep pink; "Hinodegiri," well known for its astonishing show of colour between magenta and scarlet; *"Hinomayo," bright pink, most profuse; "Kirin," pale to deep rose, double; "Kumo-no-Oye," salmon; "Kurai-no-Himo," carmine, double; "Kure-no-Yuki," double white; "Pink Treasure," pink; "Takasago," apple-blossom pink. *"Shin Seikai," cream-white. The vivid colour of "Hinodegiri" and *amœnum* looks best, I think, in company with blue-green foliage such as that of pines, and with some relieving white, such as *Choisya ternata* or *Viburnum tomentosum Mariesii*.

R. *obtusum* var. *Kæmpferi* is a deciduous bush up to 8 ft., with flowers generally bright brick-red. *"Daimio" is a form of this, valuable for flowering so late as June.

*R. *occidentale*. A deciduous bush reaching 5-6 ft., with large white-flushed flowers with a yellow blotch, strongly fragrant. It is a most beautiful plant, but needs good feeding if it is to sustain its very free flowering, and it needs some shadow if its petals are not to wilt from excess of sun. Its hybrids include some of the most unfailing and fragrant of azaleas, e.g. *delicatissima*, cream, flushed pink; *exquisita*, pink and white; *graciosa*, pink with orange spot; *magnifica*, cream, flushed pink; "Irene Koster," pink.

R. *Oldhamii*. An evergreen, said to reach 10 ft., but generally seen here as a low bush, with yellow-green foliage and brick-red flowers. Coming from Formosa, it is tender, but hardy enough for mild gardens.

R. *pentaphyllum*. A large deciduous bush with large bright-pink flowers; the leaves colour in autumn. It has the great merit of producing its lovely flowers well before the leaves.

*R. *prunifolium*, a deciduous bush 8 ft. high or more, with large blood-red flowers, as late as mid July: a splendid plant, scarce in commerce.

R. *pulchrum* var. *Maxwellii*. R. *pulchrum*, a variable species akin to *mucronatum*, is most commonly represented in gardens here by the variety *Maxwellii*, an easily grown evergreen bush reaching about 5 ft., with large magenta flowers.

R. *quinquefolium*. A bush or small tree in the style of *pentaphyllum*, but with white flowers, spotted green. A beautiful plant, but not very easy and needing shelter.

R. *reticulatum* (syn. *rhombicum* or *dilatatum*). A deciduous bush, up to 15 ft., with magenta flowers in April before the leaves. Very free-flowering and decorative in suitable company, e.g. with heaths. The white form of this should prove worth importing from Japan.

R. roseum is one of the best American species, with flowers bright warm pink, scented, early-flowering.

R. scabrum (syn. *sub-lanceolatum*). An evergreen up to 6 ft., with large rose-red to blood-red flowers, very rich in colour.

*R. Schlippenbachii. This, one of the loveliest of the whole rhododendron tribe, is a deciduous bush, about 6 ft. high (up to 15 ft. in the Korean mountains), with large frail leaves coloured in autumn, and large flowers of the clearest pale pink in April. It is supposed to need full shelter, but I have seen it thriving in some fairly windy exposures. Where it thrives no azalea is better worth planting in quantity. Give it plenty of leaf-mould.

R. Simsii (which has been confused with *R. indicum*) is a partly evergreen bush reaching 5 ft. or more in China and Formosa, on cliffs and in thin woods. The flowers, 2–3 inches across, are rose-red to dark red. This and its hybrids can be grown out of doors in mild gardens.

The hybrids comprise the range of wonderful greenhouse plants known as *Azalea indica*, which are the most effective of all pot-plants for the decoration of rooms—especially the more sophisticated kind of rooms. They are marvels of compact floweriness; and bought plants can serve year after year in the house, gaining in size and character, if repotted annually, fed with diluted cow manure when forming buds, and stood outside after making new growth.

All the following are good:

"Apollo," double scarlet; *"Blushing Bride" and "Daybreak," soft pink; "Deutsche Perle," white; also *"Perle de Gendbrugge"; "Hexe," small-flowered, vivid magenta-crimson; "Mme v. den Cruyssen," double, pink with darker blotch; *"Pauline Mardner," double, flesh pink; "Simon Mardner," deep pink; "Vuylstekeana," single crimson.

With these may be classed the remarkable Japanese variety "Gumpo" (a form of *R. Simsii eriocarpum*). This is hardy and very dwarf, not reaching more than 8 inches, but the flowers, with waved petals, are as large as 4 inches across. *Gumpo white and *Gumpo red are in commerce here; "Wada's pink" (perhaps not yet in commerce here) is said to be a pink "self" of the same colour as *Azalea Schlippenbachii*, and there are several others.

R. speciosum, from Georgia, has unscented flowers, profuse even for an azalea, generally brilliant orange or red, borne before the leaves.

R. Vaseyi. A deciduous bush, reaching 15 ft. in the wild, with flowers apple-blossom rose and deeper rose. Not difficult, and one of the best of rhododendrons. Try putting blue columbines, such as "Hensol Harebell," with a group of this. It will not stand drought or much wind.

R. *viscosum,* swamp honeysuckle. A bush 8–12 ft. high, with small flowers, white or pink, very sweet-scented, late in July; a fragrant and easily grown plant for a damp place. *Visco-sepala* is an excellent, very fragrant, white hybrid.

R. *Weyrichii.* A large bush in the style of *Schlippenbachii,* but with brick-red flowers.

R. *yedoense* var. *poukhanense,* a low bush with fragrant flowers, rose to lilac, more often grown in its cultivated but inferior double form, called "Yodogawa."

CHAPTER XV

Some Uncommon, Untried, or Tender Shrubs

FOR several centuries this country has been the home of experimental, venturesome gardeners. I cannot believe that such gardeners are extinct here; and so, in conclusion, I offer these notes on some plants that are on the border-line of being too tender for our gardens, some that are in cultivation here but still rare, and some that may not have been imported, but which, I think, deserve to be tried here. Inevitably, such a selection is based on inadequate knowledge both of the vast range of possible plants and of the behaviour of the plants in the diverse conditions which the British Isles can offer. But here is the list for what it is worth. A good many of the plants I have tried; most of them I have seen growing here or abroad; and for records of their behaviour in Cornish and other gardens I have been permitted to study the notes made by the late Mr. P. D. Williams, who visited most of the fine gardens in this country. I am sure that the list contains many very beautiful plants, and I think there is a good enough chance of success with them here to be worth experiment by those gardeners who will take a chance of extending still further our repertory of plants.

LIST F

ABELIOPHYLLUM
A. distichum. This welcome shrub, still rare here but perfectly hardy, is not showy, but is valuable because it flowers very early—from mid-January till about the end of March. It comes from Korea and is related to *forsythia.* The bush reaches 3–4 ft., with arching growths; the leaves recall those of *abelia* or the early *Forsythia ovata.* The flowers, borne in pairs near the ends of the leafless shoots, are white, with dark-brown stalks and calyces, widely tubular in shape, an inch across, almond-scented. Wilson records a pink form.

ADENANDRA
A. uniflora (miscalled *Diosma uniflora*). An evergreen shrub from the Cape (e.g. Table Mountain), making a small rounded bush 1½–2 ft. high, with small aromatic leaves, bright-red terminal

flower-buds, and white flowers like those of flax with a central star of red. This beautiful and distinguished-looking plant is only hardy enough for the mildest gardens, and will be killed by an abnormal frost such as that of December 1938. It evidently wants very good drainage.

Amongst other *adenandras* there is a pink one, *A. fragrans*, which has been tried here (by Canon Boscawen at Ludgvan, shortly before his death). This should be re-imported if lost, but it is difficult to grow, and soil requirements should be ascertained.

Agonis

A. flexuosa, from Western Australia, makes a small tree with drooping willow-like leaves and quantities of small white flowers with long stamens. Good at Tresco, and will do in mild gardens on the mainland, or in pots.

A. marginata is very different, with small leaves like box, and clusters of small white flowers with long stamens. This stands wind, is easily raised from seed or cuttings, and is worth using in coastal gardens here.

Alseuosmia

A. macrophylla, New Zealand's "bush honeysuckle," makes an evergreen bush 6 ft. high or more, 4-5 ft. across with alternate light-green leaves, variable in size up to 7 inches long. The flowers, shaped like those of weigela, are drooping, claret-red, 1½ inches long, strongly fragrant, borne singly or in threes. The shrub grows in damp forests, often as an epiphyte in a hollow tree; it comes chiefly from the Auckland district (N. of North Island) but is found locally in the South. So it is likely to need shade, a mild garden, and well-drained peaty soil. It is reputed to be difficult to grow, and is not likely to prove showy in flower here, but it is worth trying for its very pleasant scent.

Anopterus

*A. glandulosus. A large bush with long, evergreen, toothed leaves and most beautiful flowers in spring—terminal spikes of cup-shaped flowers, white, sometimes flushed with pink. This plant from Tasmanian woodlands is reputed to be fastidious, but has done well in a number of gardens in Southern England, and should certainly be tried in mild places, especially near the sea. It wants shade, shelter, and acid soil. Cuttings of very young shoots strike easily, but are apt to spend their strength in flowering. There is a pink variety (not seen here).

AOTUS

A. gracillima, a West Australian shrub with slender growths closely set with small yellow and crimson pea-flowers, is a nice cold-greenhouse plant, worth trying outside in mild gardens. At Glengariff, it proves hardy and free-flowering.

ASTERANTHERA

A. ovata. A small trailer and climber from Chilean forests, where it grows on damp banks and up mossy stumps and trunks of deciduous trees, sometimes to a height of 20 ft. Its leaves are of variable shape, up to 1½ inches long when full-grown, with serrated edge, dark green, and bristly with fine hairs. The flowers, up to 2½ inches long, tubular, with projecting upper lobes, are rosy scarlet or pure deep scarlet. It wants damp and shade, with a mossy bank, boulder, tree-trunk, or wall to cling to; given such conditions it will spread horizontally, and climb by aerial roots, self-clinging. It is hardy enough for the milder counties, and is easily propagated from cuttings.

Mr. Clarence Elliott has described it as growing in its Chilean home "very much as the common small-leaved ivy often grows in thin woodland in this country, covering the ground with a carpet of leaves and here and there running up a convenient tree-trunk" (*Gardening Illustrated,* July 1944, p. 369).

ASYSTASIA

A. bella (syn. *Mackaya bella*). An evergreen shrub, well known in cool greenhouses, with pale-lilac flowers veined with darker colour. Hardy enough for a wall in very mild gardens out of doors, and most easily grown in the greenhouse. It likes stiff loamy soil.

BANKSIA

These Australian evergreens are, generally speaking, less frost-tender than most other Australian shrubs, and they stand wind well; some of the many species, notably those which are natives of Tasmania as well as Australia, do well in mild gardens here.

B. coccinea. This has small decorative foliage, much toothed, dark green above, white underneath. The flowers, borne in cone-shaped brushes, are dark red. The plant has done well in South Devon. It likes stiff but well-drained soil.

B. grandis makes a small tree, with handsome crowns of long dentated leaves. In the middle of the crown, like a pineapple on a dish, sits the massive cylinder of flower, pale sulphur-yellow, woody in texture. This does well at Tresco and stands a good deal of wind.

B. integrifolia, the so-called white honeysuckle, comes from sandy coastal districts of Queensland, New South Wales, and Victoria. The leaves, 3–4 inches long and untoothed when mature, are dark grey-green above, white underneath. The flowers are sulphur-white cylindrical bottle-brushes. The plant makes a large bush or small tree, looks well with grey-green shrubs such as *Olearia semi-dentata*, and stands wind. It has done well in South Devon and elsewhere, and would be worth trying in mild climates such as that of North Cornwall in coastal sand. In West Cornwall it was killed in 1947.

B. marginata has long narrow leaves which look as if bitten off at the end. The flower-cones are light yellow, growing out of the stem. This is one of the hardier species.

B. serrata, a handsome tree, has long light-green leaves, softer than in the other species, with bold saw-tooth edges; the handsome flower-cones are light yellow overlaid with small lilac-blue dabs—the unopened perianths. This has done well in South Devon, and should be fairly hardy, growing in Tasmania as well as Australia.

B. verticillata, from West Australia, has large, erect, yellow flower-cones; dark foliage, white underneath. At Trebah, near Falmouth, it reached 60 ft. before being blown down by a gale in 1936; another had reached 30 ft. when it was killed by the frost of December 1938.

Others include: *B. ericæfolia*, with slender heath-like foliage and long orange-red flower-brushes; *ericoides*, a bushy species, with reddish brushes 4 inches long; *Menziesii*, with long, narrow, toothed leaves, and *speciosa*, with handsome saw-edged foliage.

BAUERA

B. rubioides, from New South Wales and from Tasmania, is generally a dwarf shrub of the undergrowth, but is said to reach

6 ft. sometimes. It has wiry heath-like growths and small, downward-looking, six-petalled flowers with crimson calyces, generally pink in the Australian form, generally white in the Tasmanian. The pink one grew for many years at Ludgvan and was seldom without flowers. Mr. H. F. Comber, who introduced the Tasmanian form, wrote thus of finding it where the forest thins at 3,000 ft.: "The groundwork of the forest," he says, "is tied together with the long wiry stems of *Bauera rubioides*, so heartily cursed by the man who has to tramp the wilds. This graceful little plant comes as a great surprise and delight, for it is many times more beautiful than the more or less tender form in cultivation, has larger fuller flowers, white or occasionally pink, and *must* be hardy, for no frost-tender plant could live up here."[1] This plant is certainly very attractive and easily grown; it proved hardy in Cornwall till 1947, and is evidently worth trying in colder counties.

B. sessiliflora, from Victoria, which reaches 4–6 ft., has pink flowers; it might well be imported for trial here, being probably more effective than *rubioides*.

BEAUFORTIA

*B. decussata. A most brilliant West Australian shrub allied to *melaleuca* and *callistemon*. It makes a bush some 4 ft. high in the open, more on a wall, with stiff growths set with small lightgreen leaves, and bottle-brush flowers at the end of each shoot, intense orange-vermilion. It is very free-flowering, hardy enough in the open for very mild gardens, and on a wall near Penzance came through the severe frosts of January 1946 undamaged. Plant it on a grey wall, not a red one.

BESCHORNERIA

B. yuccoides makes a crown of leaves like a large lax Yucca, and flower-spikes 6 ft. long or more, leaning out and curved in snaky lines; the flowers are green, but the bracts along the stems are pink and very conspicuous. Handsome in its queer exotic way, but not a good mixer in the normal English garden scene. It looks well planted in some quantity along a raised bank or on cliffs where its leaning habit and large scale are appropriate. Hardy at Exbury, and even at Winchester against a south wall.

[1] *The New Flora and Silva*, January 1931, page 98.

B. Tonelii, another Mexican species, might well be tried, if obtainable, where this succeeds. Also *B. tubiflora,* which has erect flower-scapes 5 ft. high with vermilion stems; less free-flowering than *B. yuccoides.*

BORONIA

B. megastigma. Everyone who knows it has a special affection for the brown *Boronia,* since no shrub has a sweeter, more memorable smell. The little cup-shaped flowers, maroon and dull yellow, are not brilliant; but they have a decorative pattern, hung on hair-like stalks from the slender arching sprays, and they pour out that scent, so unmistakable and delicious that a whiff of it would halt one walking in the street. Before the war it was common as a pot-plant, reaching about 3 ft Out of doors it is not easy to keep, but it has reached 7 ft. in a sheltered corner in a cold Cornish garden, and has done well in South-west Ireland. Try it in sandy peat.

The 80 species of *Boronia* are mostly Australian, but five are Tasmanian and therefore likely to be hardier.

The following species have done well out of doors in the milder counties.

B. elatior. This showy plant from West Australia is fairly hardy and much easier to keep than *B. megastigma.* It makes an upright bush, generally about 4 ft., but reaching 7–8 ft. at Glengariff (Bantry Bay). The leaves are narrow like a heath's and the small flowers bright carmine-magenta.

B. heterophylla, deeper and more carmine in colour, has likewise reached 7–8 ft. at Glengariff.

B. polygalifolia, with lilac-pink four-petalled flowers, is another which thrives at Glengariff.

Others which, so far as I know, have not been tried here include *falcifolia,* an Australian coastal plant with heath-like foliage and beautiful red flowers; and *pinnata,* with small arching sprays of nodding pink flowers, evidently an attractive plant.

BOUGAINVILLEA GLABRA, so splendidly magenta against sunlit white walls in such a climate as Southern France's, is just too tender for outdoors in this country save in very exceptional conditions. It has flowered well at Trebah, near Falmouth, and grew for many years in one place at Tresco. Give it dry conditions and full sun. The carmine one, more beautiful in colour, is even more tender.

BRACHYSEMA LATIFOLIA is a pretty climber or trailer with small grey-green leaves and deep-red pea-flowers in the leaf-axils; very long flowering. It comes from sandy soil in West Australia, and thrives on a sunny wall in some mild gardens.

BRUGMANSIA (syn. Datura)
B. arborea. The white "Datura," with its huge dangling trumpets, is one of the noblest of shrubs for a cool or cold greenhouse; it makes a lovely cool-looking decoration for an entrance-hall when grown in a large pot. It is very tender, and dislikes excessive wet; even in the mildest gardens it is likely to get cut down by frost after a wet season, though it often breaks up again. Strangely enough, it did well for a good many years in a sheltered place in the open in a garden near Dundee. *B. a. Knightii*, its double form, has lost some of the grace of its flaring trumpet shape.
B. sanguinea, the red Datura, is a much hardier plant than *arborea*; hardy enough for the open in mild gardens, and suited for a wall in many places. It can make a fine show when well hung with its brick-scarlet trumpets, smaller than *arborea's* white ones. It is rather a coarse-looking plant.
B. lutea, the yellow one, is also worth trying.

BUDDLEIA MADAGASCARIENSIS is very tender, only worth growing outside in the mildest gardens; but it is a most decorative plant, with long trails of leaves silvery underneath, and long flower-plumes similar in shape to those of *B. Davidii*, with white stems and buds, and flowers golden-yellow deepening to orange, borne in early spring. It is a success at Tresco and Glengariff (Bantry Bay), and has done magnificently at Trengwainton, near Penzance, reaching above the top of a 12-ft. wall and covering a wide spread. At La Mortola, on the Riviera, it is one of the outstanding plants.

BURCHELLIA
B. bubalina (syn. *B. capensis*), a shrub from the Cape, has tubular flowers of light orange-scarlet: probably never very effective here, but worth trying, if obtainable, in a sheltered corner.

BURSARIA

B. spinosa makes a very elegant small tree with a cloud of small white flowers in September; seeds like those of the weed Shepherd's Purse. A scarce plant.

CALODENDRON. CAPE CHESTNUT

C. capense. This is regarded by gardeners at the Cape as the handsomest of their native flowering trees. It is a semi-evergreen tree, covered when mature with large trusses of pale lilac-pink flowers. In parts of California it is a great success, and is recommended for "parkway" planting in the South-Western United States. At Tresco it is doing well in a fairly windy place and has now flowered for several years; it should certainly be tried in the most favoured gardens on the mainland and in Ireland.

CALOTHAMNUS

A genus of 25 West Australian shrubs, similar to *melaleuca*, but with the bottle-brush of stamens all on one side of the stem, like a tooth-brush. They are fairly hardy. *C. quadrifidus* and *C. sanguineus* have red flowers. *C. villosus* is a low bush with hairy linear leaves and densely set brushes, deep pink.

CALYTRIX

C. Sullivanii. A low heath-like shrub from the hills of Victoria, with myrtle-scented leaves and lovely little white or pink flowers freely borne. It might well be tried.

CANDOLLEA

C. cuneiformis. An evergreen shrub for a sheltered wall, with wedge-shaped blunt-ended leaves and yellow flowers rather like those of *Helianthemum formosum*. An extraordinarily persistent flowerer. This has done well in some Cornish gardens. It is only hardy enough for the mildest gardens, but is easily propagated and well worth some trouble.

CANTUA

C. buxifolia. A shrub from the Peruvian Andes, for a hot wall, with hanging clusters of from five to eight tubular flowers, brilliantly coloured magenta-carmine and tawny red. Very good on the Riviera and at Mt. Usher in County Wicklow, but seldom, if ever, sufficiently free-flowering in this climate, and apt to look poor in foliage. At Glengariff, for instance, though growing for many years, it has never flowered.

CARRIEREA
C. calycina. A deciduous tree 20–30 ft. high from West and Central China; leaves up to 5 inches long, reddish when young, then dark glossy green; white cup-shaped flowers an inch across, in terminal panicles. I understand that this tree, which E. H. Wilson thought highly of, is at last beginning to show its worth in our gardens. Hardy.

CERATOPETALUM
C. gummiferum, New South Wales Christmas bush. This very beautiful plant, the glory of the bush in New South Wales, is probably just beyond the reach of our gardens, but may be worth trying in the mildest places. It makes a large shrub or a tree in its home, with lanceolate leaves and terminal panicles of small white flowers, followed by vivid red bracts. It resents root disturbance and seems difficult to get started here.

CHAMÆLAUCIUM
C. ciliatum (syn. *C. uncinatum*), Geraldton wax plant. A slender shrub, 4–7 ft. high (probably less here), with narrow sharply-bent leaves $\frac{1}{2}$ inch long; the flowers, hung on thread-like stalks, have five pale-pink or white petals round a darker central saucer, like a glorified *leptospermum,* and they last well when cut. This very beautiful West Australian plant does well in California. I have not seen it here; its importation is specially desirable, but the seed is very fine and most difficult to collect.

CHORIZEMA
C. cordatum. A West Australian climber or trailer with heart-shaped leaves and long trails of small pea-flowers with brick-orange standards, magenta wings, and a fleck of yellow between the two colours which reconciles them. It is a most decorative plant for a wall in mild gardens, and one of the best cold-greenhouse plants. Trails of it make a beautiful decoration for a high mantelpiece. It is easily propagated from the seed it bears. It likes the soil rammed tight round the roots.
C. ilicifolium is similar, with leaves toothed like holly.

Clethra

C. arborea. This is certainly one of the very best large shrubs that can be grown in this country, but it is only suitable for the mildest gardens. It makes a very handsome evergreen bush, reaching tree size at Tresco and in favoured Cornish gardens; in August–September it is covered with clustered sprays of white flower rather like lily-of-the-valley, scented (a little too like the smell of scented soap). A good plant of this in flower is an unforgettable sight. The plant grows fast, flowers early in life, and reproduces itself freely by seed; even if cut down it may break again. So this is one of the plants most strongly recommended for very mild gardens, especially where woodland shelter is available.

The immense bush which was for many years one of the chief glories of Ludgvan Rectory garden was cut to the ground in December 1938, apparently killed, but broke again from ground level; and a number of large trees have survived in other Cornish gardens, at least until 1947.

Coleonema

C. album (often miscalled *Diosma ericoides*). One of the most aromatic plants, making a rounded bush 1–2 ft. high with slender growths, very small leaves, and small, starry, white flowers freely borne. The foliage when bruised has a smell as memorable as that of lemon verbena but quite different. It is tender, but stands a good deal of wind, and is easily propagated by cuttings. It comes from rocky ground at the Cape.

C. pulchrum (syn. *C. virgatum*) has taller, less compact growths, and small pink flowers. It is hardy enough for the mildest gardens, but the tips of the slim growths are likely to get nipped.

Convolvulus

C. floridus, from the Canaries, is a shrub about 8 ft. high, upright, but with a lax showering habit. Willowy growths carry narrow grey-green leaves and end in very large bunches of small white flowers like those of the lovely little convolvulus-weed of our cornfields. This most beautiful plant is good at Tresco, and is well worth trying, I think, on a hot wall on the mainland. Propagate from seed. It is well pictured in *The New Flora and Silva*, vol. V, p. 236.

Correa

C. Harrisii. This very beautiful shrub, a hybrid of *C. cardinalis*, is hardy enough for mild gardens against a wall. It has hanging tubular flowers, rose-red, very profusely borne for about four months in spring. For many years a large plant of this, dripping with flowers, was notable in Ludgvan Rectory garden against a sheltered half-shady wall; and I have seen it red all over, in full sun, against a retaining wall near Penzance. Not difficult to propagate from cuttings.

C. cardinalis, with vermilion flowers tipped with pale green, and with small dark leaves, is an even more distinguished-looking plant, but unfortunately now very rare. A splendid plant of this long flourished in one garden on the south coast here, and survived the frost of 1938; it grew in full sun, with a south-west exposure, in stony peat. It is apt to get lanky unless well-pruned. Propagation is difficult.

C. pulchella (carnea), a dwarf hybrid with pale-pink bells, is a charming plant in its quiet way; tender but easily propagated.

C. magnifica, with greenish-cream well-shaped flowers, is another good hybrid; and *C. virens*, the hardiest species, nearly always carrying some of its pale green-tinted flowers, is an attractive glittering evergreen, much used at Tresco for stopping draughts, and able to thrive in windy exposures and to grow through a mat of needles of *Pinus radiata*.

C. ventricosa, pink tipped with green, is long-flowering, prolific, and fairly hardy, but much less attractive than *Harrisii*.

Cyathea

C. dealbata, the silver tree fern from New Zealand, is one of the loveliest of ferns, with fronds that do not droop much and are milk-white underneath. It does well in Cornwall and South-west Eire, but, of course, needs wind shelter.

(*C. medullaris*, black tree fern, unfortunately probably too tender, has the underside green.)

Cyathodes

C. robusta is a bush from Chatham Island with leaves like pine-needles, and conspicuous claret-red or white berries, $\frac{1}{2}$ inch across; this is the best berrying sort.

C. acerosa is similar, but pungent, less free-flowering, slenderer, with narrower leaves.

DARWINIA

D. macrostegia (syn. *Genetyllis tulipifera*). A most beautiful West Australian shrub, generally a 2–3-ft. bush here, but reaching 10 ft. in the wild. It has small dark leaves, each branchlet ending in a nodding flower like a small "bizarre" tulip, 1½ inches long, the flower and its bracts cream-white streaked with carmine. This did well for many years at Ludgvan Rectory, and was a success for some time in the writer's garden. It may be lost to cultivation here at present and, if so, should certainly be re-imported (I wish I could get it again). Fertile seed appears to be difficult to get. There are other species, including the pink *D. fimbriata*.

DODONÆA

D. viscosa. A shrub or small tree, with long, thin, evergreen leaves, lightly borne, strikingly purple in one form. The bunches of flat seeds are quite decorative. It comes from New Zealand, Australia, and many parts of the Pacific: wind-hardy, but frost-tender. In New Zealand it grows close to the sea, often swept by spray.

DRYANDRA

D. formosa. A West Australian bush of the *Protea* family, with hard foliage like a *Banksia's* and honey-brown flower-cones freely borne. Wind-hardy. It does well at Tresco, and is worth trying on the mainland in gardens by the sea.
D. floribunda has wedge-shaped leaves and small light-yellow flowers.

ECHIUM

Among the most striking of the plants available for mild coastal gardens are these great borages from the Canary Islands, Madeira, and Teneriffe. Some are biennial, others perennial. The biennials include *E. Auberianum*; *E. Pininana*, which makes a single spike of light-blue flowers 6–12 ft. high, and has even reached 23 ft. 4 inches at Tresco; *E. simplex*, and *E. Wildpretii*, which makes a large rosette of woolly foliage in its first season, and then, in the second year, throws up a towering spike, 10–12 ft. high, coral-pink. It grows wild at an altitude of 7,000 ft. in soil consisting almost entirely of volcanic cinders; yet it manages to thrive also in the damp soil of Cornwall, the Scillies, and the Channel Islands.

The perennials include *E. callithyrsum*, blue, with longish red stamens; the white *E. candicans*; and the blue *E. fastuosum*, in which the red stamens are suppressed. The last is often washy in colour, but selected forms, propagated by cuttings, are magnificently blue and effective.

Best of all, perhaps, is a hybrid between *callithyrsum* and *Pininana*, raised at Tresco and named *E. scilloniensis*, which has the perennial character of *callithyrsum*, and magnificent spikes of blue flowers, 3 ft. long or more.

The bigger *Echiums* look too huge in scale, too coarse, in a small tame garden scene; but on rocky ground, as at St. Michael's Mount, or making an avenue, as at Tresco, in strong spring sunlight, they look not only astonishing and exotic but lovely and at home.

EPACRIS

In the days when Cape heaths and other shrubs were much grown in greenhouses, the *epacrises* from Australasia were among the most valued of winter-flowering plants for this purpose. Today they are little grown and scarce; but they can be grown successfully out of doors in very mild gardens, and few shrubs of their stature are more rewarding, although most of them are not very long-lived. Cut back after flowering.

E. impressa, with spikes 2 ft. or 3 ft. high of white or red heath-like bells, should be one of the hardiest, coming from Tasmania and New Zealand as well as from Australia; a lovely plant.

E. longiflora (syn. *miniata*) is generally a straggling plant with long weak branches, but is sometimes a fairly erect 5-ft. bush; it has drooping tubular flowers, carmine-scarlet with white tips. It is hardy enough for mild gardens, and one of the most long-flowering shrubs. Against a half-shaded wall it was for many years a delightful sight in Canon Boscawen's garden; but it comes from barren hilltops of the coast and Dividing Range of New South Wales, so it might well be tried in full sun in a hot exposure.

E. purpurascens is a bushy white-flowered species; and there is a double form of it with little white rosettes in spring, very long-flowering and reliable. Grow it in stony well-drained soil in full sun.

There are other species, such as *acuminata* and *pulchella*.
The garden varieties include:
E. magnifica, which makes erect spikes, 3 ft. high or more, hung for most of their length with longish bells of a clear bright pink. This was one of the best plants in Canon Boscawen's garden at Ludgvan; I shall not forget the tall plumes of it as they grew there in a sheltered corner, or as they appeared, lavishly cut, at Truro Flower Show in April. It is a long-flowering plant, not very long-lived, easy to grow in a heath soil in a mild climate. E. "Diadem" is another most beautiful sort, not so tall, with rose-red flowers very early in spring. "Mont Blanc" is a large-flowered white.

Other *epacrises* which have been grown out of doors in the British Isles with more or less prolonged success, e.g. at Glengariff, include: *E. hyacinthiflora acuminata*, carmine, 2–3 ft.; *hyacinthiflora candidissima*, white; *alba odorata*, white; *ardentissima*, salmon-pink, a good plant; and *lævigata*, blush. Other garden varieties are probably lost to cultivation now; but gardeners in the mildest counties would do well, I believe, to experiment with these plants, and such a demand may encourage their propagation from cuttings, which is slow and requires special care.

EPIGÆA

E. repens, the cherished "mayflower" of New England woods, is a very dwarf creeping evergreen, with clusters of small scented flowers, white touched with pink, in spring. A lovely plant in its discreet way. It needs leaf-mould and shade; in many gardens it is very recalcitrant. There is a pink form.

E. asiatica, the Japanese counterpart of the North American *E. repens*, is similar, but with pink flowers: where *repens* will not thrive, this may succeed. "Aurora" is a good hybrid between the two species, with clear-pink flowers, shown more above the leaves.

ERICA

The hundred species of heath from the Cape peninsula, with their hybrids, include some of the most beautiful shrubs in the world; and over a century ago, when some people had plenty of money to spend on gardening, and when labour and fuel were plentiful, many of these heaths were grown in greenhouses in

England. A book such as *The Greenhouse*, by Charles McIntosh (1838), with its lists of greenhouse plants and details about their cultivation, shows what a wealth of plants we have lost, and how much knowledge, e.g. as to restraint in the watering of Cape heaths, has passed out of the average gardener's repertory. In McIntosh's book, the "Select List of Heaths" comprises no fewer than 224, classified according to height and colour.

As for cultivation out of doors, the great majority of Cape heaths are very unlikely to succeed for more than a very few years. Our climate is too damp for them. But a few do prove sufficiently hardy and enduring to be worth trying outside in favoured gardens. A notable case is the lovely *E. canaliculata*, described on page 124. The following are amongst those worth trial:

E. caffra, white. Plants of this, about 2½ ft. high, are still in good health at Glengariff (Ilnacullin Island) after twelve years.
E. glandulosa, pink, one of the most reliable.
E. hyacinthiformis, white, very feathery and elegant.
E. ventricosa, pink, and its varieties *magnifica*, *Bothwelliana*, and "King Edward VII."
E. Vilmoreana, familiar in greenhouses, which bears upright plumes of long-tubed furry flowers, rose shading to white. In my own damp garden this did well out of doors for five years, and in sandy peat and a hotter exposure it might prove more durable.

Others worth considering include:
E. Cavendishiana, a yellow hybrid.
E. gracilis, reddish-purple, 1 ft.
hiemalis, pink; *persoluta densiflora*, purplish-pink; *regerminans ovata*, red; *Pageana*, bright yellow, slightly fragrant, which has done well for a time at Caerhays and elsewhere, but is easily killed by a shock; *verticillata major*, brick-red; and the lovely *cerinthoides major*, whose large vermilion bells, in small bunches, are so bright that one might think there was light inside. This did well with me for some years.

ERIOSTEMON

Beautiful and long-flowering Australian dwarf shrubs; of the seventy species, six spread into Tasmania and are likely therefore to be hardier than the rest. Several species have done very well in the open in Cornwall, but they are all liable to be killed by an abnormal winter in our damp climate, and they need special technique in propagation. Eriostemons are amongst the plants that are likely to be extremely scarce here after the war years, but it is worth taking trouble to get them restarted.

E. buxifolius is a 1–2-ft. bush, from sandy hills in New South Wales. It is very floriferous, with pink-tipped buds and white waxy stars of flower set all along the dark-green sprigs.

E. Crowei is a little bush 1–1½ ft. high, with narrow willow-like leaves and a solitary red star in each leaf-axil.

E. lanceolatus, the pink wax flower, from sandy coastal country in New South Wales, Victoria, and Queensland, is one of the best. It has narrow grey-green leaves and quite large pink or white flower-stars very freely borne along the bending sprays. Not difficult in a sheltered place, and worth trying in coastal sand.

E. neriifolius (syn. *myoporoides*), a bush 2–3 ft. high, has narrow leaves, slightly wrinkled, and white or pink star-flowers in threes in the leaf axils; the flowers have woolly stamens. A lovely and long-flowering plant.

A good many other species used to be grown in greenhouses in this country.

EUGENIA

E. myrtifolia is an Australian tree or tall bush, with glossy foliage, coppery when young, and red berries. It makes a very handsome upright evergreen, and is planted very extensively in California. It grows at Tresco: I have not seen it on the mainland.

E. Smithii, "Lilly pilly," is another symmetrical upright tree, sometimes 80–100 ft. high in New South Wales and Victoria, with drooping shoots of copper-tinted myrtle leaves and pale or deep blue-purple berries in winter. This fine plant thrives at Tresco. Young plants on the mainland were killed in 1938, but the species may prove just hardy enough if the wood is hard before it is planted out.

EUTAXIA

E. myrtifolia. A West Australian shrub with sprays of small pea-flowers, yellow, marked with brown; killed here by a hard winter, but worth trying in a mild garden; quite good as a cold-greenhouse plant.

Freylinia

F. cestroides. An evergreen bush some 12 ft. high, with narrow opposite leaves, and slim flower-spikes near the ends of the shoots, orange-yellow, fragrant. It is a South African, hardy enough for the south-west, but needing all the heat it can get.

Furcræa

F. longæva. This plant, after flowering, drops small bulb-like offsets which quickly grow into a crown of sword-like leaves like a magnified *yucca*. After from 20 to 35 years[1] a green spike thrusts from the middle of the crown, reaching a great height—sometimes as much as 40 ft.—with drooping branchlets hung with bell-shaped flowers, cream-yellow and green. In 1944 no fewer than fifty-seven of these colossal chandeliers flowered in Tresco Abbey garden, a sight not merely astonishing but beautiful and appropriate to the setting. The illustration shows some plants flowering in an avenue: the one beside which the gardener can be seen was over 40 ft. high. Even finer, perhaps, was the effect of an informal planting on the rocky slopes of a quarry-like space, the more distant plants showing through the nearer ones like fountains seen through fountains.

The plant comes from Mexico, and needs all the heat and sunlight it can get, in well-drained soil. It has, I believe, done well in some mainland gardens, and should certainly be tried in mild places where there is ample space and no hurry for immediate effect. But it is not a plant for the gentle domestic English scene. And when it dies, as it always does after flowering, the carcass remains unsightly unless violently rooted out with a jack.

Gordonia

G. anomala (syn. *G. axillaris*). A beautiful evergreen, reaching 25 ft. in West China; glossy leathery leaves; flowers like opening camellias, $2\frac{1}{2}-3\frac{1}{2}$ inches across, milk-white, with yellow stamens. In China it flowers in late summer and autumn; here the season is variable, generally late autumn to early spring. It is hardy enough for Cornwall, in woodland shelter, but may get

---

[1] The report that this plant lives "for from four hundred to five hundred years before it ends in a burst of glory," referred to in Dr. Salisbury's *The Living Garden*, is quite unfounded, judging from experience at Tresco and La Mortola.

severely cut. If it does, do not grub it up for two years, since it may break from the base.

G. *Lasianthus*, Loblolly bay, is an evergreen similar to G. *anomala*, but it comes from the South-east United States, and is rather more tender. It reaches 75 ft. in the wild, in acid lowland soil. It has fissured russet bark, dark shining leaves slightly toothed; and five-petalled cupped white flowers with yellow anthers, borne in the axils on short stalks, lasting only a day, in winter.

G. *pubescens* (*Franklinia alatamaha,*). This was originally found in Georgia in 1765, but has never been found wild since 1790. It makes a deciduous tree 20–30 ft. high; in autumn its large leaves turn splendidly red before falling. The flowers, borne a few at a time from August till late autumn, are white, 3 inches across, never opening flat, but remaining incurved round the stamens. It is hardy, but not easy to satisfy, and I have not seen it open its flowers sufficiently.

G. *chrysandra*. This evergreen species from China has fragrant cream-white flowers 2 inches across. Many plants here were killed or apparently killed by the 1938 frost; but it is probable that some were grubbed up too soon, for others, left in the ground, have sprung up again from the base. At Caerhays this is now about 30 ft. high; but it does not appear likely to prove a very effective flowering plant.

GREVILLEA

Besides G. *alpina*, *rosmarinifolia*, and *sulphurea* (referred to in Chapter IV), the following species, more tender than the others, are worth trying in favoured gardens.

G. *oleoides*, with long grey leaves and fine red flowers, is a beautiful bush about 4 ft. high, hardy enough for a mild garden.

G. *obtusifolia* is a prostrate evergreen carpeter with red flowers like those of G. *Thelemanniana*. I have seen this effectively used on sandy slopes near the sea in California: it would be worth trying here.

G. *ornithopoda*, with light-green cascading foliage and pendulous masses of cream-white flowers, is a decorative plant for such a position as the angle of a warm wall. It has done very well in some gardens here.

G. *punicea*, with light-green foliage and flowers of a fine red, is a scarce and tender plant; it did well on a wall at Ludgvan Rectory.

‡†G. *Thelemanniana* (*Preissiana*), a tender one, has elegant drooping growths of fine-cut leaves, and drooping bunches of red yellow-tipped flowers. It does well at the foot of a south wall in a very mild garden.

All these, belonging to the *protea* family, resent root disturbance and should be left alone after planting.

GUEVINA

G. avellana has most decorative, evergreen, pinnate foliage, something like that of *Berberis Bealei*, with racemes of white flowers, and red fruit like cherries (very seldom produced here). It comes from the forests of Southern Chile, where *Embothrium coccineum* and *lomatia* are its neighbours. Here it does well in many of the larger gardens in the mild counties, in woodland conditions; it has reached 45 ft. with a great spread, and has flowered and fruited at Trewidden, near Penzance. It is another proteaceous plant, so avoid root disturbance.

HAKEA

H. acicularis (syn. *H. sericea*). An evergreen shrub from Australia and Tasmania, making a bush sometimes 12 ft. high. The leaves are long spines (one might suppose it was an odd kind of conifer); and in the leaf axils come small, fragrant, white flowers, curled like those of a *grevillea*, followed by a few large wooden seed-capsules. *H. a. lissosperma* is a Tasmanian mountain form which is likely to be hardy; and the type, hardy and wind-resistant in Cornwall, is probably hardy enough for any mild garden.

H. gibbosa (syn. *H. pubescens*), makes a tight prickly bush with spine-like leaves, small milk-white flowers, and horned woody capsules.

H. laurina (syn. *H. eucalyptoides*), probably the most decorative of the *hakeas*, has flat leaves shaped like those of *Acacia melanoxylon*, often with a red line at the margin. The round flower-heads, set close against the stems, are the size of golf-balls, crimson, with white stamens protruding as if from a pin-cushion. This makes a handsome tall bush or small tree. Coming from Western Australia, it is only suited for the mildest gardens here. It likes sandy soil.

H. saligna, the willow-leaved *hakea*, has long narrow leaves and a profusion of small white flowers in the axils. It makes a sturdy upright bush near Penzance, and will stand up to 20° of frost.
H. suaveolens, with dark-green needle-like leaves like a pine, has small, white, fragrant flowers, and makes a good informal hedge.
H. dactyloides and *H. epiglottis* thrive at Glengariff.

HARDENBERGIA

H. Comptoniana. A slender twiner, with small purple pea-flowers just after Christmas. Tender, but easily propagated from seed or cuttings, and good for a sheltered wall. It did well for many years at Tregothnan, trailing through other climbers on a south-west wall.

HEERIA

H. elegans (syn. *Schizocentron elegans*) is a very dwarf creeper, with four-petalled flowers of the brightest magenta. A wide spread of this, in a half-shaded southward-facing hollow, was for many years one of the pleasures of the garden at Ludgvan Rectory, and the plants have there survived the great frost.

HESPERALOE

H. parviflora, red yucca, makes a basal crown of narrow leaves, purplish-green, with white filaments, and light branching spikes 6 ft. or 7 ft. high, with very many small flowers, coloured like those of *echeveria*—gentle orange-scarlet with yellow. This is a most decorative plant, like a giant *heuchera* in effect. It comes from Texas and is very hardy, standing temperatures below zero in Oklahoma, where I have seen it growing in quantity. It has flowered in the open in the writer's garden and at Winchester, and is well worth trial in mild gardens in a hot position.

HIBBERTIA

H. dentata is a trailing shrub from East Australia, with toothed leaves, brown underneath, and yellow five-petalled flowers 1½–2 inches across.
H. volubilis, of twining habit, comes from coastal sand-dunes of New South Wales and Queensland. It has bronzed young growths and fine yellow flowers 2 inches across, five-petalled, borne for a long season; the seed-capsules open, showing red

seeds. This does well in mild gardens, twining up through another shrub on a high sunny wall. If cut down by frost, it will often break again from the base.

HYMENOSPORUM

H. flavum. A tree or tall bush related to the *pittosporums*, with dark evergreen leaves like *pittosporum* and sprays of nankeen-yellow flowers like a large jasmine. The flowers, very fragrant and borne during a long season, open pale, and deepen to full yellow after their pollen is shed. The plant's home is Queensland and New South Wales, so it is almost if not quite too tender for the mainland; but it does splendidly at Tresco, and few of the borderline plants are more worth taking trouble over. In California, trees of this holding up their flowers against the sky are a memorable sight. Try growing it on till it has made hard wood before planting it out.

IXERBA

*I. brexioides. One of the best of all New Zealand's small trees of the forest. A tree 20–40 ft., arbutus-like in growth, with long, narrow, serrated leaves, and large flowers, waxy-white, profusely borne, in terminal clusters. Reputed to be difficult to grow: Major Dorrien Smith, of Tresco, has found it very hard to raise seeds or to get young plants started. I do not know of its having been tried in Cornwall. It comes from North Island, especially the upland forest of the Coromandel peninsula, so it is one of the more tender New Zealand plants; it needs shade.

JASMINUM

Several of the more tender species of jasmine are most fragrant as well as beautiful, and specially deserve trial in hot gardens.

*J. angulare, Cape jasmine. This is the best of all. Leaves in three leaflets; large white flowers in sprays of three, very fragrant, and extraordinarily freely borne. It whitens a hot wall at Tresco. It is most easily grown in a cold greenhouse, and is probably just hardy enough outside in favoured gardens on the mainland.

J. azoricum. This, too, is very good, though not so exceptionally free-flowering. Glossy bright-green leaves, heart-shaped; very fragrant white flowers. A rampant grower, easy in a cold greenhouse, hardy outside at Tresco, and probably just hardy enough for mild gardens.

J. odoratissimum, from Madeira, has deep-green, glossy, blunt-ended leaves on brownish stems; flowers yellow, jonquil-scented.

*J. polyanthum, from Yunnan, is hardy enough for a wall in mild gardens and is likely to be an outstanding addition. The evergreen leaflets, five or seven together, are green-bronzed in young growths. The very fragrant flowers are white, of good rounded shape, with carmine buds and tubes, borne in large loose panicles of thirty or forty; the profusion of flowers makes it much more decorative in effect than the common jasmine. It should be carefully trained, to prevent its making too dense a growth with dead wood at the back. Try this in a cold greenhouse if not out of doors.

KNIGHTIA

K. excelsa is a columnar tree, 40–80 ft. in New Zealand, where it grows on steep slopes, chiefly in North Island. Narrow, leathery, toothed leaves and curious crimson flower-heads, with florets curled up like shavings, and white stamens. Being of the *Protea* family, it probably resents root disturbance. Give it good drainage. It grew well for many years at Ludgvan Rectory, but I believe never flowered there. A rare plant in this country, but common enough in New Zealand. Here at Zennor it did not suffer from the frosts of February 1946, but was killed in 1947.

KUNZEA

K. ambigua (syn. *K. corifolia*). An Australian bush with heath-like foliage and small white flowers, mostly stamens, borne nearly all the year. A pretty shrub, good in woodland at Tresco, and hardy enough for mild gardens on the mainland. It comes from Tasmania as well as from Queensland, Victoria, and New South Wales. Easily raised from seed.

LAGERSTROEMIA

L. indica, Crêpe Myrtle. This very beautiful Chinese tree, with pink, white, or red flowers, is an outstanding plant in such a climate as that of the Italian lakes. It is hardy enough for mild gardens here, but needs a hotter summer than ours generally is, if it is to ripen its wood and flower properly. According to Bean's *Trees and Shrubs*, it "should succeed on many sunny walls in the

Southern and Western maritime counties": and I have seen it doing so in a small way in several places, e.g. at Winchester.

LASIANDRA

L. macrantha (syn. *Tibouchina semidecandra* or *Pleroma macrantha*). This magnificent plant is hardier than is generally supposed, and should be tried in any very mild garden which can give it a south wall, as well as in cold greenhouses. It has furry leaves, scarlet buds, and flat flowers, 3 inches across, of the most brilliant violet-purple, produced over a long season. Against the wall of a two-storied house at Trengwainton, near Penzance, it has reached the eaves—a wide plant in perfect health, free from the straggliness common to it when grown indoors. It was temporarily spoilt but not seriously hurt by the severe frosts of February 1946.

Another *lasiandra* much valued in California and worth trying here is *L. laxa* (syn. *Pleroma scandens*), with smaller, deep-coloured flowers very freely borne, and a half-trailing habit, without the legginess common in *L. macrantha*.

LEUCADENDRON

L. argenteum, silver tree. This very striking tree from Table Mountain is all covered with silver fur, and carries big silver and yellow flower-cones at the end of its great shoots. A wonderful sight against a deep-blue sky. It flourishes in California as far north as Santa Barbara, and reached some 10 ft. at Penberth, in South-west Cornwall, before being killed by the great frost of 1938. It can be raised from seed, and is worth trying in the driest, hottest positions. It needs careful watering from below when a seedling, and should never be given manure.

LINDERA

L. megaphylla. A very handsome, evergreen, bushy tree, with glittering leaves, very dark green, like a large smooth-edged holly; young shoots bright red, as showy as those of *Photinia serrulata*.

LUCULIA

L. gratissima. This is a large bush or small tree from Nepaul and the Burmese hills, with large soft leaves and large terminal heads of pink flowers in December, like some glorified phlox, with a delicious scent (which they retain even when dried). It has flowered very well in the open against a wall at Trengwainton, near Penzance, and has, though temporarily injured, survived the frosts of February 1946; it flourished for many years in an open border at Tresco. I have seen a magnificent plant in a cold greenhouse in Cornwall.

L. Pinceana, from the Khasia Hills, may be rather hardier than *L. gratissima*, but like it, is a plant for the greenhouse except in the mildest gardens. The leaves are narrower and stiffer, the flowers larger, with raised growths in the centre of each flower around the corolla-tube. Like *gratissima*, it is extremely sweet-scented.

These plants used to be much commoner in greenhouses than they are now, and they might well be used again in unheated greenhouses in the mild counties, planted out, not kept in pots. They should be pruned after flowering, and then kept with little water for several months, till growth begins again (about April), during the summer they need plenty of water.

Plants raised from Chinese seed recently show considerable differences of leaf, so it is possible that new species of *Luculia*, in hardier forms, will become available.

LYONOTHAMNUS

L. asplenifolius, Santa Cruz ironwood, is an evergreen tree of medium size, with narrow dark-green leaves of beautiful design like the fern, *Asplenium marinum*, and red bark that shreds off in strips. The small white flowers are borne in large flat heads, rather like a big *laurustinus* cluster. The plant grew for many years in the open at Kew, in a southward-facing corner outside the Temperate House. I used there to admire the distinguished pattern of its growth, and enjoyed it even more later when I saw the plant silhouetted against the blue of a Californian sky. It was for long regarded as difficult to propagate, but it can be propagated readily enough from seed if this is properly stratified first. It is now, I am glad to know, in commerce in England. Its natural distribution is narrowly restricted, being confined to the Southern Californian islands, Santa Cruz and Santa Rosa, which one sees looking westward from Santa Barbara. The tree grows there on steep sides of valleys, and does equally well in cultivation in similar situations in California. It appears to be easy to grow and would be a fine addition to mild gardens with steep slopes such as Glendurgan or Trebah, beside Helford river in Cornwall. At Bodnant it was killed by a zero frost even on a wall: at Exbury (Hants) it has survived on a wall. Seed should be soaked in water at a temperature of 140°; seedlings grow rapidly and resent root disturbance.

L. floribunda, the Catalina ironwood, is similar except that its leaves are entire, not dentated like the fern. It is very rare.

MELALEUCA

These Australian shrubs and trees, with brushes of stamens like the bottle-brush (*callistemon*), are in most cases too tender for cultivation here; but a few are well worth a trial.

M. squarrosa, pale yellow, probably the hardiest, has been referred to on page 154.

M. armillaris (syn. *M. ericæfolia*) is a bush 7–8 ft. high with decorative heath-like foliage and white flower-bushes in June. Hardy at Glengariff, but sensitive to wind.

**M. lateritia*, a good deal more tender, deserves special care, for it has flowers of extraordinary brilliance, orange-vermilion. It did well for a good many years in Canon Boscawen's garden at Ludgvan in Cornwall, and thrives at Glengariff.

Amongst other species, *M. hypericifolia* is fairly hardy and easy to grow, with leaves like a small-leaved St. John's Wort, and flowers of a weak orange-red, disappointing in effect. *M. styphelioides*, which makes some show at Tresco, must be an effective plant in New South Wales and Queensland when well covered with its pure white fuzz of flower; it makes a light-green tree, reaching 20–30 ft., with white trunk and papery bark. *M. Wilsonii* is a pleasant plant, with blue-green heath-like leaves and small mauve brushes.

M. Leucadendron is a graceful tree, with weeping branches and small white flowers: it does well at Tresco. Like most others of this family, it likes a hot exposure.

M. elliptica, a West Australian, is a bushy plant, with handsome deep-pink flower-brushes.

M. squamea has almost linear foliage and small cream-white brushes in June. At Glengariff it has reached 9 ft.

MELICYTUS

M. ramiflorus is a New Zealand bush about 15 ft. high, with numerous small blue berries on whitish branches; it does well in some Cornish gardens.

Michelia

These are closely related to the magnolias, but bear flowers in the leaf axils, not terminally.

M. doltsopa comes from the forests of Nepal and the Eastern Himalayas, and extends to Burma and Yunnan; it is hardy enough for the mildest maritime counties here, but experience at Caerhays shows that here, as in Burma, according to Kingdon Ward's observation, it does best on a northward-facing slope. (Presumably the sap is not encouraged to rise so early in the colder aspect, and so the bark is less liable to get split by frost.) It makes a large bush, becoming a bushy tree leafy to the ground, eventually (in its native lands at least) a tree 50–60 ft. high. In Burma, in the lower and middle temperate forest, at altitudes of 6,000–7,000 ft., it is "just but only just evergreen," the flowers being "borne among the rusty part-worn foliage of the previous year, which in early April is being rapidly shed to make way for the new" (Kingdon Ward, *Gardener's Chronicle*, August 13, 1932). The flower-buds, in long sheaths of golden-brown fur, are borne very freely in the axils of the dark leaves 6–7 inches long, and open into milk-white flowers, greenish at the base, sweet-scented, shaped like small magnolias, with from 12 to 16 petals. (It is figured in *Botanical Magazine*, plate 9645 t.) Kingdon Ward describes it as flowering in February and March, "foaming white with blossom in March," and presenting "a wonderful appearance." He noted that when one lot of bloom was killed off by snow and frost, another took its place. The same happens here: if frost browns the open flowers in March–April, the buds, protected by their fur coats, soon provide an abundant fresh crop. Plants in Cornwall have reached 35 ft. It is fine for woodland gardens in the mildest maritime counties, but needs plenty of room and shelter. It recovered perfectly from the 1947 frosts at Caerhays.

Other species of similar stature now growing here in mild gardens are *M. grandiflora, excelsa, Hookeri, insignis,* and *Forrestii,* but *doltsopa* is the most effective in flower.

M. fuscata, well known as a greenhouse shrub, has small flowers with petals maroon on the outside, powerfully scented like peardrop sweets. It is hardy enough in the open in mild gardens, but only worth growing, I think, if one enjoys its smell.

Two allied genera, *manglietia* and *talauma*, may yield some noble plants for mild woodland gardens; but I will not attempt to deal with these here.

MYOPORUM

M. lætum. Used in the Scillies for wind-shelter; a quick-growing bush, with bright-green glazed leaves speckled all over with transparent oil-glands; small white flowers. May be worth growing for shelter in the mildest coastal gardens.

PARSONSIA

P. heterophylla. A New Zealand climber, with leaves long and narrow when young, elliptic and shorter on mature growths; small white flowers in large bunches, sweet-scented; a beautiful plant, probably hardy in the mildest gardens, since it comes from the extreme South of New Zealand as well as the North. It has been grown successfully in Guernsey. Try growing it up a tree. It seems to dislike much sunlight.

PASSIFLORA

Several Passion-flowers, besides the familiar blue and the white, are worth trying in favoured gardens. There is a very beautiful hybrid, *P. racemosa* × *P. cœrulea*, with flowers of a muted pink—rather like the colour of martagon lilies. This grew for many years against the grey stone south wall of Ludgvan Rectory; lovely in colour.

Another hybrid of outstanding beauty is *P. Allardii* (*P. quadrangularis* × *P. cœrulea* var. "Constance Elliott"), raised at the University Botanic Garden, Cambridge, by the late Mr. Allard. It thrives in a cold greenhouse in Cornwall, but will probably do outside in a favoured spot. The large flowers have five violet petals alternating with the five white sepals, and the corona is vivid ultramarine; in warm air the flowers have a subtle delicious scent.

PENTAPTERYGIUM

P. serpens. This curious and beautiful plant has narrow evergreen leaves regularly set along arching sinuous stems. All along the underside of the growths hang little five-sided lanterns an inch long, constricted at the mouth, gentle vermilion in colour, pencilled with acute angles of darker red. Singular in its snaky habit but lovely in detail, and very long-flowering. It is only suited for the mildest counties, but a bush of it 6 ft. high was for many years notable at Ludgvan Rectory, till the frost of 1938.

P. rugosum is a stiff upright bush, not sinuous: the leaves are larger and much broader than those of *serpens*, and slightly toothed at the edge. The flowers have a dull-red calyx, and the lanterns are horn-coloured, shaded with red, and conspicuously pencilled with obtuse angles of red. The plant is rare and slow-growing. A good specimen is a discerning gardener's treasure. It is probably hardier than *serpens*: at Ludgvan it survived the 1938 frost.

P. "Ludgvan Cross." A beautiful hybrid between the two species has lately been raised by Miss G. Talbot at Ludgvan, in Cornwall. This is intermediate in habit between the two species, not stiff like *rugosum*, but with arching growths much less trailing than those of *serpens*. The flowers are slightly longer than 1 inch, with crimson-red calyx, the lantern of a more crimson-red than that of *serpens*, with the acute-angled pencilling of *serpens* and a greenish-white lip as in *rugosum*. The plant has the curious nodules on the root which characterise *serpens*. The leaf is intermediate between the two, slightly toothed at the edge. The plant is not so brilliant in colour as *serpens*, but has the advantage of being a much heartier grower than *rugosum* and of having a less lax habit than *serpens*. It is a very vigorous and free-flowering plant, easily propagated from cuttings.

PHARBITIS

P. Learii (*Ipomœa Learii*) is the magnificent large blue perennial convolvulus commonly seen in gardens of the Riviera. Probably too tender for our mild gardens outside, but worth trying.

Failing this, we can grow the annual *Ipomœa rubro-cœrulea grandiflora præcox* (lamentable name), the most beautiful of annual climbers. Plant it where it can be trained up a wall that catches the sun and is seen at breakfast-time. Easily raised from seed.

PITTOSPORUM

P. daphniphylloides, from West China, makes a small tree of open habit, with large deep-green leaves (6–9 inches long): the milk-white flowers are sweet-scented. It is tender, and needs full shelter from wind.

P. eugenioides makes an upstanding bushy tree up to 40 ft. high, with light-green waved leaves and flowers pervasively scented of honey. Its variegated form is one of the few first-rate variegated shrubs. Noble trees of this species were killed in Cornwall by the 1947 frosts. They should be replaced.

P. phillyræoides, from West Australia, Northern Victoria, New South Wales, and Queensland, is a bushy 30-ft. tree, with streaming branches like a weeping-willow, narrow leaves, starry lemon-yellow flowers, and very decorative orange seed-capsules the size of peas, strung all down the pendent sprays. It should be given the hottest, driest position possible, in a mild garden.

P. rhombifolium, another Australian, is a small tree with fine lozenge-shaped foliage and clusters of orange seed-capsules.

P. undulatum. This deserves a special effort. It makes a very handsome tree or bush, branched down to the ground, with glittering foliage like that of a small-leaved orange, with ivory-white flowers strongly scented like orange-blossom, and showy orange seed-capsules. It is wind-hardy, stands clipping, and is a favourite plant in California, Tasmania, and Australia. For others, see Chapter II.

P. floribundum is, I believe, even more fragrant than *undulatum*.

Plumbago

P. capensis. This familiar greenhouse plant, with lovely clusters of light-blue flowers, is too tender for any but the most favoured gardens here. It has done well outside in Guernsey, but needs a sunny season if it is to flower well. If it gets cut down by frost, it may spring up again. Excellent for a cool greenhouse.

Podalyria

P. calyptrata. A tree from woodlands at the Cape, with silky grey-green foliage and large pea-flowers in May, light violet, most beautiful in colour with the leaves. This does well at Tresco, and is one of the most attractive plants there; but it is very fastidious and tender.

Another of the five species, *P. sericea*, makes a small shrub, grey-green, with mauve pea-flowers.

P. canescens is a 6-ft. bush, with round silvery leaves and mauve flowers, from the lower foothills at the Cape.

UNCOMMON, UNTRIED, OR TENDER SHRUBS

POMADERRIS

P. elliptica. A bush or small tree from New Zealand, Tasmania, and Australia; leaves white beneath; small light-yellow flowers in large terminal heads. A showy plant, but the yellow is not free from greenish tinge. It likes stiff soil.

PRIONOTES

P. cerinthoides. This Tasmanian climber, at present very rare in this country, is evidently a treasure worth every effort by gardeners in the mild counties. Though a plant of the *epacris* family, it is an epiphyte, growing on mossy trees and boulders in damp Tasmanian forests at altitudes from 1,500 to 2,500 ft. It is evergreen, with long white suckers and fine rootlets, slender leafy stems with toothed leaves $\frac{1}{2}$–$\frac{3}{4}$ inch long, bright-red young growths, crimson buds, and flowers hanging in clusters from the axils of leaves on the previous year's growth. The flowers, $\frac{3}{4}$ inch to an inch long, are tubular, rather like those of *correa*, with a rolled-back five-lobed rim; in one form they are deep pink, in another paler pink but larger; in this country they are borne from June till September.

The plant has flowered freely at the Royal Botanic Gardens, Edinburgh. Being an epiphyte, it may prove difficult to establish, and it is probably too tender for outdoor cultivation except in the mild maritime counties. Mr. H. F. Comber, writing in the *New Flora and Silva*, January 1931, about his Tasmanian expedition, says: "Though the flowers may be browned by frost if exposed, the plant does not appear to be affected," [i.e. in Tasmania] "though it definitely requires a moist, shady environment, similar to that favoured by the Chilian *Mitraria coccinea*, to which it bears a very remarkable resemblance in many ways." The beauty of the plant may be imagined from the illustration given by Mr. Comber, and from a photograph of the plant at Edinburgh in *Gardening Illustrated*, December 1942.

PROSTANTHERA

Besides *P. rotundifolia* and *P. cuneata*, referred to in Chapter IV, there are many species of *Prostanthera*, some of them worth trying here in favoured gardens, in sandy peat, in a hot sheltered spot. *P. lasianthos*, from Tasmania and Australia, makes a large bush (20 ft. high or more in its home country), with effective panicles of pale-heliotrope flowers, spotted red in the throat, larger than those of *P. rotundifolia*. This has flowered in some Cornish gardens and thrives in the open at Glengariff. *P. nivea* has white, blue-tinted flowers; a beautiful shrub, but on the borderline of being too tender.

P. Sieberi is a very effective one, with large pale-lilac flowers, and should certainly be used here—in a mild greenhouse if it proves just too tender outside. It does quite well on a wall near Penzance.

P. coccinea, with small scarlet flowers, is unrewarding out of doors, being too tender even for our mildest gardens.

PROTEA

Several species of these wonderful shrubs from the Cape do very well at Tresco, where they grow in sandy peat, sharply drained. One species there (*P. Susanniæ*) has flower-heads as big as pæonies, with a central core of anthers, surrounded by pink bracts fringed with white. None is likely to be reliably hardy on the mainland out of doors, except perhaps *P. scolymocephala*, a small-flowered species, pretty but not striking.

PSORALEA

P. pinnata. A large evergreen shrub, with narrow pinnate leaves and campanula-blue pea-shaped flowers in June. This showy plant is only hardy enough for very mild gardens, and will be killed by a severe winter; but it is easily propagated from seed or cuttings, grows fast, stands a lot of wind if well staked, and is well worth a position on or near a sunny wall. Growing so fast, it is liable to become top-heavy and break.

P. aphylla, with narrow foliage like *P. pinnata's*, has blue and white flowers from May onwards, and proves hardy at Glengariff. Both of these are South African.

P. glandulosa, a South American, is an erect grower with light-blue flowers, very floriferous. It reaches 7–8 ft. at Glengariff.

PUYA

P. alpestris. This Chilean, like a dwarf version of *P. cœrulea*, makes rosettes like the top of a pineapple, the leaves being grey-green, recurved, with hooked prickles along the margins. The flower-scape, 3 ft. high, is densely set with flowers of a strange beautiful blue-green. Give it sun, good drainage, and dry conditions. At Glengariff it proves quite hardy.

Uncommon, Untried, or Tender Shrubs

P. chilensis makes a prickly jungle of 3-ft. leaves in rosettes; the hooked spines on the leaf margins reverse their direction half-way down the leaf, so that the plant is most difficult to handle. The flower-scapes, 4–5 ft. tall, end in a massive cone of flowers, greenish-yellow and orange.

P. cærulea makes huge, very prickly, crowns of hard recurved leaves, like an *Agave*. From these crowns the massive scapes shoot up, 5–6 ft. high, packed with flowers of a metallic blue-green with orange-yellow anthers. This striking plant appears to be quite hardy in the mildest counties, and has long been a feature of Ludgvan Rectory garden; but it is too rampant, prickly, and barbaric for the average English garden scene.

Schima

**S. khasiana*. A tall, evergreen, bushy tree from the Khasia Hills, with very handsome, large, dark-green leaves, and camellia-like flowers in September–October, 2½ inches across, opening wide, with five milk-white petals and a central tuft of yellow stamens. This magnificent plant, probably not yet in commerce, is superb in some Cornish gardens (Caerhays, Trewithen, and Trengwainton), where some plants have reached about 50 ft. It is hardy enough for sheltered gardens in the mild counties, but flowers so late that its beauty may be spoilt by rough weather.

S. argentea. Another tall evergreen, now over 30 ft. in Cornish gardens, with terminal trusses of white flowers, smaller and less effective than those of *S. Khasiana*. It comes from West China.

Solanum

S. aviculare, kangaroo apple, from New Zealand, Tasmania, and Australia, is a rather effective shrubby-herbaceous plant, generally about 5 ft. high here, with purple flowers an inch across; easily grown from seed.

S. lycioides, more attractive than *S. aviculare*, makes a lax bush freely sprinkled all over with lilac-blue flowers rather like *Convolvulus mauritanicus* in effect.

S. Rantonetii is similar but more upright, deeper in colour, and less effective.

S. Wendlandii. This magnificent climber, with clusters of huge lilac-blue potato-flowers like a much-glorified *Solanum crispum*, has flowered out of doors in a few Cornish gardens (e.g. Trewidden); but it is very tender, and must be regarded as outside the range of our mildest counties unless perhaps temporarily and in very exceptional circumstances.

SOLLYA

S. Drummondii (syn. *S. parviflora*). A slender Australian twining climber, with small, nodding, five-petalled bell-flowers, brightest blue, on hair-like stems.

S. heterophylla. Similar to *Drummondii*, but with thicker leaves, and larger Cambridge-blue flowers, more of them in each small cluster. Fairly hardy and easily raised from seed. Climbing through another wall plant, it will reach 8 ft. or more.

SPARRMANIA [1]

S. africana used to be a favourite pot-plant in Victorian greenhouses, since it flowers in mid-winter. In woodland at Tresco it makes a thicket of rampant growths, 8–10 ft. high, with large leaves and handsome white flowers with a central brush of red and yellow; it does well, too, in a sheltered place on St. Michael's Mount, and should prove hardy enough for favoured gardens.

STERCULIA

S. acerifolia, flame tree, another borderline plant from Victoria, New South Wales, and Queensland, is worth trial in the mildest gardens. It has done quite well at Garinish Island, Kerry, and thrives at Stanford, near San Francisco. It is deciduous, with glossy maple-like leaves, and vivid red flowers in summer.

S. diversifolia (syn. *Brachychiton populneum*), bottle tree. This comes from Victoria and South Australia, as well as from New South Wales, and is hardier than *S. acerifolia*. The trunk narrows suddenly towards the top, like a bottle-neck. The flowers, hanging in decorative trails, are like lily-of-the-valley in shape, greenish-cream outside, pink-flushed within.

TACSONIA

*T. *mollissima*. A lovely climber, with foliage like that of the Passion-flower, and large pendent flowers of a glowing salmon-pink. The plant is a rampant grower, and flowers very freely for

[1] Note the spelling: not *Sparmannia*.

a long season until late in autumn; it is hardy enough for warm walls in the mildest maritime counties, and in gardens near Penzance is one of the most valued wall-plants.

TELOPEA

T. speciosissima, " Waratah." This very striking plant, the handsomest of its genus, is a small tree with upright growths, leathery toothed foliage, and large crimson heads of flowers and bracts on top of the growths, in effect rather like one of those formal chrysanthemums with narrow curled petals. It is reputed to be difficult to grow; probably, like other Proteaceous plants, it dislikes root-disturbance; and, coming from New South Wales, it is on the edge of hardiness for our favoured gardens. It has flowered well at Ludgvan Rectory, and should be tried elsewhere.
T. oreades, the Gippsland waratah, comes from Victoria and New South Wales, where it reaches 30–40 ft. The leaves are entire, not toothed, and the flowers smaller than those of *speciosissima*. This, too, flowered at Ludgvan.
**T. truncata*, the Tasmanian waratah, generally reaches about 20 ft., with flowers midway between the other two; thick entire leaves, some of them curiously truncated and notched at the end; young shoots covered with silky rust-coloured fur. Coming from Tasmania, it is certainly hardier than the others; and to judge from its behaviour in other southern counties, at Winchester as well as in Cornwall, it seems likely to prove a very satisfactory and free-flowering plant for the milder counties. I have not found it at all sensitive to root disturbance, and it stands rough weather here as it does in the Tasmanian mountain forest at 3,000 ft.

TRISTANIA

T. neriifolia, from New South Wales, is a slender shrub, 5 ft. or more here, but sometimes a small tree in the wild: it has narrow leaves 3 inches long, and sprays, near the ends of the growths, of small, five-petalled, yellow stars. This pretty shrub has done well near Penzance, but is liable to be killed by a severe winter.

WAKKATAKA

W. sinensis (syn. *Dregea sinensis*). A very vigorous climber with ovate leaves, downy underneath, and umbels, $2\frac{1}{2}$ inches across, of fragrant wax-white flowers, freckled with pink in the centre.

The flowers recall the lovely but tender *Hoya carnosa*. As to its hardiness, Mr. Hillier writes: "Against a West wall this plant has survived two or three winters at Winchester, and in an unheated conservatory it is a very rampant climber, producing, from June to August, a quantity of *Hoya*-like sweetly-scented flowers. It is certainly a good rampant climber for milder areas, and under favourable conditions, judging from its vigour in my conservatory, it would hold its own with such plants as *polygonum, actinidia*, etc."

WEINMANNIA

W. trichosperma. An upright evergreen tree, reaching 40 ft. or more in the Chilean Andes, with brown shoots, very decorative pinnate foliage with winged leaf-stalks, and small spikes in May of white staminate flowers with pink anthers. The flowers are not showy, but the beautiful patterned leaves and trim columnar habit make this a valued plant in mild gardens.

W. racemosa, and the similar *W. sylvicola*, both from New Zealand, are other species, less attractive.

Other plants worth considering include the following, many of them on, if not over, the edge of being too tender for our gardens:

Agapetes buxifolia; Aster fruticosus; Atherospermum moschatum; Bignonia Tweediana; Colquhounia coccinea and *vestita; Corynocarpus lævigatus; Elliottia racemosa; Entelea arborescens; Hoya carnosa; Lhotzskya ericoides; Macleania insignis; Oxera pulchella; Pandorea jasminoides* (syn. *Tecoma jasminoides); Rhodoleia Championi; Richea scoparia; Sutherlandia frutescens; Virgilia capensis; Streptosolen Jamesonii; Templetonia retusa; Oxypetalum cœruleum; Russelia juncea; Rehdersodendron macrocarpum; Olea fragrans*.

I have omitted from the foregoing lists some outstanding plants which, to the best of my belief, are too tender to succeed out of doors for any length of time in the mainlands of the British Isles: plants such as *Jacaranda ovalifolia* (syn. *mimosæfolia*), *Solandra grandiflora, Stenocarpus sinuatus* (the firewheel tree). May some fortunate gardener prove my pessimism mistaken.

I have mentioned with a warning a few splendid plants, such as *Metrosideros tomentosa* and *Eucalyptus ficifolia*, which I fear must be counted as over the borderline, but which may be worth further trial.

I have included some plants such as *Buddleia madagascariensis*, *Luculia gratissima*, and *Lasiandra macrantha*, which gardeners generally would regard as suitable only for the greenhouse; for I have myself seen these plants doing well enough, for long enough, out of doors in favourable conditions, to feel justified in including them here. And this category of plants just on the right side of the borderline—the category in which estimates are most difficult to make—will doubtless be considerably enlarged by fortunate and experienced gardeners.

If my estimates are over-cautious in some cases, gardeners, not easily discouraged, are likely to expose the errors before long. If, on the other hand, they lead to disappointment, let me claim in excuse that this chapter is an essay in a field of gardening about which not much has been published, and that in any case estimates of this kind can only afford at best an approximate guide, in a climate so diverse and so incalculable as ours. Many of the plants here mentioned are likely to have been killed or crippled, in many places, by the exceptionally severe and prolonged frosts of January–February 1947; but that does not mean that they were not worth recommending. The experimenters, the venturesome gardeners, for whom this chapter was written, will not be deterred from their happy enterprise by one or two disasters.

With the ending of the war, we may hope that the flow of new species and hybrids will be fully renewed before long; and in peacetime we can be sure that experimental gardening will continue in this country in small gardens, even if the large ones are hard-pressed. May this chapter, defective as it is, serve as a stimulus to that enterprise, which has in the past proved so fruitful, especially in "the milder counties."

Addendum—Plant Name Changes

by **Peter Clough**, NDH, *horticulturist with vast practical experience of many western seaboard gardens, and former head gardener at Achamore House, Isle of Gigha, Tresco Abbey Garden, and Inverewe*

W. Arnold-Forster's naming of plants was researched carefully for correctness when the book was first published (1948). Since then, many changes have been made in the taxonomy of plants, and the following list is provided to help the reader find more easily the plants referred to in the text. The names have been updated to those used in the year 2000. Plant-naming has become more subject to international agreement, and as far as possible the list follows the current International Taxonomic Code.

ARNOLD-FORSTER 1948	2000
A	
ABIES georgei	ABIES forrestii var. georgei
ABIES nobilis	ABIES procera
ABUTILON speciosum	ABUTILON x hybridum
ACACIA armata	ACACIA paradoxa
ACACIA cyanophylla	ACACIA saligna
ACACIA glaucescens	ACACIA binervia
ACACIA juniperina	ACACIA ulicifolia
ACACIA longifolia Sophorae	ACACIA sophorae
ACER dasycarpum	ACER saccharinum
ACER nikoense	ACER maximowiczianum
ACER opulus	ACER opalus
AEGLE sepiaria	PONCIRUS trifoliata
ALBIZZIA Julibrissin	ALBIZIA julibrissin
ALBIZZIA lophantha	PARASERIANTHES lophantha
ALNUS oregana	ALNUS rubra
AMELANCHIER oblongifolia	AMELANCHIER canadensis
AMELANCHIER vulgaris	AMELANCHIER ovalis
AMYGDALUS communis	PRUNUS dulcis
AMYGDALUS Pollardii	PRUNUS x amygdalopersica 'Pollardii'
ANEMONE japonica	ANEMONE x hybrida
ANEMONE 'Queen Charlotte'	ANEMONE x hybrida 'Konigin Charlotte'
AZARA gilliesii	AZARA petiolaris

Addendum of Plant Name Changes

B
BEAUFORTIA decussata
BERBERIS xanthoxylon
BETULA japonica var. szechuanica
BETULA verrucosa var. dalecarlica
BRUGMANSIA arborea Knightii
BRUGMANSIA lutea
BUDDLEIA variabilis

BEAUFORTIA sparsa
BERBERIS manipurana
BETULA szechuanica

BETULA pendula 'Laciniata'

BRUGMANSIA x candida 'Knightii'
BRUGMANSIA aurea
BUDDLEJA davidii

C
CALCEOLARIA violacea
CAMELLIA Arajishi
CAMELLIA japonica
  A. M. Hovey
  Chandleri Elegans
  Compton's Brow Cherry
  Devona
  Donckelarii
  Kelvingtoni
  Lady Clare
  Magnoliaeflora
  Magnoliaeflora Alba
  Nagasaki
CAMELLIA japonica x saluenensis
CANDOLLEA cuneiformis
CARPINUS Betulus pyramidalis
CARYOPTERIS mastacanthus
CASSIA corymbosa
CASSINIA fulvida

CATALPA Duclouxii
CEANOTHUS austromontanus

CEANOTHUS dentatus
CEANOTHUS floribundus

CEANOTHUS rigidus

JOVELLANA violacea
CAMELLIA rusticana 'Arajishi'
CAMELLIA japonica
  'C. M. Hovey'
  'Elegans'
  'Gauntlettii'
  'Devonia'
  'Masayoshi'
  'Gigantea'
  'Akashigata'
  'Hagoromo'
  'Miyakodori'
  'Mikenjaku'
CAMELLIA x williamsii

HIBBERTIA cuneiformis
CARPINUS betulus 'Fastigiata'
CARYOPTERIS incana
SENNA corymbosa
CASSINIA leptophylla subsp. fulvida
CATALPA fargesii f. duclouxii
CEANOTHUS foliosus var. austromontanus
CEANOTHUS x lobbianus
CEANOTHUS dentatus var. floribundus
CEANOTHUS cuneatus var. rigidus

Addendum of Plant Name Changes

CEANOTHUS sorediatus	CEANOTHUS oliganthus var. sorediatus
CEANOTHUS thyrsiflorus griseus	CEANOTHUS griseus
CESTRUM Newellii	CESTRUM fasciculatum 'Newellii'
CHIMONANTHUS fragrans	CHIMONANTHUS praecox
CISTUS corbariensis	CISTUS x hybridus
CISTUS ladaniferus 'Maculatus'	CISTUS ladanifer 'Albiflorus'
CISTUS Loretii	CISTUS x dansereaui
CLEMATIS balearica	CLEMATIS cirrhosa var. balearica
CLEMATIS glauca akebioides	CLEMATIS akebioides
CLEMATIS macropetala Markhami	CLEMATIS macropetala 'Markham's Pink'
CLEMATIS rubro-marginata	CLEMATIS x triternata 'Rubromarginata'
CLEMATIS spooneri	CLEMATIS montana var. sericea
CLERODENDRON foetidum	CLERODENDRUM bungei
CLERODENDRON trichotomum	CLERODENDRUM trichotomum
CONVOLVULUS mauritanicus	CONVOLVULUS sabatius
COPROSMA baueri buddleoides	COPROSMA repens buddlejoides
CORDYLINE australis var. lentiginosa	CORDYLINE australis 'Atropurpurea'
CORNUS alba Atrosanguinea	CORNUS alba 'Sibirica'
COROKIA cheesemanii	COROKIA x virgata 'Cheesemanii'
CORONILLA emerus	HIPPOCREPIS emerus
CORONILLA glauca	CORONILLA valentina subsp. glauca
CORREA Harrisii	CORREA 'Mannii'
CORREA virens	CORREA reflexa virens
CORYLOPSIS platypetala	CORYLOPSIS sinensis var. calvescens
COTONEASTER adpressa	COTONEASTER adpressus
COTONEASTER bullata	COTONEASTER bullatus
COTONEASTER buxifolia	COTONEASTER buxifolius
COTONEASTER conspicua	COTONEASTER conspicuus
COTONEASTER divaricata	COTONEASTER divaricatus

Addendum of Plant Name Changes

COTONEASTER floccosa	COTONEASTER floccosus
COTONEASTER frigida	COTONEASTER frigidus
COTONEASTER glaucophylla	COTONEASTER glaucophyllus
COTONEASTER henryana	COTONEASTER henryanus
COTONEASTER integerrima	COTONEASTER integerrimus
COTONEASTER lactea	COTONEASTER lacteus
COTONEASTER microphylla	COTONEASTER microphyllus
COTONEASTER m. cochleata	COTONEASTER cochleatus
COTONEASTER m. thymaefolia	COTONEASTER linearifolius
COTONEASTER multiflora	COTONEASTER multiflorus
COTONEASTER pannosa	COTONEASTER pannosus
COTONEASTER perpusilla	COTONEASTER perpusillus
COTONEASTER rotundifolia	COTONEASTER rotundifolius
COTONEASTER rugosa	COTONEASTER rugosus
COTONEASTER salicifolia	COTONEASTER salicifolius
COTONEASTER serotina	COTONEASTER serotinus
CRATAEGUS Carrierei	CRATAEGUS x lavallei 'Carrierei'
CRATAEGUS cordata	CRATAEGUS phaenopyrum
CRATAEGUS oxyacantha	CRATAEGUS laevigata
CRATAEGUS prunifolia	CRATAEGUS persimilis 'Prunifolia'
CUPRESSUS Lawsoniana	CHAMAECYPARIS lawsoniana
CYDONIA japonica	CHAENOMELES speciosa
CYDONIA japonica superba	CHAENOMELES x superba
CYDONIA lagenaria	CHAENOMELES speciosa
CYDONIA Maulei	CHAENOMELES japonica
CYTISUS albus	CYTISUS multiflorus
CYTISUS monspessulanus	GENISTA monspessulana
CYTISUS 'Porlock'	GENISTA 'Porlock'
CYTISUS racemosus	GENISTA x spachiana

D

DAPHNE Dauphinii	DAPHNE x hybrida
DAVIDIA Vilmoriniana	DAVIDIA involucrata var. vilmoriniana
DICTAMNUS fraxinella	DICTAMNUS albus var. purpurea
DIPLACUS glutinosus	MIMULUS aurantiacus
DRIMYS andina	DRIMYS winteri var. andina
DRIMYS aromatica	DRIMYS lanceolata
DRIMYS winteri latifolia	DRIMYS winteri var. chilensis

E

ECHIUM fastuosum	ECHIUM candicans
ERICA codonodes	ERICA lusitanica
ERICA mediterranea	ERICA erigena
ESCALLONIA exoniensis	ESCALLONIA x exoniensis
ESCALLONIA 'Iveyana'	ESCALLONIA 'Iveyi'
ESCALLONIA macrantha	ESCALLONIA rubra var. macrantha
ESCALLONIA montevidensis	ESCALLONIA bifida
ESCALLONIA newryensis	ESCALLONIA 'Newry'
ESCALLONIA organensis	ESCALLONIA laevis
ESCALLONIA punctata	ESCALLONIA rubra
EUPATORIUM micranthum	EUPATORIUM ligustrinum
EUPHORBIA wulfeni	EUPHORBIA characias ssp. wulfeni

F

FABIANA imbricata minor	FABIANA imbricata 'Prostrata'
FABIANA violacea	FABIANA imbricata f. violacea
FEIJOA sellowiana	ACCA sellowiana
FITZROYA patagonica	FITZROYA cupressoides
FREMONTIA californica	FREMONTODENDRON californicum
FREMONTIA mexicana	FREMONTODENDRON mexicanum

G

GAULTHETTYA wisleyensis	GAULTHERIA x wisleyensis
GENISTA monosperma	RETAMA monosperma
GENISTA virgata	GENISTA tenera
GERANIUM anemonaefolium	GERANIUM palmatum
GUEVINA avellana	GEVUINA avellana

H

HAKEA acicularis	HAKEA lissosperma
HAKEA saligna	HAKEA salicifolia
HEERIA elegans	HETEROCENTRON elegans
HIBBERTIA volubilis	HIBBERTIA scandens
HYDRANGEA 'Blue Prince'	HYDRANGEA 'Blauer Prinz'
HYDRANGEA 'Blue Wave'	HYDRANGEA 'Mariesii Perfecta'

Addendum of Plant Name Changes

HYDRANGEA Bretschneideri	HYDRANGEA heteromalla Bretschneideri
HYDRANGEA 'Gen. Vicomte de Vibraye'	HYDRANGEA 'Generale Vicomtesse de Vibraye'
HYDRANGEA petiolaris	HYDRANGEA anomala subsp. petiolaris
HYDRANGEA sargentiana	HYDRANGEA aspera subsp. sargentiana
HYMENANTHERA crassifolia	MELICYTUS crassifolius
HYPERICUM leschenaultii	HYPERICUM addingtonii
HYPERICUM patulum Forrestii	HYPERICUM forrestii
HYPERICUM patulum grandiflorum	HYPERICUM kouytchense

J

JASMINUM heterophyllum	JASMINUM subhumile
JASMINUM primulinum	JASMINUM mesnyi
JASMINUM revolutum	JASMINUM humile 'Revolutum'

L

LARIX leptolepis	LARIX kaempferi
LASIANDRA macrantha	TIBOUCHINA urvilleana
LAURUS maderensis	LAURUS azorica
LEPTOSPERMUM Chapmanii	LEPTOSPERMUM scoparium 'Chapmanii'
LEPTOSPERMUM ericoides	KUNZEA ericoides
LEPTOSPERMUM flavescens	LEPTOSPERMUM glaucescens
LEPTOSPERMUM flavescens var. obovatum	LEPTOSPERMUM obovatum
LEPTOSPERMUM rodwayanum	LEPTOSPERMUM grandiflorum
LHOTZKYA ericoides	CALYTRIX ericoides
LIPPIA citriodora	ALOYSIA triphylla
LITHOSPERMUM prostratum	LITHODORA diffusa
LITHOSPERMUM rosmarinifolium	LITHODORA rosmarinifolia
LIRIODENDRON tulipifera pyramidale	LIRIODENDRON tulipifera 'Fastigiata'
LONICERA syringantha	LONICERA rupicola var. syringantha

M

MAGNOLIA grandiflora 'Exoniensis'	MAGNOLIA grandiflora 'Exmouth'
MAGNOLIA mollicomata	MAGNOLIA campbellii subsp. mollicomata
MAGNOLIA parviflora	MAGNOLIA sieboldii
MAGNOLIA sinensis	MAGNOLIA sieboldii subsp. sinensis
MAGNOLIA Soulangeana nigra	MAGNOLIA liliflora 'Nigra'
MAGNOLIA watsoni	MAGNOLIA x wiesneri
MAHONIA Bealei	MAHONIA japonica Bealei Group
MALUS aldenhamensis	MALUS x purpurea 'Aldenhamensis'
MALUS Eleyi	MALUS x purpurea 'Eleyi'
MALUS Lemoinei	MALUS x purpurea 'Lemoinei'
MALUS sargentii	MALUS toringo subsp. sargentii
MANDEVILLA suaveolens	MANDEVILLA laxa
METROSIDEROS albiflora	METROSIDEROS albiflorus
METROSIDEROS diffusa	METROSIDEROS diffusus
METROSIDEROS florida	METROSIDEROS floridus
METROSIDEROS hypericifolia	METROSIDEROS hypericifolius
METROSIDEROS lucida	METROSIDEROS umbellatus
METROSIDEROS perforata	METROSIDEROS perforatus
METROSIDEROS polymorpha	METROSIDEROS polymorphus
METROSIDEROS robusta	METROSIDEROS robustus
METROSIDEROS tomentosa	METROSIDEROS excelsus
METROSIDEROS villosa	METROSIDEROS villosus
MICHELIA fuscata	MICHELIA figo
MYRTUS bullata	LOPHOMYRTUS bullata
MYRTUS chequen	LUMA chequen
MYRTUS lechleriana	AMOMYRTUS luma
MYRTUS luma	LUMA apiculata
MYRTUS ugni	UGNI molinae

N

NEPETA macrantha	NEPETA sibirica
NOTHOFAGUS cliffortioides	NOTHOFAGUS solanderi var. cliffortioides
NOTHOFAGUS solandri	NOTHOFAGUS solanderi

O

OLEARIA albida	OLEARIA 'Talbot de Malahide'
OLEARIA Forsteri	OLEARIA paniculata
OLEARIA gunniana	OLEARIA phlogopappa
OLEARIA gunniana splendens	OLEARIA phlogopappa Splendens Group
OLEARIA ilicifolia x lacunosa	OLEARIA x mollis 'Zennorensis'
OLEARIA lineata	OLEARIA virgata var. lineata
OLEARIA mollis	OLEARIA ilicifolia x moschata
OLEARIA x scilloniensis	OLEARIA stellulata
OLEARIA semidentata	OLEARIA 'Henry Travers'
OLEARIA subrepanda	OLEARIA phlogopappa var. subrepanda
OSMANTHUS aquifolium	OSMANTHUS heterophyllus
OSMANTHUS Forrestii	OSMANTHUS yunnanensis
OSMAREA burkwoodii	OSMANTHUS x burkwoodii
OXYPETALUM caeruleum	TWEEDIA caerulea

P

PACHYSTEGIA insignis	OLEARIA insignis
PASSIFLORA racemosa x coerulea	PASSIFLORA x violacea
PAULOWNIA fargesii	PAULOWNIA tomentosa 'Lilacina'
PENTAPTERYGIUM rugosum	AGAPETES rugosum
PENTAPTERYGIUM serpens	AGAPETES serpens
PERNETTYA furiens	GAULTHERIA insana
PERNETTYA leucocarpa	GAULTHERIA leucocarpa
PERNETTYA macrostigma	GAULTHERIA macrostigma
PERNETTYA mucronata	GAULTHERIA mucronata
PERNETTYA nigra	GAULTHERIA nigra
PERNETTYA pumila	GAULTHERIA pumila
PERNETTYA rigida	GAULTHERIA rigida
PERNETTYA tasmanica	GAULTHERIA tasmanica
PHARBITIS Learii	IPOMOEA indica
PHILADELPHUS delavayi var. calvescens	PHILADELPHUS purpurascens
PHILADELPHUS grandiflorus	PHILADELPHUS inodorus var. grandiflorus
PHILLYREA decora	OSMANTHUS decorus
PHOTINIA serrulata	PHOTINIA serratifolia

Addendum of Plant Name Changes

PICEA excelsa	PICEA abies
PIMELEA coarctata	PIMELEA prostrata
PIMELEA laevigata	PIMELEA prostrata
PINUS Laricio	PINUS nigra subsp. laricio
PINUS Laricio nigricans	PINUS nigra subsp. nigra
montana	mugo
montana uncinata	mugo subsp. uncinata
mugho	mugo var. mugo
PLATANUS acerifolia	PLATANUS x hispanica
PLUMBAGO capensis	PLUMBAGO auriculata
POLYGONUM vaccinifolium	PERSICARIA vaccinifolia
POPULUS Eugenei	POPULUS x candicans 'Eugenei'
PRUNUS Amygdalus	PRUNUS dulcis
PRUNUS conradinae	PRUNUS hirtipes
PRUNUS Kiku Shidare	PRUNUS Kiku-Shidare-zakura
PRUNUS 'Kwansan'	PRUNUS 'Kansan'
PRUNUS Pollardii	PRUNUS x amygdalopersica 'Pollardii'
PRUNUS Rhexii	PRUNUS cerasus 'Rhexii'
PRUNUS serrulata var. pubescens	PRUNUS x verecunda
var. spontanea	PRUNUS jamasakura
PSEUDOTSUGA taxifolia	PSEUDOTSUGA menziesii

Q

QUERCUS conferta	QUERCUS frainetto
QUERCUS densiflora	LITHOCARPUS densiflorus
QUERCUS fastigiata	QUERCUS robur 'Fastigiata'
QUERCUS Lucombeana	QUERCUS x hispanica 'Lucombeana'
QUERCUS Mirbeckii	QUERCUS canariensis
QUERCUS pedunculata	QUERCUS robur
QUERCUS sessiliflora	QUERCUS petraea

R

RAPHIOLEPIS Delacourii	RHAPHIOLEPIS x delacourii
RAPHIOLEPIS indica	RHAPHIOLEPIS indica
RAPHIOLEPIS japonica	RHAPHIOLEPIS umbellata f. ovata
RHAMNUS Alaternus variegata	RHAMNUS alaternus 'Argenteovariegata'

Addendum of Plant Name Changes

RHODODENDRON bullatum
RHODODENDRON caloxanthum
RHODODENDRON cantabile
RHODODENDRON chaetomallum
RHODODENDRON chartophyllum
RHODODENDRON chasmanthum
RHODODENDRON coeruleum
RHODODENDRON concatenans

RHODODENDRON crassum

RHODODENDRON crebriflorum

RHODODENDRON croceum
RHODODENDRON Cubittii

RHODODENDRON delavayi

RHODODENDRON deleiense

RHODODENDRON desquamatum
RHODODENDRON diaprepes

RHODODENDRON didymum

RHODODENDRON discolor

RHODODENDRON drumonium
RHODODENDRON eriogynum
RHODODENDRON euchaites

RHODODENDRON eximium

RHODODENDRON exquisitum

RHODODENDRON edgeworthii
RHODODENDRON campylocarpum subsp. caloxanthum
RHODODENDRON russatum
RHODODENDRON haematodes subsp. chaetomallum
RHODODENDRON yunnanense

RHODODENDRON augustinii subsp. chasmanthum
RHODODENDRON rigidum
RHODODENDRON cinnabarinum subsp. xanthocodon Concatenans Group
RHODODENDRON maddenii subsp. crassum
RHODODENDRON cephalanthum subsp. cephalanthum Crebriflorum Group
RHODODENDRON wardii
RHODODENDRON veitchianum Cubittii Group
RHODODENDRON arboreum subsp. delavayi
RHODODENDRON tephropeplum
RHODODENDRON rubiginosum Desquamatum Group
RHODODENDRON decorum subsp. diaprepes
RHODODENDRON sanguineum subsp. didymum
RHODODENDRON fortunei subsp. discolor
RHODODENDRON telmateium
RHODODENDRON facetum
RHODODENDRON neriiflorum subsp. neriflorum Euchaites Group
RHODODENDRON falconeri subsp. eximium
RHODODENDRON oreotrephes Exquisitum Group

Addendum of Plant Name Changes

RHODODENDRON fargesii	RHODODENDRON oreodoxa subsp. fargesii
RHODODENDRON fictolacteum	RHODODENDRON rex subsp. fictolacteum
RHODODENDRON flavum	RHODODENDRON luteum
RHODODENDRON glaucum	RHODODENDRON glaucophyllum
RHODODENDRON haemaleum	RHODODENDRON sanguineum subsp. sanguineum var. haemaleum
RHODODENDRON hanceanum var. pygmaeum	RHODODENDRON hanceanum Nanum Group
RHODODENDRON imperator	RHODODENDRON uniflorum var. imperator
RHODODENDRON japonicum	RHODODENDRON molle subsp. japonicum
RHODODENDRON keleticum	RHODODENDRON calostrotum subsp. keleticum
RHODODENDRON ledoides	RHODODENDRON trichostomum Ledoides Group
RHODODENDRON litiense	RHODODENDRON wardii subsp. wardii Litiense Group
RHODODENDRON Maddenii	RHODODENDRON maddenii subsp. maddenii
RHODODENDRON muliense	RHODODENDRON chryseum
RHODODENDRON myrtilloides	RHODODENDRON campylogynum Myrtilloides Group
RHODODENDRON oleifolium	RHODODENDRON racemosum 'Oleifolium'
RHODODENDRON prostratum	RHODODENDRON saluenense subsp. chamaeunum Prostratum Group
RHODODENDRON pulchrum Maxwellii	RHODODENDRON 'Maxwellii'
RHODODENDRON radicans	RHODODENDRON calostrotum subsp. keleticum Radicans Group
RHODODENDRON radinum	RHODODENDRON trichostomum Radinum Group
RHODODENDRON ravum	RHODODENDRON cuneatum Ravum Group

Addendum of Plant Name Changes

RHODODENDRON repens	RHODODENDRON forrestii subsp. forrestii Repens Group
RHODODENDRON rhabdotum	RHODODENDRON dalhousieae var. rhabdotum
RHODODENDRON riparium	RHODODENDRON calostrotum subsp. riparium
RHODODENDRON roseum	RHODODENDRON prinophyllum
RHODODENDRON Roylei	RHODODENDRON cinnarbarinum 'Roylei'
RHODODENDRON rupicolum	RHODODENDRON rupicola
RHODODENDRON scintillans	RHODODENDRON polycladon
RHODODENDRON scottianum	RHODODENDRON pachypodum
RHODODENDRON speciosum	RHODODENDRON flammeum
RHODODENDRON sphaeranthum	RHODODENDRON trichostomum Radinum Group
RHODODENDRON timeteum	RHODODENDRON oreotrephes Timeteum Group
RHODODENDRON Tsangpoense	RHODODENDRON charitopes
RHODODENDRON villosum	RHODODENDRON tricanthum subsp. tsangpoense
RHODODENDRON zeylanicum	RHODODENDRON arboreum subsp. zeylanicum
RHUS cotinus	COTINUS coggygria
ROBINIA Descaisneana	ROBINIA x ambigua 'Descaisneana'
ROSA anemonoides	Rosa 'Anemone'
ROSA 'Fortune's Yellow'	ROSA x odorata 'Pseudindica'
ROSA hispida	ROSA pimpinellifolia var. hispida
ROSA hugonis	ROSA xanthina f. hugonis
ROSA rubrifolia	ROSA glauca
ROSA sino-Wilsoni	ROSA longicuspis var. sinowilsonii
ROSA spinosissima lutea	ROSA x harisonii 'Lutea Maxima' Rosa
ROSA Willmottiae	ROSA gymnocarpa var. willmottiae
ROSMARINUS officinalis pyramidalis	ROSMARINUS officinalis 'Miss Jessop's Upright'
RUSSELIA juncea	RUSSELIA equisetiformis

S

SALIX caerulea	SALIX alba subsp. caerulea
SALIX Matsudana	SALIX babylonica var. pekinensis
SALIX Salomonii	SALIX x sepulcralis
SALIX vitellina britzensis	SALIX alba subsp. vitellina 'Britzensis'
SALVIA Grahamii	SALVIA microphylla var. microphylla
SALVIA rutilans	Salvia elegans 'Scarlet Pineapple'
SALVIA turkestanica	SALVIA sclarea var. turkestanica
SARCOCOCCA humilis	SARCOCOCCA hookeriana var. humilis
SCHIMA argentea	SCHIMA wallichii subsp. noronhae var. superba
SCHIMA khasiana	SCHIMA wallichii subsp. wallichii var. khasiana
SCHIZANDRA chinensis	SCHISANDRA chinensis
SCHIZANDRA rubriflora	SCHISANDRA rubriflora
SENECIO Bidwillii	BRACHYGLOTTIS bidwillii
SENECIO compactus	BRACHYGLOTTIS compacta
SENECIO elaeagnifolius var. Buchanani	BRACHYGLOTTIS elaeagnifolia BRACHYGLOTTIS buchananii
SENECIO greyi	BRACHYGLOTTIS greyi
SEENECIO laxifolius	BRACHYGLOTTIS 'Sunshine'
SENECIO Monroi	BRACHYGLOTTIS monroi
SENECIO rotundifolius	BRACHYGLOTTIS rotundifolia
SKIMMIA Foremannii	SKIMMIA japonica 'Veitchii'
SKIMMIA Fortunei	SKIMMIA japonica ssp. reevesiana
SOPHORA vicifolia	SOPHORA davidii
SORBUS hybrida Fastigiata	SORBUS x thuringiaca 'Fastigiata'
SPIRAEA aitchisonii	SORBARIA tomentosa var. angustifolia
SPIRAEA bracteata	SPIRAEA nipponica
SPIRAEA discolor	HOLODISCUS discolor
SPIRAEA lindleyana	SORBARIA tomentosa
STERCULIA acerifolia	BRACHYCHITON acerifolius

Addendum of Plant Name Changes

STERCULIA diversifolia	BRACHYCHITON populneus
STEWARTIA koreana	STEWARTIA pseudocamellia Koreana Group
STRANSVAESIA davidiana	PHOTINIA davidiana
STRANSVAESIA salicifolia	PHOTINIA davidiana
STYRAX hemsleyanum	STYRAX hemsleyanus
STYRAX japonica	STYRAX japonicus

T

TACSONIA mollissima	PASSIFLORA mollissima
TAMARIX pentandra	TAMARIX ramosissima
THALICTRUM dipterocarpum	THALICTRUM delavayi
THUYA	THUJA
THYMUS lanuginosus	THYMUS pseudolanuginosus
TILIA vulgaris	TILIA x europea
TRACHELOSPERMUM japonicum	TRACHELOSPERMUM asiaticum
TRICUSPIDARIA dependens	CRINODENDRON patagua
TRICUSPIDARIA lanceolata	CRINODENDRON hookerianum

U

ULEX nanus	ULEX minus
ULMUS campestris	ULMUS procera
ULMUS montana	ULMUS glabra
ULMUS montana fastigiata	ULMUS glabra 'Exoniensis'
ULMUS stricta	ULMUS angustifolia cornubiensis
ULMUS Wheatleyi	ULMUS x sarniensis

V

VACCINIUM mortinii	VACCINIUM floribundum
VACCINIUM pennsylvanicum	VACCINIUM angustifolium laevifolium
VERONICA Andersoni	HEBE x andersonii
VERONICA 'Aoira'	HEBE recurva 'Aoira'
VERONICA 'Autumn Glory'	HEBE 'Autumn Glory'
VERONICA 'Blue Gem'	HEBE x franciscana 'Blue Gem'
VERONICA 'Bowles Hybrid'	HEBE 'Bowles Hybrid'
VERONICA brachysiphon	HEBE brachysiphon
VERONICA Cookiana	HEBE stricta var. macroura Cookiana

Addendum of Plant Name Changes

VERONICA dieffenbachii	HEBE dieffenbachii
VERONICA elliptica	HEBE elliptica
VERONICA gigantea	HEBE gigantea
VERONICA Headfortii	HEBE 'Headfortii'
VERONICA hulkeana	HEBE hulkeana
VERONICA lavaudiana	HEBE lavaudiana
VERONICA leiophylla	HEBE leiophylla
VERONICA longiracemosa	HEBE longiracemosa
VERONICA parviflora	HEBE parviflora var. angustifolia
VERONICA macrocarpa	HEBE macrocarpa
VERONICA salicifolia	HEBE salicifolia
VERONICA speciosa	HEBE speciosa
VERONICA traversii	HEBE brachysiphon
VIBURNUM fragrans	VIBURNUM farreri
VIBURNUM Opulus sterile	VIBURNUM opulus 'Roseum'
VIBURNUM tomentosum Lanarth	VIBURNUM plicatum 'Lanarth'
VIBURNUM tomentosum Mariesii	VIBURNUM plicatum 'Mariesii'
VIBURNUM tomentosum plicatum	VIBURNUM plicatum f. tomentosum
VIBURNUM tomentosum 'Rowallane'	VIBURNUM plicatum Rowallane
VITIS henryana	PARTHENOCISSUS henryana

W
WELLINGTONIA	SEQUOIADENDRON giganteum
WESTRINGIA rosmariniformis	WESTRINGIA fruticosa
WISTERIA venusta	WISTERIA brachybotrys

X
XANTHOCERAS sorbifolia	XANTHOCERAS sorbifolium

Z
ZELKOVA crenata	ZELKOVA carpinifolia
ZENOBIA pulverulenta nuda	ZENOBIA pulverulenta f. nitida

Index

Figures in heavy type indicate main reference to species or variety concerned.

Abelia, 80
  floribunda, 80
  grandiflora, 80
  Schumannii, 80
  triflora, 80
Abeliophyllum *distichum*, 314
Abies, 9–10
  cephalonica, 10
  Forrestii, 10
  Georgei, 10
  grandis, 10
  nobilis, 10
  pectinata, 10
  Pinsapo, 10
Abutilon, 80
  megapotamicum, 81
  Milleri, 80
  speciosum, 81
  vitifolium, 80
Acacia, 188–192
  acinacea, 192
  armata, 190
  Baileyana, 189
  cultriformis, 190
  cyanophylla, 190
  dealbata, 189
  decurrens var. *normalis*, 189
  Farnesiana, 190
  floribunda, 191
  glaucescens, 192
  Hanburyana, 190
  hispidissima, 190
  juniperina, 192
  longifolia, 190
  melanoxylon, 191
  myrtifolia, 191
  podalyriæfolia, 191
  pycnantha, 191
  pulchella, 190
  retinodes, 191
  Riceana, 192
  salicina, 192
  saligna, 192
  terminalis, 190
  Veitchiana, 192
  verticillata, 192
Acacia, False, see *Robinia*, 63
Acer, **54**, 81–82
  campestre, 54
  cappadocicum, 54

Acer (cont.)
  dasycarpum, 54
  griseum, 81
  niloense, 82
  Opulus, 54
  Osakazuki, 81
  palmatum septemlobum, 81
  platanoides, 54
  Pseudo-platanus, 54
Adenandra, 314–315
  fragrans, 315
  uniflora, 314
Aegle *sepiaria*, 82
Aesculus, **54**, 82
  Hippocastanum, 54
  indica, 54
  parviflora, 82
  plantierensis, 54
Agonis, 315
  flexuosa, 315
  marginata, 315
Ailanthus, 55
Albizzia, 192
  Julibrissin, 192
  lophantha, 193
Alder, see *Alnus*, **10**, 55
Amelanchier, 66, **82**
  asiatica, 82
  grandiflora, 82
  lævis, 66, **82**
  oblongifolia, 66, **82**
  vulgaris, 66
Almond, see *Amygdalus*, 66, **270**
Alnus, **10**, 55
  cordata, 55
  glutinosa, **10**, 55
  oregana, 10
Alseuosmia *macrophylla*, 315
Amygdalus, 66, **270**
  communis, 66
  Pollardii, 270
Anopterus *glandulosus*, 315–316
Aotus *gracillima*, 316
Apple, see *Malus*, 278–279
  Crab, see *Malus*, 279
Arbutus, 10, 66, **82**
  Menziesii, 82–83
  Unedo, 10, 66, **82**
Arctostaphylos *manzanita*, 83
Aronia, 281

Aronia (cont.)
  arbutifolia, 281
  melanocarpa, 281
Ash, see Fraxinus, 17, 57
Asteranthera ovata, 316
Asystasia bella, 316
Atriplex Halimus, 10
Azaleas, 282–283, **307–313**
  alabamense, 308
  Albrechtii, 308
  amœnum, see obtusum, 310
  arborescens, 308
  atlanticum, 308
  calendulaceum, 309
  Ghent, see luteum
  japonicum, 309
  Kæmpferi, see obtusum, 310
  ledifolium, see mucronatum, 310
  luteum, 309
  molle, 310
  mucronatum, 310
  oblongifolium, 310
  obtusum, 310–311
  occidentale, 311
  Oldhamii, 311
  pentaphyllum, 311
  pulchrum, 311
  quinquefolium, 311
  reticulatum, 311
  roseum, 311
  scabrum, 311
  Schlippenbachii, 312
  Simsii, 312
  speciosum, 312
  Vaseyi, 312
  viscosum, 312
  Weyrichii, 313
  yedoense, 313
  yellow, see Rhododendron Flavum, 73
Azara, 83–84
  Browneæ, 84
  dentata, 83
  Gilliesii, 84
  integrifolia, 84
  lanceolata, 84
  microphylla, 84

Baccharis patagonica, 11
Banksia, 316–317
  coccinea, 316
  ericæfolia, 317
  ericoides, 317
  grandis, 317
  integrifolia, 317
  marginata, 317
  Menziesii, 317
  serrata, 317
  speciosa, 317
  verticillata, 317

Bauera, 317–318
  rubioides, 317
  sessiliflora, 318
Beaufortia decussata, 318
Beech, see Fagus, 17, 56–57
  Southern Beeches, see Nothofagus, 58, 257–260
Berberidopsis corallina, 84
Berberis, 11, 66, **84–87**
  Darwinii, 11, 66, **84**
  chilensis, 86
  dictyophylla, 87
  for berry, 85
  for leaf colour, 85
  Forrestii, 87
  Jamesiana, 67
  japonica, see Mahonia
  Knightii, see xanthoxylon
  linearifolia, 85
  lologensis, 85
  montana, 86
  stenophylla, 67, **86**
  Thunbergii, 67
  vulgaris, 67, **87**
  xanthoxylon, 67
Beschorneria, 318–319
  Tonelii, 319
  tubiflora, 319
  yuccoides, 318
Betula, 55
  albo-sinensis septentrionalis, 55
  Ermani, 55
  japonica szechuanica, 55
  nigra, 55
  papyrifera, 55
  pubescens, 55
  verrucosa, 55
Billardiera longifolia, 88
Birch, see Betula, 55
Boronia, 319
  elatior, 319
  falcifolia, 319
  heterophylla, 319
  megastigma, 319
  pinnata, 319
  polygalifolia, 319
Bottle-Brush, see Callistemon, 90–91
Bougainvillea Glabra, 319–320
Bowkeria Gerrardiana, 88
Brachyglottis repanda, 11
Brachysema latifolia, 320
Broom, see Cytisus, 69, **111–113**
Brugmansia, 320
  arborea, 320
  lutea, 320
  sanguinea, 320
Bupleurum fruticosum, 11
Buckthorn, see Hippophæ, 18, **70**
Buddleia, 11, 67, **88–89**
  alternifolia, 67, **88**

Index

Buddleia (cont.)
 auriculata, 88
 Colvilei, 88
 Davidii, 11, 88
 globosa, 11, 89
 madagascariensis, 320
 variabilis, 67
Burchellia bubalina, 320
Bursaria, spinosa, 89, 321

Cæsalpinia, 89
 Gilliesii, 89
 japonica, 89
Calceolaria, 89–90
 integrifolia, 90
 violacea, 89
Callistemon, 90–91
 citrinus, 90
 linearis, 90
 rigidus, 90
 salignus, 90
 speciosus, 90
Calluna vulgaris, 125
Calodendron capensis, 321
Calothamnus, 321
 quadrifidus, 321
 sanguineus, 321
 villosus, 321
Calythrix Sullivanii, 321
Camellia, 194–205
 " Cornish Snow," 195
 cuspidata, 195
 japonica, 195
  pink varieties, 202–203
  red varieties, 203–204
  white varieties, 204–205
 J. C. Williams, 197
 maliflora, 196
 oleifera, 196
 Pitardii, 197
 reticulata, 197
  semi-plena, 198
 saluenensis, 199
  and varieties, 199
 Sasanqua, 199
 taliensis, 200
Campsis, 91
 grandiflora, 91
 radicans, 91
 Tagliabuana, 91
Candollea cuneiformis, 321
Cantua buxifolia, 321–322
Carmichaelia, 91–92
 australis, 91
 Enysii, 92
Carpenteria californica, 92
Carpinus Betulas, 55
Carrierea calycina, 322
Caryopteris, 92
Cassia corymbosa, 92

S.M.C.—24

Cassinia, 11
 fulvida, 11
 retorta, 11
Castanea sativa, 56
Catalpa, 92–93
 bignonioides, 92
 Duclouxii, 93
 speciosa, 93
Ceanothus, 206–216
 arboreus, 209
 austromontanus, 210
 cœruleus, 210
 cordulatus, 210
 crassifolius, 210
 cuneatus, 210
 cyaneus, 210
 dentatus, 211
 foliosus, 211
 gloriosus, 211
 griseus, 211
 History, cultivation, hardiness, colour, habit, scent, 206–209
 Hybrids, 215–216
 impressus, 212
 integerrimus, 212
 Lobbianus, 212
 megacarpus, 212
 oliganthus speciosus, 212
 papillosus, 212
 prostratus, 213
 purpureus, 213
 ramulosus fascicularis, 213
 rigidus, 213
 sonomensis, 214
 sorediatus, 214
 spinosus, 214
 thyrsiflorus, 214
  griseus, 214
 Veitchianus, 214
 verrucosus, 214
Celastrus, 93
 Loeseneri, 93
 orbiculatus, 93
 Rosthornianus, 93
Cerasus, see Prunus, 272
Ceratopetalum gummiferum, 322
Ceratostigma, 93
 Griffithii, 94
 Willmottianum, 93
Cercidiphyllum, 94
 japonicum, 94
 sinense, 94
Cercis, 94
 chinensis, 94
 racemosa, 94
 Siliquastrum, 94
Cestrum, 94
 elegans, 94
 Newellii, 94
 Parqui, 94

Cherry, see *Prunus*, 60-61, 71-72, **271-278**
  Bird, see *Prunus padus*, 61, 72, 277
  Spring, see *Prunus Subhirtella*, 275-276
Chestnut
  Cape, see *Calodendron*, 321
  Horse, see *Aseculus*, **54**, 82
  Spanish, see *Castanea*, 56
Chamælaucium ciliatum, 322
Chimonanthus fragrans, 94
Chionanthus, 95
  retusa, 95
  virginica, 95
Choisya ternata, 95
Chorizema, 322
  cordatum, 322
  ilicifolium, 322
Cistus, 12, 67, **95-96**
  corbariensis, 12, 67
  ladaniferus, 96
  laurifolius, 12, 67
  Loretii, 96
  populifolius, 12, 96
  pulverulentus, 12, 96
  salvifolius, 67, 96
  see also *Halimium*
Clematis, 12, **96-102**
  aristata, 97
  Armandii, 96
  alpina, 98
  balearica, 98
  campaniflora, 98
  cirrhosa, 98
  Flammula, 12, **99**
  florida, 100
  glauca akebioides, 99
  Hybrids, large flowering, 99
  indivisa, 97
  Jackmanii, 99
  lanuginosa, 100
  macropetala, 99
  Meyeniana, 97
  montana, 97
  paniculata, 99
  patens, 100
  Planting positions, 100
  Propagating, 100
  Pruning, 100
  Rehderiana, 99
  Spooneri, 97
  tangutica obtusiuscula, 99
  texensis, 102
  vedrariensis, 98
  Veitchiana, 99
  Viticella, 99
  viticella group, 100
  Wilt of, 100
Clerodendron, 102
  fœtidum, 102
  Fargesii, 102
  trichotomum, 102

Clethra, **102**, 323
  arborea, 323
  alnifolia, 102
  barbinervis, 102
  Delavayi, 102
  monostachya, 102
Clianthus puniceus, 103
Coleonema, 323
  album, 323
  pulchrum, 323
Convolvulus, **103**, 323
  Cneorum, 103
  floridus, 323
  mauritanicus, 103
Coprosma, 12, **103**
  acerosa, 103
  Baueri, 12, 103
  nitida, 103
  Petriei, 103
Cordyline, 12, **103-104**
  australis, 12, 103
  Banksii, 104
  indivisa, 104
Cornel, see *Cornus*, 104
Cornus, 12, 69, **104-105**
  alba atrosanguinea, 69, **104**
  capitata, 12, **104**
  florida, 105
  Kousa, 105
  mas, 69, **105**
  Nuttalli, 105
  stolonifera, 12
Corokia, 12, **106**
  Cotoneaster, 106
  buddleoides, 106
  Cheesemanii, 106
  macrocarpa, 12, **106**
  virgata, 12, **106**
Coronilla, 106
  glauca, 106
  Valentina, 106
  Emerus, 106
Correa, 324
  cardinalis, 324
  Harrisii, 324
  magnifica, 324
  pulchella, 324
  ventricosa, 324
  virens, 104
Corylopsis, 107
  glabrescens, 107
  pauciflora, 107
  platypetala, 107
  sisensis, 107
  spicata, 107
  Veitchiana, 107
  Willmottiae, 107
Cotoneaster, 13, 67-69, **107-110**
  adpressa, 109
  aldenhamensis, 107

Index

Cotoneaster (cont.)
  bullata, 68, **108**
  buxifolia, 108
  cornubia, 68, **107**
  conspicua, 68, **109**
  Dammeri, 68, **109**
  divaricata, 108
  Dwarf growers, 68, **109–110**
  Franchettii, 68, **108**
  frigida, 68, **107**
  glaucophylla, 66, **108**
  Henryana, 68, **108**
  horizontalis, 68, **109**
  integerrima, 13
  lactea, 13, 68, **108**
  Medium growers, 68, **108–109**
  microphylla, 69, **110**
  multiflora, 68
  pannosa, 13, 68, **108**
  præcox, 68
  rotundifolia, 108
  salicifolia, 68, **107**
  serotina, 68, **108**
  Simonsii, 68, **109**
  St. Monico, 68
  Tall growers, 68, **107**
  Wardii, 69, 109
  Watereri, 68, **107**
Crataegus, 13, **69**
  cordata, 13, 69
  Carrierei, 69
  Crus-galli, 69
  mollis, 69
  monogyna, 13, **69**
  Oxyacantha, 13, **69**
  prunifolia, 13, **69**
Cupressus, **13**, **56**
  Lawsoniana, **13**, 56
  macrocarpa, **13**, 56
Cyathea dealbata, 324
Cyathodes, 324
  acerosa, 324
  robusta, 324
Cydonia, 69, **110–111**
  cathayensis, 69, **111**
  japonica, 110
    Knap Hill Scarlet, 110
  lagenaria, 111
    Cardinalis, 111
    Rowallane seedling, 111
  Simonii, 110
Cytisus, 69, **111–113**
  albus, 69, **111**
  Battandieri, 111
  Porlock Broom, 112
  proliferus, 112
  racemosus, 112
    elegans, 112
  scoparius, 69, **112**
    decumbens, 112

Cytisus (cont.)
  kewensis, 112
  præcox, 112
Daboecia cantabrica azorica, 124
Daphne, 113–115
  arbuscula, 113
  aurantiaca, 113
  Blagayana, 113
  Buckwoodii, 113
  Cneorum, 113
  collina, 114
  japonica, 114
  Mezereum, 114
  odora, 114
  petræa grandiflora, 115
  retusa, 115
  tangutica, 115
Darwinia macrostegia, 325
Davidia, 56, **115**
  involucrata, 56, **115**
  Vilmoriniana, 56, **115**
Dendromecon rigida, 115
Desfontainea, 116
  Hookeri, 116
  spinosa, 116
Deutzia, 116
  Hybrids and Species
    Pink, 117
    White, 117
Dicksonia antarctica, 117
Diervilla, see Weigela, 186
Dipelta, 117
  floribunda, 117
  ventricosa, 117
Diplacus glutinosus, 117
Douglas Fir, see Pseudotsuga, 29
Dodonæa viscosa, 325
Dryandra, 325
  floribunda, 325
  formosa, 325
Drimys, 118
  andina, 118
  aromatica, 118
  Winteri, 118
    var. latifolia, 118

Eccremocarpus scaber, 118
Echium, 325–326
  Auberianum, 325
  callithyrsum, 326
  candicans, 326
  fastuosum, 326
  Pininana, 325
  simplex, 325
  Wildpretti, 325
Elæagnus, 14, **119**
  angustifolia, 119
  glabra, 14, **119**
  macrophylla, 14, **119**
  pungens, 14

Elæocarpus dentatus, 119
Elm, see *Ulmus*, 33, **64**
Embothrium, 119–121
 coccineum, 119
  var. *lanceolatum*, 120
  var. *longifolium*, 120
Enkianthus, 121
 cernuus rubens, 121
 deflexus, 121
 perulatus, 121
Epacris, 326–327
 acuminata, 327
 impressa, 326
 longiflora, 326
 magnifica, 327
 and hybrids, 329
 pulchella, 327
 purpurascens, 326
Epigæa, 327
 asiatica, 327
 repens, 327
Ercilla volubilis, 121
Erica, 71, 121–126, **327–328**; see also
 Daboecia, 124, and *Calluna*, 125
 arborea, 123
 australis, 123
 caffra, 328
 canaliculata, 124
 carnea, 70, **122**
 cerinthoides, 328
 ciliaris, 125
 cinerea, 124
 codonodes, 70
 darleyensis, 122
 glandulosa, 328
 gracilis, 328
 hiemalis, 328
 hyacinthiformis, 328
 mediterranea, 70, **123**
  varieties, 123
 multiflora, 125
 Pageana, 328
 persoluta densiflora, 328
 regerminans, 328
 terminalis, 125
 Tetralix, 125
 umbellata, 126
 vagans, 70, **125**
 ventricosa, 328
 verticillata major, 328
 Villmoreana, 328
Eriostemon, 328–329
 buxifolius, 329
 Crowei, 329
 lanceolatus, 329
 neriifolius, 329
Erythrina Crista-gallii, 126
Escallonia, **14–16**, 70, 126
 exoniensis, 16
 Hybrids, garden, 16

Escallonia (cont.)
 Iveyana, 16
 macrantha, **15**, 70
 montevidensis, 126
 newryensis, 16
 organensis, 16
 pterocladon, 16
 revoluta, 16
 rubra, 15
Eucalyptus, 16, 217–227
 acervula, 220
 aggregata, 227
 amygdalina, see *Salicifolia*
 Archeri, 227
 Beauchampiana, 221
 cæsia, 227
 cinerea, 227
 citridora, 225
 coccifera, 16, **221**
 cordata, 221
 crebra, 227
 Dalrympleana, 222
 Deanii, 222
 delegatensis, 222
 Economic value, flowers, growth, hardiness, leaves, scent, 217–220
 ficifolia, 226
 Forrestiana, 227
 gigantea, 222
 globulus, 222
 Gunnii, 16, **223**
  var. *montana*, 16, **223**
 hemiphloia, 227
 Johnstoni, 227
 Lehmannii, 227
 leucoxylon, 226
 Macarthuri, 224
 Muelleri, see *subcrenulata*
 obliqua, 227
 pauciflora, 224
 Perriniana, 224
 Preissiana, 227
 polyanthemos, 227
 pulchella, 225
 pulverulenta, 224
 punctata, 227
 radiata, 224
 regnans, 224
 rostrata, 227
 rubida, 220, 227
 rudis, 227
 salicifolia, 224
 sideroxylon, 227
 Species, 220–227
  Hardiest, 220–225
  Tender, 225–227
 subcrenulata, 224
 tereticornis, 227
 torquata, 227
 urnigera, 225

INDEX 371

Eucalyptus (cont.)
  unialata, 224
  vernicosa, 225
  viminalis, 225
  virgata, 225
Eucryphia, 126–128
  cordifolia, 126
  glutinosa, 127
  intermedia, 128
  lucida, 128
  Moorei, 128
  Nymansensis, 128
Eugenia, 329
  myrtifolia, 329
  Smithii, 329
Euonymus, 17, **70**, 128
  alatus, 128
  europæus, 70
  japonicus, 17, **70**
  latifolius, 70
  planipes, 128
Eupatorium micranthum, 129
Euphorbia, 129
  mellifera, 129
  Wulfenii, 129
Eutaxia myrtifolia, 329
Exochorda, 129
  Giraldii, 129
  Korolkowii, 129
  macrocantha, 129

Fabiana, 129
  imbricata, 129
  minor, 129
  violacea, 129
Fagus Sylvatica, 17, **56**
Feijoa Sellowiana, 130
Fendlera rupicola, 130
Fire Bush, see *Embothrium*, 119
Fir, Silver, see *Abies*, 9–10
Forsythia, 130–131
  Giraldiana, 131
  intermedia,
    var. *spectabilis*, 130
  ovata, 131
  suspensa, 130
  viridissima, 130
Fothergilla, 131
  major, 131
  monticola, 131
Fraxinus, 17, **57**
  angustifolia, 57
  excelsior, 17, **57**
  Ornus, 57
Fremontia, 131
  californica, 131
  mexicana, 131
Freylinia cestroides, 330
Fringe Tree, see *Chionanthus*, 95

Fuchsia, 17–18, **131–134**
  corallina, 132
  gracilis, 18
  Hybrids and varieties, 131–134
  magellanica, 131
  Riccartonii, 17
  microphylla, 132
  procumbens, 133
  pumila, 132
  triphylla, 133
Furcræa longæva, 330

Garrya, 18
  elliptica, 18
  Thuretii, 18
Gaulthettya wisleyensis, 134
Gaultheria, 134–135
  antipoda, 134
  cuneata, 134
  depressa, 134
  Forrestii, 134
  fragrantissima, 134
  hispida, 134
  Hookeri, 134
  oppositifolia, 134
  Shallon, 134
  tetramera, 135
  tricophylla, 135
  Veitchiana, 135
Gelsemium sempervirens, 135
Genista, 18, 70, **135–136**
  æthnensis, 135
  cinerea, 70, **136**
  hispanica, 18, 70, **136**
  lydia, 136
  monosperma, 136
  pilosa, 136
  virgata, 70, **136**
Geranium, see *Pelargonium*, 136, 160
  anemonæfolium, 136
Gordonia, 330–331
  anomala, 330
  chrysandra, 331
  Lasianthus, 331
  pubescens, 331
Gorse, see *Ilex*, 33
Griselinia, 18
  littoralis, 18
  lucida, 18
Grevillea, **136–137**, 331
  alpina, 136
  obtusifolia, 331
  oleoides, 331
  ornithopoda, 331
  punicea, 331
  rosmarinifolia, **136**, 331
  sulphurea, **137**, 331
  Thelemanniana, 332
  thyrsoides, 137
Guevina avellana, 332

Hakea, 332–333
    acicularis, 332
    dactyloides, 333
    epiglottis, 333
    gibbosa, 332
    laurina, 332
    saligna, 333
    suaveolens, 333
Halesia, 137
    carolina, 137
    monticola, 137
Halimiocistus, 96
    halimifolium, 96
    lasianthum, 96
    ocymoides, 96
    sahucii, 96
    wintonensis, 96
Halimium, see Cistus, 96
Hamamelis, 137
    japonica, 137
    mollis, 137
    Zuccariniana, 137
Hardenbergis Comptoniana, 333
Heath, see Erica, 121
Heeria elegans, 333
Hesperaloe parviflora, 333
Hibbertia, 333–334
    dentata, 333
    volubilis, 333
Hibiscus syriacus, 137–138
Hippophæ rhamnoides, 18, 70
Hoheria, 71, 138–139
    angustifolia, 71, 138
    glabrata, 71, 138
    Glory of Amlwch, 139
    Lyallii, 138
    populnea, 139
    sexstylosa, 71, 139
Holbœllia, 140
    coriacea, 140
    grandiflora, 140
    latifolia, 140
Holly, see Ilex, 19
Honeysuckle, see Lonicera, 71
Hornbeam, see Carpinus, 55
Hydrangea, 19, 140–143
    arborescens grandiflora, 142
    aspera, 142
    Bretschneideri, 142
    Garden varieties, 141–143
    hortensis, see macrophylla
    macrophylla, 141
    paniculata, 142
    petiolaris, 143
    Sargentiana, 143
    serrata, 143
    strigosa, 142
    vestita, 142
    villosa, 142
Hymenanthera crassifolia, 19

Hymenosporum flavum, 334
Hypericum, 143–144
    Leschenaultii, 143
    patulum, 143
    Rodgersii, 143
    Rowallane Hybrid, 144

Ilex, 19, 71
    Aquifolium, 19, 71
    cornuta, 19
    crenata major, 19
    glabra, 19
Ixerba brexioides, 334

Jasmine, see Jasminum, 144–145, 334–335
Jasminum, 144–145, 334–335
    angulare, 334
    azoricum, 334
    Beesianum, 144
    fruticans, 144
    heterophyllum glabricymosum, 144
    nudiflorum, 144
    odoratissimum, 335
    officinale grandiflorum, 144
    Parkeri, 144
    polyanthum, 335
    primulinum, 144
    revolutum, 144
Judas Tree, see Cercis, 94
Juglans, 57
    nigra, 57
    regia, 57
Juniperus, 19, 145–146
    communis, 146
    conferta, 145
    horizontalis, 145
    Pfitzeriana, 19
    rigida, 146
    sabina, 146
    sabina tamariscifolia, 145
    scopulorum, 146
    squamata, 145
Juniper, see Juniperus, 19, 145–146

Kalmia latifolia, 146
Kerria japonica, 146
Knightia excelsa, 335
Kolkwitzia, 146
Kunzea ambigua, 335

Laburnum, 147
    alpinum, 147
    Vossii, 147
    Watereri, 147
Lagerstrœmia indica, 335–336
Lapageria rosea, 147
Larch, see Larix, 20
Larix leptolepis, 20
Lasiandra, 336
    laxa, 336
    macrantha, 336

INDEX

Laurel, see *Prunus Laurocerasus*, 28
Laurus, 20
  maderensis, 20
  nobilis, 20
Lavatera, **20**, 147–148
  arborea, 20
  assurgentiflora, 20
  olbia rosea, 147
Leonotis Leonurus, 148
Leptodermis pilosa, 148
  oblonga, 148
  Purdomii, 148
Leptospermum, 148–150
  baccatum, 148
  ericoides, 148
  flavescens, 149
  lævigatum, 149
  Liversidgei, 149
  nitidum, 150
  pubescens, 149
  Rodwayanum, 149
  scoparium, 149
    Chapmanii, 150
    eximium, 150
    flore-pleno, 150
    grandiflorum, 150
    Keatleyi, 150
    Nichollsii, 150
    prostratum, 150
    stellatum, 150
Leucadendron argenteum, 336
Ligustrum, 20, **150**
  confusum, 150
  ionandrum, 20
  lucidum, 150
  ovalifolium, 20
  sinense, 150
Lilac, see *Syringa*, 151, 178
Lime, see *Tilia*, 64
Lindera magaphylla, 336
Ling, see *Calluna vulgaris*, 125
Lippia, citriodora, 151
Liriodendron Tulipifera, 57
Lithospermum, 151
  prostratum, 151
  rosmarinifolium, 151
Locust Tree, see *Robinia*, 63
Lomatia ferruginea, 151–152
Lonicera, 21, 71, **152–154**
  americana, 152
  arboreus, 153
  Bushes, 153
  Climbers, 152–153
  etrusca, 152
  fragrantissima, 152
  Hildebrandtiana, 152
  japonica Halliana, 152
  nitida, 21, **153**
  Periclymenum belgica, 71, **152**
  pileata, 153

Lonicera (cont.)
  sempervirens, 152
  Standishii, 152
  syringantha, 153
  tatarica, 153
  Tellmanniana, 152
  tragophylla, 153
  yunnanensis, 21, **153**
Lilac, see *Syringa*, 151, 178
Luculia, 336–357
  gratissima, 336
  Pinceana, 337
Lupin, see *Lupinus*, 71, **153**
Lupinus arboreus, 71, **153**
Lycium chinense, 21
Lyonothamnus, 337–338
  asplenifolius, 337
  floribunda, 338

Magnolias, 228–248
  Alexandrina, 243
  Brozzonii, 243
  Campbellii, 231
  Dawsoniana, 233
  Delavayi, 244
  denudata, 238
  Fraseri, 248
  globosa, 236
  grandiflora, 246
  Kobus, 239
  Lennei, 243
  liliflora, 234
  macrophylla, 247
  mollicomata, 232
  nitida, 245
  obovata, 238
  officinalis, 239
  parviflora, 235
  rostrata, 239
  salicifolia, 240
  Sargentiana, 230
    robusta, 231
  sinensis, 236
  Soulangeana, 241
  Sprengeri diva, 233
  stellata, 240
  Thompsoniana, 248
  Veitchii, 243
  virginiana, 248
  Watsonii, 237
  Wilsonii, 235
Mahonia, 86–87 (see under *Berberris*)
  Aquifolium, 87
  Bealei, 87
  japonica, 86
  lomariifolia, 87
  napaulensis, 87
  pinnata, 87
Mallow Tree, see *Lavatera*, 20

INDEX

Malus, 72, **278–279**
  aldenhamensis, 278
  Apples, 278
    Crab, 279
  atrosanguinea, 278
  baccata, 72
  cornaria, 278
  Eleyi, 279
  floribunda, 278
  hupehensis, 72, **279**
  Hybrids, Pink, 278
    Wine-red, 278–279
  Lemoinei, 278
  pumila, 279
  purpurea, 278
  Sargentii, 279
  spectabilis, 279
Mandevilla, 154
  suaveolens, 154
  Tweedicana, 154
Maple, see Acer, **54**, 81–82
Medicago arborea, 21
Melaleuca, 154, **338**
  armillaris, 338
  elliptica, 338
  hypericifolia, 338
  lateritia, 338
  Leucadendron, 338
  styphelioides, 338
  squamea, 338
  squarrosa, 154, **338**
  Wilsonii, 338
Melicytus ramiflorus, 338
Mespilus, Snowy, see Amelanchier, 66, 82
Metrosideros, 21, **249–256**
  albiflora, 255
  Colensoi, 256
  diffusa, 254
  florida, 255
  hypericifolia, 255
  lucida, 21, 249
  Parkinsonii, 254
  perforata, 255
  polymorpha, 256
  robusta, 21, 251
  tomentosa, 252
  villosa, 254
Mexican Orange Blossom, see Choisya, 95
Michelia, 339–340
  doltsopa, 339
  excelsa, 339
  Forrestii, 339
  fuscata, 339
  grandiflora, 339
  Hookeri, 339
  insignis, 339
Mitraria coccinea, 154
Mountain Ash, see Sorbus, 73
Muehlenbeckia complexa, 21
Mutisia, 155

Mutisia (cont.)
  Clematis, 155
  decurrens, 155
  ilicifolia, 155
Myoporum lætum, 340
Myrsine africana, 21
Myrtle, see Myrtus, 155–157
Myrtus, 155–157
  bullata, 155
  chequen, 155
  communis, 155
  Lechleriana, 156
  Luma, 156
  Ugni, 157

Nandina, domestica, 157
Nerium, 157–158
Notelæa excelsa, 22
Nothofagus—Southern Beeches, 58, 257–260
  antarctica, 258
  betuloides, 258
  Blairii, 258
  cliffortioides, 258
  Cunninghamii, 259
  Dombeyi, 259
  fusca, 259
  Gunnii, 259
  Menziesii, 259
  Moorei, 260
  obliqua, 260
  procera, 260
  pumilio, 260
  Solandri, 260
  truncata, 259
Notospartium Carmichæliæ, 158

Oak, see Quercus, 29, **61–63**
Oleander, see Nerium, 157
Olearia, 21–23, 71, **261–268**
  albida 21, 71, **261**
  angustifolia, 261
  arborescens, 262
  argophylla, 262
  avicenniæfolia, 21, 71, **262**
  chathamica, 262
  Colensoi, 262
  Cunninghamii, 268
  dentata, 263
  erubescens, 263
  excorticata, 263
  floribunda, 268
  Forsteri, 22, **263**
  furfuracea, 263
  glutinosa, 263
  Gunniana, 263
  flavescens, 264
  Haastii, 264
  ilicifolia, 23, **264**
  lacunosa, 265
  lineata, 265

INDEX

Olearia (cont.)
  Lyallii, 265
  lyrata, 266
  macrodonta, 22, 71, **268**
  mollis, 266
  moschata, 266
  oleifolia, 266
  pachyphylla, 266
  persoonioides, 268
  ramulosa, 267
  Rossii, 267
  scilloniensis, 267
  semi-dentata, 267
  Solandri, 23, 268
  speciosa, 268
  stellulata, 268
  subrepanda, 268
  Traversii, 23, 71, **268**
Oleaster, see *Elæagnus*, 14, **119**
Osmanthus, 158
  Aquifolium, **158**
  Delavayi, 158
  Forrestii, 158
Osmarea Burkwoodii, 158
Osteomeles Schweriniæ, 159
Oxydendrum arboreum, 159

Palms, 159
  canariensis, 159
  Chamærops Fortunei, 159
  C. excelsa, 159
  C. humilis, 159
  Phœnix reclinata, 159
Parrot's Beak, see *Clianthus*, 103
Parsonsia heterophylla, 340
Passiflora, 159, **340**
  Allardii, 340
  cærulea, 340
  racemosa, 340
Passion Flower, see *Passiflora*, 159, **340**
Paulownia, 159
  Fargesii, 160
  tomentosa, 159
Pearl Bush, see *Excohorda*, 129
Pear, see *Pyrus*, 61
Pelargonium, 160
Pentapterygium, 340–341
  Ludgvan Cross, 341
  rugosum, 341
  serpens, 340
Pernettya, 160–161
  furiens, 160
  leucocarpa, 160
  macrostigma, 160
  mucronata, 160
  nigra, 161
  pumila, 161
  rigida, 161
  tasmanica, 161
Perovskia atriplicifolia, 161

Pharbitis Learii, 341
Philadelphus, 161–163
  Burfordensis, 162
  Delavayi, 162
  grandiflorus, 162
  insignis, 162
  microphyllus, 162
  pubescens, 162
Philesia magellanica, 162–163
Phillyrea, 24
  angustifolia, 24
  decora, 24
  latifolia, 24
Phormium Tenax Cookianum, 24
Photinia, 163
  serrulata,-163
  villosa, 163
Phygelius capensis, 163
Picea, 24, 58
  alba, 24
  excelsa, **24**, 58
  nigra, 24
  Omorika, 58
  sitchensis, 24
Pieris, 163–164
  floribunda, 163
  formosa, 163
  Forrestii, 163
  japonica, 163
  taiwanensis, 164
Pileostegia viburnoides, 164
Pimelea, 164
  coarctata, 164
  ferruginea, 164
  lævigata, 164
Pine, see *Pinus*, 24–27, 58
Pinus, **24–27**, 58
  contorta, 25
  halepensis, 25
  Laricio, **24**, 58
  nigricans, 25
  montana, 25
  muricata, 26
  Pinaster, **26**, 58
  radiata, **24**, 58
  sylvestris, 58
  Thunbergii, 27
Pittosporum, **27–28**, 341–342
  Buchanani, 27
  bicolor, 27
  colensoi, 27
  crassifolium, 27
  Dallii, 28
  daphniphylloides, 341
  Fairchildii, 27
  Kirkii, 28
  phillyræoides, 342
  Ralphii, 27
  rhombifolium, 342
  tenuifolium, 27

Pittosporum (cont.)
  Tobira, 28
  undulatum, 341
Plane, see *Platanus*, 59
Planting, 1–187
  Country Roadsides, shrubs and small trees, 65–74
  General, 79–187
  Roadsides and Towns, 39–78
  Roadsides and Towns, large trees, 54–65
  Town, trees and shrubs, 74–78
  Wind and Shelter, 6–38
Platanus, 59
  acerifolia, 59
  orientalis, 59
Plumbago capensis, 342
Plum, see *Prunus cerasifera*, 72
Podalyria, 342
  calyptrata, 342
  canescens, 342
  sericea, 342
Polygala, 164–165
  myrtifolia, 164
  virgata, 165
Pomaderris elliptica, 343
Pomegranate, see *Punica*, 165
Poplar, see *Populus*, 28, **59–60**
  Aspen, 60
  Balsam, 60
  Black, 60
  White, 60
Poppy, Californian tree, see *Romneya*, 168
Populus, 28, **59–60**
  alba nivea, 28, **60**
  berolinensis, 60
  Bolleana, 60
  candicans, 60
  canescens, 60
  Eugenei, 60
  nigra, 60
    betulifolia, 28, **60**
  robusta, 60
  tremula, 60
  tremuloides, 60
  trichocarpa, 28, **60**
Potentilla, 165
  fruticosa, 165
  Vilmoriniana, 165
  Wardii, 165
Prionotes cerinthoides, 343
Privet, see *Ligustrum*, 20, **150**
Prostanthera, 165, **343–344**
  coccinea, 344
  cuneata, 165, **343**
  lasianthos, 343
  nivea, 344
  rotundifolia, 165, **343**
  Sieberi, 344
Protea, 344
  scolymocephala, 344

Protea (cont.)
  Susanniæ, 344
Prunus, 28, 60, 71–72, **269–278**
  Almonds, 270–271
  Amygdalus, 270
  Apricots, 271
  Armeniaca, 271
  Avium, 61, **271**
  cerasifera, 61, 72, **271**
  cerasus, 272
  Cherries, 271–273
    Bird, 277
    Japanese, see *P. serrulata*, 72, 273–275
    Laurels, 277–278
    Spring, see *P. subhirtella*, 275–277
  conradinæ, 72, **272**
  incisa, 272
  Laurocerasus, 28, **277**
  lusitanica, 29, **278**
  padus Albertii, 72, 277
    „ *Watereri*, 61, 72, **277**
  Peaches, 270–271
  Persica sanguinea plena, 270
  Plums, 271
  Rhexii, 272
  serrulata, 273
  subhirtella, 72, **275–276**
  tenella, 270
  triloba multiplex, 270
  Zabeliana, 278
Pseudotsuga taxifolia, 29
Psoralea, 344
  aphylla, 344
  glandulosa, 344
  pinnata, 344
Punica Granatum, 165
Puya, 344–345
  alpestris, 344
  chilensis, 345
  cœrulea, 345
Pyracantha, 72, **166**
  angustifolia, 166
  atalantioides, 72, **166**
  coccinea, 166
  Lalandii, 72
  Rogersiana, 72, **166**
Pyrus, 61, **279**
  communis, 61
  Malus, 72, 269–279
  salicifolia pendula, 279

Quercus, 29, **61–63**
  agrifolia, 63
  Cerris, 62
  coccinea, 62
  conferta, 62
  densiflora, 63
  fastigiata, 62
  Ilex, 29, **62**
  pendunculata, 62

INDEX

Quercus (cont.)
  phillyræoides, 29
  rubra, 62
  sessiliflora, 29, **62**
  Suber, 63
Quince, Japanese, see *Cydonia*, 110

Raphiolepis, 166
  indica, 166
  japonica, 166
Rhamus Alaternus variegata, 166
Rhododendron, 29, 73, **282–313**
  General:
    Dwarf species and hybrids, 284–291
      Lilac-blue and Purple, 284–285
      Magenta and Pink, 285–288
      Red, 290–291
      White, 288–289
      Yellow, 289–290
    Larger species and hybrids, 295–302
    Medium species and hybrids, 291–294
      Blue, lavender, lilac-mauve, 291–292
      Heather pink, 292
      Red, 294
      White and pure pink, 292–293
      Yellow and orange, 293–294
    Scented species and hybrids, 302–306
    Cultivation, 282–283
    Planting, 73, 282–284
      Roadsides and Towns, 73
      Wind-breaker, 283
  Hybrids:
    Baryclayi, 301
    Beauty of Littleworth, 300
    Betty Wormald, 302
    Blue Diamond, 284
    Blue Tit, 284
    Bric-à-brac, 289
    Britannia, 301
    cilpinense, 289
    Cornish Cross, 299
    Cornubia, 295
    Damaris, 296
    Earl of Athlone, 301
    Elizabeth, 290
    Fusilier, 297
    Hawk, 301
    J. G. Millais, 301
    King George, 301
    Lady Alice Fitzwilliam, 304
    Lady Chamberlain, 297
    Lady Rosebery, 297
    Loderi, 299
    Loders White, 299
    Matador, 299
    May Day, 291, 299
    Mother of Pearl, 300
    Penjerrick, 296
    Polar Bear, 295
    præcox, 288

Rhododendron (cont.)
  Hybrids : (cont.)
    Princess Alice, 305
    Raoul Millais, 302
    Red Cap, 290
    Romany Chal, 298
    Royal Flush, 296
    Sir Charles Lemon, 295
    Tally Ho, 298
    Venapens, 290
  Species:
    arboreum, 295
    ambiguum, 293
    Augustinii, 291
    auriculatum, 295
    barbatum, 295
    bullatum, 303
    cæruleum, 291
    callimorplum, 292
    calophytum, 295
    calostrotum, 286
    caloxanthum, 293
    campanulatum, 295
    campylocarpum, 296
    cantabile, 285
    catacosmum, 294
    chætomallum, 294
    chamætortum, 287
    charitopes, 288
    chartophyllum, 292
    chasmanthum, 291
    chryseum, 289
    ciliatum, 289, 303
    ciliicalyx, 303
    cinnabarinum, 293
    crassum, 303
    crebreflorum, 286
    croceum, 293
    Cubittii, 303
    Dalhousiæ, 303
    Davidsonianum, 292
    decorum, 297
    Delavayi, 295
    deleiense, 287
    desquamatum, 292
    diaprepes, 297
    dichroanthum, 293
    didymum, 290
    discolor, 297
    drumonium, 284
    Edgarianum, 284
    Edgeworthii, 304
    Elliottii, 297
    emasculum, 288
    eriogynum, 298
    euchaites, 294
    eximium, 298
    exquisitum, 292
    Falconeri, 298
    Fargesii, 298

Rhododendron (cont.)
  Species : (cont.)
    fastigiatum, 284
    fictolacteum, 298
    flavidum, 290
    flavum, 73
    fragrantissimum, 304
    formosum, 304
    Forsterianum, 304
    Fortunei, 297
    fulgens, 294
    glaucum, 287
    grande, 298
    Griersonianum, 298
    Griffithianum, 299
    hæmaleum, 291
    hæmatodes, 291
    Hanceanum, 289
    hippophæoides, 285
    Hookeri, 294
    impeditum, 284
    imperator, 286
    intricatum, 284
    Johnstoneanum, 304
    keleticum, 286
    Kyawi, 300
    lacteum, 300
    ledoides, 287
    leucaspis, 288
    Lindleyi, 305
    litiense, 293
    lutescens, 294
    Lyi, 305
    Macabeanum, 300
    Maddenii, 305
    mallotum, 300
    meddianum, 294
    megacalyx, 305
    megeratum, 289
    mollicomum, 287
    moupinense, 288
    mucronulatum, 292
    muliense, 289
    myrtilloides, 286
    neriiflorum, 294
    Nuttallii, 305
    oleifolium, 287
    orbiculare, 293
    oreodoxa, 293
    oreotrephes, 292
    orthocladum, 284
    pemakoense, 286
    pocophorum, 294
    ponticum, 29, 73, **283-284**
    prostratum, 286
    prunifolium, 285
    racemosum, 287
    radicans, 285
    radinum, 287
    ravum, 287

Rhododendron (cont.)
  Species : (cont.)
    repens, 290
    rhabdotum, 306
    rubiginosum, 292
    rupicolum, 285
    russatum, 285
    saluenense, 286
    sanguineum, 291
    Sargentianum, 289
    Scottianum, 306
    scintillans, 285
    sesterianum, 306
    sino-grande, 300
    Soulici, 293
    Species:
      Dwarf, 284
      Larger, 295–302
      Medium, 291–294
      Scented species and hybrids, 302–306
    sperabile, 294
    sperabiloides, 294
    sphæranthum, 287
    Stewartianum, 293
    suave, 306
    supranubium, 306
    sutchuenense, 301
    Taggianum, 306
    telmateium, 284
    tephropeplum, 287
    Thomsonii, 301
    timeteum, 292
    tsangpoense, 288
    Valentinianum, 290
    Veitchianum, 306
    venator, 301
    villosum, 292
    Wardii, 301
    Williamsianum, 288
    yakusimanum, 289
    yunnanense, 293
    zaleucum, 292
    zeylanicum, 301
Rhus, 167
  cotinoides, 167
  Cotinus, 167
  trichocarpa, 167
  typhina, 167
Ribes, 167
  sanguineum splendens, 167
  speciosum, 167
Robinia Pseud Acacia, 63
Romneya, 168
  Coulteri, 168
  trichocalyx, 168
Rosa, 73
  filipes, 73
  Helenæ, 73
  highdownensis, 73
  moschata, 73

INDEX

Rosa (cont.)
  Moyesii, 73
  Willmottiæ, 73
  Rosmarinus, 171–172
    corsicus, 171
    officinalis, 171
    prostratus, 171
    Tuscan Blue, 171
  Rosemary, see Rosmarinus, 30, 171–172
  Rose, 30, **168–171**
    Albertine, 171
    anemonoides, 169
    Banksiæ, 170
    bracteata, 168
    Fargesii, 169
    filipes, 170
    Fortune's yellow, 170
    highdownensis, 169
    Hillieri, 169
    hispida, 170
    Hugonis, 169
    Lady Waterlow, 171
    lævigata, 169
    Mermaid, 169
    moschata, 170
    Moyesii, 169
    multibracteata, 171
    primula, 170
    rubrifolia, 171
    rugosa, 30
    sino-Wilsoni, 170
    spinosissima altaica, 170
    spinosissima, lutea, 170
    virginiana, 30
    Willmottiæ, 170
    xanthina spontanea, 170
  Rubus deliciosus, 172

Salix, 30, 63
  acutifolia, 30
  alba, 63
  babylonica, 64
  Caprea, 30
  cœrulea, 63
  daphnoides, 30, **63**
  Matsudana, 63
  Salamonii, 64
Salvia, 172
  Grahamii, 172
  Greggii, 172
  rutilans, 172
Santolina Chamæcyparissus, 172
Sarcococca, 172
  Hookeriana, 172
  humilis, 172
  ruscifolia, 172
Schima, 345
  argentea, 345
  Khasiana, 345
Schizandra, 173

Schizandra (cont.)
  chinensis, 173
  rubriflora, 173
Schizophragma, 173
  hydrangeoides, 173
  integrifolium, 173
Semele androgyna, 173
Senecio, 30, 173
  Bidwillii, 32
  compactus, 32
  elæagnifolius, 31
  Greyii, 32
  laxifolius, 32
  Monroi, 32
  rotundifolius, 30
  scandens, 173
Skimmia, 32, **173–174**
  Foremanii, 173
  Fortunei, 173
Solanum, 174, **345–346**
  aviculare, 345
  crispum, 174
  jasminoides, 174
  lycioides, 345
  Rantoneti, 345
  Wendlandii, 345
Sollya, 346
  Drummondii, 346
  heterophylla, 346
Sophora, 174–175
  japonica, 174
  macrocarpa, 175
  microphylla, 174
  secundiflora, 175
  tetraptera, 175
  viciifolia, 175
Sorbus, 73, **269–281**
  Aria, 73, **281**
    Decaisneana, 281
    intermedia, 281
    lutescens, 281
  Aronia, 281
    arbutifolia, 281
    melanocarpa, 281
  Aucuparia, 73, **280–281**
    commixta, 280
    Conradinæ, 280
    discolor, 280
    domestica, 280
    Esserteauiana, 280
    hupehensis, 280
    scalaris, 281
    Sargentiana, 281
    Vilmorinii, 281
Sparrmania africana, 346
Spartium, junceum, 73
Spiræa, 175–176
  Aitchisonii, 176
  arguta, 175
  bracteata, 175

Spiræa (cont.)
  decumbens, 175
  discolor, 176
  japonica, 175
  Lindleyana, 176
  prunifolia, 175
  sorbifolia, 176
  trichocarpa, 175
  Veitchii, 176
Spruce, see Picea, 24, 58
Stachyurus, 176
  chinensis, 176
  præcox, 176
Staphylea, 176
  colchica, 176
    var. Coulombieri, 176
  holocarpa, 176
  pinnata, 176
Sterculia, 346
  acerifolia, 346
  diversifolia, 346
Stewartia, 176–177
  koreana, 176
  malacodendron, 177
  monodelpha, 177
  ovata, 177
  Pseudo-Camellia, 177
  serrata, 177
  sinensis, 177
Stranvæsia, 32, 176
  Davidiana, 32, 176
    var. undulata, 176
  salicifolia, 32, 176
Strawberry Tree, see Cornus, 104
Styrax, 177–178
  Hemsleyanum, 178
  japonica, 177
  Obassia, 178
  Wilsonii, 178
Syringa, 151, 178
  Marshal Foch, 178
  Rouen lilac, 178
  Sweginzowii superba, 178
  Vestale, 178

Tacsonia mollissima, 346–347
Tamarisk, see Tamarix, 32–33
Tamarix, 32–33, 73
  anglica, 33
  gallica, 33, 73
  hispida, 33
  parviflora, 33
  pentandra, 33
Tecoma, see Campsis, 91
Telopea, 347
  oreades, 347
  speciosissima, 347
  truncata, 347
Teucrium fruticans, 178–179

Thorn, see Cratægus, 13
Tilia, 64
  euchlora, 64
  petiolaris, 64
  vulgaris, 64
Trachelospermum, 179
  asiaticum, 179
  japonicum, 179
  jasminoides, 179
Tree of Heaven, see Ailanthus, 55
Tricuspidaria, 179–180
  dependens, 180
  lanceolata, 179
Tristania neriifolia, 347
Tulip Tree, see Liriodendron, 57

Ulmus, 33, 64
  campestris, 33, 64
  montana, 33, 64
  stricta, 33
Ulex, 33, 64
  europæus, 33, 73
  europæus flore-pleno, 73

Vaccinium, 180–181
  arctostaphylos, 180
  corymbosum, 180
  Delavayi, 180
  glauco-album, 181
  Mortinia, 181
  ovatum, 181
  pennsylvanicum, 181
  stamineum, 181
  virgatum, 181
  Vitis-idæa, 181
Veronica, 34–36, 73, 181–182
  Andersonii, 34
  Autumn Glory, 34
  Bowles Hybrid, 181
  Blue Gem, 34
  brachysiphon, 34
  Dieffenbachii, 34, 73
  elliptica, 34, 73
  gigantea, 35
  Headfortii, 181
  Hulkeana, 182
  lavaudiana, 182
  leiophylla, 182
  macrocarpa, 35
  parviflora, 182
  salicifolia, 35, 73
  speciosa, 35, 182
    and hybrids, 182
  Traversii, see V. brachysiphon
Viburnum, 73–74, 182–185
  Berrying, 185
  betulifolium, 73, 185
  bitchiuense, 183
  bodnantense, 184
  Carlesii, 182

INDEX

Viburnum (cont.)
  Flowering, 182
  fragrans, 183
  grandiflorum, 184
  hupehense, 185
  Juddii, 183
  Lantana, 74, **183**
  lobophyllum, 185
  macrocephalum grandiflorum, 184
  Opulus, 74
  opulus sterile, 184
  tinus, 184
  tomentosum plicatum, 184
    var. Lanarth, 184
    var. Mariesii, 184
    var. Rowallane, 184
Vinca difformis, 186
Vitex Agnus-castus, 185

Wakkataka sinensis, 347–348
Walnut, see *Juglans*, 57
Weigela japonica and varieties, 186
Weinmannia, 348–349
  racemosa, 348
  sylvicola, 348
  trichosperma, 348
Westringia, 186

Westringia (cont.)
  rigida, 186
  rosmariniformis, 186
Whitebeam, see *Sorbus*, 73
Willow, see *Salix*, **63**, 130
Winter Sweet, see *Chimonanthus*, 94
Wisteria, 186
  floribunda, 186
  japonica, 186
  sinensis, 186
  venusta, 186
Witch Hazel, see *Corylopsis*, 107

Xanthoceras sorbifolia, 187

Yucca, 187
  filamentosa, 187
  flaccida, 187
  gloriosa, 187
  recurvifolia, 187
  Red, see *Hesperaloe parviflora*, 333
  vomerensis, 187
  Whipplei, 187

Zenobia, 187
  nuda, 187
  pulverulenta, 187